ATTRIBUTION THEORY:
An Organizational Perspective

Editor

Mark J. Martinko, Ph.D.

Department of Management
Florida State University
Tallahassee, Florida

S^t_L

St. Lucie Press
Delray Beach, Florida

79.95

Copyright ©1995 by St. Lucie Press

Printed and bound in the U.S.A. Printed on acid-free paper.

Library of Congress Cataloging-in-Publication Data

Attribution theory : an organizational perspective / edited by Mark
   Martinko : with special contributions from Bernard Weiner, Robert
   Lord.
    p.   cm.
   Includes bibliographical references and index.
   ISBN 1-884015-19-0 (alk. paper)
   1. Organizational behavior. 2. Attribution (Social psychology)
I. Martinko, Mark J. II. Weiner, Bernard, 1935– . III. Lord,
Robert G. (Robert George), 1946– .
HD58.7.A87 1995
302.3′5—dc20   94-17213
                                             CIP

Direct all inquiries to St. Lucie Press, Inc., 100 E. Linton Blvd., Suite 403B, Delray Beach, Florida 33483.

Phone: (407) 274-9906
Fax: (407) 274-9927

S_L^t

Published by
St. Lucie Press
100 E. Linton Blvd., Suite 403B
Delray Beach, FL 33483

CONTENTS

SECTION III
Applying Attribution Theory to Organizational Issues
Part A: Intrapersonal Behavior

Part B: Leadership

Part C: Group Dynamics

PREFACE

Development of This Book

The idea for this book evolved from a series of doctoral seminars on leadership and attribution theory conducted at Florida State University. At the conclusion of the seminars, many of the students expressed a continued interest in attribution theory, and an informal symposium series was formed in which the group members presented and discussed papers and ideas for papers. The group met about twice a year over a period of about six years. Eventually, these informal meetings included participants from around the Southeast, including the University of Mississippi, Georgia Southern University, and Florida International University. Members of this initial group included William L. Gardner, Russell Kent, Constance Campbell, Sherry Moss, and Elizabeth Rozell. As the meetings evolved, various members of the group presented their work at regional and national conferences and had their work published in respected journals such as the *Academy of Management Journal, Academy of Management Review,* and *Journal of Management.* Despite these individual successes, as a group we were still concerned about the apparent lack of integration of attribution theory within the organizational sciences. Although we were aware of a number of excellent works describing the nature, function, and applications of attribution theory within the social sciences (Brewin and Anataki, 1987; Graham and Folkes, 1990; Seligman, 1991; Weiner, 1986; Weiner et al., 1971; Zelen, 1991),* no such integrated collection of papers exists in the organizational sciences. This book emerged to fill that need.

---

*Brewin, L.R. and Anataki, C. (1987). *Journal of Social and Clinical Psychology,* 5(1):79–98; Graham, S. and Folkes, V.S. (Eds.). (1990). *Attribution Theory: Applications to Achievement, Mental Health, and Interpersonal Conflict,* Hillsdale, N.J.: Erlbaum; Seligman, M. (1991). *Learned Optimism,* New York: Alfred A. Knopf; Weiner, B. (1986). *An Attribution Theory of Motivation and Emotion,* New York: Springer-Verlag; Weiner, B., Frieze, I., Kukla, A., Reed, L., Rest, S., and Rosenbaum, R.M. (1971). Perceiving the causes of success and failure. in *Attribution: Perceiving the Causes of Behavior,* E.E. Jones, D.E. Kanouse, H.H. Kelley, R.E. Nisbett, S. Valins, and B. Weiner (Eds.), Morristown, N.J.: General Learning Press; Zelen, S.L. (Ed.). (1991). *New Model, New Extensions of Attribution Theory,* New York: Springer-Verlag.

In developing the current volume, a call for papers was circulated, and papers were submitted to a blind review process. All of the members of the review board served voluntarily and, as the list of reviewers indicates, many well-known scholars in both the social and organizational sciences participated. The group of papers that was eventually accepted includes contributions from Australia, Canada, and universities across the United States. In addition, Bernard Weiner and Robert Lord were invited to write the first and next-to-last chapters, respectively, and both contributed, despite extremely demanding schedules.

Organization of the Chapters

The book was organized to expand from specific issues to more global ones. Section II begins with a discussion of measurement issues, focusing on the measurement and validity of the concept of attributional style. The three chapters in this section describe the major issues involved in measuring attributional styles, explore the validity of trait-like measures of attributional style, and present and evaluate a scale for measuring attributional style within organizational contexts.

In Section III Part A, the application of attributional theory in the context of intrapersonal behavior in organizations is explored. As a group, the chapters in this section demonstrate relationships between attributions, affective states such as negative affectivity, and performance-related behaviors such as absenteeism, job retention, and the mastery of computer-related skills.

The focus of attribution theory shifts from self to other attributions in the chapters on leadership in Section III Part B. As a group, these chapters describe and demonstrate how attributional biases, information, and the characteristics of organizational tasks influence attributions and evaluations of others. In particular, these chapters show that hedonic relevance, psychological closeness, and the sheer amount of information that evaluators must process influence both attributions and the consequent evaluations of others.

Chapters 13 to 17 represent the largest stretch for attribution theory. These chapters, in Section III Part C on group dynamics, begin to depart from traditional intraindividual models of information processing. They address not only how individuals process information within group contexts but also begin to suggest additional dynamics that may occur as the result of the synergy of interactive group contexts. Included in these chapters are discussions of how an attributional analysis may clarify the difference between politics and citizenship behaviors, how ingroup versus outgroup status affects attributions for group performance, the role that attributions play in deciding whether to cooperate or compete, the effects of demographic diversity on group attributions and performance expectations, and how varying levels of power and group performance affect group attributions and distributive justice norms. Importantly, these chapters move beyond traditional paradigms and demonstrate how attribution theory can contribute to and explain the dynamics that occur in groups and organizations.

Clearly, it would be impossible for a single book or set of papers to fully represent the wide range and potential of both the theories and applications of attribution theory in the organizational sciences. However, this book may suggest the potential that is inherent in attributional perspectives of organizational behavior and point out some of the directions for exploration that will be most beneficial.

Acknowledgments

When beginning this book, like most editors, I wondered what the final product would look like and whether or not the book would receive the support and cooperation that was needed. I am happy to report that all of my surprises were pleasant and positive. One interaction in particular characterizes the degree of commitment and support the project received. After "cold calling" on Bernard Weiner to serve as a reviewer, I later asked him if he would write an introductory chapter or preface for the book. After describing a very demanding schedule, he agreed to participate. I was astonished, however, to receive his contribution within a week of our initial conversation. All of the authors demonstrated high levels of commitment and professionalism and it was a pleasure working with each one of them.

In addition to the reviewers and authors, the support of my department chair, Pamela Perrewé, and Melvin Stith, Dean of the College of Business at Florida State University, is greatly appreciated. From the inception of this project to its conclusion, both Pam and Mel have been unhesitatingly supportive and encouraging. Dennis Buda, of St. Lucie Press, and Sandy Pearlman, who coordinated the production, demonstrated the flexibility and professionalism that were needed to place the finishing touches on the book. Finally, I would like to again thank the reviewers who did an outstanding job of providing critical but constructive suggestions to the authors.

Mark J. Martinko
Florida State University

EDITOR

Dr. Mark J. Martinko is currently Professor of Management at Florida State University, Tallahassee, Florida. He received his bachelor's degree in psychology from Muskingum College, his master's degree in educational psychology from the University of Iowa, and his Ph.D. in business from the University of Nebraska.

His research is concerned with the development and testing of models for explaining and understanding intrapersonal and interpersonal behavior in organizations. This interest has resulted in research focusing on the observation of managerial behaviors, leadership behaviors, impression management, learned helplessness, and leadership decision styles.

In addition to his academic background, Dr. Martinko has consulted or worked for a wide variety of both private and public sector organizations including Western Electric Corporation; Omaha Public Power District; the State of Nebraska; National Cash Register; Sheller-Globe Corporation; U.S. Steel; Florida Department of Law Enforcement; Appalachee Community Mental Health; Guinness Group Sales, Ltd., Ireland; Wal-Mart Corporation; and W.R. Grace and Company.

Dr. Martinko is the co-author of two previous books, *The Practice of Supervision and Management* and *The Power of Positive Reinforcement,* and more than forty research articles. His research includes publications in the *Academy of Management Review, Academy of Management Journal, American Educational Research Journal, Journal of Management,* and the *Journal of Management Studies.* He served two consecutive terms on the editorial board of the *Academy of Management Review* and is currently a member of the editorial boards of the *Journal of Organizational Behavior Management* and *Organizational Dynamics.*

REVIEWERS

Hector Betancourt
Loma Linda University

Constance Campbell
Georgia Southern University

Margaret M. Clifford
University of Iowa

Gregory H. Dobbins
University of Tennessee

Donald F. Fedor
Georgia Institute of Technology

Jack Feldman
Georgia Institute of Technology

Gerald R. Ferris
University of Illinois at Urbana-Champaign

William L. Gardner III
University of Mississippi

John W. Henry
Georgia Southern University

Eileen A. Hogan
Valdosta State University

Jerry Hunt
Texas Tech University

K. Michele Kacmar
Florida State University

Russell L. Kent
Georgia Southern University

Robert C. Liden
University of Illinois at Chicago

Robert G. Lord
University of Akron

Fred Luthans
University of Nebraska

Roger C. Mayer
Notre Dame

James C. McElroy
Iowa State University

Sherry E. Moss
Florida International University

Pamela Perrewé
Florida State University

Mark F. Peterson
Texas Tech University

Elizabeth J. Rozell
Missouri Southern State College

Bernard Weiner
University of California, Los Angeles

Robert Zmud
Florida State University

AUTHORS

Keith G. Allred
The Anderson Graduate School of
    Management
University of California, Los Angeles
Los Angeles, California

Neal M. Ashkanasy
Commerce Department
The University of Queensland
Brisbane, Australia

Dharm P.S. Bhawuk
Institute of Labor and Industrial Relations
University of Illinois at Urbana–
    Champaign
Champaign, Illinois

Michael E. Bitter
M.E. Rinker, Sr. Institute of Tax and
    Accountancy
Lynn School of Business Administration
Stetson University
DeLand, Florida

Dana M. Broach
FAA Civil Aeromedical Institute
Oklahoma City, Oklahoma

Constance Campbell
Department of Management
College of Business
Georgia Southern University
Statesboro, Georgia

Katherine Farquhar
School of Public Affairs
The American University
Washington, D.C.

Donald F. Fedor
School of Management
Georgia Institute of Technology
Atlanta, Georgia

Walter J. Ferrier
College of Business and Management
University of Maryland
College Park, Maryland

Gerald R. Ferris
Institute of Labor and Industrial
    Relations
University of Illinois at Urbana–
    Champaign
Champaign, Illinois

William L. Gardner III
Department of Management and
    Marketing
School of Business Administration
University of Mississippi
University, Mississippi

Chan M. Hellman
Oklahoma City Community College
Oklahoma City, Oklahoma

John W. Henry
Department of Management
College of Business
Georgia Southern University
Statesboro, Georgia

Thomas F. Hilton
FAA Civil Aeromedical Institute
Oklahoma City, Oklahoma

Timothy A. Judge
Center for Advanced Human Resource
  Studies
New York State School of Industrial and
  Labor Relations
Cornell University
Ithaca, New York

Leonard Karakowsky
Faculty of Management
University of Toronto
Toronto, Ontario, Canada

Russell L. Kent
Department of Management
Georgia Southern University
Statesboro, Georgia

Robert G. Lord
University of Akron
Akron, Ohio

Karen J. Maher
School of Business Administration
University of Missouri–St. Louis
St. Louis, Missouri

Mark J. Martinko
Department of Management
College of Business
Florida State University
Tallahassee, Florida

Joseph J. Martocchio
Institute of Labor and Industrial Relations
University of Illinois at Urbana–
  Champaign
Champaign, Illinois

Don Michael McDonald
Department of Sociology
Texas A&M University
College Station, Texas

Terence R. Mitchell
Department of Management
College of Business Administration
University of Washington
Seattle, Washington

Kenneth J. Rediker
College of Business Administration
University of Houston
Houston, Texas

Elizabeth J. Rozell
School of Business Administration
Missouri Southern State College
Joplin, Missouri

J.P. Siegel
Faculty of Management
University of Toronto
Toronto, Ontario, Canada

Ken G. Smith
College of Business and Management
University of Maryland
College Park, Maryland

Bernard Weiner
Department of Psychology
University of California, Los Angeles
Los Angeles, California

L. Alan Witt
Barnett Banks, Inc.
Jacksonville, Florida

Section I

INTRODUCTION: THE ROLE AND FUNCTION OF ATTRIBUTION THEORY IN THE ORGANIZATIONAL SCIENCES

1

ATTRIBUTION THEORY IN ORGANIZATIONAL BEHAVIOR: A RELATIONSHIP OF MUTUAL BENEFIT

Bernard Weiner

The history of attribution theory originated in the writings of four main authors: Fritz Heider (1958), who wrote about dyadic relationships; Edward Jones and his collaborators (Jones and Davis, 1965; Jones and Nisbett, 1972), who researched dispositional ascriptions; Harold Kelley (1967), concerned with personal interdependence and inferential processes; and Julian Rotter (1966), who investigated individual differences in causal perceptions. From these beginnings, the conceptual approach of attribution theory has become incorporated into the study of virtually all aspects of psychology, from clinical to cognitive, from the examination of schizophrenia to an understanding of schema. Attributional interpretation has also spread beyond its psychological boundaries, as proven in this and prior volumes (see Antaki and Brewin, 1982; Graham and Folkes, 1990; Jaspars et al., 1983).

As evidenced by some chapters in this book, attributional development, in principle, could have started with an analysis of organizational behavior and then branched out to the interpretation of individual and dyadic phenomena. This is because the concepts, issues, and ideas of attribution theory lend themselves so well to phenomena ingrained in organizational settings. Some of the chapters in this book include discussions of credit and blame, expectation, cooperation, disposition and situational attributions, and emotion—the very foundation of earlier attributional research and thinking on the personal and dyadic levels that was the focus of Heider, Kelley, and others.

Research in organizations, however, provides the opportunity for more than what could be provided given an individual or dyadic unit of analysis. Thus, it could result in important empirical and conceptual advances that both challenge and further prior research. This is illustrated briefly in the following discussion, which includes topics advanced by students of the University of California, Los Angeles, Graduate School of Management that relate to research described by Weiner (1985, 1986, 1993).

It is reasonably well established that perceptions of individual responsibility are influenced by variables such as freedom of choice, personal controllability, intentionality, foresight, and ability to tell right from wrong. Thus, for example, one is more responsible for a crime to the extent that the criminal act was freely engaged in (as opposed to being forced, as when a victim aids the robber in collecting money from other victims), the cause was under volitional control (as opposed to a "crime of passion"), the act was done intentionally (rather than by accident), the person envisioned the outcome (as opposed to not realizing the potential damage of the action), and the actor could distinguish right from wrong (as opposed to an infant or an insane individual, who might not be capable of this differentiation).

However, consider the allocation of responsibility in organizational settings, where organizational structure can influence such moral inferences. For example, given company failure, does the responsibility of the highest executive increase or decrease as a function of the number of levels or layers in the hierarchy? Whatever the answer is, it is evident that an entirely new aspect of judgments of responsibility has been uncovered and that structure will have to be related to dynamics. In so doing, a host of theoretical, empirical, and even philosophical questions are raised pertinent to an understanding of the concept of responsibility, one of the core themes within attribution theory.

Perceptions of responsibility for a negative, self-related outcome can give rise to anger. For example, students are angry at roommates who play the radio so loud that they cannot study or who do not help to keep the apartment clean. In these instances, there is perceived freedom to act, and the actions are subject to volitional alteration. On the other hand, when an other-related aversive outcome cannot be controlled by the other individual, then the response is sympathy. Hence, we are sympathetic to someone living in a totalitarian society, someone with a debilitating handicap, or the very aged. There are relations between cognitive appraisals and emotions, such that thoughts are sufficient determinants of feelings (see Weiner, 1985, 1986).

When evaluating these ideas in an organizational setting, other factors must be taken into account:

1. Is the responsibility–anger linkage altered because of the power relationship between the transgressor and the person experiencing the emotion? For example, if a superior has committed a transgression against a subordinate, will that subordinate experience the same degree of anger as would be true of the superior given a transgression by the subordinate?

2. Will this linkage be influenced by whether or not the transgressor and the transgressed are members of the same group?

3. Will the emotional climate of the organization (i.e., whether the atmosphere is competitive or cooperative) alter the association between perceptions of responsibility and emotional reactions?

This is not an exhaustive list of factors that might affect thinking–feeling associations, but rather an illustration of the ways in which organizational variables can be brought to bear upon what is thought to be an invariant union. Taking such factors under consideration expands our conception of the ingredients necessary for formulating a theory of emotion. These potential moderator variables would not be considered when the unit of analysis is only the individual.

Putting attribution theory in the context of organizational behavior should be of great benefit not only to those individuals working within this field, but also to those attribution theorists (like myself) who have approached this conceptual framework with a rather narrow outlook.

REFERENCES

Antaki, C. and Brewin, C. (Eds.). (1982). *Attributions and Psychological Change,* New York: Academic Press.

Graham, S. and Folkes, V.S. (Eds.). (1990). *Attribution Theory: Applications to Achievement, Mental Health, and Interpersonal Conflict,* Hillsdale, N.J.: Erlbaum.

Heider, F. (1958). *The Psychology of Interpersonal Relations,* New York: Wiley.

Jaspars, J., Fincham, F.D., and Hewstone, M. (Eds.). (1983). *Attribution Theory and Research: Conceptual, Developmental, and Social Dimensions,* New York: Academic Press.

Jones, E.E. and Davis, K.E. (1965). From acts to dispositions: The attribution process in person perception. in *Advances in Experimental Social Psychology,* Vol. 2, L. Berkowitz (Ed.), New York: Academic Press, pp. 219–266.

Jones, E.E. and Nisbett, R.E. (1972). The actor and the observer: Divergent perceptions of the causes of behavior. in *Attribution: Perceiving the Causes of Behavior,* E.E. Jones, D.E. Kanouse, H.H. Kelley, R.E. Nisbett, S. Valins, and B. Weiner (Eds.), Morristown, N.J.: General Learning Press, pp. 79–94.

Kelley, H.H. (1967). Attribution theory in social psychology. in *Nebraska Symposium on Motivation,* D. Levin (Ed.), Lincoln: University of Nebraska Press, pp. 192–238.

Rotter, J.B. (1966). Generalized expectancies for internal versus external control of reinforcement. *Psychological Monographs,* 80(No. 609).

Weiner, B. (1985). An attribution theory of achievement motivation and emotion. *Psychological Review,* 92:548–573.

Weiner, B. (1986). *An Attributional Theory of Motivation and Emotion,* New York: Springer-Verlag.

Weiner, B. (1993). On sin versus sickness: A theory of perceived responsibility and social motivation. *American Psychologist,* 48:957–965.

2

THE NATURE AND FUNCTION OF ATTRIBUTION THEORY WITHIN THE ORGANIZATIONAL SCIENCES

Mark J. Martinko

As indicated in the preface and Chapter 1, the appearance and integration of attribution theory within the organizational sciences is a relatively recent phenomenon. Although many readers will have experience and background in attribution theory, the notion of attribution theory will be relatively new for many others. Therefore, the purpose of this chapter is to provide a general discussion of the basic nature and characteristics of attribution theory, as well as the nature of its current contribution within the organizational sciences. There are several sources that provide excellent introductions and discussions of attribution theory. These include Graham and Folkes (1990), Kelley and Michela (1980), Martinko (in press a and b), Green and Mitchell (1979), Weiner (1986), Weiner et al. (1971), and Zelen (1991). The discussion presented here is not intended to be comprehensive, but rather it is intended to provide a basic introduction to this area, as well as identify some of the major issues, challenges, and opportunities associated with attribution theory.

©St. Lucie Press CCC 1-884015-19-0 1/95/$100/$.50

NATURE OF ATTRIBUTIONS

Attribution theory concerns people's causal explanations for events (Martinko, in press a). Stimulated by the early writings of Heider (1958), social psychologists have become increasingly concerned with the processes by which people explain their own successes and failures (Weiner, 1987) and those of others (Jones, 1976; Kelley and Michela, 1980). Heider's basic premise was that people have an innate need to understand and control their environments. Thus, individuals function as "naive psychologists," developing causal explanations for significant events. These beliefs about causation influence expectations, which, in turn, influence subsequent behavior. Thus, attribution theorists are concerned with the perceived causes of events and the consequences of those perceptions. For example, an employee who attributes the failure to make a sale to lack of ability will have a lowered expectation of future success and is unlikely to expend effort on sales in the future. On the other hand, if an employee attributes the failure to make a sale to an inappropriate presentation, that person may change his or her presentation with the expectation that a better presentation will result in success in the future. The premise that our beliefs about ourselves and others influence our behavior is not new. The ability of attribution theory to articulate how this process occurs, however, provides a basis for understanding and theory building that translates into practical action and motivation strategies which can empower both self and others.

Several aspects of attribution theory deserve attention and explanation.

Focus and Target

As Kelley and Michela (1980) have observed, there is no single "theory of attribution" but rather a number of differing attributional perspectives. The majority of these perspectives can be classified as self- or other attribution theories. Weiner's theory of achievement motivation (1986) is an example of a self-attribution theory. This theory is primarily concerned with how individuals explain their own successes and failures and the consequences of those explanations.

On the other hand, Kelley's ANOVA model (1967) and Green and Mitchell's (1979) model of leader behavior focus primarily on how observers assign responsibility for the outcomes of others. Essentially, these models describe the process by which observers decide whether an individual is personally responsible for an outcome or situational factors outside of the control of the individual are causally related to the event. As an example, the research of Mitchell and Wood (1980) and Wood and Mitchell (1981) demonstrates that leaders' beliefs about individuals' responsibilities for causing events influence the type of disciplinary actions they select.

It should be noted that although the majority of the theory developed up to this point focuses on how individuals process information regarding the causes of their own and others' events, a theory that attempts to develop and explain causal reasoning within group and interactive contexts is beginning to emerge. For an introduction to this theory, see Chapters 13 through 17.

Functions

The major function of attributions is generally considered to be causal analysis. However, as Brewin and Antaki (1987) note, attributions may serve other purposes, such as labeling or description, moral evaluation, and self-presentation. Similarly, Lord and Smith (1983) have noted that there are three different types of attributions: those that function to identify the cause of an event, those that seek to identify the responsibility for an event, and those that refer to personal qualities such as leadership or trustworthiness. For example, attribution theory has addressed the issue of why some individuals are labeled as leaders whereas others are not (Staw and Ross, 1980). Similarly, consumers' attributions regarding product characteristics such as quality and reliability have also been the target of attribution theories (Folkes, 1988). Thus, although a large number of attribution theories are concerned with achievement motivation and assessing the actions of others, attribution theories have also been developed to explain other perceptual and behavioral domains.

It is important to note that the purposes mentioned above need not be mutually exclusive; in fact, these purposes may often confound each other. Thus, an executive's account of the prior year's performance may serve the dual functions of both causal analysis and impression management. As can be inferred from this example, ascertaining the exact nature and purpose of the attribution is an important practical as well as theoretical problem.

ATTRIBUTIONS AND ATTRIBUTIONAL DIMENSIONS

As indicated above, attributions are specific causal explanations for events. Typical self-attributions for achievement include ability, effort, task difficulty, or chance/luck. Thus, one person may attribute the failure to be promoted to a lack of ability whereas another may believe that the failure was due primarily to luck or chance. It is generally believed that underlying these specific attributions are attributional dimensions that represent the individual's cognitive structure. Thus, for example, Weiner et al. (1971) classified the attributions above within two dimensions: locus of causality and stability. Locus of causality refers to whether individuals believe the cause resides within themselves or outside of themselves. Stability indicates the degree to which the cause is anticipated to change over time. Stable causes do not change, whereas unstable causes do. Using these two dimensions, the four specific attributions indicated earlier are typically classified as follows:

Attribution	Locus of causality	Stability
Ability	Internal	Stable
Effort	Internal	Unstable
Task difficulty	External	Stable
Chance/luck	External	Unstable

It is the underlying cognitive structure rather than the specific attribution that is believed to shape expectancies. As Russell (1982) has pointed out, a subject's classification of an attribution may not always match that of the experimenter. Thus, whereas most researchers classify ability as an internal and stable attribution, some subjects may believe that their abilities are malleable and can be enhanced. If a person believes that his or her ability is changeable, he or she is more likely to expend effort at the task in the future. Thus, it is the underlying cognitive dimension that represents the individual's beliefs about the nature of the attribution that is believed to be the key to the motivating properties of attributions.

Many other performance attributions are possible in addition to the ones described above. Examples include mood, health, strategy, and fatigue. Hypothetically, an exhaustive taxonomy of attributional dimensions would enable the classification of all specific attributions. However, from a conceptual level, such a taxonomy may not be either possible or realistic, since the subjects may not classify their attributions mutually exclusively. Some individuals may believe that portions of their ability are stable while other parts are unstable.

Finally, it should be noted that there are numerous attributional dimensions other than the ones suggested above. These dimensions include controllability, universality versus specificity, and intentionality. To a large extent, the relevant attributional dimensions depend upon the domain of interest. Thus, intentionality is most relevant to attributions for the actions of others and less so within the self-attribution context.

EMPHASIS IN THE ORGANIZATIONAL LITERATURE

Various types of attribution theories have received varying degrees of emphasis in the organizational literature. For the most part, responsibility assignment models that describe how people make attributions for the behavior and outcomes of others have dominated the organizational literature. The theoretical paper by Green and Mitchell (1979) and the empirical work that followed (e.g., Wood and Mitchell, 1981; Mitchell and Wood, 1980; Liden and Mitchell, 1985), describing how leaders react to subordinate behaviors, are typical of this body of work. Similarly, the work of Dobbins and Russell (1986a, 1986b), Knowlton and Ilgen (1980), and Feldman (1981), describing the role of attributional biases in performance appraisal situations, is also exemplary of this type of attributional research. Thus, responsibility assignment models are most typical of the attributional research conducted in organizations.

Although the achievement-oriented intrapersonal attributional models have been a major focus of attention in psychology, less attention has been devoted to the achievement-oriented models in organizational contexts. A number of conceptual papers (e.g., Evans, 1986; Martinko and Gardner 1982, 1987) have described the role and nature of attributions from the perspective of intrapersonal motivation, but empirical research investigating the role of attributions from the perspective of achievement motivation has been more limited, although there are some examples (Campbell and Martinko, 1994; Henry et al., 1993; Seligman and Schulman, 1986).

This relative emphasis on interpersonal versus intrapersonal attributional models is reflected in recent organizational behavior textbooks. In an informal survey of twenty popular organizational behavior texts, it was found that, with few exceptions (e.g., Martinko, in press b), attribution theory was virtually never mentioned in the chapters on motivation. The texts did, however, usually offer some explanation of attribution theory in the chapters on perception. In addition, research that includes aspects of attribution theory was usually discussed in the chapters on leadership and selection, but attribution theory as a theoretical body of work was frequently ignored.

A partial explanation for the lack of attention to the intrapersonal aspects of attribution theory within organizational behavior may be attributed to the nature of the field. Although intrapersonal behavior has always been a part of the field of organizational behavior, the dyadic and group behavior that is an integral part of the nature of behavior in organizations has probably received more emphasis. Thus, the nature of the problems associated with leading and managing cooperative group efforts within organizations can be seen as stimulating the development of interpersonal attributional perspectives.

The current emphasis on interpersonal attribution models in organizational behavior should not be viewed as a weakness. This emphasis, which is somewhat different from the general intrapersonal orientation of psychology, forces both organizational psychologists and researchers in organizational behavior to develop new theories and concepts to explain interpersonal behavioral domains. Therefore, many of the chapters in the current volume break new ground in their attempt to explain and explore areas of interpersonal and group behavior not previously considered.

As noted previously, very little attention is afforded to attributional perspectives in chapters on intrapersonal motivation in traditional organizational behavior texts. This lack of attention may be because attribution theory has been viewed and labeled as a theory of perception rather than as a motivation theory. As indicated earlier in the discussion of multiple purposes and functions of attributions, attribution theories address both domains. In particular, attributional theories of achievement motivation are a natural extension of expectancy theory and both explain and account for the development of expectancies. More specifically, research has repeatedly emphasized the direct links between attributions and expectancies (Abramson et al., 1978; Weiner, 1986). Since it is well accepted that expectancies have a strong influence on behavior, attributions may be viewed as the key to influencing expectancies. Research on the learned helplessness paradigm generally supports the notion that attributions are associated with expectancies, affective states, and passive as well as motivated behavior (Abramson et al., 1978; Martinko and Gardner, 1982, 1987). In general, the learned helplessness paradigm has demonstrated that attributional styles are associated with motivated behavior. More specifically, people with optimistic attributional styles characterized by specific, external, and unstable attributions for failure and global, internal, and stable attributions for success have been found to have higher levels of expectancies, express more positive affect, and achieve at higher levels of performance than their more pessimistic counterparts (e.g., Campbell and Martinko, 1994; Henry et al., 1993; Limpaphayom et al., 1992; Seligman and Schulman, 1986). Although this research is still developing, it would seem that attribution theory may have much to add to the theoretical understanding and explanation of employee empowerment and motivation in general.

REFERENCES

Abramson, L.Y., Seligman, M.E., and Teasdale, J.D. (1978). Learned helplessness in humans: Critique and reformulation. *Journal of Abnormal Psychology,* 87(1):49–74.

Brewin, L.R. and Antaki, C. (1987). *Journal of Social and Clinical Psychology,* 5(1):79–98.

Campbell, C. and Martinko, M.J. (1994). An attributional analysis of learned helplessness in an organization: A multi-method field study. *Proceedings of the Southeast Decision Science Institute,* pp. 110–112.

Dobbins, G.H. and Russell, J.M. (1986a). Self-serving biases in leadership: A laboratory experiment. *Journal of Management,* 12(4):475–483.

Dobbins, G.H. and Russell, J.M. (1986b). The biasing effects of subordinate likeableness on leaders' responses to poor performers: A laboratory and a field study. *Personnel Psychology,* 39(4):759–777.

Evans, M.G. (1986). Organizational behavior: The central role of motivation. *Journal of Management,* 2(2):203–222.

Feldman, J.M. (1981). Beyond attribution theory: Cognitive processes in performance appraisal. *Journal of Applied Psychology,* 66(2):127–148.

Folkes, V. (1988). Recent attribution research in consumer behavior: A review and new directions. *Journal of Consumer Research,* 14(1):548–565.

Graham, S. and Folkes, V.S. (Eds.). (1990). *Attribution Theory: Applications to Achievement, Mental Health, and Interpersonal Conflict,* Hillsdale, N.J.: Erlbaum.

Green, S.G. and Mitchell, T.R. (1979). Attributional processes of leaders in leader–member interactions. *Organizational Behavior and Human Performance,* 23(3):429–458.

Heider, F. (1958). *The Psychology of Interpersonal Relations,* New York: Wiley.

Henry, J., Martinko, M.J., and Pierce, M.A. (1993). Attributional style as a predictor of success in a first computer science course. *Computers in Human Behavior,* 9:341–352.

Jones, E.E. (1976). How do people perceive the causes of behavior? *American Scientist,* 64(3):300–305.

Kelley, H.H. (1967). Attribution theory in social psychology. in *Nebraska Symposium on Motivation,* D. Levine (Ed.), Lincoln: University of Nebraska Press, pp. 192–238.

Kelley, H.H. and Michela, J.L. (1980). Attribution theory and research. *Annual Review of Psychology,* 31:457–501.

Knowlton, W.A., Jr. and Ilgen, D.R. (1980). Performance attributional effects on feedback from superiors. *Organizational Behavior and Human Performance,* 25(3):441–456.

Liden, R.C. and Mitchell, T.R. (1985). Reactions to feedback: The role of attributions. *Academy of Management Journal,* 28(2):291–308.

Limpaphayom, P., Martinko, M.J., and Perrewé, P.L. (1992). Organizationally induced helplessness: An alternative explanation for job strain. *Proceedings of the Decision Science Institute.*

Lord, R.G. (1985). An information processing approach to social perceptions, leadership and behavioral measurement in organizations. *Research in Organizational Behavior,* 7:87–128.

Lord, R.G. and Maher, K.J. (1990). Alternative information-processing models and their implications for theory, research, and practice. *Academy of Management Review,* 15(1): 9–28.

Lord, R.G. and Smith, J.E. (1983). Theoretical, information processing, and situational factors affecting attribution theory models of organizational behavior. *Academy of Management Review,* 8(1):50–60.

Martinko, M.J. (in press a). Attribution theory. in *The Blackwell Dictionary of Organizational Behavior,* N. Nicholson (Ed.), London: Blackwell Publishers.

Martinko, M.J. (in press b). Basic motivation. in *Organizational Behavior, Praxis Edition,* F. Luthans (Ed.), New York: McGraw-Hill.

Martinko, M.J. and Gardner, W.L. (1982). Learned helplessness: An alternative explanation for performance deficits. *Academy of Management Review,* 7(2):195–204.

Martinko, M.J. and Gardner, W.L. (1987). The leader/member attribution process. *Academy of Management Review,* 12(2):235–249.

Mitchell, T.R. and Wood, R.E. (1980). Supervisor's responses to subordinate poor performance: A test of an attributional model. *Organizational Behavior and Human Performance,* 25:123–138.

Russell, D. (1982). The causal dimension scale: A measure of how individuals perceive causes. *Journal of Personality of Social Psychology,* 42:1137–1145.

Seligman, M. (1991). *Learned Optimism,* New York: Alfred A. Knopf.

Seligman, M. and Schulman, P. (1986). Explanatory style as a predictor of productivity and quitting among life insurance agents. *Journal of Personality and Social Psychology,* 50(4):832–838.

Staw, B.M. and Ross, J. (1980). Commitment in an experimenting society: A study of the attribution of leadership from administrative scenarios. *Journal of Applied Psychology,* 65(3):249–260.

Weiner, B. (1986). *An Attribution Theory of Motivation and Emotion,* New York: Springer-Verlag.

Weiner, B. (1987). The social psychology of emotion: Applications of a naive psychology. *Journal of Social and Clinical Psychology,* 5(4):405–419.

Weiner, B., Frieze, I., Kukla, A., Reed, L., Rest, S., and Rosenbaum, R.M. (1971). *Perceiving the Causes of Success and Failure,* Morristown, N.J.: General Learning Press.

Wood, R.E. and Mitchell, T.R.(1981). Manager behavior in a social context: The impact of impression management on attributions and disciplinary actions. *Organizational Behavior and Human Performance,* 28(3):356–378.

Zelen, S.L. (Ed.). (1991). *New Model, New Extensions of Attribution Theory,* New York: Springer-Verlag.

Section II

MEASURING ATTRIBUTIONAL PROCESSES IN ORGANIZATIONAL CONTEXTS

3

THE MEASUREMENT OF ATTRIBUTIONS IN ORGANIZATIONAL RESEARCH

Russell L. Kent and Mark J. Martinko

ABSTRACT

Attributional research in organizational behavior has flourished in recent years. A major criticism of this research concerns the measurement of attributions. Issues that researchers need to consider when measuring attributions are identified and discussed in this chapter.

INTRODUCTION

In recent years, attribution theory, which is concerned with the process by which individuals assign causes to events, has been applied to a variety of organizational phenomena. For example, it has increased our understanding of processes such as leadership (McElroy, 1982), leader–member relations (e.g., Martinko and Gardner, 1987; Mitchell and Wood, 1980), motivation (e.g., Brockner and Guare, 1983; Dorfman and Stephan, 1984; Teas and McElroy, 1986; Weiner, 1985a), organizationally induced helplessness (Martinko and Gardner, 1982, 1987), goal setting (Chacko and McElroy, 1983), and the performance satisfaction relationship (Adler, 1980; Norris and Niebuhr, 1984). It has also been suggested that attribution theory can be applied to other areas of concern to organizational researchers and practitioners such as turnover (Seligman and Schulman, 1986), performance appraisal and feedback (e.g., Feldman, 1981; Liden and Mitchell, 1985), organizational conflict (Baron, 1988), organizational strategy (Ford, 1985), and overall organizational/group performance (Bettman and Weitz, 1983; Brown, 1984). Obviously, attribution theory plays a major role in present and future research in organizational behavior.

Although a great deal of attention has been given to developing attributional theories in organizational behavior, little emphasis has been placed on the measurement of attributions in organizational research. In fact, one major criticism of attributional research in organizational behavior is the lack of psychometrically sound instruments for measuring attributions (Ilgen and Klein, 1988). However, before instruments can be developed, several fundamental issues need to be addressed. One of these issues is whether the instruments are concerned with "causal explanations" or "causal dimensions." Causal explanations are the actual attributions made by individuals (e.g., luck, ability, effort, task difficulty), whereas causal dimensions refer to the causal structure underlying the nearly endless list of possible attributions for an event (e.g., locus of causality, stability). Both have received considerable attention in the organizational behavior literature and are discussed in this chapter.

A second area relating to how attributions are measured concerns the construct of "attributional style" in assessing the relationship between attributions and a number of outcome variables. Peterson et al. (1982, p. 288) define attributional style as "the extent to which individuals show characteristic attributional tendencies." Although this construct has received considerable attention in other disciplines, it has only been given minimal consideration in organizational research (e.g. Seligman and Schulman, 1986).

The purpose of this chapter is to review existing methods used to assess causal attributions in organizational research. It begins with a discussion of the distinction between causal explanations and causal dimensions. Measurement concerns when assessing both causal explanations and causal dimensions are discussed, and the construct of an "attributional style" is presented. Issues concerning the validity of this construct and its cross-situational characteristics, stability, and measurement are also discussed. The chapter concludes with a summary of issues presented and proposes additional issues that warrant attention before selecting a process for measuring attributions.

CAUSAL EXPLANATIONS VERSUS CAUSAL DIMENSIONS

An interesting feature of the attribution research in the organizational literature is the use of both causal explanations and causal dimensions when assessing how attributions are made or the impact of making certain types of attributions on other outcome variables. The term "causal explanation," or, as Weiner (1985a) refers to it, "causal description," is used here to mean the specific causal attributions individuals use to explain their past success and failure experiences. This implies that there is a nearly endless list of possible attributions individuals may make, including attributions to effort, ability, task difficulty, luck, one's own mood, the mood of others, acts of God, and a number of other variables having to do with oneself, other people, or other situational events.

Although the study of these specific causal attributions is in itself interesting, the demands of theory construction often require researchers to go beyond these specific causal explanations for a given outcome to the underlying causal structure. Identifying the causal dimensions along which this myriad of causal explanations vary is necessary to identify the similarities and differences in the various causal explanations. Identification of these similarities and differences facilitates empirical study and leads to the discovery of relationships that contribute to the meaning and significance of cause. An example of this is in the study of the reformulated learned helplessness model of depression (Abramson et al., 1978). This model predicts that individuals who make internal, stable, and global attributions for failure tend to become helpless and suffer from depression to a greater extent than those exhibiting a different attributional style. To test this hypothesized relationship, the researcher must go from the specific causal attribution made by the subject to an assessment of the underlying causal dimensions of internality, stability, and globality.

Studies assessing both causal explanations and causal dimensions can be found in the organizational literature, although the majority appear to focus on assessing causal dimensions (e.g., Dorfman and Stephan, 1984; Seligman and Schulman, 1986). Because both "explanations" and "dimensions" appear to be of interest to researchers, measurement issues concerning each are discussed below.

THE ASSESSMENT OF CAUSAL EXPLANATIONS

Elig and Frieze (1979) presented one of the most thorough examinations of the different methods of measuring causal explanations. In this examination, they compared the use of open-ended attributions (the subject simply states the reason for success or failure), measures of percentage of causality (subjects are given a list of potential attributions and told to indicate how much each cause contributed to their success or failure), and measures of importance of different causes (subjects are given a list of potential attributions and told to rate the importance of each one on a separate scale). They concluded that the latter approach of using importance ratings seemed to be the method of choice, although open-ended measures may be appropriate for novel or new situations.

Examples of each of the methods for assessing causal explanations described by Elig and Frieze (1979) can be found in the organizational literature. Seligman and Schulman (1986) looked at open-ended attributions in their study of attributions and productivity. Adler (1980) used the percentage of importance method in his investigation of attributions and job satisfaction. The importance rating method was used by Dorfman and Stephan (1984) in their investigation of attributions, satisfaction, and performance. In addition to the three methods identified by Elig and Frieze (1979), organizational researchers have adopted a fourth method that uses a forced choice format. That is, the subject is given a list of possible causal explanations and forced to choose the one that is most appropriate for a given situation.

Several problems with the above methods appear obvious. First, with the exception of the open-ended method, all of the methods limit the attributions the subject can make. It would seem that there is an almost endless list of possible attributions for any given situation. Limiting the choice to just a few (normally four) may not accurately assess the individual's actual explanation for why an event occurred. Second, all of the methods described have either questionable or completely unknown psychometric properties. Finally, the use of a variety of methods in the different studies makes it extremely difficult to aggregate findings across studies in order to gain a more complete understanding of the role of attributions in organizations.

THE ASSESSMENT OF CAUSAL DIMENSIONS

Often, the need for testing predictions from attributional models makes it necessary for researchers to look beyond the specific causal explanations to the underlying causal dimensions (e.g., locus of control, stability). To accomplish this, researchers often "force" different causal explanations into a dimension or set of dimensions. Use of this approach to assess causal dimensions is questionable for several reasons. First, since the causal explanations being forced are normally identified using one of the methods discussed above, all of the problems associated with the above methods appear to apply to the assessment of causal dimensions as well. Second, using this approach assumes that the researcher and the person making the attribution assign the same meaning to the causal explanation. Making the transition from causal explanations to causal dimensions often results in what Russell (1982) has termed the "fundamental attribution researcher error." An example of this may involve an attribution to one's ability. Normally, based on the conceptualization provided by Weiner (1974), the researcher would classify this causal explanation as internal and stable. However, it is also plausible that a subject may believe that ability is unstable and able to be changed by additional training or experience. The end result would be the incorrect assignment of the attribution to the internal, stable category by the researcher when the individual meant something entirely different. To prevent this problem, Russell (1982) and others (Ronis et al., 1983; Russell et al., 1987) have suggested focusing on a more direct assessment of the underlying meaning of causal explanations. Examples of where this approach has been used success-fully can be found in studies of depression (Peterson et al., 1982) and in a variety of studies regarding achievement situations that use the Causal Dimension Scale (Russell, 1982; McAuley et al., 1992). The approach used on these scales is to ask the respondent to assign a cause for a success or failure event. The subject (as opposed to the researcher) is then asked to rate the cause along the dimensions of interest (e.g., internal/external, stability). This method of directly assessing causal dimensions appears to be more accurate than methods that rely on using the theoretical meaning of causal attributions (Russell et al., 1987).

Another issue warranting attention is the fundamental question "Does an identifiable causal structure underlie the numerous causal explanations given by individuals and, if so, along what dimensions do these causal explanations vary?" For example, in his attributional theory of achievement motivation, Weiner (1985a) suggests that attributions for success and failure vary along the dimen-sions of stability, locus of causality (internal/external), and controllability. In the reformulated learned helplessness model of depression, Abramson et al. (1978) also identify the attributional dimensions of stability and locus of causality but use "globality" as a third dimension and disregard the dimension of controllabil-ity. When applying attribution theory to the study of a variety of relationships, organizational researchers use a number of different dimensions, but provide little justification as to why certain dimensions are thought to relate to the phenomenon under study. Because of the importance of this issue, it is discussed in more detail below.

CAUSAL DIMENSIONS

The purpose of this section is to discuss the different causal dimensions identified in the literature and the appropriateness of using the different dimen-sions in the study of organizational issues.

Weiner (1985a) discussed five underlying causal dimensions identified in previous research: an internal/external (locus) dimension, a stability dimension, a controllability dimension, a global/specific dimension, and a dimension re-ferred to as intentionality. These dimensions are discussed in turn here.

Locus of Causality

The internal/external dimension appears to be the most widely accepted dimension along which attributions are thought to vary. In fact, the analysis of structure of causality began with an internal/external dimension. This causal dimension pertains to the distinction between factors "inside" the person and factors "outside" the person or in the environment. It gained further acceptance with the work of Rotter (1966) and plays a leading role in most attributional theories (Abramson et al., 1978; Weiner, 1985a). Empirical support for this dimension is fairly convincing (Sweeney et al., 1986; Weiner, 1985a). More specifically, in the seven empirical studies identified by Weiner (1985a), six reported a locus of causality dimension. More recently, in their meta-analysis of attributional style and depression, Sweeney et al. (1986) found a relatively large effect size (–0.36) for the internal attribution dimension in explaining depression. These empirical findings, combined with a logical analysis of causal structure, strongly support the contention that locus of causality is an underlying dimension of perceived causality.

Before discussing the next dimension, a few additional comments concerning the internal/external dimension may be helpful. First, the use of an internal/external dimension normally implies that both physical and mental attributes of the person are to be considered when looking at internal elements. It should be noted that at least one study (Wimer and Kelley, 1982) makes the distinction between physical and mental attributes. Their findings suggest that the internal dimension is one of psychological internality and only those causes located "in the person's mind" are of interest when assessing the internal dimension. However, the majority of the research seems to support the broader definition of internality.

A second additional comment concerning the internal/external dimension deals with the label "locus of causality." With the wide acceptance of Rotter's (1966) work, the term "locus of control" has been widely used when discussing the internal/external dimension. Because a dimension to be considered later concerns the issue of controllability, using the term "locus of control" may be confusing. As Weiner (1985a) points out, this distinction may be necessary because an event can be internal yet uncontrollable (e.g., mood). To avoid confusion, Weiner (1985a) suggests that the term "locus of causality" be used instead of "locus of control."

A final comment on the internal/external dimension has to do with the assumed inverse relationship between internal (dispositional) and external (situational) factors. Solomon (1978) suggests that internal and external attributions are not inversely related and that only studies that report these dimensions separately allow us to draw unambiguous conclusions. This same approach is suggested by Peterson and Villanova (1988) in the study of attributional style. In their expanded Attributional Style Questionnaire, internal consistency for the internal/external dimension, although improved over the original scale, was still only 0.66. One explanation is that in the study of explanatory style, locus of causality is actually multi-dimensional. Future studies may want to consider investigating the multi-dimensionality of locus of causality by treating internality and externality as two separate dimensions. Nevertheless, the overall findings regarding this dimension, combined with a logical analysis of causal structure, strongly support the notion that locus of causality is a primary dimension of perceived causality.

Stability

A second dimension that has received wide acceptance was proposed by Weiner et al. (1971). This dimension addresses the variability of cause over time and is referred to as the stability dimension. For example, ability and mood are both internal factors. However, they differ in that ability is normally thought to be relatively stable over time whereas mood is thought to vary. Evidence supporting the validity of the stability dimension is again fairly convincing. Four of seven studies reviewed by Weiner (1985a) clearly identified a stability dimension, and Sweeney et al. (1986) reported medium effect sizes (–0.25) of stability in the study of depression. Weiner (1985a) has identified the stability of a cause as the major determinant of expectancy shifts, which is a key element in his theory of achievement motivation. Thus, as with the locus of causality dimension, the stability dimension has received wide support both empirically (Sweeney et al., 1986) and by its inclusion in a number of attributional theories and models (e.g., Abramson et al., 1978; Martinko and Gardner, 1982; Weiner, 1985a).

Controllability

Although both locus of causality and stability share widespread acceptance by attribution theorists and researchers, several other dimensions not receiving this same level of acceptance have been identified in various attributional theories. In his attribution theory of achievement motivation, Weiner (1979) included a third dimension referred to as "controllability," which represents the extent to which a cause is seen as being under the control of the individual. Rosenbaum (1972), using the same deductive reasoning that characterized the development of attribution theory, recognized that although mood and effort were both internal and unstable factors, they were distinguishable because of control. That is, effort is under the volitional control of the individual whereas mood is not. Weiner (1985a) found five empirical studies that identified controllability as a causal dimension and concluded that it should be used in the causal analysis of attributions. Although controllability was not included in the Abramson et al. (1978)

reformulated model of learned helplessness and depression, Anderson et al. (1983, p. 135) concluded that controllability is very important in understanding attributional styles. This suggests that although controllability is not explicitly included in the model of Abramson et al. (1978), its inclusion in learned helplessness research may contribute to our understanding of this phenomenon.

Although a reasonable level of support for a controllability dimension exists, there are several concerns regarding its inclusion in causal analysis. Controllability and locus of causality have been found to be highly intercorrelated (Kent and Martinko, 1995; Russell et al., 1987). On the other hand, some studies have reported that locus of causality and control liability are uncorrelated (e.g., Russell et al., 1985). More recently, in assessing the psychometric properties of a revised Causal Dimension Scale, McAuley et al. (1992) provided convincing evidence that the locus of causality and controllability dimensions were empirically distinct. To explain inconsistent findings, Russell et al. (1987) have suggested that the relation between locus of causality and the controllability dimensions varies from situation to situation. Thus, for example, controllability may emerge as a separate factor in studies of social motivation (e.g., Weiner, 1993), but fail to be distinguished as a separate factor in a study of self-attributions. It appears, therefore, that the behavioral domain and the specific environment in which the behavior occurs determine the dimensions likely to emerge from causal analyses. In addition, both Weiner (1985a) and Anderson et al. (1983) note that a failure to find orthogonality at the empirical level does not invalidate separation at a conceptual level. Given these general findings, researchers should be particularly careful to identify and confirm which dimensions are relevant when they generalize and apply theory to different contexts.

Globality

Another dimension that has been proposed by Abramson et al. (1978) in their reformulated learned helplessness model pertains to a global/specific characteristic of attributions. They claim that it is orthogonal to the previously proposed locus of causality and stability dimensions and include it in their model to determine if helplessness is cross-situational or if it applies only to the original situation. For example, an individual may perform poorly in a training course that requires an aptitude for math. Two possible attributions can be made that are both internal and stable: lack of intelligence or lack of mathematical skills. An attribution to lack of intelligence is more global and implies that failure will occur in a number of situations. According to the theory, this leads to "global" or cross-situational helplessness. If the individual attributes poor performance in the training course to a lack of mathematical skills, future failure should only occur in those situations involving mathematical skills and helplessness should be situation-specific.

While Abramson, Seligman, and their colleagues have found support for the role of the global/specific dimension in their model (Alloy et al., 1984) and continue to include it in their research, a number of criticisms of this dimension have been raised. Although he states that the dimension has face validity, Weiner (1985a) notes that a global/specific dimension did not emerge in a single study he reviewed. He questions whether this distinction is actually made by laypersons or only by attribution theorists.

In the study of organizational phenomenon, arguments for and against this dimension can be made. For example, one could argue that because the emphasis is on a single situation (work-related), a dimension to evaluate cross-situational consistency is unnecessary. On the other hand, a strong case can be made that a number of situations exist in the work environment (e.g., pay, promotions, and supervisor relations). Because of this, cross-situational consistency is a concern and should be included, at least initially, in investigations of attributional style in the workplace.

Intentionality

The final dimension discussed by Weiner (1985a) has been labeled "intentionality" (Weiner, 1979). He describes intentionality as the property that best describes the difference between effort and strategy. That is, insufficient effort and improper strategy are both internal, unstable attributions for an event. The difference between these two is that one does not intentionally use an improper strategy, whereas one may intentionally not exert sufficient effort. The case of a manager who fails due to spending too much time on the golf course and not enough time at work (effort) versus a manager who works very hard but fails to do "the right things" is an example of this distinction.

Although not identifying it as the causal dimension of intentionality, Clifford (1984, 1986) has stressed the importance of strategy attributions in achievement situations. Clifford's research has demonstrated the importance of a causal explanation that is more stable than effort and less stable than ability. She assigned the label "strategy" to this explanation and defines it as methods and techniques used to develop skills. It should be noted that Clifford (1984) acknowledges the fact that strategy attributions are rare. However, she has also demonstrated that when strategy attributions are made, they produce very constructive results in influencing future achievement situations (Clifford, 1986). Although people may not readily make strategy attributions, adding this to their repertoire of attributional responses to failure situations may be a productive training approach.

However, several criticisms of including intentionality as a dimension have also been raised (Weiner, 1985a). First, intent and control generally covary highly. Second, Weiner (1985a) presents the conceptual argument that intent is an action, not a cause. His example is that of aptitude: it can be described as internal or stable, but can it be described as unintentional?

More recent research on the intentionality dimension suggests that this dimension is particularly relevant to the context of social motivation (Weiner, 1993; Betancourt and Blair, 1992). In particular, the work of Betancourt and Blair (1992) provides empirical evidence that attributions of intentionality relate to reactions of anger and violence. Thus, at least within some contexts, intentionality emerges as a relevant dimension.

Conclusions

This section has examined the differences between causal explanations and causal dimensions and the respective methodologies for measuring each of these constructs. Several conclusions appear appropriate. First, there appears to be a general consensus in the literature that causal reasoning is most appropriately assessed by evaluating causal dimensions. There are sound theoretical reasons for this position. According to models suggested by Weiner (1986), Abramson et al. (1978), and Martinko and Gardner (1982), it is the causal dimensions rather than the specific attributional explanations that are believed to influence expectancies. More specifically, it is not the individual's belief in a lack of ability per se that is theorized to cause lowered expectations, but rather it is the individual's belief that the cause is stable and cannot be changed that results in the lowered expectation. In addition, from a logical standpoint, it is clear that by classifying explanations along attributional dimensions, attributions can be compared and contrasted. Nevertheless, it should be acknowledged that there are few or no studies that directly compare the proportion of variability in expectancies attributable to causal explanations versus causal dimensions within a specific behavioral domain. It is possible that, because of internal scripts and experience (Lord and Maher, 1990), some individuals may automatically employ causal explanations without any explicit consideration of causal dimensions. Thus, it is possible that scales using causal explanations may be more reliable and account for more variability in some contexts than scales that assess causal dimensions. More empirical work would help clarify which, if any, situations are more appropriately assessed by evaluating causal explanations as opposed to causal dimensions. Thus, although the literature appears to support the superiority of assessing causal dimensions rather than causal explanations, additional research would be helpful to more clearly delineate the relative efficacy of focusing on one or the other of these constructs.

Another issue suggested above is the issue of whether or not causal dimensions are a reasonable representation of the structures that individuals use to process information about causation. Stated another way, it is possible that causal dimensions are more an artifact of the process by which researchers classify information than an accurate representation of subjects' causal reasoning processes. As Lord and Maher (1990) have suggested, causal reasoning can be depicted as a cybernetic process and may not typically involve the rational processes depicted by the majority of attribution theories. If this is the case, alternative measurement procedures and methods of inquiry may be warranted, particularly in organizational contexts. At this point in theory development, qualitative approaches to studying and assessing causal reasoning (e.g., Campbell and Martinko, 1994) may yield important insights into the nature and function of attributional processes, whereas adherence to more traditional questionnaire methodologies may inhibit theory development.

Another issue not yet raised, particularly with respect to the Causal Dimension Scale (Russell, 1982; McAuley et al., 1992), is that many of the current measures force subjects to describe dimensions that apply to a single cause. In reality, subjects probably frequently perceive multiple causes. Thus, researchers should consider developing and adapting measurement procedures that more accurately reflect causal reasoning processes.

Finally, if causal dimensions are the focus of measurement, some comment on the relevant dimensions is appropriate. Although Weiner (1985a) has probably done the most thorough analyses of causal dimensions, the majority of this work and research focuses on self-attributions in achievement-oriented situations. As other domains are explored in organizations (e.g., group and observer attributions), additional dimensions may become relevant. Thus, for example, intentionality is probably more relevant to the measurement of observer attributions than it is to self-attributions. Therefore, researchers should anticipate that causal structures and dimensions may not be replicated across behavioral domains. The relevant dimensions for assessment are likely to change depending upon the domain of interest.

ATTRIBUTIONAL STYLE

One alternative approach to assessing the role of causal attributions is the construct of attributional style. Attributional style (AS) as a construct derived from the reformulated theory of learned helplessness (Abramson et al, 1978). This individual difference construct refers to the systematic ways in which people explain their own successes and failures. The basic idea is that people differ in their AS and that AS differences contribute to motivational, performance, and affective reactions to various life experiences (Anderson et al., 1988). In their model of learned helplessness, Abramson et al. (1978) predicted that individuals who attributed their failure to internal, stable, and global factors were more prone to depression than those individuals making other types of attributions. It was also predicted that depression-prone individuals would attribute success to external, unstable, and specific factors. The suggestion was that AS was debilitating because the combination of these attributional reactions to success and failure would permit the integration of bad but not good outcomes into the structure of beliefs about the self (Sweeney et al., 1986).

A review of the literature on the AS construct shows that the relationship between AS and depression is by far the most heavily researched, although the relationship between AS and other outcomes has also been studied (e.g., Seligman and Schulman, 1986; Henry et al., 1993). In their meta-analysis of the relation of AS to depression, Sweeney et al. (1986) identified over 100 studies for inclusion in their review. The results of the meta-analysis provide fairly convincing support for the attributional model of learned helplessness and depression presented by Abramson et al. (1978). In addition to the numerous studies focusing on depression, a number of other measures of AS have been developed (e.g., Anderson et al., 1983; Escovar et al., 1982; Furnham et al., 1992; Gong-Guy and Hammen, 1980; Ickes and Layden, 1978; Peterson et al., 1982; Peterson and Villanova, 1988; Russell, 1982; McAuley et al., 1992), although the Attributional Style Questionnaire (ASQ) appears to be the most widely accepted.

As with any psychological construct, a major concern in studying AS is construct validity. At least some evidence of the construct validity of an individual AS is provided by the research on the relationship between attributions and depression as hypothesized in the reformulated learned helplessness model. In general, the research in this area has been supportive of the model. Most convincing is the meta-analysis conducted by Sweeney et al. (1986), which concluded that the literature as a whole supports predictions that depression is positively related to internal, stable, and global attributions for failure and external, unstable, and specific attributions for success. Investigations of the relationship between attributions and other outcomes such as loneliness (Anderson et al., 1983), burnout (Wade et al., 1986), hardiness (Hull et al., 1988), stress (Mikulincer and Solomon, 1983), and turnover (Seligman and Schulman, 1986) have also produced findings supporting the construct validity of AS.

Although past research seems to provide some level of support for the construct validity of an individual AS, several studies question the concept of a cross-situationally consistent, trait-like AS (Arntz et al., 1985; Cutrona et al., 1984). It has also been suggested that individuals may only demonstrate attributional consistency across a fairly narrow range of events (Cutrona et al., 1984).

In responding to the criticisms raised by Cutrona et al. (1984) and others, Anderson et al. (1988) addressed three questions: (1) Is AS a valid construct? (2) Is a person's AS general across types of situations, or is it so situation-specific that it would be inappropriate to use it as an individual difference construct? (3) Does AS have important effects in complex social settings, or do situational influences render it impotent? Instead of using the ASQ, Anderson et al. (1988)

measured AS using the Attributional Style Assessment Test (ASAT) (Anderson, et al., 1983). Data from six previous studies (both published and unpublished) were included in the analysis in an attempt to eliminate the "publication bias" that may have been present in previous reviews (e.g., Sweeney et al., 1986). Based on their results, several conclusions were reached: (1) AS does seem to be a valid construct, (2) AS does not appear to be as cross-situationally consistent as originally thought, and (3) AS is not so situationally specific as to cease being a meaningful construct. They also suggested that a person's AS is cross-situationally consistent only across situations that are similar in psychologically meaningful ways. In summary, the results provide some evidence of convergent and discriminant validity for an AS when assessed at an intermediate level of specificity, rather than a more general AS.

In addition, however, the research by Henry and Campbell (1995), reported in this book, indicates that both situational and trait measures (i.e., AS measures) demonstrated reasonable reliability and validity as predictors of performance. Moreover, in a situation that was reasonably specific, there was no clear difference in the validity and reliability of the situational versus AS measures of attributions. Both measures performed reasonably well in terms of reliability and validity. Thus, at this point in the process of theory development, measuring AS appears to be a worthwhile endeavor, and both situational and more general measures appear to be worth exploring.

THE MEASUREMENT OF ATTRIBUTIONAL STYLE

The final area relating to AS concerns the measurement of the construct. In past research, most researchers have used combined scores to assess an individual's AS. That is, scores for the separate dimensions (e.g., locus of causality, stability, globality) were combined to form a single score that was purported to measure AS. The primary reason for this was the low internal consistencies of the separate dimensions (0.4 to 0.7) reported on the most commonly used measure of AS (ASQ, Peterson et al., 1982). Internal consistency reported for the combined scores in the initial investigation of the ASQ was 0.75 for good events and 0.72 for bad events. Because of this, most researchers using the ASQ have followed the advice of the scale developers and reported only composite scores. More recently, however, Peterson and Villanova (1988) have presented an expanded ASQ and report considerably higher reliabilities for the separate dimensions (0.66 to 0.88). Because of these higher reliabilities, the relationship between the separate dimensions and outcome variables was reported, rather than using a composite score. This approach is also supported by Carver (1989), who argues against using a composite score when assessing AS. According to Carver (1989), the main shortcoming of the use of composite scores is the loss of information that occurs. A second interesting point raised by Carver is that there appears to be no rationale for assuming that the dimensions are additive. In fact, he suggests an interactive effect of the different dimensions on various outcomes. Specifically, in the learned helplessness model of depression (Abramson et al., 1978), it is hypothesized that for depression to occur, high levels of both stability and globality must be present. Thus, since the impact of one variable on some outcome is dependent on the level of a second variable, this implies an interactive model. Carver suggests that the need to test for an interaction between attributional dimensions appears to be a logical next step.

Based on the preceding discussion, several conclusions concerning the construct of AS appear reasonable. First, AS does seem to be a valid construct. There is at least some evidence of both the convergent and discriminant validity of AS. Second, AS does not appear to be totally cross-situationally consistent. However, AS is a useful construct when assessed across a narrower range of activities. In organizational research, the situation can be narrowed considerably by using only work-related events. Next, AS appears to be related to a number of variables (e.g., turnover, stress, burnout) that are of interest to organizational researchers and is therefore worthy of some discussion and evaluation in an organizational context. Finally, not only should a composite score of AS be considered, but the relationship between the individual causal dimensions, causal explanations, and other variables should be assessed. Both the additive and interactive characteristics of these relationships should be tested.

SUMMARY AND CONCLUSIONS

This chapter has summarized and discussed the major concerns and issues regarding the measurement of attributions and AS. Several practical and theoretical limitations were discussed relating to the measurement of causal explanations. Also, there appeared to be a general consensus in the literature that, for both theoretical and practical purposes, causal dimensions yielded more information regarding causal reasoning than the assessment of causal explanations. Nevertheless, it was noted that causal explanations are still worthy of attention and investigation and, in some contexts, may explain as much variance in behavior as causal dimensions. In addition, it was noted that focusing on causal dimensions as the primary method for measuring attributions may detract from the development of theory that more accurately describes the process of causal reasoning. Thus, more qualitative and exploratory methods of measuring and describing attributional processes may be appropriate.

AS was also discussed as an alternative method of exploring causal reasoning. As the review indicated, almost all of the scales developed employ assessment of causal dimensions rather than causal explanations. There do not appear to be any studies that employ causal explanations as the primary method for classifying AS. As in the case of the general problem of assessing causal reasoning, it would seem that comparisons and contrasts between causal dimensions and causal explanations might be helpful. In addition, there remains some controversy over whether general measures or measures that are more specific to a particular behavioral domain are more efficacious. The mixed results suggest that both types of measures warrant further consideration.

REFERENCES

Abramson, L., Seligman, M., and Teasdale, J. (1978). Learned helplessness in humans: Critique and reformulation. *Journal of Abnormal Psychology,* 87:49–74.

Adler, S. (1980). Self-esteem and causal attributions for job satisfaction and dissatisfaction. *Journal of Applied Psychology,* 65:327–332.

Alloy, L., Peterson, C., Abramson, L., and Seligman, M. (1984). Attributional style and the generality of learned helplessness. *Journal of Personality and Social Psychology,* 46(3):681–687.

Anderson, C. (1983). The causal structure of situations: The generation of plausible causal attributions as a function of type of event situation. *Journal of Experimental Social Psychology,* 19:185–203.

Anderson, C., Horowitz, L., and French, R. (1983). Attributional style of lonely and depressed people. *Journal of Personality and Social Psychology,* 45(1):127–136.

Anderson, C., Jennings, D., and Arnoult, L. (1988). Validity and utility of the attributional style construct at a moderate level of specificity. *Journal of Personality and Social Psychology,* 55(6):979–990.

Arnold, H. (1985). Task performance, perceived competence, and attributed causes of performance as determinants of intrinsic motivation. *Academy of Management Journal,* 28(4):876–888.

Arntz, A., Gerlsma, C., and Albersnagel, F. (1985). Attributional style questioned: Psychometric evaluation of the ASQ in Dutch adolescents. *Advances in Behavior Research Therapy,* 7:55–89.

Baron, R. (1988). Attributions and organizational conflict: The mediating role of apparent sincerity. *Organizational Behavior and Human Decision Processes,* 41:111–127.

Betancourt, H. and Blair, I. (1992). A cognition (attribution)-emotion model of violence in conflict situations. *Personality and Social Psychology Bulletin,* 18(3):343–350.

Bettman, J. and Weitz, B. (1983). Attributions in the board room: Causal reasoning in corporate annual reports. *Administrative Science Quarterly,* 28:165–183.

Brockner, J. and Guare, J. (1983). Improving the performance of low self-esteem individuals: An attributional approach. *Academy of Management Journal,* 26(4):642–656.

Brown, K. (1984). Exploring group performance: An attributional analysis. *Academy of Management Review,* 2:54–63.

Campbell, C. and Martinko, M.J. (1994). An attributional analysis of learned helplessness in an organization: A multi-method field study, *Proceedings of the Southeast Decision Science Institute.*

Carver, C. (1989). How should multi-faceted personality constructs be tested? Issues illustrated by self- monitoring, attributional style, and hardiness. *Journal of Personality and Social Psychology,* 56(4):577–585.

Chacko, T. and McElroy, J. (1983). The cognitive component in Locke's theory of goal setting: Suggestive evidence for a causal attribution interpretation. *Academy of Management Journal,* 26(1):104–118.

Clifford, M. (1984). Thoughts on a theory of constructive failure. *Educational Psychologist,* 19(2):108–120.

Clifford, M. (1986). The effects of ability, strategy, and effort attributions for educational, business, and athletic failure. *British Journal of Educational Psychology,* 56:169–179.

Cutrona, C., Russell, D., and Jones, R. (1984). Cross-situational consistency in causal attributions: Does attributional style exist? *Journal of Personality and Social Psychology,* 47:1043–1058.

Dorfman, P. and Stephan, W. (1984). The effects of group performance on cognitions, satisfaction, and behavior: A process model. *Journal of Management,* 10:173–192.

Elig, T. and Frieze, l. (1979). Measuring causal attributions for success and failure. *Journal of Personality and Social Psychology,* 37(4):621–634.

Escovar, L., Brown, G., and Rodriguez, R. (1982). Development and Evaluation of an Attributional Style Questionnaire for Affiliative Behavior, paper presented at the annual meeting of the American Psychological Association, Washington, D.C.

Feldman, J. (1981). Beyond attribution theory: Cognitive processes in performance appraisal. *Journal of Applied Psychology,* 66:127–148.

Ford, J. (1985). The effects of causal attributions on decision makers' responses to performance downturns. *Academy of Management Review,* 10(4):770–786.

Furnham, A., Sadka, U., and Brewin, C. (1992). The development of a scale to measure occupational attributional style. *Journal of Organizational Behavior,* 13:27–39.

Gong-Guy, E. and Hammen, C. (1980). Causal perceptions of stressful events in depressed and nondepressed outpatients. *Journal of Abnormal Psychology,* 89:662–669.

Henry, J. and Campbell, C. (1995). A comparison of the validity, predictiveness and consistency of a trait versus situational measure of attributions. in *Attribution Theory: An Organizational Perspective,* M.J. Martinko (Ed.), Delray Beach, Fla.: St. Lucie Press.

Henry, J., Martinko, M.J., and Pierce, M.A. (1993). Attributional style as a predictor of success in a first computer science course. *Computers in Human Behavior,* 9:341–352.

Hull, J., Van Treuren, R., and Propsom, P. (1988). Attributional style and the components of hardiness. *Personality and Social Psychology Bulletin,* 14(3):505–513.

Ickes, W. and Layden, M. (1978). Attributional styles. in *New Directions in Attribution Research,* Vol. 2, J.H. Harvey, W. Ickes, and R.F. Kidd (Eds.), Hillsdale, N.J.: Erlbaum, pp. 119–152.

Ilgen, D. and Klein, H. (1988). Organizational behavior. *Annual Review of Psychology,* 40:327–351.

Ilgen, D. and Knowlton, W. (1980). Performance attributional effects on feedback from superiors. *Organizational Behavior and Human Performance,* 25:441–456.

Kent, R. and Martinko, M. (1995). The development and evaluation of a scale to measure organizational attributional style. in *Attribution Theory: An Organizational Perspective,* M.J. Martinko (Ed.), Delray Beach, Fla.: St. Lucie Press.

Liden, R. and Mitchell, T. (1985). Reactions to feedback: The role of attributions. *Academy of Management Journal,* 28(2):291–308.

Lord, R.G. and Maher, K.J. (1990). Alternative information-processing models and their implications for theory, research, and practice. *Academy of Management Review,* 15(1):9–28.

Martinko, M. and Gardner, W. (1982). Learned helplessness: An alternative explanation for performance deficits. *Academy of Management Review,* 7(2):195–204.

Martinko, M. and Gardner, W. (1987) . The leader–member attribution process. *Academy of Management Review,* 12(2):235–249.

McAuley, E., Duncan, T.E., and Russell, D.W. (1992). Measuring causal attributions, the revised causal dimension scale (CDSII), *Personality and Social Psychology Bulletin,* 18(5):566–573.

McElroy, J. (1982). A typology of attribution leadership research. *Academy of Management Review,* 7:413–417.

Mikulincer, M. and Solomon, Z. (1988). Attributional style and combat-related stress disorder. *Journal of Abnormal Psychology,* 97(3):308–313.

Mitchell, T. and Wood, R. (1980). Supervisor's responses to poor performance: A test of an attributional model. *Organizational Behavior and Human Performance,* 25:123–138.

Norris, D. and Niebuhr, R. (1984). Attributional influences on the job performance–job satisfaction relationship. *Academy of Management Journal,* 27(2):424–431.

Peterson, C. and Villanova, P. (1988). An expanded Attributional Style Questionnaire. *Journal of Abnormal Psychology,* 97(1):87–89.

Peterson, C., Semmel, A., von Bayer, C., Abramson, L., Metalsky, G., and Seligman, M. (1982) . The Attributional Style Questionnaire. *Cognitive Therapy and Research,* 6(3): 287–300.

Ronis, D., Hansen, R., and O'Leary, V. (1983). Understanding the meaning of achievement attributions: A test of derived locus and stability scores. *Journal of Personality and Social Psychology,* 77:702–711.

Rosenbaum, R. (1972). A Dimensional Analysis of the Perceived Causes of Success and Failure, unpublished doctoral dissertation, University of California, Los Angeles; cited in Weiner, B. (1979). A theory of motivation for some classroom experiences. *Journal of Educational Psychology,* 71:3–25.

Rotter, J. (1966). Generalized expectancies for internal versus external control of reinforcement. *Psychological Monographs,* 70(1).

Russell, D. (1982). The causal dimension scale: A measure of how individuals perceive causes. *Journal of Personality of Social Psychology,* 42:1137–1145.

Russell, D., Lenel, J., Spicer, C., Miller, J., Albrecht, J., and Rose, J. (1985). Evaluating the handicapped: An attributional analysis. *Personality and Social Psychology Bulletin,* 11:23–31.

Russell, D., McAuley, E., and Tarico, V. (1987). Measuring causal attributions for success and failure: A comparison of methodologies for assessing causal dimensions. *Journal of Personality and Social Psychology,* 52(6):1248–1257.

Seligman, M. and Schulman, P. (1986). Explanatory style as a predictor of productivity and quitting among life insurance agents. *Journal of Personality and Social Psychology,* 50(4):832–838.

Solomon, S. (1978). Measuring situational and dispositional attributions. *Personality and Social Psychology Bulletin,* 4:589–593.

Sweeney, P., Anderson, K., and Bailey, S. (1986). Attributional style in depression: A meta-analytic review. *Journal of Personality and Social Psychology,* 50:974–991.

Teas, R. and McElroy, J. (1986). Causal attributions and expectancy estimates: A framework for understanding the dynamics of salesforce motivation. *Journal of Marketing,* 50(January):75–86.

Wade, D., Cooley, E., and Savicki, V. (1986). A longitudinal study of burnout. *Children and Youth Services Review,* 8(2):161–173.

Weary, G., Stanley, M., and Harvey, J. (1989). *Attribution,* New York: Springer-Verlag.

Weiner, B. (1974). *Achievement Motivation and Attribution Theory,* Morristown, N.J.: General Learning Press.

Weiner, B. (1979). A theory of motivation for some classroom experiences. *Journal of Educational Psychology,* 71:3–25.

Weiner, B. (1985a). An attributional theory of achievement motivation and emotion. *Psychological Review,* 92(4):548–573.

Weiner, B. (1985b). "Spontaneous" causal thinking. *Psychological Bulletin,* 97(1):74–84.

Weiner, B. (1986). *An Attributional Theory of Motivation and Emotion,* New York: Springer-Verlag.

Weiner, B. (1993). A theory of perceived responsibility and social motivation. *American Psychologist,* 48(9):957–965.

Weiner, B. and Kukla, A. (1970). An attributional analysis of achievement motivation. *Journal of Personality and Social Psychology,* 15:1–20.

Weiner, B., Frieze, I., Kukla, A., Reed, L., Rest, S., and Rosenbaum, R. (1971). *Perceiving the Causes of Success and Failure,* Morristown, N.J.: General Learning Press.

Wimer, S. and Kelley, H. (1982). An investigation of the dimensions of causal attribution. *Journal of Personality and Social Psychology,* 43:1142–1162.

4

A COMPARISON OF THE VALIDITY, PREDICTIVENESS, AND CONSISTENCY OF A TRAIT VERSUS SITUATIONAL MEASURE OF ATTRIBUTIONS

John W. Henry and Constance Campbell

ABSTRACT

This chapter explores the issues of validity, predictiveness, and consistency of a trait versus situational measure of attributions. Before these types of instruments can be used in organizational settings to select employees and develop training programs, it is necessary to demonstrate their generalizability from research settings to organizational adoption. It is argued in this chapter that this adoption may be premature. Further research should be conducted and the measures refined before they are standardized for use in organizational settings. The results of this study do provide support for past research and show that these instruments do exhibit a relatively high degree of validity and consistency, but their predictive validity is questionable. The results also show that the use of both a general attributional style questionnaire and a situationally based measure can add insight into behavior and performance. The study suggests that both trait and situational measures should be used to predict behavior.

©St. Lucie Press CCC 1-884015-19-0 1/95/$100/$.50

INTRODUCTION

Recent literature includes a great number of discussions on the relative merits of treating attributions about a person's experience as situationally specific explanations for events or as traits (Russell, 1991). There are many proponents of both approaches. Moreover, there have been attempts to measure attributions in organizational settings in order to predict employee behavior, with mixed results (Seligman and Schulman, 1986). The validity of the measures used in these investigations is of central concern. Both trait and situational approaches may have merit, but neither approach has been conclusively examined and sufficiently validated to allow its use in organizational contexts.

With the increasing use of instruments measuring attributions in organizational settings and its impact on major decisions such as the selection of employees (Seligman and Schulman, 1986) and the development of training programs, issues of reliability, predictive power, and consistency assume greater importance. To date, these issues have not been fully addressed. This chapter presents an exploratory investigation of these issues and suggests that further study be conducted before relying on these instruments in organizational settings.

TRAIT VERSUS SITUATIONAL MEASURES

The situational approach to measuring attributions argues that attributions should be measured by examining the interpretations of respondents based on several underlying causal dimensions regarding a single specific situation (Russell, 1991). Thus, this method involves the assessment of causal attributions for specific events. Proponents of this approach often use the Causal Dimension Scale (CDS) to measure attributions (Russell, 1982). In contrast, the trait approach to measuring attributions proposes that individuals possess an "attributional style" that is consistent across situations and heavily influences attributions for specific situations (Russell, 1991). This is typically evaluated by examining the respondent's interpretations based on several causal dimensions with a series of hypothetical events. Proponents of this approach often use the Attributional Style Questionnaire (ASQ) to measure attributions (Peterson et al., 1982).

The ASQ is not specifically related to the context in which performance is measured. That is, the questions are general-purpose questions intended to apply across a variety of situations. In addition, the questionnaire presents only hypothetical situations to the respondent, rather than allowing the respondent to evaluate an actual situation. The respondents are presented with the hypothetical situation and asked to state its cause, assuming it happened to them. They are then asked to rate the cause on a Likert-type scale based on locus of causality (internal versus external), globality, and stability. The premise of this measure is that respondents who tend to blame themselves for negative events, who think that the cause will occur in different contexts, and who think that it will last into the future are labeled as having a "pessimistic" attributional style. Those who rate the situations in the opposite fashion are labeled as having an "optimistic" attributional style (Seligman and Schulman, 1986).

On the other hand, the CDS (Russell, 1991) is directly related to the context in which an event occurs. Like the ASQ, the CDS asks respondents to rate an event based on locus of causality (or internality) and stability, in addition to controllability, but the CDS asks the respondent about an actual situation, rather than a hypothetical one. Both of these approaches have received extensive research attention.

Comparisons of trait and situational approaches to measuring attributions have also been conducted. For example, Russell (1991) compared trait and situational measures of attributions, examining the relationship between attributional styles and attributions for a particular situation. Although he found trait measures to relate to variables such as affect, there was not a direct relation between attributional style and causal explanations for a particular event. Russell's study (1991) examined the relationship between attributional style and attributions for a specific event. However, this method does not tell the researcher whether that attributional style for a specific situation is a better predictor of performance than general attributional style. We have found no studies that compare instruments for measuring trait versus state in relation to performance. This is especially important, since the organizational work with attributions has focused on performance (Seligman and Schulman, 1986). Thus, it is imperative that the instruments be validated before they are used on organizational members. For example, if an employee and supervisor make different attributions for performance, it could lead to firing (or not hiring) a valuable employee or wasting monies on unnecessary training programs. If attributions are assumed to be related to performance and if organizations use attributional measures to enhance training and job design, additional research is warranted.

A key issue in examining measuring instruments is to examine their psychometric adequacy. At a minimum, the instrument should demonstrate adequate reliabilities; however, this has not always been the case in previous studies. Reliabilities of the general-purpose ASQ, which has been used in most prior research on attributions (cf. Peterson and Villanova, 1988), are generally low (cf. Cutrona, 1983). Barnett and Gottlib (1988) referred to the reliabilities obtained in previous uses of the ASQ as woefully inadequate. This poses a problem, in that the researcher is unable to tell whether the results are valid or were obscured by the inadequacies of the measuring instrument. Moreover, Anderson et al. (1988)

stated that a more accurate measure of attributional style would focus on a smaller domain of situations. They suggest developing attributional style measures with a "moderate level of specificity." Employing this notion, researchers would measure attributional style relative to academic performance in general, or performance with computers in general, and not specific academic events or performance with specific software packages.

Beyond the basic issue of reliability, there are still questions about the construct validity of the ASQ and CDS (Russell, 1991; Abramson et al., 1978; Cutrona et al., 1985). Neither the convergent validity of these measures nor their predictive validity has been adequately demonstrated. Currently only a few studies relating attributional style to performance measures exist, resulting in a need for greater evidence in this area (Seligman and Schulman, 1986; Henry et al., 1993).

Finally, the idea that attributional style is a trait that demonstrates consistency over time has not been fully addressed. Only a few studies have attempted to examine consistency of attributional style over time, rather than across situations, and we have found no studies that examine attributional style measured at different times in relation to performance variables. This is especially important, because if attributional style is indeed a trait, it would be expected that the ASQ and similar measures would demonstrate a higher degree of consistency than the CDS, a measure of an attribution for a specific situation. Consistent with this reasoning, the ASQ could be viewed as an antecedent to a specific attribution that would be predictive of attributions over time, whereas the CDS could be viewed as a measure of an attribution for a specific situation that would show variations that correlate with the variation in situations.

To examine these issues, two types of construct validity were examined in addition to the consistency of scores across time. Convergent validity of the two measures was obtained by correlating scores on the ASQ with scores on the CDS. Predictive validity was measured by comparing the relative ability of the ASQ and the CDS to predict performance. Finally, the consistency of scores on the ASQ and CDS and their subscales across time was measured.

METHOD

Participants

The participants in this study were 256 undergraduate students enrolled in a Principles of Management course at a large southeastern university. Most of the students were business majors (91%) who are Caucasian (88%), and there were roughly equivalent percentages of men (55%) and women (45%). The students were recruited from two classes, and participation was voluntary.

Materials

The two measures used in this study were modified versions of the ASQ (Peterson et al., 1982) and the CDS (Russell, 1991). The items on the modified ASQ were grouped according to the underlying causal dimensions identified by Seligman and Schulman (1986), and the items on the modified CDS were grouped according to the underlying causal dimensions identified by Russell (1991). The complete modified ASQ and CDS measures are provided in the appendix to this chapter. Controllability was not measured on the modified CDS, because in past (Russell, 1991) and current research it did not meet the criteria for reliability of 0.70 set by Nunnally (1970).

The ASQ was modified to include only events related to academics, ten positive and ten negative events. For example, one item was the following: "You give a presentation in class and receive a favorable grade." After reading the description of the hypothetical event, the student wrote a cause for the event and then rated the stated cause based on stability, globality, and internality. A stable cause is viewed as being permanent; an unstable cause is viewed as being temporary. A global cause is viewed as affecting a wide variety of situations; a specific cause is viewed as affecting only one situation. An internal cause is viewed as coming from within the respondent; an external cause is viewed as being due to other people or circumstances.

Seven scales were constructed from the ASQ by summing the stability, globality, and internality rating across academic events. The subscales for internal/external (I/E), stable/unstable (S/U), and global/specific (G/S) ratings of events form the bases for measure of negative events (CoNeg), positive events (CoPos), and the composite score (CPCN) representing a general attributional style. The CoNeg score was computed by summing the stability, globality, and internality ratings for the ten negative academic events, and the CoPos score was computed by summing the stability, globality, and internality rating for the ten positive academic events. The CPCN score is the CoPos minus the CoNeg score (Seligman and Schulman, 1986). In addition, the subscales for I/E negative and positive events and S/U negative and positive events were examined.

The modified CDS is similar in format to the ASQ; however, as mentioned earlier, the CDS pertains to actual situations, while the ASQ refers to hypothetical ones. On the CDS, respondents selected one of four specific attributions for their performance in the course: ability, task difficulty, effort, and luck/chance. These four causes were used so that the respondents would focus on factors directly attributable to them or to the course, rather than making excuses for performance. For example, the authors' past research has shown that students will write down causes such as "I didn't have enough time" or "the library was closed." These causes are not directly related to internal factors or something specific about the course.

After selecting one of the four specific attributions mentioned previously for their performance in the course, respondents then evaluated the cause of their performance on Likert scales as either internal or external and as either stable or unstable. For example, one item was the following: "Is the cause of [your performance in this course] due to something about you or something about other people or circumstances?" An internal scale score, a stability scale score, and a composite score were calculated. All scores on both the ASQ and CDS were calculated using the procedures described by the authors of the instruments.

Procedure

The ASQ and CDS were administered at the start of the class period near the beginning (time 1) and end (time 2) of a 16-week semester. One could argue that the ASQ was inappropriately used at time 1 since the students had little experience with the course. However, the students were assumed to have had previous experience evaluating the reasons for their performance in school work. In fact, they had been evaluating their performance for 13 to 14 years before taking this course. It is important to note that the CDS asks about their performance, not grade, in the course. Although this was a rather liberal interpretation of how the CDS should be used, it was felt to be appropriate since the practical usefulness of describing the causes for events after the events have occurred is debatable.

The participants were given both brief instructions about how to fill out an accompanying scoring form and directions written on the questionnaire itself. No participant indicated difficulty in interpreting instructions. Participants' questionnaires were matched from time 1 to time 2 using their social security numbers.

Analysis

In order to examine the precision of measurement of the modified ASQ and CDS measures, reliabilities were calculated using Cronbach's alpha (1951). Convergent construct validity was examined using correlations of the two scales. Predictive validity was examined by regressing the ASQ and CDS scales and subscales on grades for the course. Based on methods used in past research in this area (Russell, 1991) and because of the possibility of multicollinearity in the data, six separate hierarchical multiple regression analyses were conducted so that the predictive power of the subscales and the composite scores could be compared on the two tests. To examine the consistency of the ASQ and CDS over time, correlations were computed for the scales and subscales at time 1 and time

2. In addition, a composite CDS scale for time 1 and time 2 was constructed by summing all the CDS items. All scales and subscales were numbered 1 or 2 to represent time 1 and time 2, where appropriate. All the scales and subscales used in this study are shown in Table 4.1 using abbreviations for each scale and subscale. For example, CDS-Comp1 refers to the CDS composite scale at time 1.

RESULTS

Basic Statistics, Correlations, and Reliabilities

Out of 256 participants, 205 completed the questionnaires at both time 1 and time 2 and received a final grade in the course. Basic statistics for the two measures at time 1 and time 2 are shown in Table 4.1, and the reliabilities for all scales and subscales are shown in Table 4.2.

As shown in Table 4.2, the subscales on both tests demonstrated higher reliabilities than in previous studies, which have been in the range of 0.50 to 0.70 (Barnett and Gottlib, 1988). In fact, most are above Nunnally's (1970) criteria of acceptability of 0.70. Comparing the reliabilities from the ASQ and CDS on the same subscales (I/E and S/U) indicates that the reliabilities are similar on the two scales, with the CDS having higher reliabilities on the I/E subscale and the ASQ having higher reliabilities on the S/U subscale.

Convergent and Discriminant Validity

The convergent and discriminant validity of the ASQ and CDS was examined in order to determine the degree of differentiation (Anastasi, 1982). Assuming the modified ASQ and CDS measured trait and situational attributions, respectively, two results were expected. First, it was expected that the correlations between the composite scales and subscales would not exceed 0.30 (Stone, 1978) and that the correlations would be smaller at time 2 than at time 1, due to the fact that the situational measure (i.e., the CDS) would be a more accurate measure of attributions for a specific event than of a general attributional style. This was accomplished by examining the pattern of correlations of the composite scores and the subscales at time 1 and time 2. Although there were exceptions to the 0.30 rule, the pattern of correlations in Table 4.1 indicates that there is a higher degree of discriminant validity between the measures at time 2 than at time 1, as expected. For example, at time 1 the composite score on the ASQ (the ASQ-CPCN1) and the composite score on the CDS (the CDS-Comp1) were significantly correlated, whereas at time 2 the correlation was not significant.

TABLE 4.1 Basic Statistics for the ASQ and CDS

	Time 1 and Time 2				
	Time 1			**Time 2**	
Test/scale	x	SD		x	SD
1. ASQ (CPCN)	3.33	2.65		3.10	2.65
2. ASQ-I/E-Neg	5.12	0.85		5.08	0.87
3. ASQ-I/E-Pos	5.79	0.67		5.78	0.66
4. ASQ-S/U-Neg	4.12	1.00		4.18	1.00
5. ASQ-S/U-Pos	5.51	0.69		5.37	0.74
6. ASQ-G/S-Pos	5.49	0.76		5.37	0.82
7. ASQ-G/S-Neg	4.18	1.00		4.10	1.19
8. ASQ-CoNeg	13.44	2.19		13.43	2.27
9. ASQ-CoPos	16.76	1.83		16.51	1.94
10. CDS-Comp	39.40	7.83		38.17	7.90
11. CDS-Int	5.77	1.30		5.65	1.31
12. CDS-Stab	5.46	1.09		5.10	1.20

Correlation Matrix

Test/scale	1	2	3	4	5	6
1. ASQ-CPCN1						
2. ASQ-CPCN2	0.61*					
3. ASQ-I/E-Neg1	−0.26*	−0.21*				
4. ASQ-I/E-Neg2	−0.13	−0.28*	0.65*			
5. ASQ-I/E-Pos1	0.49*	0.25*	0.31*	0.30*		
6. ASQ-I/E-Pos2	0.22*	0.56*	0.19*	0.32*	0.46*	
7. ASQ-S/U-Neg1	−0.64*	−0.39*	0.08	0.07	−0.09	−0.03
8. ASQ/S/U-Neg2	−0.47*	−0.59	0.12	0.12	−0.06	−0.07
9. ASQ-S/U-Pos1	0.57*	0.28*	0.08	0.10	0.60*	0.26*
10. ASQ-S/U-Pos2	0.27*	0.51*	0.05	0.08	0.34*	0.62*
11. ASQ-CoNeg1	−0.74*	−0.52*	0.49*	0.34*	0.06	0.01
12. ASQ-CoNeg2	−0.70*	−0.70*	0.32*	0.45*	0.05	0.01
13. ASQ-CoPos1	0.57*	0.25*	0.21*	0.20*	0.80*	0.35*
14. ASQ-CoPos2	0.26*	0.54*	0.10	0.15**	0.40*	0.78*
15. CDS-Comp1	0.31*	0.17**	0.17**	0.23*	0.26*	0.19*
16. CDS-Comp2	0.19*	0.14	0.19*	0.24*	0.23*	0.27*
17. CDS-Int1	0.25*	0.13	0.21*	0.27*	0.26*	0.19*
18. CDS-Int2	0.20*	0.15**	0.18*	0.25*	0.25*	0.28*
19. CDS-Stab1	0.36*	0.21*	0.06	0.13	0.20*	0.16**
20. CDS-Stab2	0.11	0.08	0.14**	0.17**	0.16**	0.18*

Test/scale	7	8	9	10	11	12	13
1. ASQ-CPCN1							
2. ASQ-CPCN2							
3. ASQ-I/E-Neg1							
4. ASQ-I/E-Neg2							
5. ASQ-I/E-Pos1							
6. ASQ-I/E-Pos2							
7. ASQ-S/U-Neg1							
8. ASQ/S/U-Neg2	0.69*						
9. ASQ-S/U-Pos1	0.05	0.08					
10. ASQ-S/U-Pos2	0.15**	0.21*	0.52*				
11. ASQ-CoNeg1	0.81*	0.64*	0.05	0.10			
12. ASQ-CoNeg2	0.55**	0.83*	0.09	0.20*	0.69*		
13. ASQ-CoPos1	0.04	0.09	0.91*	0.52*	0.13	0.14**	
14. ASQ-CoPos2	0.11	0.17**	0.46*	0.93*	0.11	0.22*	0.50*
15. CDS-Comp1	−0.11	−0.03	0.33*	0.28*	−0.09	0.00	0.36*
16. CDS-Comp2	−0.01	0.05	0.28*	0.33*	0.02	0.10	0.31*
17. CDS-Int1	−0.13	−0.04	0.27*	0.25*	−0.06	0.03	0.30*
18. CDS-Int2	−0.05	−0.00	0.26*	0.30*	−0.02	0.07	0.28*
19. CDS-Stab1	−0.08	−0.04	0.36*	0.27*	−0.13	−0.05	0.38*
20. CDS-Stab2	0.05	0.11	0.22*	0.29*	0.07	0.13	0.28*

Test/scale	14	15	16	17	18	19	20
1. ASQ-CPCN1							
2. ASQ-CPCN2							
3. ASQ-I/E-Neg1							
4. ASQ-I/E-Neg2							
5. ASQ-I/E-Pos1							
6. ASQ-I/E-Pos2							
7. ASQ-S/U-Neg1							
8. ASQ/S/U-Neg2							
9. ASQ-S/U-Pos1							
10. ASQ-S/U-Pos2							
11. ASQ-CoNeg1							
12. ASQ-CoNeg2							
13. ASQ-CoPos1							
14. ASQ-CoPos2							
15. CDS-Comp1	0.22*						
16. CDS-Comp2	0.29*	0.45*					
17. CDS-Int1	0.20*	0.95*	0.41*				
18. CDS-Int2	0.27*	0.41*	0.93*	0.39*			
19. CDS-Stab1	0.22*	0.87*	0.42*	0.69*	0.36*		
20.CDS-Stab2	0.25*	0.39*	0.84*	0.33*	0.58*		0.40*

Note: SD = standard deviation. $* = p < 0.01$, $** = p < 0.05$.

TABLE 4.2   Reliabilities of the ASQ and CDS

	Time 1	Time 2
ASQ-I/E-Neg	(0.67)	(0.70)
ASQ-I/E-Pos	(0.62)	(0.69)
ASQ-S/U-Neg	(0.81)	(0.85)
ASQ-S/U-Pos	(0.75)	(0.80)
ASQ-CoNeg	(0.84)	(0.86)
ASQ-CoPos	(0.86)	(0.89)
ASQ-CPCN	—	—
CDS-I/E	(0.90)	(0.90)
CDS-S/U	(0.68)	(0.69)
CDS-Comp	(0.89)	(0.87)

Predictive Validity

Two approaches were chosen to examine the predictive validity of the ASQ and CDS. First, correlations of the scales and subscales with grades were examined, as shown in Table 4.3. Table 4.3 indicates that the composite scales from both the ASQ (ASQ-CPCN1 and 2) and CDS (CDS-Comp1 and 2) were correlated with the students' grades.

TABLE 4.3   Correlation of ASQ and CDS Scores with Grades

	Time 1	Time 2
ASQ-I/E-Neg	−0.10	−0.09
ASQ-I/E-Pos	0.11	0.06
ASQ-S/U-Neg	−0.02	−0.11
ASQ-S/U-Pos	0.21*	−0.02
ASQ-CoNeg	−0.10	−0.09
ASQ-CoPos	0.19*	0.15**
ASQ-CPCN	0.20*	0.19*
CDS-Comp	0.15**	0.24*
CDS-Int	0.13	0.21*
CDS-Stab	0.14**	0.22*

Note: $* = p < 0.01$, $** = p < 0.05$.

TABLE 4.4   Impact of Trait and Situational Measures on Grade

	Predictor	Beta	R^2
1.	CDS-Comp2	0.220	0.05*
	ASQ-CPCN2	0.159	0.02***
2.	CDS-Comp1	0.094	0.02***
	ASQ-CPCN1	0.166	0.02***
3.	CDS-Int2	0.104	0.04**
	CDS-Stab2	0.140	0.02****
	ASQ-CoPos2	0.091	0.01
4.	CDS-Int1	0.043	0.01****
	CDS-Stab1	0.055	0.01
	ASQ-CoPos1	0.157	0.02***
5.	CDS-Int2	0.084	0.04**
	CDS-Stab2	0.168	0.01****
	ASQ-CoNeg2	−0.116	0.01****
6.	CDS-Int1	0.058	0.01****
	CDS-Stab1	0.094	0.00
	ASQ-CoNeg1	−0.081	0.00
7.	CDS-Int2	0.094	0.04**
	CDS-Stab2	0.157	0.01****
	ASQ-CPCN2	0.163	0.03***
8.	CDS-Int1	0.055	0.01****
	CDS-Stab1	0.047	0.00
	ASQ-CPCN1	0.165	0.02***

Note: The dependent variable is the grade. * = $p < 0.001$, ** = $p < 0.01$, *** = $p < 0.05$, ****
= $p < 0.10$.

To further examine predictive validity, several hierarchical multiple regression analyses were conducted, similar to Russell's (1991) analysis. The purpose was twofold: to determine if the trait measures (ASQ) explained any variance in the students' grades beyond that explained by the CDS and to determine the amount of variance explained by each measure. Thus, the first set of variables entered in the regression were the composite and subscales from the CDS. In this case, only the internal and stable scales were used. All analyses indicated that the ASQ scales and subscales were significant contributors to the variance explained in the students' grades. The results are displayed in Table 4.4.

These results support Russell's (1991) and are in the expected direction.

That is, since the CDS measures attributions for an actual event, it would be expected to correlate most highly with performance at time 2, when the students had the most recent information about their grades. However, the fact that the CPCN score on the ASQ correlated significantly with performance at both times is suggestive of the predictive validity of attributional style as a general trait that has at least some impact on performance. Of particular interest are the regressions (1, 2, 4, 5) that demonstrate the contribution of the ASQ (CPCN) to the variance explained in addition to the CDS, thus demonstrating the existence of an attributional style separate from the situational measure of attributions (CDS).

Consistency

The correlations of the scales and subscales from time 1 to time 2 were all significant at the 0.01 level and are shown in Table 4.5. These results indicate a high level of consistency in attributional style for both positive and negative life events, on both tests, over the 16-week semester. Moreover, the CDS demonstrated consistency from time 1 to time 2. However, as shown in Table 4.3, the correlations of the CDS scale and subscales significantly increased at time 2, suggesting an increase in the predictive validity of the CDS as the time between administering the questionnaire and the actual event (receiving a grade) became shorter. The correlations of the ASQ and subscales with the students' grades at time 1 and time 2 were virtually identical.

TABLE 4.5   Correlations of ASQ and CDS Scores from Time 1 to Time 2

ASQ/I/E-Neg	0.65*
ASQ-I/E-Pos	0.46*
ASQ-S/U Neg	0.69*
ASQ-S/U-Pos	0.52*
ASQ-CoNeg	0.69*
ASQ-CoPos	0.50*
ASQ-CPCN	0.61*
CDS-Int	0.39*
CDS-Stab	0.40*
CDS-Comp	0.45*

Note: * = p <0.01.

DISCUSSION

This research addressed the issues of the validity, predictiveness, and consistency of a trait measure of attributions, the ASQ, versus a situational measure of attributions, the CDS. Using a modified ASQ with a "moderate level of specificity" in this study, both the ASQ and the CDS possessed adequate reliabilities.

Moreover, with respect to the construct validity of the ASQ and the CDS, the degree of differentiation between the trait and situational measures became greater from time 1 to time 2. Thus, as students gained more information about their grades through feedback from tests and assignments during the semester, their attributions were no longer based on expectations, but on actual knowledge about their performance level in the course. Thus, as Table 4.3 indicates, it is likely that the situational aspects were more prominent in their cognitive interpretation of the causes for their performance in the course versus their general "attributional style."

The second issue addressed in this research was the impact of the predictive validity of the modified ASQ and CDS, which is pertinent to the generalizability to organizational settings. In this study, there were mixed results on this issue. Not all of the scales on the ASQ and CDS were significant predictors of performance (grades) in the course, although the composite scales from each measure proved to be valid predictors.

The evidence in this study indicated consistency in attributional style and provides support for the notion of attributional style as a trait that is present over time (Anderson et. al., 1988). As previous researchers have surmised, it may be that attributional style did not appear as a trait in previous studies due to psychometric inadequacies of the ASQ (Cutrona, 1983) and that, as measuring instruments are improved, the ability to measure consistency of attributional style will increase. The critical finding of consistency of attributional style indicates that attributional style is a variable meriting further exploration. For organizational researchers, it will be important in the future to determine the consequences in the work setting of having a particular attributional style.

There can be several explanations for the results of this study. One factor to be considered is the validity of measures of attributions and attributional style. Although both instruments appear to be reliable and to produce consistent results over time, the question still remains as to what is truly being measured by them. The two instruments used in this study contain two similar subscales, internal/external and stable/unstable. However, even though the subscales are comparable, the results were not comparable between them. That is, the ASQ-S/U-Pos from time 1 was the only scale significantly correlated with grades on the ASQ, whereas all scales on the CDS were significantly correlated, except the CDS-Int scale at time 1. If the scales measure the same thing, it would be expected that the correlation of those scales with grades would be very similar. Since one instrument deals with hypothetical situations and the other deals with actual experience, it is possible that the two instruments may be measuring different cognitive interpretations of events. The validity of measures of attributions is a topic that merits further research.

Another possible explanation for these results is that this particular means of measuring attributions (questionnaires) is not the best method. Problems such as common methods variance and social desirability responding often bias the results of questionnaires. Perhaps other methods such as interviews would be a better way to ascertain the attributional style of an individual. Further studies could use multiple methods to compare attributions and determine the most effective measurement method. Nonetheless, since the composite scores on the ASQ and the scale scores on the CDS were related to performance in the course, this suggests the possibility of a relationship between performance and attributional style.

Organizational researchers could extend this area by exploring the impact of attributional styles on such factors as turnover, job satisfaction, and job performance. Current research is being conducted, for example, using attributions as a predictor of performance with computer-related technology (Martinko et al., 1993).

CONCLUSIONS

The measures of attributional style used in this study possessed an adequate level of reliability, and participants' responses on the questionnaires demonstrated consistency in attributional style over the 16-week semester. However, there were mixed results regarding the relationship of attributional style to performance in a course. The current study suggests directions for future research in the use of questionnaire measures of attributional style to predict performance, not only in academic settings but in organizations. The validity and practical importance of the ASQ constructed at a moderate level of specificity can only be demonstrated in future research that compares the predictive power of other organizational personality measures and the ASQ to the important organizational variables of turnover, quitting, job satisfaction, and job performance.

APPENDIX

Modified Attributional Style Questionnaire

1. You cannot get all the reading done that your instructor assigns. Write down the one major cause _____

   Is the cause of this due to something about you or something about other people or circumstances?
   Totally due to others **1**   **2**   **3**   **4**   **5**   **6**   **7**   Totally due to me

   In the future, will this cause again be present?
   Never present   **1**   **2**   **3**   **4**   **5**   **6**   **7**   Always present

   Is this cause something that affects just this type of situation, or does it also influence other areas of your life?
   Just this situation   **1**   **2**   **3**   **4**   **5**   **6**   **7**   All situations

2. You give a presentation in class and you receive a favorable grade.

3. You fail an examination.

4. An instructor praises your work in class.

5. You receive a poor grade on a surprise quiz in class.

6. You make a higher grade than expected on an examination.

7. You are placed on academic probation.

8. You receive an academic scholarship.

9. You do not have high enough grades to switch to your desired major.

10. You are one of the few students who successfully completed a project for extra credit.

11. You are dropped from the university because your grades are too low.

12. You are caught up on your class assignments.

13. You cannot get started writing a paper.

14. You are assigned a set of 20 homework problems and successfully complete them all.

15. You get a "D" in a course required for your major.

16. A fellow student comes to you with a problem and you are able to help.

17. You cannot understand the points a lecturer makes.

18. You make the dean's list.

19. You receive an incomplete in a course.

20. You fully understand the course material.

Modified Causal Dimension Scale

Please answer the following questions, based on the major cause you chose that you believe will determine your performance in this course. (Causes were restricted to ability, effort, course difficulty, luck/chance).

1. Is the cause something that:

    Reflects an aspect   1   2   3   4   5   6   7   Reflects an aspect
    of the situation   of yourself

2. Is the cause of this due to something about you or something about other people or circumstances?

    Totally due to others   1   2   3   4   5   6   7   Totally due to me

3. Is the cause something that is:

    Outside of you   1   2   3   4   5   6   7   Inside of you

4. Is the cause:

    Something about   1   2   3   4   5   6   7   Something about
    you   others

5. Is the cause something that is:

    Temporary   1   2   3   4   5   6   7   Permanent

6. In the future, will this cause again be present?

    Never present   1   2   3   4   5   6   7   Always present

7. Is the cause something that:

    Changes over time   1   2   3   4   5   6   7   Is stable over time

REFERENCES

Abramson, L.Y., Seligman, M.E.P., and Teasdale, J. (1978). Learned helplessness in human beings: Critique and reformulation. *Journal of Abnormal Psychology,* 87:49–74.

Anastasi, A. (1982). *Psychological Testing,* 5th edition, New York: Macmillan.

Anderson, C.A., Arnoult, L.H., and Jennings, D.L. (1988). Validity and utility of the attributional style construct at a moderate level of specificity. *Journal of Personality and Social Psychology,* 55(6):979–990.

Bagozzi, R.P., Davis, F.D., and Warshaw, P.R. (1992). Development and test of a theory of technological learning and usage. *Human Relations,* 45(7):659–686.

Barnett, P.A. and Gottlib, I.H. (1988). Psychosocial functioning and depression: Antecedents, concomitants, and consequences. *Psychological Bulletin,* 104(1):97–126.

Cronbach, L.J. (1951). Coefficient alpha and the internal structure of tests. *Psychometrika,* 16:297–334.

Cutrona, C.E. (1983). Causal attributions and perinatal depression. *Journal of Abnormal Psychology,* 47(5):1043–1058.

Cutrona, C.E., Russell, D., and Jones, R.D. (1985). Cross-situational consistency in causal attributions: Does attributional style exist? *Journal of Personality and Social Psychology,* 47:1043–1058.

Henry, J.W., Martinko, M.J., and Pierce, M.A. (1993). Attributional style as a predictor of success in a first computer science course. *Computers in Human Behavior,* 9:341–352.

Martinko, M.J., Henry, J.W., and Zmud, R.W. (1993). Individual Reactions to Technology in the Workplace, unpublished manuscript.

Nunnally, J.C., Jr. (1970). *Introduction to Psychological Measurement,* New York: McGraw-Hill.

Peterson, C. and Villanova, P. (1988). An expanded attributional style questionnaire. *Journal of Abnormal Psychology,* 97(1):87–89.

Peterson, C., Semmel, A., vonBaeyer, C., Abramson, L.Y., Metalsky, G.I., and Seligman, M.E.P. (1982). The Attributional Style Questionnaire. *Cognitive Therapy and Research,* 6(3):287–300.

Russell, D. (1982). The Causal Dimension Scale: A measure of how individuals perceive causes. *Journal of Personality and Social Psychology,* 42(6):1137–1145.

Russell, D.W. (1991). The measurement of attribution process: Trait and situational approaches. in *New Models, New Extensions of Attribution Theory,* S.L. Zelen (Ed.), New York: Springer-Verlag.

Russell, D.W., McAuley, E., and Tarico, V. (1987). Measuring causal attributions of success and failure: A comparison of methodologies for assessing causal dimensions. *Journal of Personality and Social Psychology,* 52(6):1248–1257.

Seligman, M.E.P. and Schulman, P. (1986). Explanatory style as a predictor of productivity and quitting among life insurance sales agents. *Journal of Personality and Social Psychology,* 54(4):832–838.

Stone, E.F. (1978). *Research Methods in Organizational Behavior,* Glenview, Ill.: Scott, Foresman.

5

THE DEVELOPMENT AND EVALUATION OF A SCALE TO MEASURE ORGANIZATIONAL ATTRIBUTIONAL STYLE

Russell L. Kent and Mark J. Martinko

ABSTRACT

This chapter provides an evaluation of a questionnaire designed to measure organizational attributional style. Internal consistency and test–retest reliabilities were acceptable, especially as compared to other attributional style measures. The organizational attributional style was multi-dimensional, including the dimensions of stability and control.

INTRODUCTION

Although considerable attention has recently been given to developing attribution theories in organizational contexts, a major criticism of this area has been the failure to develop psychometrically sound instruments for measuring attributions (Ilgen and Klein, 1988). This shortcoming is addresses, in part, in this

---

chapter by presenting the results of a study designed to develop and psychometrically evaluate an instrument for measuring organizational attributional style (OAS).

BACKGROUND

Construct Validity

Peterson et al. (1982, p. 288) define attributional style (AS) as "the extent to which individuals show characteristic attributional tendencies." AS evolved from the reformulated learned helplessness (LH) theory of depression (Abramson et al., 1978), which is concerned with individual differences in people's explanations of success and failure. The basic thesis is that differences in AS are related to differences in motivation, performance, and affective reactions (Anderson et al., 1988). In their meta-analysis of over 100 studies, Sweeney et al. (1986) provide convincing support for the role of AS in the LH process. Investigations of the relationship between attributions and other outcomes such as burnout (Wade et al., 1986), hardiness (Hull et al., 1988), stress (Mikulincer and Solomon, 1988), productivity (Anderson, 1983; Seligman and Schulman, 1986), motivation (Anderson, 1983), and turnover (Seligman and Schulman, 1986) also support the construct validity of AS.

Although research has supported the construct validity of AS, two studies question the concept of a cross-situationally consistent AS (Arntz et al., 1985; Cutrona et al., 1984). Using the Attributional Style Questionnaire (ASQ) (Peterson et al., 1982), both of these studies suggested that the concept of AS may not be valid and that situational explanations of attributional processes may be more appropriate. It should be noted, however, that although Cutrona et al. (1984) concluded that their study provided little support for a broad construct of AS, they did report some evidence for cross-situational consistency of attributions, particularly for the stability and globality dimensions. They therefore suggested that individuals may be expected to demonstrate attributional consistency within narrower attributional categories such as "health-related events" (p. 1055). This rationale provides a conceptual basis for exploring ASs associated with work-related issues.

A later study confirms that investigations of work-related situations may be appropriate. In responding to the criticisms raised by Cutrona et al. (1984) and others, using the Attributional Style Assessment Test (ASAT) (Anderson et al., 1983), Anderson et al. (1988) concluded that (1) AS appears to be a valid construct, (2) AS is not as cross-situationally consistent as originally thought, and (3) AS is not so situationally specific as to cease being a meaningful construct. They suggested that a person's AS is cross-situationally consistent only across situations that are similar in psychologically meaningful ways. In summary, the results provide evidence for the convergent and discriminant validity of AS when assessed at an intermediate level of specificity such as an organizational context.

The Measurement of Attributional Style

Before proceeding with the development of the questionnaire, it is important to recognize several key issues concerning the measurement of AS. As indicated above, the focus of most attributional theories is on *causal dimensions* as distinguished from *causal explanations.* The term *causal explanation,* or, as Weiner (1985) refers to it, *causal description,* is used here to mean the specific explanations people make concerning the causes of prior outcomes. This implies numerous attributions including effort, ability, task difficulty, luck, mood, strategy, acts of God, and other explanations related to self, others, and situational events. Although the study of specific attributions is interesting, the identification of the underlying causal dimensions along which this myriad of causal explanations vary is necessary if a theory regarding the similarities, differences, and significance of the various attributions is to emerge.

The next issue concerns the appropriate method for assessing AS. In the organizational behavior area, researchers often "force" their data by classifying subjects' attributions along some predetermined set of causal dimensions. This procedure assumes that the researcher and the subject assign the same meaning to the causal explanation and results in what Russell (1982) has termed the "fundamental attribution researcher error." As an example, although ability is typically viewed by researchers as internal and stable (Weiner, 1974), some subjects may view ability as unstable if they feel that it can be changed by additional training or experience. As a result of such conflicts, researchers may assign attributions to dimensions that are entirely different from those perceived by the subjects. To prevent this, Russell (1982) and others (Ronis et al., 1983; Russell et al., 1987) have suggested using more direct assessments of the dimensions of causal explanations. Examples of this approach are the ASQ (Peterson et al., 1982), which has been used in the study of depression, the Occupational Attributional Style Questionnaire (Furnham et al., 1992), which has been used in work-related situations, and the Causal Dimension Scale (CDS) (Russell, 1982), which has been used in a variety of achievement situations. The approach used on these scales is to ask the respondent to assign a cause for a success or failure event. Then the subject (as opposed to the researcher) classifies the cause according to dimensions (e.g., internal/external or stability). This method of assessing causal dimensions appears to be more accurate than methods that rely on using the theoretical meaning of causal attributions (Russell et al., 1987).

A final note concerning the measurement of AS relates to existing measures. Although several measures of general AS are available, for example, ASQ (Peterson et al., 1982) and CDS (Russell, 1982), only one measure of work-related attributions was identified (Furnham et al., 1992). This measure has received limited use in the field and has several potential shortcomings, such as questionnaire length and structure, marginal reliability, and a lack of substantiated construct validity. Because of this, additional work is needed to develop a measure of OAS.

Causal Dimensions

Assuming causal structures underlie attributions, appropriate dimensions must be identified. Numerous authors (e.g., Abramson et al., 1978; Weiner, 1985) have suggested a variety of dimensions. These dimensions and their appropriateness to the study of organizational issues are discussed in this section.

Locus of Causality

This dimension was first identified by Heider (1958) and indicates a distinction between factors "inside" and "outside" the person. It gained further acceptance with the work of Rotter (1966) and plays a leading role in most attributional theories (Abramson et al., 1978; Weiner, 1985). In a review of the empirical research on the causal structure of attributions, Weiner (1985) convincingly argues that locus of causality (LOC) should be included in any analysis of the causal structure of attributions. More importantly, in a recent meta-analysis of AS and depression, Sweeney et al. (1986) found a relatively large effect size (–0.36) for the internal dimension. Thus, there is strong support for LOC as a causal dimension.

One concern about this dimension is the assumed inverse relationship between internal and external factors. Solomon (1978) asserts that the dimensions are not inversely related. Peterson and Villanova (1988) also suggested the independence of these two dimensions after they were unsuccessful in increasing the internal consistency for the internal/external dimension in an expanded version of the ASQ. Thus, there is an expanding body of work supporting the independence of the internal and external dimensions.

Stability

The stability dimension, suggested by Weiner et al. (1971), addresses variability of causation over time. For example, ability is often perceived as stable, whereas mood is thought to vary over time. The evidence supporting the stability dimension is convincing. Four of seven studies reviewed by Weiner (1985) clearly identified a stability dimension. More recently, Sweeney et al. (1986) reported medium effect sizes (–0.25) for stability in the study of depression. Stability, therefore, has received wide support both empirically and conceptually as a major dimension in most attributional theories and models (i.e., Abramson et al., 1978; Weiner, 1985).

Controllability

In his theory of achievement motivation, Weiner (1979) included a third dimension referred to as *controllability*. Similarly, Rosenbaum (1972) suggested that although mood and effort were both internal and unstable factors, they were distinguishable because of control. That is, effort is often perceived to be volitional whereas mood is not. Although controllability was not included in the LH model of Abramson et al. (1978), Anderson et al. (1983, p. 135) later concluded that "controllability is quite important to our understanding of the attributional styles..." Finally, Weiner (1985) found five empirical studies that identified controllability as a causal dimension and concluded that it should be included in the causal analysis of attributions. The research and conceptual literature strongly suggests, therefore, that the controllability dimension may contribute to the understanding of LH.

One important criticism of the controllability dimension is that it may not be independent of the LOC dimension, although the evidence is somewhat equivocal. More specifically, Russell et al. (1987) reported a correlation between LOC and controllability of 0.928 when using the CDS. However, in an earlier study, Russell et al. (1985) found the LOC and controllability scores from the CDS to be uncorrelated ($r = –0.048$). To explain this, Russell et al. (1987) suggest that the relation between LOC, stability, and controllability varies from situation to situation. In addition, both Weiner (1985) and Anderson et al. (1983) note that a failure to find orthogonality at the empirical level does not invalidate separation at the conceptual level.

Globality

Another dimension which has been proposed by Abramson et al. (1978) pertains to the global/specific characteristics of attributions. They claim globality is orthogonal to the LOC and stability dimensions and that it is included in their model to determine if LH is cross-situational or situation specific. Thus, global attributions for failure suggest that failure will occur in all similar situations, whereas specific attributions blame failure on the specific set of circumstances. According to the theory, global attributions lead to cross-situational LH.

Although Abramson and Seligman and their colleagues have found support for the role of the global/specific dimension in their model (i.e., Alloy et al., 1984), criticisms of this dimension have been raised. Weiner (1985) notes that a global/specific dimension did not emerge in a single study he reviewed and questions whether this distinction is only made by attribution theorists. It should also be noted that this dimension has not been included in attribution theories or models other than those based on the LH model.

Intentionality

Weiner (1985) describes intentionality as the property that best differentiates between effort and strategy. That is, although insufficient effort and improper strategy are both internal, unstable attributions for an event, improper strategy is unintentional, whereas insufficient effort may be intentional. However, Weiner (1985) also raises several criticisms of including intentionality as a dimension. He notes that intent and control generally covary. In addition, he asserts that intent is an action, not a cause, and is therefore beyond the scope of attributional theories of causation. Regardless of this, however, there appears to be enough support for this dimension that it deserves consideration.

Characteristics of Organizational Attributional Style

Tentative parameters for exploring an OAS construct are suggested in this section. First, based on the preceding discussion, it is suggested that individual OASs will vary over time, but should be stable enough over short periods to be measurable constructs. Second, it appears that OASs will be multi-dimensional. Specifically, six dimensions (internality, externality, stability, controllability, globality, and intentionality) appear appropriate for preliminary exploration. The relationships between scores on individual dimensions as well as a composite score are considered. Finally, it is anticipated that OAS will be correlated to other AS measures as well as to variables identified in previous research such as job satisfaction, burnout, and work-related depression.

METHODS

Sample

Questionnaires were developed and then administered during class to 289 undergraduate and graduate business students who had worked at least three months on a recent job. The demographics of the sample, which were fairly typical, were as follows: 62% males, 38% females, 33% under age 20, 57% between 21 and 25 years, 10% over 25 years, 43% with 3 months to 1 year tenure, 24% with 1 to 2 years tenure, 38% with more than 2 years tenure, 67% operational employees, and about 20% supervisors or managers.

Measures

Organizational Attributional Style Questionnaire

OAS was measured using the Organizational Attributional Style Questionnaire (OASQ), an instrument developed for this study. As indicated earlier, both individual scores on each dimension and composite scores were developed. The questionnaire consists of 16 work situations receiving considerable attention in the organizational literature (see the appendix to this chapter). Particular attention was given to items included in Martinko and Gardner's (1982) attributional model of organizationally induced helplessness. Items were reviewed by a panel of organizational researchers prior to final selection. The format of the questionnaire is similar to that used in other AS scales (i.e., Peterson et al., 1982; Peterson and Villanova, 1988). More specifically, the subjects are presented with negative situations and instructed to imagine these events happening to them. They are then asked to write down one major cause of the event and answer six questions asking them to identify the causes in terms of the six dimensions described above.

Other Measures

The ASQ (Peterson et al., 1982) was used to assess general AS. The ASQ contains 12 events assessed across three dimensions (LOC, stability, and globality). The ASQ has reliabilities ranging from 0.40 to 0.70 for individual dimensions and from 0.72 to 0.75 for combined scores.

Job satisfaction was measured using the General Job Satisfaction Scale (Hackman and Oldham, 1975). The five-item scale has reliabilities of 0.74 to 0.80.

Burnout was measured by asking the subjects to respond to seven questions related to job burnout. These same seven items were used in a previous study by Hochwarter et al. (1990) and had a reported reliability of 0.80.

Depression was measured using the Depressed Mood at Work scale (Quinn and Shepard, 1974). This nine-item scale has a reported internal consistency of 0.71. The scale was modified slightly by using a five-point response scale instead of the four-point scale in the original questionnaire.

TABLE 5.1 Description Statistics, Correlations, and Scale Reliabilities of the OASQ

	$\bar{x}$	SD	1	2	3	4	5	6	7
1. OASQ internal	3.87	0.86	(0.69)						
2. OASQ external	4.66	0.81	−0.49*	(0.68)					
3. OASQ stability	4.73	0.77	−0.10	0.38*	(0.80)				
4. OASQ control	3.66	0.83	0.75*	−0.46*	−0.20**	(0.70)			
5. OASQ global	4.73	0.83	0.08	0.18**	0.55*	0.09	(0.76)		
6. OASQ intent	1.90	0.77	0.14***	−0.02	0.16**	0.12***	0.03	(0.80)	
7. OASQ composite	23.58	2.30	0.52*	0.15**	0.60*	0.48*	0.66*	0.47*	(0.78)

Note: Scale reliabilities are shown on the diagonal. n = 289, SD = standard deviation. * = $p < 0.001$, ** = $p < 0.01$, *** = $p < 0.05$.

RESULTS

Descriptive statistics, correlations, and scale reliabilities for the six OASQ dimensions are shown in Table 5.1. A principal axis factor analysis with an oblique (OBLIMIN) rotation was performed on the 96 variables (16 situations with 6 dimensions each). The preliminary analysis indicated that the correlation matrix approached singularity in that no inverse for the correlation matrix was available since at least one row (or column) was a linear combination of another row (or column). The reason for the highly correlated responses appears to be the similarities between the situations and the fact that these situations were all assessed along the same six dimensions.

One potential solution was to reduce the number of situations, and the second was to reduce the number of dimensions. Since there are theoretically sound reasons for considering each of the six dimensions, it appeared most appropriate to reduce the number of situations. Rather than arbitrarily eliminating situations, it appeared most appropriate to divide the situations into two groups, factor analyze each group separately, and compare the results of the two analyses. Thus, two separate principal axis factor analyses using an OBLIMIN rotation were conducted. Because theoretical justification existed regarding the factors that should be extracted, the analyses employed attempted to force a six-factor solution. The results of both analyses were very similar, and factor loadings and correlations are shown in Tables 5.2 to 5.5.

In both analyses, one factor related to intent emerged clearly. A second factor related to stability (across time and situation) also emerged with questions relating to both stability *and* globality loading on this factor. The remaining four factors all related to control, but separate dimensions for internal LOC, external LOC, and control did not appear warranted. Instead, a single control dimension incorporating all of the above dimensions appeared most appropriate.

Since both of the partial analyses indicated only three dimensions (stability, controllability, and intent), another factor analysis, forcing a 3-factor solution, was performed using all 16 situations and only the questions relating to the dimensions of stability, control, and intent.

Results of this factor analysis showed that the three factors extracted accounted for 21.6% of the total variance (Table 5.6). The first factor, intent, accounted for 9.9% of the variance, with factor loadings for specific questions ranging from 0.30 to 0.63. Factor 2, stability, accounted for 7.6% of the variance, with loadings ranging from 0.25 to 0.55. As expected, the third factor was a control factor and accounted for 4.1% of the variance, with the loadings of individual questions ranging from 0.17 to 0.48. Intercorrelations between the factors are shown in Table 5.7.

TABLE 5.2   Factor Loadings for Questions 1 to 8

	Factor 1 (Control)	Factor 2 (Control)	Factor 3 (Stability)	Factor 4 (Intent)	Factor 5 (Control)	Factor 6 (Control)
Eigenvalue	(4.710)	(3.836)	(3.000)	(2.621)	(2.136)	(2.036)
Question 1: Performance Evaluation						
Internal LOC	0.22685	−0.00058	0.24951	−0.19869	0.10755	<u>0.28202</u>
External LOC	−0.24922	0.03313	−0.13074	0.27272	−0.11259	<u>−0.31371</u>
Stability	0.03405	−0.09745	<u>0.23072</u>	0.12394	0.01237	−0.10907
Control	0.17243	−0.03946	0.14847	−0.25416	0.19575	<u>0.27384</u>
Globality	0.05758	−0.06425	<u>0.29189</u>	0.04252	0.09216	0.02208
Intent	0.09722	0.10082	0.19648	<u>0.31873</u>	0.05510	0.04549
Question 2: Superior Relations						
Internal LOC	0.17512	−0.09048	−0.09289	0.01469	<u>0.20849</u>	0.09992
External LOC	−0.10308	0.06493	<u>0.18427</u>	0.03878	−0.07342	−0.12258
Stability	−0.14582	−0.01260	<u>0.29762</u>	0.15922	−0.15790	−0.19153
Control	0.25546	−0.05720	−0.17995	−0.02037	<u>0.34543</u>	0.23630
Globality	0.00891	0.10586	<u>0.45942</u>	0.12112	−0.02681	−0.10176
Intent	−0.08579	0.03186	0.03592	<u>0.58537</u>	−0.09735	−0.14377
Question 3: Promotion						
Internal LOC	<u>0.87342</u>	−0.05183	0.09300	−0.00248	0.25615	0.20190
External LOC	<u>−0.63112</u>	0.13406	0.08330	0.02195	−0.11312	−0.15734
Stability	−0.09562	0.12481	<u>0.36061</u>	0.17172	0.01423	−0.13685
Control	<u>0.77439</u>	−0.06080	0.07644	−0.00992	0.33250	0.18779
Globality	−0.04516	0.09227	<u>0.41484</u>	−0.00160	0.03425	−0.02747
Intent	0.23752	−0.01067	0.12205	<u>0.56920</u>	−0.05506	0.00062
Question 4: Pay						
Internal LOC	0.02746	0.12638	0.02316	0.00035	<u>0.22004</u>	0.04840
External LOC	−0.13315	−0.00789	0.12434	0.04359	<u>−0.19700</u>	−0.16189
Stability	−0.12326	0.00415	<u>0.51558</u>	0.16209	−0.09430	−0.25265
Control	0.12823	0.01385	0.01445	−0.00846	<u>0.25614</u>	0.03076
Globality	0.06563	0.05402	<u>0.34133</u>	0.06942	−0.03803	−0.12407
Intent	−0.02285	0.01425	0.13603	<u>0.49952</u>	0.10456	−0.15089
Question 5: Goal Achievement						
Internal LOC	0.19792	−0.19969	−0.07665	0.06544	0.14508	<u>0.81920</u>
External LOC	−0.20952	0.15115	0.22665	0.10606	−0.13429	<u>−0.63287</u>
Stability	−0.04098	0.10309	<u>0.42530</u>	0.17380	−0.02306	−0.34294
Control	0.23648	−0.16477	−0.13150	0.00878	0.21488	<u>0.76772</u>
Globality	0.03327	0.12300	<u>0.42628</u>	0.00671	0.01888	0.04283
Intent	0.01093	−0.00956	0.07424	<u>0.60969</u>	−0.12556	0.05163

TABLE 5.2 (continued)   Factor Loadings for Questions 1 to 8

	Factor 1 (Control)	Factor 2 (Control)	Factor 3 (Stability)	Factor 4 (Intent)	Factor 5 (Control)	Factor 6 (Control)
Question 6: Co-worker Relations						
Internal LOC	0.05004	−0.03606	0.15223	0.02040	0.17759	0.11713
External LOC	−0.20124	0.13216	0.05754	0.08860	−0.07756	−0.15634
Stability	−0.04866	0.20655	0.40404	0.09098	−0.04304	−0.14976
Control	0.11237	0.03876	0.09662	−0.03363	0.21147	0.10796
Globality	0.07537	0.05627	0.35570	0.01784	−0.01439	0.06411
Intent	−0.05148	0.09718	−0.04196	0.44924	0.00029	−0.08365
Question 7: Customer Relations						
Internal LOC	0.13493	−0.86613	0.03067	−0.03404	0.04827	0.18737
External LOC	−0.16235	0.70183	0.16783	0.07557	−0.00570	−0.15570
Stability	0.02488	0.28445	0.38544	0.19066	0.01465	−0.15725
Control	0.11662	−0.82727	−0.00369	−0.01953	0.06363	0.14954
Globality	−0.01800	−0.16074	0.39593	0.07314	0.00172	0.02202
Intent	−0.05050	−0.15124	0.05934	0.54384	0.06691	0.00555
Question 8: Training						
Internal LOC	0.11974	−0.08110	0.06995	−0.03450	0.76171	0.15797
External LOC	−0.22194	0.09923	0.17895	0.01998	−0.60131	−0.12822
Stability	0.01563	0.02383	0.54958	−0.00591	0.04892	−0.02432
Control	0.13375	−0.08020	0.09319	0.05448	0.80062	0.08212
Globality	−0.00583	−0.04606	0.58956	−0.07565	0.05365	−0.03443
Intent	−0.11270	0.04156	0.09311	0.51694	0.22343	−0.05651

TABLE 5.3   Factor Correlation Matrix for Questions 1 to 8

	Factor 1	Factor 2	Factor 3	Factor 4	Factor 5	Factor 6
Factor 1	1.00000					
Factor 2	−0.09302	1.00000				
Factor 3	0.00947	0.08002	1.00000			
Factor 4	−0.06019	0.02625	0.10840	1.00000		
Factor 5	0.24645	−0.01984	0.01895	−0.01368	1.00000	
Factor 6	0.28300	−0.12798	−0.09540	−0.16108	0.22295	1.00000

TABLE 5.4 Factor Loadings for Questions 9 to 16

	Factor 1 (Control)	Factor 2 (Control)	Factor 3 (Control)	Factor 4 (Expenses)	Factor 5 (Stability)	Factor 6 (Control)
Eigenvalue	(4.871)	(4.263)	(3.037)	(2.698)	(2.346)	(2.231)
Question 9: Layoff						
Internal LOC	<u>0.21511</u>	–0.14504	–0.17258	–0.10092	–0.03096	0.11392
External LOC	–0.15301	0.11235	0.09011	0.06196	<u>0.15698</u>	–0.04865
Stability	0.11649	–0.04214	0.14057	0.09545	<u>0.34376</u>	0.14754
Control	<u>0.19895</u>	–0.13768	–0.01485	–0.13697	0.05320	0.14536
Globality	–0.02268	–0.10783	–0.06582	0.07416	<u>0.27363</u>	–0.00852
Intent	0.17174	–0.12122	–0.03338	–0.10605	–0.00277	<u>0.43497</u>
Question 10: Expense Reimbursement						
Internal LOC	0.20731	–0.10091	–0.06652	<u>–0.87087</u>	0.04771	0.11009
External LOC	–0.16076	0.17125	0.08214	<u>0.81959</u>	0.13322	–0.16839
Stability	–0.04629	0.03168	0.09479	<u>0.45922</u>	0.26172	0.10851
Control	0.21626	–0.20156	–0.08289	<u>–0.77778</u>	0.10367	0.18608
Globality	–0.08015	0.00641	0.05920	<u>0.36542</u>	0.24662	0.05363
Intent	0.19277	–0.07148	0.09184	–0.20271	0.07952	<u>0.49516</u>
Question 11: Technology						
Internal LOC	0.06227	–0.07710	<u>–0.89675</u>	–0.05902	–0.05719	–0.01325
External LOC	0.01489	0.06410	0.78075	0.01654	<u>0.23620</u>	0.03316
Stability	0.00952	0.01323	0.08220	0.08044	<u>0.47613</u>	0.10611
Control	0.08237	–0.14808	<u>–0.83109</u>	–0.06228	–0.14866	–0.00160
Globality	–0.00489	–0.08392	0.12117	0.09155	<u>0.40127</u>	0.04016
Intent	0.07400	–0.05857	–0.07691	–0.03690	–0.01707	<u>0.53596</u>
Question 12: Pay						
Internal LOC	0.26848	<u>–0.90154</u>	–0.18045	–0.16981	0.01530	0.08706
External LOC	–0.16131	<u>0.77466</u>	0.14499	0.17116	0.11288	–0.14939
Stability	–0.03199	0.18213	0.21792	0.16598	<u>0.52224</u>	–0.07243
Control	0.20179	<u>–0.88733</u>	–0.15681	–0.17275	–0.01873	0.11073
Globality	–0.00472	–0.02482	0.04928	0.03178	<u>0.46681</u>	–0.16355
Intent	0.15461	–0.21395	–0.01999	0.05533	–0.17741	<u>0.59596</u>
Question 13: Superior Relations						
Internal LOC	0.19613	–0.22205	–0.20108	–0.12059	0.00151	<u>0.31055</u>
External LOC	–0.08552	0.18194	0.17552	0.08310	<u>0.21095</u>	–0.16620
Stability	–0.07189	0.08324	0.20396	0.13931	<u>0.51522</u>	–0.05638
Control	0.19145	–0.20966	–0.22734	–0.11603	–0.03178	<u>0.22991</u>
Globality	0.07151	0.03022	0.03492	–0.01962	<u>0.40821</u>	0.02605
Intent	0.08655	–0.05557	0.02872	–0.08386	0.03361	<u>0.67752</u>

TABLE 5.4 (continued) Factor Loadings for Questions 9 to 16

	Factor 1 (Control)	Factor 2 (Control)	Factor 3 (Control)	Factor 4 (Expenses)	Factor 5 (Stability)	Factor 6 (Control)
Question 14: Peer Relations						
Internal LOC	0.16507	–0.10669	0.00192	–0.16207	0.03873	0.08846
External LOC	–0.06570	–0.06815	0.02415	0.08179	0.09805	–0.03422
Stability	0.01768	–0.01405	0.16754	0.13354	0.57693	–0.03499
Control	0.17543	–0.13116	–0.14030	–0.15175	0.08428	0.06508
Globality	0.09140	–0.09176	–0.00329	–0.00552	0.49631	0.07377
Intent	0.11211	–0.02030	0.06669	–0.01862	0.05266	0.66327
Question 15: Superior Relations						
Internal LOC	0.27209	–0.14939	–0.09035	–0.09697	0.05407	0.25111
External LOC	–0.07788	0.09948	0.07060	0.04969	0.09783	–0.15934
Stability	–0.03607	0.07760	0.05979	0.08622	0.39345	–0.05831
Control	0.16622	–0.16336	–0.10566	–0.14351	–0.02551	0.24631
Globality	–0.07066	0.06456	0.01803	–0.01531	0.51512	–0.06764
Intent	0.14391	–0.02848	–0.05631	0.00784	0.06657	0.54480
Question 16: Accident						
Internal LOC	0.93596	–0.10691	–0.05818	–0.18369	0.05030	0.22477
External LOC	–0.65645	0.14193	0.08153	0.09966	0.10394	–0.06406
Stability	–0.11565	–0.01452	0.15576	0.00723	0.46458	0.11930
Control	0.83482	–0.12348	–0.03279	–0.17724	0.08742	0.23008
Globality	0.05550	–0.02920	0.17857	–0.06229	0.44866	0.12701
Intent	0.12031	–0.05291	0.03131	–0.02270	0.02168	0.43424

TABLE 5.5 Factor Correlation Matrix for Questions 9 to 16

	Factor 1	Factor 2	Factor 3	Factor 4	Factor 5	Factor 6
Factor 1	1.00000					
Factor 2	–0.23161	1.00000				
Factor 3	–0.13114	0.20708	1.00000			
Factor 4	–0.24817	0.14015	0.11144	1.00000		
Factor 5	–0.00517	–0.00262	0.16556	0.10412	1.00000	
Factor 6	0.26337	–0.19240	–0.04753	–0.11634	0.01697	1.00000

TABLE 5.6   Results of Three-Factor Analysis

Situation	Factor 1 (Intent)	Factor 2 (Stable)	Factor 3 (Control)
1. Received a below average performance appraisal			
Stable	0.064	0.246	−0.052
Control	−0.063	−0.074	0.327
Intent	0.307	0.092	0.074
2. Suggestions made to boss will not be implemented			
Stable	0.121	0.385	−0.176
Control	−0.026	−0.149	0.396
Intent	0.576	0.166	−0.110
3. You won't receive a promotion			
Stable	0.040	0.418	−0.101
Control	0.003	−0.001	0.356
Intent	0.449	0.080	−0.078
4. Pay inequity exists			
Stable	0.149	0.467	−0.109
Control	0.005	0.058	0.287
Intent	0.524	0.153	0.032
5. Failed to achieve all of your goals			
Stable	0.095	0.535	−0.101
Control	0.021	−0.228	0.360
Intent	0.526	0.114	−0.039
6. Difficulty getting along with co-workers			
Stable	0.025	0.409	−0.117
Control	0.053	−0.025	0.323
Intent	0.437	−0.045	0.026
7. Customer complained about your service			
Stable	0.134	0.423	−0.029
Control	0.064	−0.111	0.178
Intent	0.552	0.090	0.087
8. Not selected for advanced training			
Stable	0.051	0.514	0.071
Control	0.087	0.061	0.478
Intent	0.549	0.117	0.189

TABLE 5.6 (continued)   Results of Three-Factor Analysis

Situation	Factor 1 (Intent)	Factor 2 (Stable)	Factor 3 (Control)
9. You are laid off			
Stable	0.146	<u>0.415</u>	−0.010
Control	0.155	0.030	<u>0.311</u>
Intent	<u>0.490</u>	0.067	0.169
10. You will not be reimbursed for expenses			
Stable	0.086	<u>0.325</u>	−0.181
Control	0.135	−0.053	<u>0.372</u>
Intent	<u>0.548</u>	0.117	0.119
11. Difficulty learning to use the new computers at work			
Stable	0.044	<u>0.429</u>	−0.019
Control	−0.106	−0.280	<u>0.314</u>
Intent	<u>0.562</u>	0.012	0.037
12. Received a below average raise			
Stable	−0.017	<u>0.563</u>	<u>−0.040</u>
Control	0.041	−0.156	<u>0.474</u>
Intent	<u>0.601</u>	−0.058	0.163
13. Negative feedback from boss			
Stable	0.054	<u>0.579</u>	−0.163
Control	0.066	−0.148	<u>0.409</u>
Intent	<u>0.610</u>	0.046	0.073
14. Co-workers don't nominate you for a special award			
Stable	0.001	<u>0.535</u>	−0.003
Control	0.000	−0.068	<u>0.334</u>
Intent	<u>0.619</u>	0.100	0.051
15. Boss doesn't take you seriously			
Stable	−0.051	<u>0.416</u>	−0.071
Control	0.089	−0.120	<u>0.400</u>
Intent	<u>0.443</u>	0.070	0.226
16. Involved in an accident at work			
Stable	0.092	<u>0.411</u>	−0.019
Control	0.184	0.084	<u>0.277</u>
Intent	<u>0.502</u>	0.045	0.020

TABLE 5.7   Correlations between OASQ and Other Variables

	$\bar{x}$	SD	1	2	3	4	5	6	7	8	9	10	11
1. OASQ composite	10.30	1.38	(0.75)										
2. OASQ stability	4.73	0.77	0.51*	(0.80)									
3. OASQ control	3.66	0.83	0.57**	-0.20**	(0.70)								
4. OASQ intent	1.90	0.77	0.70*	0.16**	0.12***	(0.80)							
5. ASQ composite (negative)	12.05	1.98	0.29*	0.22*	0.25*	0.04	(0.68)						
6. ASQ LOC (negative)	3.94	0.94	0.25*	-0.01	0.38*	0.02	0.65*	(0.43)					
7. ASQ stability (negative)	4.16	0.80	0.17**	0.31*	0.00	0.02	0.68*	0.11***	(0.60)				
8. ASQ global (negative)	3.93	1.05	0.21**	0.21**	0.13***	0.04	0.80*	0.23*	0.43*	(0.62)			
9. Depression	2.26	0.56	0.12***	0.11***	0.00	0.10	0.05	0.01	0.01	0.10	(0.81)		
10. Burnout	2.56	0.71	0.12***	0.09	-0.01	0.11***	-0.09	-0.10	-0.06	-0.02	0.52*	(0.69)	
11. Job satisfaction	3.42	0.79	0.01	-0.03	0.12***	-0.07	-0.10	0.05	-0.02	0.00	-0.51*	-0.57*	(0.79)

Note: Scale reliabilities are shown on the diagonal. Mean, standard deviation, and scale reliability for OASQ composite were recalculated using only the stability, control, and intent dimensions. $n = 289$, SD = standard deviation. $* = p < 0.05$, $** = p < 0.01$, $*** = p < 0.001$.

Scale Reliability

Internal consistency and test–retest reliabilities were assessed for the three dimensions identified in the factor analysis. Scale reliabilities for the three OASQ dimensions ranged from 0.70 to 0.80 (see Table 5.7). In addition, internal consistency for the OASQ composite score was 0.75. Thus, the reliabilities, although not as high as desired, were within the range of 0.70 suggested by Nunnally (1978). Test–retest reliabilities were assessed on 85 subjects. These were found to be 0.65 for the stability dimension, 0.72 for the control dimension, 0.66 for the intent dimension, and 0.75 for the OASQ composite score.

Construct Validity

Some indication of the construct validity OAS was obtained by assessing the correlations between OASQ scores and other variables thought to be related to the construct. These correlations are shown in Table 5.7. As predicted, the OASQ composite score was positively and significantly related to the ASQ composite ($r = 0.29$, $p < 0.001$). In addition, the different dimensions of the OASQ and ASQ were correlated as expected. The OASQ stability dimension was correlated with both the ASQ stability dimension ($r = 0.31$, $p < 0.001$) and the globality dimension ($r = 0.21$, $p < 0.01$), whereas the OASQ control dimension was correlated with the LOC dimension on the ASQ ($r = 0.38$, $p < 0.001$). Thus, it appears that the construct being measured by the OASQ is similar, yet not identical, to the construct being measured by the ASQ. This relationship was anticipated and provides some evidence of the construct validity of OAS.

In addition, it was also predicted that the OASQ would be correlated with other variables such as depression, burnout, and job satisfaction. Table 5.7 shows the OASQ composite to be correlated with both depression ($r = 0.12$, $p < 0.05$) and burnout ($r = 0.12$, $p < 0.05$). The OASQ stability dimension is correlated with depression ($r = 0.11$, $p < 0.05$), and the control dimension is correlated with job satisfaction ($r = 0.12$, $p < 0.05$). These relationships are consistent with theory.

DISCUSSION

Overall, the results of this study support the reliability of the instrument and provide some initial indication of the construct validity of the OASQ. Although additional research is needed to further clarify and confirm its psychometric qualities, the OASQ appears to measure a valid construct.

Several issues deserve additional comment. One issue is the dimensions identified in the study. The stability dimension, although consistent with much of the existing attributional research (e.g., Weiner, 1985), appears to be broader than in some studies (e.g., Peterson et al., 1982). That is, the stability dimension extracted in this study includes both cross-temporal and cross-situational stability. As with the stability dimension, the control dimension identified in this study also has a broader definition, including both individual (LOC) and situational characteristics. Russell et al. (1987) reported similar results, finding a correlation between LOC and controllability of 0.928. They suggested that the relation between LOC and the traditional control dimension varies from situation to situation. Thus, in organizational contexts, it appears that situational characteristics combine with the individual characteristics of LOC, resulting in an overall level of expressed control. Interestingly, this interpretation may explain the traditionally low reliabilities of the LOC dimension in past research (e.g., Peterson and Villanova, 1988).

The third dimension identified in the study is one of intent. Although the role of intentions in organizational behavior and work motivation has recently been elaborated (Tubbs and Ekeberg, 1991), several concerns regarding intent as a dimension exist. First, although a factor related to intent appeared to emerge in the factor analysis, it is possible that it is the result of the skewness of the responses. Visual examination of the results shows that the mean response was low ($x = 1.90$, SD $= 0.77$). This would be expected, since most individuals do not intend for negative events to happen. To further investigate this dimension, a factor analysis of the 6 original dimensions on each of the 16 situations was performed. A dimension related to intent did not emerge in any one of the 16 separate factor analyses. Two dimensions consistently emerged: stability and control. The response for the intent question showed no pattern of loading on either of these two factors. Thus, it appears that support for the intent dimension is limited. It may be that the intent dimension is more appropriate for understanding attributions concerning others (e.g., actor–observer).

Several possible shortcomings of this study should be noted. First, the subjects were students. However, this may not be a major limitation in that all had held their most recent job for at least three months. In future research, more heterogeneous samples of people from a variety of organizations would be appropriate to develop the generalizability of the results. A second concern about this study is that it provided relatively limited information concerning the construct validity of OAS. This problem is not viewed as critical, in that a single study is rarely adequate to establish construct validity. Reliable construct validity will only be established after more extensive research supports the relationships between OAS and the many variables suggested by existing theory. Nonetheless, this study provides some evidence in support of construct validity of OAS and the OASQ.

A final issue concerns the general nature of the OASQ. Although a definite pattern of factor loadings emerged, the loadings were not as high as desired. Additional research is needed to further explore the cross-situational characteristics of OAS. Differences across organizations as well as differences in OAS concerning different situations (e.g., performance issues, interpersonal issues, etc.) in the same organization need to be considered.

In summary, this study addressees one of the major criticisms of past attributional research by contributing to the development and psychometric evaluation of an AS instrument within an organizational context. More importantly, the results provide support for the existence of an OAS and suggest procedures for measuring and evaluating OASs. The results of this study are intended to facilitate researchers in the development of methods that further enhance our ability to acquire knowledge of how attributional processes contribute to critical organizational phenomena such as performance, satisfaction, burnout, turnover, and LH.

Appendix
OASQ SITUATIONS

Subjects were asked to respond to the following questions concerning each of the 16 situations below.

a. Major cause _____

b. To what extent is this cause due to something about you?
    Nothing to do with me **1 2 3 4 5 6 7**   Totally due to me

c. To what extent is this cause due to something about other people or circumstances?
    Nothing to do with **1 2 3 4 5 6 7** Totally due to other
    other people or   circumstances
    circumstances

d. Will this cause be present in future situations which are similar?
    Never present **1 2 3 4 5 6 7** Always present

e. To what extent is this cause under your control?
    Not at all under **1 2 3 4 5 6 7** Completely under my
    my control   control

f. Is this cause something that affects just this type of situation or does it affect other situations at work?
    Just this type of **1 2 3 4 5 6 7** All types of situations
    situation

g. To what extent is this cause something you intended to happen?
    Not what I intended **1 2 3 4 5 6 7** Exactly what I intended

SITUATIONS

1. You recently received a below average performance evaluation from your supervisor.

2. Today, you were informed that suggestions you made to your boss in a recent meeting would not be implemented.

3. You recently learned that you will not receive a promotion that you have wanted for a long time.

4. You recently discovered that you are being paid considerably less than another employee holding a position similar to yours.

5. You recently received information that you failed to achieve all of your goals for the last period.

6. You have a great deal of difficulty getting along with your co-workers.

7. You just discovered that a customer recently complained about the service you provided them.

8. You were not selected for advanced training which you wanted to attend.

9. A large layoff has been announced at your company and you are told that you will be one of the those laid off.

10. You just learned that you will not be reimbursed for expenses you recently submitted.

11. You are having a great deal of difficulty learning how to use the new computers at work.

12. You recently received a below average raise.

13. All of the feedback you have received lately from your boss concerning your performance has been negative.

14. Your co-workers (peers) failed to nominate you for a special award which you would like to receive.

15. You feel your boss doesn't take you seriously.

16. You are involved in a serious accident at work.

REFERENCES

Abramson, L., Seligman, M., and Teasdale, J. (1978). Learned helplessness in humans: Critique and reformulation. *Journal of Abnormal Psychology,* 87:49–74.

Alloy, L., Peterson, C., Abramson, L., and Seligman, M. (1984). Attributional style and the generality of learned helplessness. *Journal of Personality and Social Psychology,* 46(3):681–687.

Anderson, C. (1983). The causal structure of situations: The generation of plausible causal attributions as a function of type of event situation. *Journal of Experimental Social Psychology,* 19:185–203.

Anderson, C., Horowitz, L., and French, R. (1983). Attributional style of lonely and depressed people. *Journal of Personality and Social Psychology,* 45(1):127–136.

Anderson, C., Jennings, D., and Arnoult, L. (1988). Validity and utility of the attributional style construct at a moderate level of specificity. *Journal of Personality and Social Psychology,* 55(6):979–990.

Arntz, A., Gerlsma, C., and Albersnagel, F. (1985). Attributional style questioned: Psychometric evaluation of the ASQ in Dutch adolescents. *Advances in Behavior Research Therapy,* 7:55–89.

Brown, K. (1984). Exploring group performance: An attributional analysis. *Academy of Management Review,* 9:54–63.

Carver, C. (1989). How should multi-faceted personality constructs be measured? Issues illustrated by self-monitoring, attributional style, and hardiness. *Journal of Personality and Social Psychology,* 56(4):577–585.

Cutrona, C., Russell, D., and Jones, R. (1984). Cross-situational consistency in causal attributions: Does attributional style exist? *Journal of Personality and Social Psychology,* 47:1043–1058.

Escovar, L., Brown, G., and Rodriguez, R. (1982). Development and Validation of an Attributional Style Questionnaire for Affiliative Behavior, paper presented at the annual meeting of the American Psychological Association, Washington, D.C.

Furnham, A., Sadka, V., and Brewin, C. (1992). The development of an occupational attributional style questionnaire. *Journal of Organizational Behavior,* 13:27–39.

Gong-Guy, E. and Hammen, C. (1980). Causal perceptions of stressful events in depressed and nondepressed outpatients. *Journal of Abnormal Psychology,* 89:662–669.

Hackman, J. and Oldham, G. (1975). The Job Diagnostic Survey: An Instrument for the Diagnosis of Jobs and the Evaluation of Job Redesign Projects, Tech Report 4, New Haven, Conn.: Yale University, Department of Administrative Sciences.

Heider, F. (1958). *The Psychology of Interpersonal Relations,* New York: John Wiley & Sons.

Hochwarter, W., Perrewé, P., and Kent, R. (1993). The impact of persistence on the stressor-strain and strain-intentions to leave relationships: A field examination. *Journal of Social Behavior and Personality,* 8(3):389–404.

Hull. J., Van Treuren, R., and Propsom, P. (1988). Attributional style and the components of hardiness. *Personality and Social Psychology Bulletin,* 14(3):505–513.

Ickes, W. and Layden, M. (1978). Attributional styles. in *New Directions in Attribution Research,* Vol. 2, J.H. Harvey, W. Ickes, and R.F. Kidd (Eds.), Hillsdale, N.J.: Erlbaum, pp. 119–152.

Ilgen, D. and Klein, H. (1988). Organizational behavior. *Annual Review of Psychology,* 40:327–351.

Lowe, C., Medway, F., and Beers, S. (1979). Individual Differences in Causal Attribution: The Personal-Environmental Causal Attribution (PECA) Scale, paper presented at the annual meeting of the Eastern Psychological Association, Baltimore.

Martinko, M.J. and Gardner, W.L. (1982). Learned helplessness: An alternative explanation for performance deficits. *Academy of Management Review,* 7(2):195–204.

Mikulincer, M. and Solomon, Z. (1988). Attributional style and combat-related stress disorder. *Journal of Abnormal Psychology,* 97(3):308–313.

Nunnally, J.C. (1978). *Psychometric Theory,* 2nd edition, New York: McGraw-Hill.

Peterson, C. and Villanova, P. (1988). An expanded Attributional Style Questionnaire. *Journal of Abnormal Psychology,* 97(1):87–89.

Peterson, C., Semmel, A., von Bayer, C., Abramson, L., Metalsky, G., and Seligman, M. (1982). The Attributional Style Questionnaire. *Cognitive Therapy and Research,* 6(3): 287–300.

Quinn, R. and Shepard, L. (1974). *The 1972–1973 Quality of Employment Survey,* Ann Arbor, Mich.: Institute for Social Research.

Ronis, D., Hansen, R., and O'Leary, V. (1983). Understanding the meaning of achievement attributions: A test of derived locus and stability scores. *Journal of Personality and Social Psychology,* 77:702–711.

Rosenbaum, R. (1972). A Dimensional Analysis of the Perceived Causes of Success and Failure, unpublished doctoral dissertation, University of California, Los Angeles; cited in Weiner, B. (1979). A theory of motivation for some classroom experiences. *Journal of Educational Psychology,* 71:3–25.

Rotter, J. (1966). Generalized expectancies for internal versus external control of reinforcement. *Psychological Monographs,* 70(1).

Russell, D. (1982). The causal dimension scale: A measure of how individuals perceive causes. *Journal of Personality of Social Psychology,* 42:1137–1145.

Russell, D., Lenel, J., Spicer, C., Miller, J., Albrecht, J., and Rose, J. (1985). Evaluating the handicapped: An attributional analysis. *Personality and Social Psychology Bulletin,* 11:23–31.

Russell, D., McAuley, E., and Tarico, V. (1987). Measuring causal attributions for success and failure: A comparison of methodologies for assessing causal dimensions. *Journal of Personality and Social Psychology,* 52(6):1248–1257.

Seligman, M. and Schulman, P. (1986). Explanatory style as a predictor of productivity and quitting among life insurance agents. *Journal of Personality and Social Psychology,* 50(4):832–838.

Solomon, S. (1978). Measuring situational and dispositional attributions. *Personality and Social Psychology Bulletin,* 4:589–593.

Sweeney, P., Anderson, K., and Bailey, S. (1986). Attributional style in depression: A meta-analytic review. *Journal of Personality and Social Psychology,* 50:974–991.

Tubbs, M. and Ekeberg, S. (1991). The role of intentions in work motivation: Implications for goal-setting theory and research. *Academy of Management Review,* 16(1):180–199.

Wade, D., Cooley, E., and Savicki, V. (1986). A longitudinal study of burnout. *Children and Youth Services Review,* 8(2):161–173.

Weary, G., Stanley, M., and Harvey, J. (1989). *Attribution,* New York: Springer-Verlag.

Weiner, B. (1974). *Achievement Motivation and Attribution Theory,* Morristown, N.J.: General Learning Press.

Weiner, B. (1979). A theory of motivation for some classroom experiences. *Journal of Educational Psychology,* 71:3–25.

Weiner, B. (1985). An attributional theory of achievement motivation and emotion. *Psychological Review,* 92(4):548–573.

Weiner, B. (1986). *An Attributional Theory of Motivation and Emotion,* New York: Springer-Verlag.

Weiner, B., Frieze, I., Kukla, A., Reed, L., Rest, S., and Rosenbaum, R. (1971). *Perceiving the Causes of Success and Failure,* Morristown, N.J.: General Learning Press.

Section III

APPLYING ATTRIBUTION THEORY TO ORGANIZATIONAL ISSUES

Part A:
Intrapersonal Behavior

6

THE INTERACTIVE EFFECTS OF NEGATIVE AFFECTIVITY AND A CAREER-IMPACTING PERFORMANCE OUTCOME ON SELF-SERVING ATTRIBUTIONS OF CAUSALITY

L. Alan Witt, Dana M. Broach,
Thomas F. Hilton, and Chan M. Hellman

ABSTRACT

Subjects were 114 federal employees in an eight-week resident training program. It was hypothesized that scores on a measure of negative affectivity (NA) collected on the first day of the program would moderate the relationship between a pass/fail job-training outcome and self-serving attributions of causality regarding that outcome collected on the final day. To rule out likely competing explanations for the hypothesized effect, a higher-order interaction was also examined to include positive affectivity (PA): NA × PA performance outcome. Initial regression analyses partially confirmed the hypothesis, and the plotting of the significant higher-order interaction suggested that the interaction between NA and the performance outcome on causal attributions varied substantially among employees at different levels of PA. Results support four models previously introduced to explain the self-serving bias and deviations from it: the classic, depressed, realist, and optimist models.

INTRODUCTION

Attribution theory is predicated on a "thinking person" assumption, in that the individual is seen as motivated "to attain a cognitive mastery of the causal structure of his environment" (Kelley, 1967, p. 193) and is based on three assumptions. First, individuals will attempt to assign causes for important instances of behavior (e.g., receiving an appraisal of poor performance) and, when necessary, seek additional information in order to do so (e.g., talk with peers about the problem). Second, individuals will assign causal explanations in a systematic manner. Third, the particular cause that an individual assigns to an event has important consequences for his/her subsequent behavior (Jones et al., 1972). Thus, attribution theory pertains to the processes used by individuals to interpret events by using causal explanations. The issue is "why" as opposed to "what" or "what if" (Weiner, 1972). In other words, the issue of interest is the relationship between the circumstance (e.g., being fired) and the reasons (i.e., causes) for the circumstance. The attribution process involves post hoc reasoning, whereby a person infers the causes of behavior from the observation of the behavior or event (Steers and Mowday, 1981). This process is important, because causal attributions play a vital role in providing the input to action and the bases for deciding among alternative courses of action (Kelley, 1973).

These "thinking person" assumptions do not imply that attributional errors are not possible. Rather, they reflect the desire of individuals to accurately comprehend their social environment (Kelley, 1971). Indeed, while the desire to accurately comprehend the environment is strong, individuals will ultimately act in accordance with their attributions, regardless of the accuracy of perceptions of the causes of circumstances. This is an important point, as understanding others' attribution processes is a key to interpersonal success on and off the job.

Adapting different motivational styles to fit the personalities of subordinates is a critical element of managerial performance (Davis et al., 1992), and identifying how an individual makes attributions is an important element of determining the person–motivation style fit. One factor limiting managers is the failure to recognize the facts that (1) individuals differ in their attributional processes and (2) people act on the basis of their attributions rather than someone else's "reality." Once these facts are accepted, however, the difficult task is to identify and understand how each subordinate makes attributions about critical outcomes. The purpose of the present study was to assess the extent to which the predisposition to experience negative affect (i.e., "negative affectivity") and positive affect (i.e., "positive affectivity") influences causal attributions regarding an important work outcome.

OUTCOMES AND ATTRIBUTIONS

Although Ash (1980) reported that self-assessments of ability strongly predicted performance, a consensus developed years ago that self-appraisals of job performance are sufficiently riddled with measurement problems (Heneman, 1980) to render them useless for practical use in organizations. Levine (1980) stressed that research on the process of self-assessment is needed in order to determine where the problems lie. He suggested that self-appraisals may falter on the basis of an inadequate judgment process. Researchers in social psychology have been examining self-assessment problems since Heider (1958) argued that individuals, in explaining the causality of an event, will place great importance on protecting their own self-esteem.

Social psychologists have focused on the self-serving bias effect (Arkin et al., 1980). The notion is simple: individuals, in explaining success and failure outcomes, are more likely to attribute success to personal qualities such as ability or effort and to attribute failure to situational characteristics, such as luck or difficulty of the task (e.g., Weary-Bradley, 1978; Weiner and Kukla, 1970; Zaccaro et al., 1987). However, evidence suggests that individuals in some situations hold themselves more responsible for failures than for successes (Rotter, 1966; Ross et al., 1974). Furthermore, there is a basic antinomy between the desire to preserve familiar and valued cognitive schemas and the degree to which such schemas are open to change (James et al., 1978). Indeed, the cost of self-enhancing distortions is high, because misperceptions can render us less able to remedy situations that cause us problems than do accurate perceptions (Nisbett and Ross, 1980). Given this cost, why do people distort events to protect their self-esteem? Recent work on negative affectivity might shed some light on individual differences in the attribution process.

AFFECTIVITY

Personality influences on the attribution process have received relatively little emphasis in the literature. One notable exception is a study of high school students by Meyer (1970), who demonstrated the effect of individual differences in achievement motivation on the impact of success and failure on causal attributions.

In contrast, researchers (e.g., Weiner et al., 1978, 1979) have emphasized the effects of specific outcomes on *state* affect (i.e., mood). Golwitzer and Stephan (Golwitzer et al., 1982; Stephan and Golwitzer, 1981), however, focused on affect as an antecedent rather than as an outcome, showing that *state* negative affect influences causal attributions. Recent developments in the affect literature, however, suggest that affective *predisposition* influences responses to situations, which may also help explain some causal attributions.

In studies of self-reported mood, negative affect and positive affect have consistently emerged as two separate and relatively independent dimensions (Diener and Emmons, 1985; Watson and Tellegen, 1985). Watson and Clark (1984) argued that the tendencies to experience negative or positive affect reflect stable dispositions—negative affectivity (NA) and positive affectivity (PA). Studies on twins reared apart suggest that both PA and NA are inherited (Tellegen et al., 1988). Evidence suggests that PA and NA are key reasons why individuals experience positive and negative moods (Costa and McCrae, 1980; Watson and Clark, 1984). Watson and Clark (1984) noted that persons high in PA are characterized by high energy, full concentration, and active engagement, whereas low-PA individuals typically experience sadness and lethargy.

Marco and Suls (1993, p. 1060) suggested that "NA is first and foremost a prevailing state in that high NAs experience greater baseline levels of negative affect even in the absence of stress." High-NA individuals focus on their disappointments, shortcomings, and mistakes, adopting a more negative view of life experiences. Low-NA persons, on the other hand, tend to be more self-secure, satisfied, and calm, focusing less on daily frustrations and adopting a more resilient approach to setbacks (Watson and Clark, 1984).

In contrast to researchers linking neuroticism with NA (e.g., Bolger and Schilling, 1991), we concur with Watson and Clark's (1984) view that NA represents subjective differences in temperament, mood, and cognitive orientation rather than an index of psychological health.

Previous research suggests that in conditions of failure, high-NA individuals might make more internal attributions than low-NA persons. In a study of the affective states of 24 college students, Sharp and Tennen (1983) found that depressed students assigned greater personal responsibility for failure than those who were not depressed. They argued that high-NA personnel have a depressed attributional style, such that they identify causes that are most unfavorable to themselves. Other research, which indicates that persons high in NA are more reactive to situational cues (Larsen and Ketelarr, 1991; Marco and Suls, 1993; Parkes, 1990; Witt, 1991, 1994), also suggests that high-NA individuals would report disproportionately higher levels of internal causality for failure. Their findings, however, offer an alternative explanation: high-NA individuals experiencing failure might be more likely to overemphasize their own shortcomings and mistakes because of an overreaction to failure.

Unfortunately, it is not clear how NA might affect the self-serving bias in conditions of success. If the depressed attributional style of high-NA persons leads them to identify causes that are most unfavorable to themselves (Sharp and Tennen, 1983), then they are likely to attribute their success to external factors. In contrast, if individuals high in NA are more sensitive to situations (Larsen and Ketelarr, 1991), then they might tend to overreact and overestimate the impact of their efforts when succeeding (i.e., make more internal attributions).

Alternatively, Levin and Stokes (1989) argued that high-NA people may be able to make more realistic appraisals of their job experiences than low-NA people. Accordingly, they might be less prone to making self-enhancing distortions and thus be better able to address problems.

The literature, then, is not clear as to the effect of NA on the self-serving bias effect: depressed attributional style, greater sensitivity to situational cues, or greater accuracy in assessing events at work? The purpose of the present study was to investigate this issue.

> **Hypothesis 1:** Following research showing moderating effects of NA on situation–behavior relationships (e.g., Parkes, 1990) and Sharp and Tennen's (1983) college student study suggesting a "depressed attributional style," it was hypothesized that NA would moderate the relationship between outcome and causal attributions. However, due to the conflicting findings in the literature, the form of the interaction was not predicted.

Assessing the "depressed attributional style" explanation requires the measurement of PA. The individuals predisposed to experience depressive states would likely report both low PA (low levels of activation) and high NA (high levels of anger and anxiety).

> **Hypothesis 2:** Based on Sharp and Tennen's (1983) notion of "depressed attributional style," it was hypothesized that PA would moderate the NA × outcome interaction. Specifically, employees likely predisposed to experience depressive states (i.e., those high in NA and low in PA) will make comparatively more internal attributions for failure and external attributions for success than employees at other points on the PA and NA continua.

POSSIBLE CONFOUNDS

Consistent with previous findings of an expectancy–attribution link (see Weiner, 1986), the individual's expectancy for success could potentially confound the effect that was hypothesized. An important component of expectancy is the individual's history of reinforcement. This has been generally conceptualized in terms of locus of control (Phares, 1976), which reflects a person's experienced-based conclusion about the extent to which positive and negative outcomes are within the parameters of one's control. Persons classified as "internals" generally view themselves as having influence over outcomes, whereas "externals" typically see luck, fate, and other forces as dominant. Research suggests that locus of control is relatively stable over time (Wofle and Robertshaw, 1982). Internals might be predisposed to make internal attributions and externals to make external attributions. A locus of control measure was included to statistically control for individual differences in expectancies.

METHOD

Subjects

Participants were civilian federal government employees in a two-month, full-time government job training program. Employees who successfully completed this program by passing a series of paper-and-pencil tests and laboratory simulations were awarded with continued full-time government employment and received a salary increase. Those who failed the assessments, however, were terminated from federal employment. Of the 185 who began the program, 114 employees (61.62%, 74% males, M age = 26) provided full and complete data for the study. Of these, 73 succeeded (coded as a 2), and 41 failed (coded as a 1).

Procedure and Measures

On the first day of the program, the subjects were asked to complete three personality measures. One was the widely used Rotter (1966) internal–external locus of control measure ($\alpha = 0.68$). High scores reflect externality in locus of control. The means and standard deviations for this and the other measures are included in Table 6.1. The others were the Watson et al. (1988) ten-item (e.g., "distressed") NA scale ($\alpha = 0.83$) and ten-item (e.g., "active") PA scale ($\alpha = 0.83$). Response options were presented on a five-point Likert-type scale (1 = very slightly or not at all, 2 = a little, 3 = moderately, 4 = quite a bit, and 5 =

extremely). High scores reflect high NA and PA, respectively. Organ and Konovsky's (1989) operationalization of the NA scale asked subjects to indicate how they felt at work, which may have confounded NA with work-related affect and cognitions. In order to reduce the influence of effects specific to the workplace on NA and PA, all subjects in the study were instructed to indicate how they felt generally.

Two months later, on the final day of the program, minutes after being informed of the outcome (pass or fail), employees who passed were asked, "Why did you pass?" and those who failed were asked, "Why did you not pass?" They were then asked to consider the cause(s) they wrote and then respond to the three-item internal–external causality subscale ($\alpha = 0.88$) of the Russell (1982) Causal Dimension Scale, which was presented on a nine-point bipolar scale: (1) Is/are the cause(s) something that (1 = reflects an aspect of yourself, 9 = reflects an aspect of the situation [reverse scored]), (2) Is/are the cause(s) (1 = outside of you, 9 = inside of you), (3) Is/are the cause(s) (1 = something about you, 9 = something about others [reverse scored]). High scores reflect internal attributions of causality.

Analyses

To test the hypothesis, a hierarchical moderated multiple regression analysis (Cohen and Cohen, 1983) was conducted. For the purposes of examining the effect size of a moderator, Stone and Hollenbeck (1989) advocated examining the ΔR^2 brought about by entering the cross-product term of the predictor and moderator. However, some researchers (e.g., Champoux and Peters, 1987; McClelland and Judd, 1993) have asserted that the ΔR^2 insufficiently indicates the impact of the moderator variable. Alternative measures of the effect size of the interaction, such as Champoux and Peters' (1987) standardized impact of the moderator on the regression slope and Cohen's (1978) semi-partial correlation of the interaction term, provide conservative estimates of the effect size of the interaction term because they also assess the effect across the entire range of values of the predictor variable (Witt, 1994).

Cohen (1977) identified three categories of effect sizes: 0.20 = small, 0.50 = medium, and 0.80 = large. Using these criteria, the effect of the moderator variable (NA) in terms of the differential impact of the moderator on the criterion was assessed at the two levels of the predictor: success and failure.

In order to identify the form of the interaction, a procedure advocated by Stone and Hollenbeck (1989) was followed. Three slopes were plotted graphically, one low in NA (one standard deviation below the mean), one average in NA (at the mean), and one high in NA (one standard deviation above the mean).

RESULTS AND DISCUSSION

The intercorrelation matrix is included in Table 6.1. As shown there and consistent with previous findings of a self-serving bias effect, the outcome had a considerable effect on the attributions ($r = 0.69$, $p <0.01$). However, neither NA ($r = -0.03$) nor PA ($r = 0.07$) was significantly related to attribution scores.

To test the first hypothesis, locus of control, the outcome, PA, and NA scores were entered at the first step. Next, the cross-product (i.e., NA × outcome) term was entered, which accounted for significant variance ($R^2 = 0.52$, $p <0.00001$; $\Delta R^2 = 0.018$, $p <0.05$) over and above the main effects; this effect size (ΔR^2) is within the range for moderator effects in nonexperimental studies (Champoux and Peters, 1987; Chaplin, 1991). Thus, the relationship of outcome with attributions of causality varied significantly as a function of the respondents' degree of NA.

In terms of Cohen's (1977) criteria of effect size, NA yielded the following differences at one standard deviation below the mean of NA compared to one standard deviation above the mean of NA in predicted values of attributions of causality divided by the standard deviation of attributions of causality (standardized group differences): (1) 0.42 standard units of attributions of causality scores among students who failed and (2) 0.14 standard units of attributions of causality scores for those who succeeded. Thus, the effect of NA on causal attribution scores varied at the different levels of the outcome. They were small among employees who failed the program but trivial among employees who passed the program.

Figure 6.1 graphically presents the disordinal form of the interaction. As shown there, among the employees who failed the program, those high in NA reported more internal attributions than those low in NA. This is consistent with the findings that individuals high in NA overreact to negative situational cues (Witt, 1994) and that persons high in NA assigned greater personal responsibility

TABLE 6.1   Means, Standard Deviations, and Intercorrelation Matrix

Variable	Mean	SD	1	2	3	4
1. Negative affect	17.33	5.18				
2. Locus of control	8.54	3.12	0.08			
3. Causality	17.29	7.07	−0.03	−0.07		
4. Performance outcome	1.65	0.48	−0.04	0.03	0.69	
5. Positive affect	41.16	5.28	−0.39	−0.22	0.07	−0.01

Note: $r <0.26$, $p <0.01$.

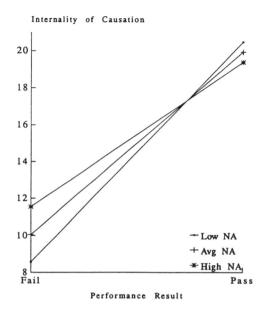

Moderating Effect of NA
Across All Employees

FIGURE 6.1 Attribution of causality scores regressed on pass/fail outcome among all subjects: low, average, and high NA levels. Note: $Y = (17.4 - 0.41f)X + (0.77f - 15.3)$. Low NA = one standard deviation below the mean of NA; avg NA = the mean of NA; high NA = one standard deviation above the mean of NA.

for failure (Sharp and Tennen, 1983). The trivial effect size of NA among employees who passed did not permit assessment of the appropriateness of these competing explanations. Figure 6.1 also does not rule out the explanation based on work by Levin and Stokes (1989) suggesting that high-NA people make more realistic appraisals of their job experiences. The slopes reflect that the self-serving bias effect was weakest among high-NA employees.

Conducting the second set of regression analyses to test the second hypothesis, seven variables were entered at the first step: locus of control, the outcome, PA, NA, the NA × outcome cross-product, the PA × outcome cross-product, and the NA × PA cross-product. Next, the PA × NA × outcome interaction term was entered, which accounted for significant variance ($R^2 = 0.53$, $p < 0.00001$; $\Delta R^2 = 0.017$, $p = 0.05$) over and above the main effects and other interaction terms. This suggests that the interaction of the outcome with NA on attributions of causality varied significantly as a function of the respondents' degree of PA.

In order to identify the form of the higher-order interaction, the regression

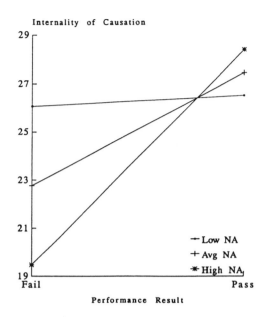

FIGURE 6.2 Attribution of causality scores regressed on pass/fail outcome among subjects low in PA: low, average, and high NA levels. Note: $Y = (-7.45 - 0.66f)X + (-1.19f - 39.85)$. Low NA = one standard deviation below the mean of NA; avg NA = the mean of NA; high NA = one standard deviation above the mean of NA.

analysis procedure used to test the first hypothesis was repeated for three groups of employees. In the first group, among employees with PA scores at or below one standard deviation below the mean, the NA × outcome cross-product term added substantial variance ($\Delta R^2 = 0.05$). This disordinal interaction is presented in Figure 6.2. The size of the effect of NA on causal attributions was large among students who failed (1.03 standard units of causal attributions scores) and small for those who succeeded (0.29 standard units of causal attributions scores). These effect sizes permit assessment of the competing explanations among both passing and failing employees. The individuals who reported low PA (high levels of sadness and lethargy) and high NA (high levels of anger and anxiety)—the ones most prone to experience depressive states—were in the group who manifested the strongest self-serving bias. This does not support the argument that persons predisposed to experience depression make unfavorable attributions, which is based on Sharp and Tennen's (1983) finding. The low-NA (calm) group showed virtually no self-serving bias. The findings that the outcome affected the attributions of the high-NA group rather than the low-NA group are not consistent with the argument that high-NA personnel make more realistic appraisals of job performance (Levin and Stokes, 1989). Among these employees, who are at the very low end of the PA continuum, the notion that those high in NA are comparatively more reactive to the situation (Larsen and Ketelarr, 1991) might be the most relevant explanation of the effect of NA on the outcome–attributions relationship.

In the second group, among employees within ±1 standard deviation of the mean of PA, the NA × outcome cross-product term also added substantial variance ($\Delta R^2 = 0.04$). The size of the effect of NA on causal attributions was 0.40 standard units of causal attributions scores among students who failed and 0.58 standard units of causal attributions scores for those who succeeded. As shown in Figure 6.3, those high in NA made greater internal attributions for failure and external attributions for success than low-NA employees. In other

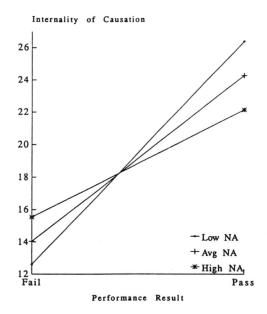

FIGURE 6.3 Attribution of causality scores regressed on pass/fail outcome among subjects within ±1 standard deviation of the mean of PA: low, average, and high NA levels. Note: $Y = (23.91 - 0.76f)X + (-1.2f - 19.4)$. Low NA = one standard deviation below the mean of NA; avg NA = the mean of NA; high NA = one standard deviation above the mean of NA.

words, the high-NA employees were least likely to manifest the self-serving bias. Because these high-NA employees are not at the low end of the PA scale, it is likely that they are not predisposed to depression. Thus, rather than making the unfavorable attributions common among persons experiencing states of depression, they simply might have been comparatively more accurate than persons low in NA. This finding, which represents the majority of the sample (i.e., those in between the extreme scores of PA), supports the explanation that high-NA people make more realistic appraisals of job performance (Levin and Stokes, 1989).

In the third group, among employees with PA scores at or above one standard deviation above the mean, the NA × outcome cross-product term added little variance ($\Delta R^2 = 0.007$). This plot, presented in Figure 6.4, clearly shows a main effect for the self-serving bias, with high-NA individuals making more internal attributions in both success (effect size = 0.58) and failure (effect size = 0.29) conditions.

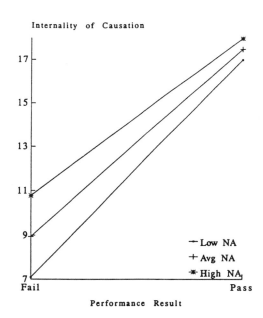

FIGURE 6.4   Attribution of causality scores regressed on pass/fail outcome among subjects high in PA: low, average, and high NA levels. Note: $Y = (13.33 - 0.26f)X + (0.71f - 12.44)$. Low NA = one standard deviation below the mean of NA; avg NA = the mean of NA; high NA = one standard deviation above the mean of NA.

CONCLUSIONS

These findings offer a new perspective of attribution theory. Over the years, several models have been introduced to account for attribution results for subgroups not conforming to the classic self-serving bias model, in which attributions for success are internal and attributions for failure are external (Jones et al., 1972). Researchers introduced the depression model to explain results that were the opposite of the classic model predictions (see review by Sweeney et al., 1986). The depression model identified mental health as a possible moderator. The realist model was introduced to explain results showing a low propensity to externalize except when realistic to do so (e.g., Alloy and Ahrens, 1987; Watson and Clark, 1984). The realist model added explanations including self-esteem, mood, and self-efficacy/control. In contrast, the optimist/hopeful model was introduced as an explanation of results showing a low propensity to internalize (Seligman, 1990; see also discussion by Taylor and Brown, 1988). The optimist model adds notions such as learned pessimism/ optimism and social adjustment. The results of the study indicate that affectivity might be sufficient to account for the predictions of each model.

Figure 6.5 presents a grid depicting the attribution patterns predicted on the

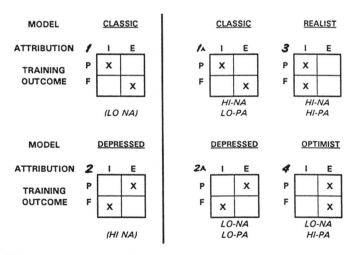

FIGURE 6.5 Four "models" of attributions. Note: Scheme depicting attribution predictions for each possible 2 × 2 (pass/fail × internal/external attribution) combination. Model 1 depicts the classic model, and Model 2 depicts the depression model; these models do not account for positive affectivity. Models 1A, 2A, 3, and 4 depict model predictions for each model discussed and the actual pattern of responses for NA and PA subgroups.

basis of the preceding four models: classic, depressed, realist, and optimist. When affectivity is ignored, the classic model (1) emerges. When NA alone is examined, the classic and depression models (1 and 2) emerge. However, when PA is included, two additional patterns emerge. The third is consistent with the realist model (3) and the fourth with the optimist model (4). Paradoxically, the role of NA shifts from the depression model to the classic one when PA is considered. This indicates that in normal people, a depressive attributional style may be less due to high NA than to low PA (Hall, 1977, cited in Watson and Tellegen, 1985). The inclusion of both PA and NA trait measures, consistent with Watson and Tellegen (1985), adds an explanatory dimension that accounts for all possible combinations of subgroup attributions. Moreover, affectivity accounts for attributions more parsimoniously by avoiding appeal to complex underlying factors such as mental health, self concept, mood, or social adjustment.

At first glance, it may seem odd that only now has a single study been able to account for all possible 2 × 2 attribution subgroups using the explanatory moderation of self-reported affectivity. A casual perusal of the psychology and organizational science literature, however, reveals that more attention has been paid to NA than PA and that when both are addressed, PA is less likely the focus of attention. Additionally, most attribution research has used student subjects often in contrived situations (DeVader et al., 1986). By testing for attributions in an actual work context, reactions to results that were highly salient to the subjects could be addressed in two ways. First, outcomes were linked to job fate (pass: stay vs. fail: separate), and outcomes had high rewards/costs (pass: high-pay future vs. fail: unemployment and lost investment due to quitting the job to compete for a new one), so it can be safely assumed that effort was high. Second, subjects knew that they were a highly select group representing the top 3 to 4% of thousands of tested applicants. Therefore, pass/fail outcomes realistically should be due to effort. Also, the training program was both competitive and difficult. These manipulations might have enabled emergence of the realist and optimist models at a measurable level. Finally, due to the safety-sensitive nature of the job assigned following training, subjects were medically screened out for clinical depression and other psychiatric disorders as part of the hiring process for trainees. Consequently, NA scores are not likely confounded with depression as in many studies, although mood remained uncontrolled.

In addition to the manipulation of linking performance to highly salient outcomes, by measuring self-reported affectivity and causal attributions eight weeks apart, substantial control for method variance associated with self-report was achieved. Of course, the study had its limitations. Considering that there were only 114 subjects—a third of whom experienced failure—these data should be considered preliminary. A larger work sample needs to be studied, and multiple measures of personality and mood should be employed to cross-check whether subjects in the depressed, realist, and optimist model subgroups evidence other indicators besides affectivity to verify classification accuracy. A second limitation deals with the fact that attributions were scored relatively. For a particular level of affectivity, internality/externality attributions were determined only relative to others within their affectivity subgroup. Therefore, responses may vary along the internality spectrum such that one's internal attribution may be more external than another group's external attribution. Nevertheless, these data showed that all attributions within an affectivity subgroup were in the predicted direction.

Earlier, it was suggested that it is important for managers to identify how an individual makes attributions, because it is an important element of determining the person–motivation style fit. The literature (Taylor and Brown, 1988) suggests that most employees are likely to act consistent with the classic well-adjusted model (1A). Managers should be able to place these individuals in a broad spectrum of jobs with expectations for both success and a self-serving bias in attributions of performance. Seligman (1990) argued that managers should avoid hiring model 2A (depressed) employees in favor of more positive, optimistic employees, because they tend to have better job outcomes and are psychologically resilient and stress resistant. Model 3 (realist) employees might be well-suited for tasks in which realism enhances outcomes, such as high-danger jobs, appraisers, and loan officers. Model 4 (optimist) employees might be well-suited for tasks in which maintaining a positive attitude in the face of failure is desired, such as service work or sports.

Finally, these data shed additional light on why self-assessments of performance tend not to correlate with objective indicators and supervisor ratings. Consistent with Levine's (1980) argument that the judgment process undermines the accuracy of self-appraisals, the four models identified here suggest that people vary in their attributions for success and failure when outcomes are self-relevant and have important consequences for them. Given that people act on the basis of their attributions rather than someone else's "reality," this awareness can help sensitize managers engaged in coaching their subordinates.

REFERENCES

Alloy, L.B. and Ahrens, A.H. (1987). Depression and pessimism for the future: Biased use of statistically relevant information in predictions for self versus others. *Journal of Personality,* 52:366–378.

Arkin, R., Cooper, H., and Kolditz, T. (1980). A statistical review of the literature concerning the self-serving attribution bias in interpersonal influence situations. *Journal of Personality,* 48:433–448.

Ash, R.A. (1980). Self-assessments of five types of typing ability. *Personnel Psychology,* 33:273–282.

Bolger, N. and Schilling, E.A. (1991). Personality and problems of everyday life: The role of neuroticism in exposure and reactivity to stress. *Journal of Personality,* 59:355–386.

Champoux, J.E. and Peters, W.S. (1987). Form, effect size, and power in moderated regression analysis. *Journal of Occupational Psychology,* 60:243–255.

Chaplin, W.F. (1991). The next generation of moderator research in personality psychology. *Journal of Personality,* 59:143–178.

Cohen, J. (1977). *Statistical Power Analysis for the Behavioral Sciences,* New York: Academic Press.

Cohen, J. (1978). Partialled products are interactions; partialled powers are curve components. *Psychological Bulletin,* 85:858–866.

Cohen, J. and Cohen, P. (1983). *Applied Multiple Regression for the Behavioral Sciences,* Hillsdale, N.J.: Erlbaum.

Costa, P.T. and McCrae, R.R. (1980). Influence of extroversion and neuroticism on subjective well-being: Happy and unhappy people. *Journal of Personality and Social Psychology,* 38:36–51.

Davis, B.L., Skube, C.J., Hellervik, L.W., Gebelein, S. H., and Sheard, J.L. (1992). *Successful Manager's Handbook,* Minneapolis: Personnel Decisions.

DeVader, C.L., Bateson, C., and Lord, R.G. (1986). Attribution theory: A meta-analysis of attributional hypotheses. in *Generalizing from Laboratory to Field Settings,* E.A. Locke (Ed.), Lexington, Mass.: D.C. Heath, pp. 63–81.

Diener, E. and Emmons, R.A. (1985). The independence of positive and negative effect. *Journal of Personality and Social Psychology,* 47:1105–1117.

Golwitzer, P.M., Earle, W.B., and Stephan, W.G. (1982). Affect as a determinant of egotism: Residual excitation and performance attributions. *Journal of Personality and Social Psychology,* 43:702–709.

Hall, C.A. (1977). Differential Relationships of Pleasure and Distress with Depression and Anxiety over a Past, Present, and Future Time Framework, unpublished doctoral dissertation, University of Minnesota; cited in Watson, D. and Tellegen, A. (1985). Toward a consensual structure of mood. *Psychological Bulletin,* 98:219–235.

Heider, F. (1958). *The Psychology of Interpersonal Relations,* New York: Wiley.

Heneman, H.G. III. (1980). Self-assessment: A critical analysis. *Personnel Psychology,* 33:297–300.

James, L.R., Hater, J.J., Gent, M.J., and Bruni, J.R. (1978). Psychological climate: Implications from cognitive social learning theory and interactional psychology. *Personnel Psychology,* 31:783–813.

Jones, E.E., Kanouse, D.E., Kelley, H.H., Nisbett, R.E., Valins, S., and Weiner, B. (1972). *Attribution: Perceiving the Causes of Behavior,* Morristown, N.J.: General Learning Press.

Kelley, H.H. (1967). Attribution theory in social psychology. in *Nebraska Symposium on Motivation,* D. Levine (Ed.), Lincoln: University of Nebraska Press, pp. 192–238.

Kelley, H.H. (1971). Moral evaluation. *American Psychologist,* 26:293–300.

Kelley, H.H. (1973). The processes of causal attribution. *American Psychologist,* 28:107–128.

Larsen, R.J. and Ketelarr, T. (1991). Personality and susceptibility to positive and negative emotional states. *Journal of Personality and Social Psychology,* 61:132–140.

Levin, I. and Stokes, J.P. (1989). Dispositional approach to job satisfaction: Role of negative affectivity. *Journal of Applied Psychology,* 74:752–758.

Levine, E.L. (1980). Introductory remarks for the symposium "Organizational applications of self appraisal and self-assessment: Another look." *Personnel Psychology,* 33:259–262.

Marco, C.A. and Suls, J.S. (1993). Daily stress and the trajectory of mood: Spillover, response assimilation, contrast, and chronic negative affectivity. *Journal of Personality and Social Psychology,* 64:1053–1063.

McClelland, G.H. and Judd, C.M. (1993). Statistical difficulties of detecting interactions and moderator effects. *Psychological Bulletin,* 114:376–390.

Meyer, W.U. (1970). Self-Concept and Achievement Motivation, unpublished doctoral dissertation, Ruhr University, Bochum, Germany; cited in Weiner, B. (1986). *An Attributional Theory of Motivation and Emotion,* New York: Springer-Verlag.

Nisbett, R. and Ross, L. (1980). *Human Inference: Strategies and Shortcomings of Social Judgment,* Englewood Cliffs, N.J.: Prentice-Hall.

Organ, D.W. and Konovsky, M. (1989). Cognitive versus affective determinants of organizational citizenship behavior. *Journal of Applied Psychology,* 74:157–164.

Parkes, K.R. (1990). Coping, negative affectivity, and the work environment: Additive and interactive predictors of mental health. *Journal of Applied Psychology,* 75:399–409.

Phares, E.J. (1976). *Locus of Control in Personality,* Morristown, N.J.: General Learning Press.

Ross, L., Bierbrauer, G., and Polly, S. (1974). Attribution of education outcomes by professional and non-professional instructors. *Journal of Personality and Social Psychology,* 29:609–618.

Rotter, J. (1966). Generalized experiences for internal versus external locus of control of reinforcement. *Psychological Monographs,* 80(1:No. 609).

Russell, D. (1982). The causal dimensions scale: A measure of how individuals perceive causes. *Journal of Personality and Social Psychology,* 42:1137–1145.

Seligman, M.E.P. (1990). *Learned Optimism: How to Change Your Mind and Your Life,* New York: Pocket Books.

Sharp, J. and Tennen, H. (1983). Attributional bias in depression: The role of cue perception. *Cognitive Therapy and Research,* 7:325–331.

Steers, R.M. and Mowday, R.T. (1981). Employee turnover and post-decision accommodation processes. in *Research in Organizational Behavior,* L.L. Cummings and B.R. Staw (Eds.), Greenwich, Conn.: JAI Press, pp. 235–283.

Stephan, W.G. and Golwitzer, P.M. (1981). Affect as a mediator of attributional egotism. *Journal of Experimental Social Psychology,* 17:444–458.

Stone, E.F. and Hollenbeck, J.R. (1989). Clarifying some controversial issues surrounding statistical procedures for detecting moderating variables: Empirical evidence and related matters. *Journal of Applied Psychology,* 74:3–10.

Sweeney, P., Anderson, K., and Bailey, S. (1986). Attributional style in depression: A meta-analytic review. *Journal of Personality and Social Psychology,* 50:974–991.

Taylor, S.E. and Brown, J.D. (1988). Illusion and well-being: A social psychological perspective on mental health. *Psychological Bulletin,* 103:193–210.

Tellegen, A., Lykken, D.T., Bouchard, T.J., Jr., Wilcox, K.J., Segal, N.L., and Rich, S. (1988). Personality similarity in twins reared apart and together. *Journal of Personality and Social Psychology,* 54:1031–1039.

Watson, D. and Clark, L.A. (1984). Negative affectivity: The disposition to experience aversive emotional states. *Psychological Bulletin,* 96:465–490.

Watson, D. and Tellegen, A. (1985). Toward a consensual structure of mood. *Psychological Bulletin,* 98:219–235.

Watson, D., Clark, L.A., and Tellegen, A. (1988). Development and validation of brief measures of positive and negative affect: The PANAS scales. *Journal of Personality and Social Psychology,* 54:1063–1070.

Weary-Bradley, G. (1978). Self-serving biases in the attribution process: A re-examination of the fact or fiction question. *Journal of Personality and Social Psychology,* 36:56–71.

Weiner, B. (1972). *Theories of Motivation: From Mechanism to Cognition,* Chicago: Markham.

Weiner, B. (1986). *An Attributional Theory of Motivation and Emotion,* New York: Springer-Verlag.

Weiner, B. and Kukla, A. (1970). An attributional analysis of achievement motivation. *Journal of Personality,* 15:1–20.

Weiner, B., Russell, B., and Lerman, D. (1978). Affective consequences of causal ascriptions. in *New Directions in Attribution Research,* Vol. 2, J.H. Harvey, H.J. Ickes, and R.F. Kid (Eds.), Hillsdale, N.J.: Erlbaum, pp. 59–88.

Weiner, B., Russell, B., and Lerman, D. (1979). The cognition emotion process in achievement-related contexts. *Journal of Personality and Social Psychology,* 37:1211–1220.

Witt, L.A. (1991). Negative affect as a moderator of role stressor-job attitude relationships. *Military Psychology,* 3:151–162.

Witt, L.A. (1994). Perceptions of Organizational Support and Affectivity as Predictors of Job Satisfaction, Technical Report # DOT/FAA/AM-94-2, Washington, D.C.: Office of Aviation Medicine, Federal Aviation Administration.

Wofle, L.M. and Robertshaw, D. (1982). Effects of college attendance on locus of control. *Journal of Personality and Social Psychology,* 43:802–810.

Zaccaro, S.J., Peterson, C., and Walker, S. (1987). Self-serving attributions for individual and group performance. *Social Psychology Quarterly,* 50:257–263.

7

ATTRIBUTIONS CONCERNING ABSENCE FROM WORK: A DISPOSITIONAL PERSPECTIVE*

Timothy A. Judge and Joseph J. Martocchio

ABSTRACT

Because the degree to which absenteeism is within or beyond an employee's control is a significant yet unresolved issue in the absence literature, it is important to understand the factors that influence employees' attributions about the causes of absence events. As a result of recent research suggesting that personality variables are important influences on work attitudes and behaviors, the present study took a dispositional approach in investigating the predictors of employee absence attributions. Using data collected from three sources, between-subjects analyses suggested a number of dispositional influences on absence attributions. Within-subjects analyses suggested that the factors leading to external attributions vary widely across individuals.

*The authors contributed equally to this chapter. The School of Industrial and Labor Relations and the Center for Advanced Human Resource Studies, Cornell University, provided partial funding for this study. We thank Amir Erez for assistance with data preparation. We also appreciate the helpful comments of three anonymous reviewers on an earlier version of this paper.

INTRODUCTION

For decades, researchers have attempted to distinguish reliably between voluntary and involuntary absenteeism (Martocchio and Harrison, 1993). Moreover, practitioners have sought out methods to lower voluntary absence levels, or absence that is within an employee's control (Ballagh et al., 1987), because of the financial burden it places on employers (Martocchio, 1992) as well as the workplace disruptions it imposes on employers and co-workers (Goodman and Atkin, 1984). However, some scholars have argued that it is difficult to infer from operational measures whether absence is voluntary or involuntary (Hammer and Landau, 1981). These absence measures are based on data extracted from personnel records, which have been shown to be contaminated for a variety of reasons (Atkin and Goodman, 1984; Hammer and Landau, 1981).

Ultimately, these problems of inference have led researchers to conclude that the meaning of absence (i.e., whether voluntary or involuntary) rests with the employee (Hammer and Landau, 1981). To better understand voluntary absence, researchers have begun to model the employee's decision to be absent from work (Hackett et al., 1989; Martocchio and Harrison, 1993; Martocchio and Judge, 1994). Accordingly, on any given work day, an individual may encounter potential absence-inducing events. For a particular set of circumstances, some individuals may choose to attend work while others may choose to be absent from work (Martocchio and Judge, 1994). Among the absent, some may attribute the circumstances to factors within their control (i.e., voluntary) and others to factors outside their control (i.e., involuntary) (Nicholson, 1977). The attributions an individual makes about the cause of an absence probably depend upon his or her dispositional state (Nicholson, 1977). However, we know little about the attributions an employee makes about absence-inducing events or the possible dispositional sources of these attributions. Accordingly, the purpose of this study is to investigate dispositional influences on the attributions employees make for the factors that contribute to a decision to be absent from work. This approach gets closer to discerning the meaning of absence for individuals (specifically, the extent to which an employee views an absence episode as within or outside his or her control) and complements existing research (Hackett et al., 1989; Martocchio and Judge, 1994; Nicholson and Payne, 1987) by shedding light on the extent to which an employee attributes absence-inducing events to factors within or outside his or her control. Hypotheses based on the most reasonable dispositional influences on absence attributions are developed in this chapter.

HYPOTHESES

The following hypotheses relate dispositional factors to the attributions employees make about the causes of absence. To date, there is insufficient conceptual research on the relationship between dispositional factors and work outcomes (Judge, 1992) and employee absence in particular (Martocchio and Harrison, 1993). Thus, dispositional variables that would fit well with the conceptualization of absence as presented earlier were selected. These factors are the following: (1) Protestant work ethic, (2) self-deception, (3) negative affectivity, (4) tendency to make excuses, (5) life controlled by chance, (6) internality, (7) attributional style, and (8) health complaints. Factors 5 and 6 are considered to be two aspects of locus of control.

Protestant Work Ethic

Values are general modes of behavior representing what an individual should or ought to exhibit (Rokeach, 1973). The Protestant work ethic (Blood, 1969) has been one of the most commonly studied work values. Individuals who endorse the Protestant ethic believe in the intrinsic value of hard work, the merit of achievement in society, and the necessity of short-term sacrifice (Blood, 1969). Although it is unclear whether work values are truly dispositional in nature, work values are relatively stable (Judge and Bretz, 1992), and evidence suggests that the Protestant work ethic is dispositional in nature (Mirels and Garrett, 1971). Because being absent from work implies a failure in one's work role obligations, individuals who endorse the Protestant ethic should be more likely to attribute absence to their own failings (internal attributions) rather than to contextual factors (external attributions). For example, one of the most interesting items Mirels and Garrett (1971) studied is the opinion that people who fail at a job usually have not tried hard enough (p. 41). This suggests that pro-Protestant work ethic individuals have little tolerance for failure at work (such as failing to attend work) and thus more likely attribute absence to failings of the person rather than the situation.

Hypothesis 1: Protestant work ethic will negatively influence external attributions regarding the cause of absence.

Self-Deception

Self-deception refers to the tendency to hold honestly held but positively biased views of oneself (Paulhus, 1986). Research shows that individuals disposed to engage in self-deception ignore minor criticisms, discount failures, and avoid negative thoughts (Sackeim and Gur, 1979). Not surprisingly, research shows that self-deceivers report lower levels of depression than other individuals (Paulhus and Reid, 1991; Roth and Ingram, 1985; Sackeim and Gur, 1979). Self-deceivers avoid aversive self-confrontation and attributions of failure (Sackeim and Gur, 1979). This supports the link between self-deception and positive attributions (at the extremes called "positive illusions") (Taylor, 1989). Sackeim and Gur argued that self-serving attributions, such as the tendency to make external attributions about negative events, may have their basis in self-deception. Furthermore, Roth et al. (1986) found that individuals with a tendency to engage in self-deception denied negative characteristics that threatened their self-image. This suggests that self-deceivers are likely to make external attributions about absence events to avoid negative self-images.

> **Hypothesis 2:**   Self-deception will positively influence external attributions regarding the cause of absence.

Negative Affectivity

According to Watson and Clark (1984), negative affectivity (NA) reflects individual differences in negative emotionality and self-concept. High-NA individuals often are distressed and upset and view themselves and the world around them negatively. NA is relevant in the case of absence attributions because research has found that depressed or high-NA individuals are more realistic and accurate in their judgments (Alloy and Abramson, 1979). These authors found that nondepressed (low-NA) subjects discounted their true degree of control over negative outcomes but overestimated their degree of control over positive outcomes (their experiments held constant the actual degree of control). Given that being absent from work is likely to be viewed negatively by co-workers and supervisors (Goodman and Atkin, 1984), these findings suggest that high-NA individuals will be more likely to attribute absence to factors within their control.

> **Hypothesis 3:**   Negative affectivity will negatively influence external attributions regarding the cause of absence.

Excuse-Making

On the basis of knowledge of the absence literature and experience in organizations studying employee absence, it appears that the vast majority of employees offer personal illness as an excuse for absence. Accordingly, employees who advance personal illness as an excuse for absence are, in a sense, making a plea to their employer to elicit pardon for what the employer may consider an unacceptable act. This view is consistent with the evolving role of personal illness as a socially acceptable excuse or reason for absence (Rushmore and Youngblood, 1979). Accordingly, employees who have a tendency to engage personal illness as an excuse for absence may be more likely to make external attributions than those who do not engage personal illness as an excuse.

> **Hypothesis 4:**   The tendency to make excuses will positively influence external attributions regarding the cause of absence.

Locus of Control:
Life Controlled by Chance and Internality

Derived from Rotter's (1954) social learning theory, locus of control is a generalized expectancy pertaining to the connection between personal characteristics or actions and experienced outcomes (Rotter, 1966). Specifically, locus of control concerns the tendency to ascribe the cause of events either to oneself or to the external environment. Accordingly, those who attribute control of events to their own behavior or to relatively permanent characteristics have an internal locus of control, whereas those who attribute control to outside forces have an external locus of control (Rotter, 1966).

Since its conception, researchers have refined the locus of control construct (Lefcourt, 1991). Levenson's (1981) refinement of the construct is widely cited. Levenson proposed that locus of control is a multi-faceted construct consisting of three factors: powerful others, life controlled by chance, and internality. He based his reconceptualization on the assumption that an individual can believe in his or her own efficacy while believing at the same time that other powerful persons also have some control, or that one can believe in the power of luck or chance happenings and still count on one's own ability to control events. In the opinion of the authors, the latter two facets—life controlled by chance and internality—are relevant to the prediction of absence attributions. (The powerful others scale was excluded because the items pertained more to control of powerful others over one's life rather than the control over events such as absence.) Life controlled by chance reflects a predisposition about the degree to which a person believes chance typically affects his or her experiences and outcomes. Internality, on the other hand, refers to the degree to which people believe they have control over their own lives. Thus, it is anticipated that employees who are of the mind that chance dictates outcomes in their lives should attribute the circumstances leading to an absence occurrence to external factors. On the other hand, it is expected that employees who typically believe they have control over the events in their lives will tend toward internal attributions about the causes leading to absence.

Hypothesis 5:   Employees who account for the occurrence of events in their lives with chance should be more willing to make external attributions for the events that lead to an absence occurrence than employees who tend not to rely on chance.

Hypothesis 6:   Employees who ascribe the occurrence of events in their lives to personal control should be less willing to make external attributions for the events that lead to an absence occurrence than employees who tend not to ascribe the occurrence of events to personal control.

Attributional Style

A key tenet of learned helplessness theory (Seligman, 1975) is that people exposed to uncontrollable events ultimately develop a relatively invariant expectation that they do not control events. Serious consequences of these expectations include motivational and cognitive deficits that are characterized by an individual's inability to perceive existing opportunities to control outcomes. In its original formulation (Seligman, 1975), learned helplessness theory did not account for individual differences in susceptibility to helplessness. Subsequent research attempted to address this issue by suggesting that when individuals face uncontrollable events, they ask why (Abramson et al., 1978). The conclusions from this research are that individuals who habitually explain (1) negative events by internal, stable, and global causes and (2) positive events by external, unstable, and specific causes will be more likely to experience general and lasting symptoms of helplessness than individuals with the opposite style. A number of studies have confirmed this conclusion (see Peterson and Seligman, 1984).

We expect that attributional style will predict employees' absence attributions. As indicated earlier, many consider absence a breach of one's duty to work that, as a rule, results in disciplinary actions against the employee (Ballagh et al., 1987). From almost any standpoint, it is reasonable to label this conception of absence as a negative event inasmuch as the act of being absent (breach of duty) and the attendant outcomes (disciplinary action) are undesirable. Accordingly, employees whose explanatory style toward negative events is characterized by internal, stable, and global causes, as opposed to external, unstable, and specific causes, are susceptible to helplessness. Helpless employees, in turn, are more likely to attribute the occurrence of negative events (including absence) as beyond their control. Martinko and Gardner (1982) argued that learned helplessness influences how individuals make causal attributions about their performance. Since attendance is a performance-related work role behavior, this suggests that helpless individuals will make internal attributions about their absenteeism.

Hypothesis 7: Employees who possess a positive explanatory style should be more willing to make external attributions for the events that lead to an absence occurrence than employees who possess a negative explanatory style.

Health Complaints

As stated earlier, employees often advance personal illness as a reason for absence (Hackett et al., 1989; Martocchio and Judge, 1994; Morgan and Herman, 1976; Nicholson and Payne, 1987). Researchers have concluded that personal illness constitutes a socially acceptable reason for absence in a particular context (Rushmore and Youngblood, 1979; Smulders, 1980). Those studies have considered personal illness at a general level such that employees advance the phrase "personal illness" as a statement of cause of absence. Left relatively unexplored has been the question of whether employees' experience of physical symptoms of illness (e.g., excessive fatigue, headaches, backaches) may influence the attributions they make about an absence occurrence. Although health and the reporting of health complaints are only quasi-dispositional in nature, health is partly genetically based, and the reporting of health complaints has been viewed from a dispositional perspective (Kobasa, 1979). It is reasonable to expect that as the number of physical symptoms mounts, it may be increasingly difficult or impossible for an employee to attend work. Coupled with the acceptability of personal illness as a cause of absence, the following hypothesis is proposed.

Hypothesis 8: Employees who report health problems should be more willing to make external attributions for the events that lead to an absence occurrence than employees whose health complaints are fewer.

CONTROL VARIABLES

Within-Subjects Manipulations

On the basis of prior research concerning the antecedents of absence decisions (Hackett et al., 1989; Martocchio and Judge, 1994; Morgan and Herman, 1976; Nicholson and Payne, 1987), it was expected that several absence-inducing events influence attributions about an absence occurrence. These events are the following: (1) personal illness, (2) kinship responsibilities, (3) pressing work demands, and (4) day of the week. The rationale for the influence of these factors follows.

Personal Illness

Nicholson and Payne (1987) found that the vast majority of employees attribute potential future absence to factors beyond their personal control (specifically, to illness) rather than to events within their own control. Several subsequent studies have replicated this finding (Hackett et al., 1989; Martocchio and Judge, 1994). Nicholson and Payne (1987) concluded that attributing absence to medical illness is consistent with evolving social beliefs about what constitutes acceptable reasons for absence in a particular context. This conclusion fits well with research which showed that medical absence relates to work and nonwork motives (Rushmore and Youngblood, 1979). Smulders (1980) suggested that absence is one element of a "sick role" (viz., Parsons, 1952), a temporal process in which an individual moves from a "well" state to a state of illness, to a coping process, and finally a return to a "well" state. According to Smulders, the interpretation of these external circumstances reflects the attitudes and opinions of relatives and medical professionals as well as sickness benefits offered by the employer and the job situation. These arguments suggest that illness will be a salient attribution regarding the cause of absence.

Kinship Responsibilities

When an employee's kinship responsibilities are pressing (such as when a child or other family member is ill), this person must choose between staying away from work to deal with the demands or attending work by leaving the responsibility with a spouse or other family member. If an employee cannot rely on others to manage a particular episode associated with kinship responsibilities, then he or she would be absent (Martocchio and Judge, 1994). In this case, it is logical to expect that the employee would attribute absence to factors outside personal control. On the other hand, if an employee can rely on others yet chooses to be absent from work, then it is still in his or her best interest to attribute the absence episode to factors outside personal control, particularly if the employee faces discipline due to absence. Often, arbiters and employers deem kinship responsibilities a mitigating or extenuating circumstance in disciplinary procedures, for absence and such circumstances usually cause the employer to lessen the penalty (Ballagh et al., 1987). Thus, employees are likely to attribute absences that are due to kinship responsibilities to factors beyond their control.

Pressing Work Demands

Consistent with Morgan and Herman's (1976) analysis based on expectancy theory, an employee is less likely to be absent from work when there are major demands that consist of a heavy work load and pressing deadlines. Recent research supports this proposition (Martocchio and Judge, 1994). When absent during high-demand work periods, an employee is more likely to fall behind in his or her responsibilities. Falling behind may result in negative outcomes such as a reprimand or poor performance evaluation because some consider absence a breach of an employee's duty to attend work regularly (Ballagh et al., 1987). Obviously, the consequences of breaching one's duty to work are likely to be more significant when work demands are substantial. Thus, when work demands are high and an absence occurs, an employee should be more willing to attribute the episode to factors beyond personal control than when work demands are not heavy. Moreover, retrospective rationality (Salancik and Pfeffer, 1978) suggests that an absent employee might conclude, "I was absent despite having pressing work, so it must have been beyond my control." Thus, it would be expected that pressing work demands will lead to external attributions regarding the cause of absence.

Break in Work

Another factor that should influence absence attributions is when absence occurs in relationship to scheduled time off such as the weekend (Chadwick-Jones et al., 1971). Martocchio and Judge (1994) found that employees were more likely to be absent from work on days adjacent to scheduled time off than during contiguous work days, and it is expected that employees' attributions will depend upon whether absence occurs within a series of contiguous scheduled work days or just before or following scheduled days off. Because absence may facilitate stress reduction for employees (Staw and Oldham, 1978), it is possible that employees would attribute absence that occurs during adjacent work days to factors outside their control, recognizing the need to take time off to regain perspective. Along these lines, employees would be likely to attribute absence that occurs next to scheduled time off to factors within personal control because there may be relatively fewer work disruptions when absences occur just before or after scheduled days off.

Between-Subjects Control Variables

On the basis of prior research, it was anticipated that additional factors would be necessary to predict attributions about the cause of absence. Organizational tenure (Hackett, 1990), age (Martocchio, 1989), actual kinship responsibilities*

---

*This variable measures the kinship responsibilities the employee actually has in general. Thus, this between-subjects variable is distinct from the within-subjects variable, which manipulated whether the employee had a family member who required care on a particular day (versus the level of kinship responsibilities in general).

(Steers and Rhodes, 1978), and occupation and race (Rhodes and Steers, 1990) represent demographic factors that many researchers have used as proxies for the possible attributional processes engaged by employees to explain their absences (Nicholson, 1977; Nicholson and Payne, 1987). Since older and more tenured workers are absent less (Hackett, 1990; Martocchio, 1989), and thus may be less likely to excuse absence, organizational tenure and age were expected to negatively influence external attributions. Because kinship responsibilities lead to increased absence rates and employees attribute them as beyond their control, actual kinship responsibilities were expected to positively influence external attributions. Finally, occupational status and race as controls were used because absence rates vary widely by occupation and race (Rhodes and Steers, 1990). However, a specific prediction is not made because the nature of the relationships is inconclusive.

METHODS

Setting, Subjects, and Procedure

Surveys were administered to a stratified random sample of employees of a large university located in the midwest. Subjects occupied a wide range of service jobs in the university, ranging from clericals to construction workers to managers. The average age of respondents was 46.7 years. Females constituted 68% of respondents, and 84% were married. Employees with one or more children under 18 years of age made up 35% of respondents. Whites constituted 95% of respondents. Average salary of respondents was $23,095. Educational background was as follows: 36% of respondents had a high school diploma, 43% had an associate's degree or completed some college work, and 21% had at least an undergraduate degree.

The surveys were sent to employees through campus mail. The cover letter informed participants that individual responses were completely confidential and that all participants were promised a $15 honorarium in return for completing the survey. Subjects also signed an informed consent form. Subjects were sampled from all departments within the university. From a potential pool of 433 responses, employees returned 138 usable surveys, representing a response rate of 32%. To compare the degree to which the sample of respondents was representative of the population, respondents' and nonrespondents' age, organizational tenure, race, gender, salary, and job type were compared. No significant differences were found with respect to these variables, suggesting that respondents were representative of the larger population of employees.

To minimize self-report bias, a "significant other" (spouse or family member) evaluated several aspects of the focal employee's disposition. The choice of which variables to measure from the perspective of a significant other rested on two considerations: (1) the need to keep the significant other's survey brief and (2) a somewhat subjective judgment of which constructs the significant other could assess best, accomplished by examining the items within each dispositional measure. The relationship of the significant others to the respondents was as follows: spouse = 74%, close friend = 19%, parent = 4%, sibling = 3%. In a further effort to reduce reliance on self-report data, relevant archival data (i.e., age, tenure, etc.) were obtained from university personnel records. These multiple sources of data should yield a more accurate, complete, and unbiased estimate of the core constructs.

Research Design

A mixed experimental design was used that incorporated both within-subjects and between-subjects components (Keppel, 1982). The factors manipulated were illness, kinship responsibilities, pressing work demands, and break in the work week. Each factor, with the exception of the illness factor, contained two levels (i.e., the factor was present or not). The illness factor contained three levels (i.e., illness was not a factor, minor illness, and major illness). With the exception of the illness factor (which was coded 0 = no illness, 1 = minor illness, and 2 = major illness), each factor was coded dichotomously, where 0 indicated the absence of the factor and 1 indicated presence of the factor. The four within-subjects independent variables were completely crossed, which permits assessment of the independent effects of each factor on absence attributions. Crossing the factors resulted in 24 ($2 \times 2 \times 2 \times 3$) scenarios that contained all possible combinations of the independent variables. Six scenarios were replicated to assess reliability of the dependent variable. To minimize order effects, the scenarios in the survey and the factors within each scenario were presented in random order. Each participant read each description as a set of factors that he or she might encounter on a scheduled work day. Below is a sample scenario.

> Assume that on a day that you are scheduled to work you have the following event(s) occurring:
>
> • You are in the middle of your scheduled work week. It's been two days since you have had time off from work, and it will be two days before you have some scheduled time off.
>
> • You need to take care of your children or have other family responsibilities.
>
> • You have a heavy work load or an important deadline at work you must meet.

- You do not feel well today and are physically unable to take on your normal duties.

Measures

External Attribution about the Cause of Absence

Belief about whether the absence occurrence depicted in each scenario was due to factors external to employees (that is, beyond the employees' control) was operationalized in the following manner: "If you were absent given the above circumstances, would this absence be within or beyond your control?" A seven-point Likert-type scale was used, anchored by 1 = totally within my control to 7 = totally beyond my control. The reliability of the dependent variable was calculated by computing reliability coefficients for each of the six replicated scenarios and then averaging the six reliability coefficients. The resulting reliability estimate of this measure was 0.87.

Life Controlled by Chance and Internality

Most researchers have measured locus of control with Rotter's (1966) scale. However, Rotter's scale has come under scrutiny because of its unidimensional conceptualization, its inherent social desirability bias, and difficulties created by its forced-choice response format (Lefcourt, 1991). Accordingly, Levenson's (1981) internality, powerful others, chance (IPC) scales were chosen to measure these factors. The IPC reflects three dimensions of locus of control: internality and chance (both of which were defined earlier) and powerful others (the degree to which people believe other persons control events in their lives). Because it did not seem relevant for the purposes of this study, the powerful others subscale was not included in the analysis. The focal employees evaluated eight statements regarding their internality (e.g., "My life is determined by my own actions."). The significant others of the respondents rated the degree to which they felt the focal employees would endorse eight statements reflecting chance ("He believes that when he makes plans, he is almost certain to make them work."). In the present study, the coefficient alpha (α) reliability estimate of the internality subscale was 0.72. For the chance subscale, $\alpha = 0.77$.

Attributional Style

Attributional style was measured with the Attributional Style Questionnaire (ASQ, Peterson et al., 1982). The ASQ measures the stable tendency of people to make attributions that signify that they are either optimistic or helpless to the world around them. The ASQ presents individuals with twelve hypothetical scenarios (e.g., "You meet a friend who acts hostile toward you." "You become very rich."). Respondents then are asked to indicate whether each event is within or beyond their control (1 = totally due to other people or circumstances to 7 = totally due to me). High scores on this measure indicate positive explanatory styles. Research has demonstrated that the ASQ possesses moderate reliability and validity (Peterson and Seligman, 1984). In the present study, $\alpha = 0.79$.

Negative Affectivity

Negative affectivity (NA) was measured with the NA portion of the Positive and Negative Affect Schedule (PANAS, Watson et al., 1988), a ten-item measure of an individual's tendency to experience aversive emotional states. As recommended by Watson et al. (1988), trait-NA was measured by using general or long-term instructions. Watson et al. reported that the PANAS displayed high degrees of reliability and convergent and discriminant validity. Furthermore, Watson et al. reported that the NA schedule was stable over time ($r = 0.71$ over a two-month period). Judge and Bretz (1993) also found that the NA schedule was relatively stable over a six-month period (corrected $r = 0.71$). For the NA schedule in the present study, $\alpha = 0.85$.

Protestant Work Ethic

The Protestant work ethic was measured with the scale developed by Blood (1969). This scale asks individuals to respond to eight statements about their general beliefs (e.g., "Hard work makes a person better"). Results by Blood suggest that the Protestant ethic scale possesses favorable psychometric properties. In the present study, the scale was modified in two ways: (1) since the significant other used the scale to evaluate the focal employee, it was modified by adding a stem that preceded the eight statements (e.g., "My significant other believes that...") and (2) the wording was made gender-neutral (i.e., "a man" was changed to "a person"). In the present study, $\alpha = 0.62$.

Self-Deception

Self-deception was measured with Paulhus' Balanced Inventory of Desirable Responding (BIDR; Paulhus, 1984), which assesses the tendency to give oneself reports that are positively biased (e.g., endorsing a statement such as, "I never regret my decisions." "I am a completely rational person."). Overall, this 20-item test appears to have desirable psychometric properties and converges with other measures of self-deception (Paulhus, 1991). In the present study, $\alpha = 0.71$.

Health Complaints

On the basis of a scale contained in the Quality of Employment Survey (QES, Quinn and Staines, 1979), a scale was formed consisting of items where significant others indicated if the focal employee had complained about a number of physical conditions in the past year, including back pain, stomach problems, headaches, excessive fatigue, and insomnia (Judge and Watanabe, 1993). The significant other rated the frequency of each symptom for the focal employee with a scale on which 1 = never to 4 = often. In the case of this study, $\alpha = 0.74$, confirming that health problems are often interrelated (Bultena and Oyler, 1971).

Excuse-Making

Five items assessed the extent to which an employee engages personal illness as an excuse for absence. Participants responded to a five-point Likert scale anchored by "strongly disagree" to "strongly agree." A sample item includes "If I was absent on a particular day due to some reason other than illness, as an excuse I might tell my supervisor I was ill." Results indicated that the resulting scale was reliable ($\alpha = 0.84$).

Demographic Variables

Data on organization tenure and age (both measured in years) and occupation (coded 0 = blue collar, 1 = white collar) were obtained from the university's archival records. The number of dependents was measured with a specific question on the focal employee survey.

Analyses

The data set used for the analysis was constructed by duplicating the individual difference variables and then appending these to the four within-subjects manipulations and corresponding attributions (30 for each individual). Conceptually, duplicating between-subjects factors is appropriate because a between-subjects factor can affect the respondent's reaction to each scenario (Judge and Bretz, 1992). For example, internality may influence an absence attribution each time an individual confronts a hypothetical choice, much like internality could influence absence attributions over time (for example, each time an individual faces an actual choice and subsequent attribution). Statistically, this is appropriate because each reaction to a scenario is an independent event, and each event becomes a dependent variable (Hays, 1981). In fact, stable characteristics are usually duplicated in time series and policy-capturing designs in the same way it was done in the present study (Feuille and Delaney, 1986; Judge and Bretz, 1992; Judge and Martocchio, in press; Rynes et al., 1989). Since each of the 138 respondents reacted to 30 scenarios, the sample size used for the analysis was 4140 (30 × 138, less cases deleted due to missing values).

The problem created when duplicating variables is that observations are no longer independent from one another. This means that there will likely be a positive correlation between error terms (autocorrelation), violating an assumption of ordinary least squares (OLS) regression (Kennedy, 1985). There are two consequences of autocorrelation. First, although OLS is still an unbiased estimator of regression coefficients, it is no longer the maximum efficiency estimator; the variance of estimates is inflated. Second, when autocorrelation is present, OLS is not an unbiased estimator of the variance of regression coefficients (standard errors). Thus, standard statistical tests of regression coefficients may be biased.

Given the autocorrelation problem, OLS estimation of standard errors is not recommended. Therefore, generalized least squares (GLS) was used to estimate the effect of the independent variables on absence attributions. GLS produces unbiased estimates of regression parameters and error terms and thus is well suited to deal with autocorrelated errors (Hanushek and Jackson, 1977). GLS corrects problems due to autocorrelation by taking into account the expected variance and covariance of the error terms. This is accomplished by weighting the variance–covariance matrix of the regression error terms. The weighting is a function of the degree of autocorrelation in the error terms, which in this case is determined by the number of duplicated scenarios.

In the present study, GLS regression was performed in two ways. GLS was used as the method of estimation in the LISREL 7 algorithm (Jöreskog and Sörbom, 1989). However, because questions have been raised about the degree to which GLS in LISREL solves the nonindependence problem (D.A. Kenny, personal communication, 1994), the time series cross-section regression (TSCSREG) procedure in SAS also was used to estimate the model (Drummond and Gallant, 1979). TSCSREG is designed to analyze pooled cross-sectional data, which seems appropriate in this case. TSCSREG uses any one of three statistical methods to analyze the data. In the case of this study, the Parks method (autoregressive method) seemed most appropriate because it assumes a first-order autoregressive error matrix with contemporaneous covariance among the cross-sections. For comparison purposes, OLS regression results also are reported.*

---

*Since same the dependent variable (absence attributions) was repeatedly measured over time (30 times for each individual), a repeated-measures analysis of variance (ANOVA) would also seem to be an appropriate analysis strategy. Although a repeated-measures ANOVA was not estimated in the present study (it would require reconstructing the data set), it is likely that the results would be similar to the TSCSREG results that are reported. This is true because the TSCSREG algorithm takes into account the repetitions of the dependent variable and the nonindependence of the cross-sectional (in this case, between-subjects) variables.

RESULTS

Test of the Hypotheses

The means, standard deviations, and intercorrelations of the study variables are shown in Table 7.1. The results of the regression analysis are displayed in Table 7.2. Among the control variables, race, organizational tenure, and age were significantly related to absence attributions; however, higher tenure predicted external attributions. Occupation was not related to attributions; number of dependents was not consistently related to attributions. As expected, personal illness, kinship responsibilities, and pressing work demands significantly predicted external attributions. Interestingly, the results for break in the week depended on the method of estimation. Break in the week was a significant predictor of absence attributions only for the TSCSREG estimation.

Most of the hypotheses regarding the influence of dispositions on the attributions made about the cause of an absence occurrence received support regardless of the method of estimation (Table 7.2). All the hypotheses were supported in two methods of estimation (OLS and GLS in LISREL). Specifically, individuals who had an external locus of control (those who believed their life was controlled by chance and had low internality), who did not endorse the Protestant work ethic, who were self-deceivers, who had positive attributional styles, had low NA, and had a tendency to make excuses were more likely to make external attributions about a particular absence event than were individuals who had the opposite pattern of traits. Using the TSCSREG procedure, however, Hypothesis 1 (Protestant work ethic) and Hypothesis 6 (internality) were not supported. This suggests that Hypotheses 2 to 5, 7, and 8 were clearly supported by the results. Hypotheses 1 and 6 were equivocally supported.

Relationships Among Dispositional Variables

Because the dispositional variables included in this study are conceptually related, it is possible that collinearity exists among the personality measures. To examine this possibility, an analysis of principal components of the eight personality measures was conducted. The results of this analysis, summarized in Table 7.3, suggested that the eight personality scales comprised three constructs (three factors had eigenvalues greater than 1.0). Cumulatively, the three factors explained 51.5% of the variance in the constructs. Although interpretation of factors is always subjective, Factor 1 is difficult to interpret holistically, as individuals scoring high on this factor have a low tendency to self-deceive and to make excuses and report few health complaints, but believe their life is controlled by chance. In most ways, they appear to be positive in their orientation. Factor 2 appears to be characterized by helplessness, where individuals

TABLE 7.1   Means (M), Standard Deviations (SD), and Intercorrelations of Study Variables

	M	SD	1	2	3	4	5	6	7	8	9	10	11	12	13	14	15	16	17	18
1. External attribution	2.77	1.66	(87)																	
2. Number of dependents	0.69	0.98	03	—																
3. Race	0.02	0.12	06	04	—															
4. White-collar occupation	0.27	0.44	02	11	06	—														
5. Organization tenure	11.41	7.90	06	-20	-05	17	—													
6. Age	46.00	10.67	-02	-50	-15	-03	36	—												
7. Pressing work	0.47	0.50	05	00	00	00	00	00	—											
8. Illness	1.10	0.83	25	00	00	00	-00	00	05	—										
9. Break in work week	0.53	0.50	-02	00	00	00	00	00	-06	-05	—									
10. Kinship responsibilities	0.47	0.50	10	-00	00	00	00	00	06	-11	-06	—								
11. Life controlled by chance[a]	17.09	5.08	04	-01	-09	11	05	02	00	00	00	00	(77)							
12. Protestant work ethic[a]	37.24	6.18	-08	01	-10	05	01	05	00	00	00	00	-01	(62)						
13. Tendency to make excuses	62.16	7.69	06	-01	-01	-20	-19	05	00	00	00	00	-08	04	(84)					
14. Attributional style	37.53	8.27	11	-08	00	09	-10	03	00	00	00	00	-02	-08	-01	(79)				
15. Negative affectivity	17.49	5.23	-06	-03	-07	04	13	01	00	00	00	00	16	-05	-13	-07	(85)			
16. Health complaints[a]	15.35	3.78	06	-11	-12	-01	-01	05	00	00	00	00	20	-11	-12	-04	10	(74)		
17. Internal locus of control	41.04	5.81	-09	-03	-04	-09	15	02	00	00	00	00	04	15	-08	-20	-19	-07	(72)	
18. Self-deception	27.54	8.26	09	20	07	-20	-16	-06	-00	00	00	00	-12	-12	14	06	-12	-20	-18	(71)

Note: Decimals are omitted from correlations. Where appropriate, coefficient alpha (α) reliability estimates are in parentheses on the diagonal. Number of observations = 4136; number of subjects = 141.

[a] Reported by significant other.

**TABLE 7.2 Alternative Regression Estimates
Predicting External Attributions Regarding Absence**

Variable	OLS	GLS LISREL	GLS TSCSREG
Demographic variables			
Number of dependents	+0.038 (0.029)*	+0.008 (0.006)	+0.071 (0.035)**
Race	+0.744 (0.208)***	+0.002 (0.005)***	+0.000 (0.000)
White-collar occupation	−0.007 (0.060)	−0.001 (0.006)	−0.031 (0.057)
Organization tenure	+0.029 (0.004)***	+0.051 (0.006)***	+0.007 (0.004)*
Age	−0.008 (0.003)***	−0.020 (0.007)***	−0.013 (0.004)***
Within-subjects factors			
Pressing work	+0.101 (0.048)**	+0.011 (0.005)**	+0.021 (0.010)**
Illness	+0.520 (0.029)***	+0.094 (0.005)***	+0.504 (0.006)***
Break in work week	+0.011 (0.048)	+0.001 (0.005)	+0.025 (0.009)***
Kinship responsibilities	+0.410 (0.048)***	+0.045 (0.005)***	+0.402 (0.009)***
Dispositional variables			
Life controlled by chance	+0.019 (0.005)***	+0.021 (0.005)***	+0.028 (0.007)***
Protestant work ethic	−0.010 (0.004)**	−0.013 (0.005)**	+0.001 (0.004)
Tendency to make excuses	+0.017 (0.003)***	+0.028 (0.006)***	+0.006 (0.004)*
Attributional style	+0.021 (0.003)***	+0.038 (0.005)***	+0.021 (0.002)***
Negative affectivity	−0.025 (0.005)***	−0.028 (0.006)***	−0.006 (0.005)*
Health complaints	+0.040 (0.007)***	+0.033 (0.006)***	+0.016 (0.009)**
Internality	−0.021 (0.005)***	−0.027 (0.006)***	−0.008 (0.008)
Self-deception	+0.016 (0.003)***	+0.029 (0.006)***	+0.011 (0.004)***

Note: Estimates are unstandardized regression coefficients. Standard errors are in parentheses. Intercept is not reported. Life controlled by chance, Protestant work ethic, and health complaints were reported by significant others. * = p <0.10 (one-tailed); ** = p <0.05 (one-tailed); *** = p <0.01 (one-tailed).

scoring high on this factor have a low work ethic, external locus of control, and a negative attributional style. Factor 3 appears to represent a negative cognitive style: individuals scoring high on this factor are high on NA and learned helplessness.

When multicollinearity is present among variables, principal components regression is recommended (Greene, 1990). Principal components regression entails constructing new variables (principal components) that are a subset of the original variables. The new variables are created by multiplying the existing variables by their factor weights from the principal components analysis. Be-

TABLE 7.3   Principal Components Analysis of Dispositional Measures

Measure	Factor loading		
	Factor 1	**Factor 2**	**Factor 3**
Tendency to make excuses	**−0.68211**	+0.07703	+0.11907
Self-deception	**−0.63728**	+0.31419	−0.02231
Life controlled by chance	**+0.57866**	+0.08094	+0.18893
Health complaints	**+0.57486**	+0.21560	+0.14230
Internal locus of control	+0.16331	**−0.73718**	−0.26530
Protestant work ethic	−0.06835	**−0.57098**	+0.01448
Attributional style	+0.06703	**+0.57683**	**+0.58688**
Negative affectivity	+0.19709	+0.20598	**+0.78854**
Eigenvalue	1.69161	1.40780	1.02171
Percent variance explained	21.1	17.6	12.8

Note: Factor loadings greater than 0.50 are in bold.

cause principal components analysis yields orthogonal (i.e., independent) factors, the new computed variables have near-zero correlations. This solves the problem of any collinearity among the original measures. Thus, three new variables were computed from the eight original personality measures, and these principal components were entered into the regression equation.

The results of the principal components regression are presented in Table 7.4.* Results in the table suggest that the three dispositional factors are highly significant predictors of attributions regardless of the method of estimation. The directional effects of the factors on absence attributions makes sense in light of the interpretations of the factors offered above. Specifically, Factor 1, the positive factor, was positively related to external attributions. This seems logical, as individuals with a disposition to be positive can maintain their positive disposition by interpreting negative events (i.e., absence events) as outside their responsibility. Similarly, it seems logical that Factor 2, the helplessness factor, positively predicted external attributions, since individuals with helplessness perceptions should have low expectancy perceptions about performance-related phenomena (Martinko and Gardner, 1982), such as absence. Finally, that Factor 3, the negative cognitive-style factor, was associated with internal attributions

---

*Because the GLS LISREL results were somewhat in between the OLS and GLS TSCSREG results, they are not reported in Table 7.4 but are available from the senior author upon request.

TABLE 7.4 Principal Components Regression Predicting External Absence Attributions

Variable	OLS	GLS TSCSREG
Demographic variables		
Number of dependents	+0.093 (0.026)***	+0.077 (0.022)***
Race	+0.326 (0.185)**	+0.000 (0.000)
White-collar occupation	−0.193 (0.052)***	−0.028 (0.037)
Organization tenure	+0.011 (0.003)***	+0.004 (0.002)*
Age	−0.008 (0.002)***	−0.010 (0.002)***
Within-subjects factors		
Pressing work	+0.076 (0.043)**	+0.025 (0.007)***
Illness	+0.567 (0.026)***	+0.507 (0.004)***
Break in work week	−0.001 (0.043)	+0.013 (0.006)**
Kinship responsibilities	+0.427 (0.044)***	+0.404 (0.006)***
Dispositional principal components		
Factor 1	+0.012 (0.003)***	+0.006 (0.002)***
Factor 2	+0.019 (0.004)**	+0.011 (0.004)***
Factor 3	−0.028 (0.003)***	−0.023 (0.003)***

Note: Estimates are unstandardized regression coefficients. Standard errors are in parentheses. Intercept is not reported. * = $p < 0.10$ (one-tailed); ** = $p < 0.05$ (one-tailed); *** = $p < 0.01$ (one-tailed).

fits with the earlier rationale that negative individuals would be more likely to attribute negative events (such as absence) to forces within their control. In sum, it can be concluded that the dispositional variables influence absence attributions even when the collinearity among the dispositional measures is taken into account.

DISCUSSION

At a theoretical level, the obtained links between the dispositional factors and absence attributions shed light on the meaning of voluntary versus involuntary absenteeism. Until now, the literature on absence, and the attributions that result from absence, has been without an examination of theoretically based antecedents. Thus, this study helps to fill an important gap in the employee absenteeism literature. Similarly, this study contributes to an emerging literature on the dispositional bases of work attitudes and behaviors. Whereas prior research has linked mood at work to absence (George, 1989), it has not considered the dispositional basis of absence attributions. The results clearly suggest that these attributions, in part, are based on personality characteristics.

The clear support of the hypotheses involving disposition highlights that attributions concerning absence are shaped in different ways, and these differences may manifest themselves in unique patterns of absence events. First, life factors controlled by chance and a positive attributional style suggest a profile of a self-concept such that effort is decoupled from the outcome. Individuals high on these dispositions are likely to exhibit chronic absenteeism because they probably believe that any number of agents impede their attendance (such as transportation problems). These individuals may not feel they possess the resources necessary to effect positive control over the factors that hinder their attendance (for example, using public transportation as a backup to using one's car) because they are likely to believe that some other agent (for example, an ill child) will lead to absence. Moreover, it is unlikely that individuals with a pessimistic attributional style and a belief that life is controlled by chance would take responsibility for their actions simply because they do not believe in the efficacy of their actions.

Second, the factors of Protestant work ethic, NA, and internality suggest a profile of positive control such that purposive input is linked to the result. When absent, these individuals will be more apt to claim responsibility. Thus, individuals who are high on these dispositions are likely to exhibit a low to modest level of absence because they believe they can effectively manage absence-inducing events.

Third, the self-deception and tendency to make excuses factors suggest a self-serving profile. Accordingly, absences will virtually always be due to external agents that are socially desirable (for example, taking care of an elderly dependent), compared to internal agents (for example, low work motivation) that are less socially desirable (for example, break in the work week). For these individuals, the motive may be an attempt to "justify" absence to mitigate the disciplinary response to the event (Martocchio and Judge, in press).

As expected, health complaints lead to external attributions. This finding lends support to the notion that there are individual differences in health that influence employee absence attributions. That significant others independently assessed health complaints makes the results stronger, minimizing a response bias toward social desirability. Thus, the results of this study suggest personal illness as a dispositional source, which complements the notion of personal illness as socially acceptable (e.g., Nicholson and Payne, 1987).

The results of a principal components analysis suggested that the eight dispositional variables comprised three general factors. These factors were highly significant predictors of absence attributions. This increases confidence in the validity of the findings. Also, three different estimations were used to account for problems of autocorrelation. It is not yet clear which of these methods is "correct," but the fact that they yielded comparable results makes the findings more persuasive.

Absence-Inducing Events

This analysis of absence-inducing factors revealed that personal illness demonstrated the greatest effects on attributions concerning absence. One explanation for this finding is that societal norms treat personal illness as an acceptable reason for absence from work (Rushmore and Youngblood, 1979) and that norms and attitudes facilitate enactment of the "sick role" (Smulders, 1980). An alternative explanation, based on expectancy theory, is that using personal illness as a reason for absence is instrumental to the attainment of motivating outcomes associated with not being in the workplace when scheduled (Morgan and Herman, 1976). Specifically, the organization under study provides individuals with a number of paid absence days for personal illness. The organization does not require proof of illness. These structural factors not only serve to legitimize absence, but also provide incentives for employees to advance personal illness as a reason when they decide to miss work when scheduled. Prior research provides indirect support for these explanations (e.g., Dalton and Perry, 1981). Finally, attributing absence to factors beyond one's personal control often mitigates the effects of disciplinary actions taken by the employer against the alleged transgressor because it is difficult for an employer to prove whether an "ill" employee was sufficiently ill to perform his or her work duties safely (Ballagh et al., 1987).

Given the perceived acceptability of personal illness as a reason for absence, it is not unreasonable to expect individuals to advance personal illness as an important factor. The confidentiality of subjects' responses and prior research findings, which show that policy capturing tends to minimize response bias toward social desirability (Arnold and Feldman, 1981), makes it reasonable to assume that the salience of personal illness was not a response artifact. Thus, the strong effect of illness on individuals' attributions concerning absence may suggest that illness does cause the majority of absences.

The next largest effect was for the presence of kinship responsibilities. Historically, attributing absence to kinship demands, whether of dependent elders or children, was common (Rhodes and Steers, 1990). As argued earlier, it was not clear whether kinship was within or outside the control of employees. However, labor force projections suggest that both spouses in a relationship increasingly will assume full-time work outside the home (Wetzel, 1990). Therefore, employees may increasingly attribute absence to kinship responsibilities because they cannot as readily rely on their spouses to deal with these demands.

Pressing work demands significantly influenced absence attributions. The positive coefficient indicates that, as expected, individuals were more likely to make external attributions for absence occurrences when they were facing pressing work demands. Finally, break in the work week was a significant predictor of absence attributions in only one of the three estimations. The regression coefficient was relatively small, which suggests that the probability of attributing absence either to internal or external factors based on when absence occurs is not significantly different. Earlier, a rationale was presented for an employee making external attributions for absences that result in a break in the work week based on the salutary effects of absence (Staw and Oldham, 1978) and internal attributions for absences that occur next to scheduled days off because these absences would be less likely to cause a disruption to work. An alternative rationale is that an employee would make external attributions for absences that occur next to scheduled days off because it may be more difficult to justify taking time off just before or after scheduled days off.

Strengths and Limitations

A strength of this study lies in the use of control variables and reliance on employees in a work context. Also, collecting data from three sources should yield a more accurate, complete, and unbiased estimate of the core constructs. Another strength is that the reliability of participants' ratings was assessed, and the ratings were quite reliable. Finally, the advance promise of confidentiality and explicit informed consent should have reduced the chance that participants provided socially desirable responses to questions.

In spite of these strengths, this study is not without limitations. One limitation is that potentially relevant dispositional variables, such as self-esteem, were excluded from this model. Although it was not feasible to include all possible dispositional variables, future research should expand the dispositional characteristics that are linked to absence attributions.

Another limitation with these results is external validity. It is possible that the factors manipulated in the study would not generalize to other organizations. Potential problems with external validity of the factors were minimized in two ways. First, the literature and an earlier study (Martocchio and Judge, 1994) were used to select the most theoretically relevant influences on absence decisions. Second, an independent sample of employees (from the same organization) generated the list of factors that contribute to absence decisions. Thus, from a theoretical and empirical perspective, the factors that were included in this study should generalize to employees in other organizations.

There is a more important concern about the external validity of these findings, however. Specifically, one might criticize these findings because subjects made absence decisions in a contrived setting rather than in the context in which they actually make absence decisions—the field. In particular, there was little resemblance between the context in which the study was conducted and the context in which an individual makes an absence decision (i.e., subjects were taking time from their jobs to respond to a survey that contained hypothetical, but realistic, scenarios rather than evaluating actual absences from work). These scenarios were not particularly holistic in that the only contextual information contained in them related to the four manipulated factors. Although it is true that subjects made these attributions in a contrived setting, results supported these hypotheses. Furthermore, the effects of the relatively stable dispositional factors, whose assessment should be unaffected by the study's context, were consistent with our hypotheses. Therefore, the correspondence between the study's context and the context in which attributions concerning absence are typically made makes generalizations to the "real-life" setting stronger (Mook, 1983).

In conclusion, this study identified absence-inducing events about which employees make attributions, and these results add insights into the meaning of voluntary and involuntary absence to employees. Also, the results demonstrated the importance of dispositions as a source of absence attributions. Future research should attempt to replicate these findings for samples of employees from different populations and settings. Moreover, research that attempts to establish links between dispositions and actual absence events is warranted.

REFERENCES

Abramson, L.Y., Seligman, M.E.P., and Teasdale, J.D. (1978). Learned helplessness in humans: Critique and reformulation. *Journal of Abnormal Psychology,* 87:49–74.

Alloy, L.B. and Abramson, L.Y. (1979). Judgment of contingency in depressed and non-depressed students: Sadder but wiser? *Journal of Experimental Psychology: General,* 108:441–485.

Arnold, H.J. and Feldman, D.C. (1981). Social desirability response bias in self-report choice situations. *Academy of Management Journal,* 24:377–385.

Atkin, R.S. and Goodman, P.S. (1984). Methods of defining and measuring absenteeism. in *Absenteeism: New Approaches to Understanding, Measuring, and Managing Absence,* P.S. Goodman and R.S. Atkin (Eds.), San Francisco: Jossey-Bass, pp. 47–109.

Ballagh, J.H., Maxwell, E.B., and Perea, K.A. (1987). *Absenteeism in the Workplace,* Chicago: Commerce Clearing House.

Blood, M.R. (1969). Work values and job satisfaction. *Journal of Applied Psychology,* 53:456–459.

Bultena, G.L. and Oyler, R. (1971). Effects of health on disengagement and morale. *Aging and Human Development,* 2:142–148.

Chadwick-Jones, J.K., Brown, C.A., Nicholson, N., and Sheppard, C. (1971). Absence measures: Their reliability and stability in an industrial setting. *Personnel Psychology,* 24:463–470.

Dalton, D.R. and Perry, J.L. (1981). Absenteeism and the collective bargaining agreement: An empirical test. *Academy of Management Journal,* 24:425–431.

Drummond, D. and Gallant, A.R. (1979). TSCSREG: A SAS Procedure for the Analysis of Time-Series Cross-Section Data, SAS Technical Report S-106, Cary, N.C.: SAS Institute.

Feuille, P. and Delaney, J.T. (1986). Collective bargaining, interest arbitration, and police salaries. *Industrial and Labor Relations Review,* 39:228–240.

George, J.M. (1989). Mood and absence. *Journal of Applied Psychology,* 74:317–324.

Goodman, P.S. and Atkin, R.S. (1984). Effects of absenteeism on individuals and organizations. in *Absenteeism: New Approaches to Understanding, Measuring, and Managing Absence,* P.S. Goodman and R.S. Atkin (Eds.), San Francisco: Jossey-Bass, pp. 276–321.

Greene, W.H. (1990). *Econometric Analysis,* New York: Macmillan.

Hackett, R.D. (1990). Age, tenure, and employee absenteeism. *Human Relations,* 43:601–619.

Hackett, R.D., Bycio, P., and Guion, R.M. (1989). Absenteeism among hospital nurses: An idiographic-longitudinal analysis. *Academy of Management Journal,* 32:424–453.

Hammer, T.H. and Landau, J.C. (1981). Methodological issues in the use of absence data. *Journal of Applied Psychology,* 66:574–581.

Hanushek, E.A. and Jackson, J.E. (1977). *Statistical Methods for Social Scientists,* Orlando, Fla.: Academic Press.

Hays, W.L. (1981). *Statistics,* 3rd edition, New York: Holt, Rinehart, and Winston.

Jöreskog, K.G. and Sörbom, D. (1989). *LISREL 7: A Guide to the Program and Applications,* Chicago: SPSS.

Judge, T.A. (1992). The dispositional perspective in human resources research. in *Research in Personnel and Human Resources Management,* Vol. 10, G.R. Ferris and K.M. Rowland (Eds.), Greenwich, Conn.: JAI Press, pp. 31–72.

Judge, T.A. and Bretz, R.D., Jr. (1992). Effects of work values on job choice decisions. *Journal of Applied Psychology,* 77:261–271.

Judge, T.A. and Bretz, R.D., Jr. (1993). Report on an alternative measure of affective disposition. *Educational and Psychological Measurement,* 53:1095–1104.

Judge, T.A. and Martocchio, J.J. (in press). The effect of fairness orientation and supervisor attributions on absence disciplinary decisions. *Journal of Business and Psychology.*

Judge, T.A. and Watanabe, S. (1993). Another look at the job-life satisfaction relationship. *Journal of Applied Psychology,* 78:939–948.

Kennedy, P. (1985). *A Guide to Econometrics,* Cambridge, Mass.: MIT Press.

Keppel, G. (1982). *Design and Analysis: A Researcher's Handbook,* 2nd edition, Englewood Cliffs, N.J.: Prentice-Hall.

Kobasa, S.C. (1979). Stressful life events, personality, and health: An inquiry into hardiness. *Journal of Personality and Social Psychology,* 37:1–11.

Lefcourt, H.M. (1991). Locus of control. in *Measures of Personality and Social Psychological Attitudes,* J.P. Robinson, P.R. Shaver, and L.S. Wrightsman (Eds.), San Diego, Academic Press, pp. 413–499.

Levenson, H. (1981). Differentiating among internality, powerful others, and chance. in *Research with the Locus of Control Construct,* Vol. 1, H.M. Lefcourt (Ed.), New York: Academic Press, pp. 15–63.

Martinko, M.J. and Gardner, W.L. (1982). Learned helplessness: An alternative explanation for performance deficits. *Academy of Management Review,* 7:195–204.

Martocchio, J.J. (1989). Age-related differences in employee absenteeism: A meta-analytic review. *Psychology and Aging,* 4:409–414.

Martocchio, J.J. (1992). The financial cost of absence decisions. *Journal of Management,* 18:133–152.

Martocchio, J.J. and Harrison, D.A. (1993). To be there or not to be there? Questions, theories, and methods in absenteeism research. in *Research in Personnel and Human Resources Management,* Vol. 11, G.R. Ferris (Ed.), Greenwich, Conn.: JAI Press, pp. 259–327.

Martocchio, J.J. and Judge, T.A. (1994). A policy capturing approach to individuals' decisions to be absent. *Organizational Behavior and Human Decision Processes,* 57:358–386.

Martocchio, J.J. and Judge, T.A. (in press). When we don't see eye to eye: Discrepancies between supervisors and subordinates in absence disciplinary decisions. *Journal of Management.*

Mirels, H.L. and Garrett, J.B. (1971). The Protestant ethic as a personality variable. *Journal of Consulting and Clinical Psychology,* 36:40–44.

Mook, D.G. (1983). In defense of external validity. *American Psychologist,* 38:379–387.

Morgan, L.G. and Herman, J.B. (1976). Perceived consequences of absenteeism. *Journal of Applied Psychology,* 62:237–240.

Nicholson, N. (1977). Absence behavior and attendance motivation: A conceptual synthesis. *Journal of Management Studies,* 14:231–252.

Nicholson, N. and Payne, R. (1987). Absence from work: Explanations and attributions. *Applied Psychology: An International Review,* 36:121–132.

Parsons, T. (1952). *The Social System,* London: Tavistock.

Paulhus, D.L. (1984). Two-component models of socially desirable responding. *Journal of Personality and Social Psychology,* 46:598–609.

Paulhus, D.L. (1986). Self-deception and impression management in test responses. in *Personality Assessment via Questionnaire,* A. Angleitner and J.S. Wiggins (Eds.), New York: Springer-Verlag, pp. 143–165.

Paulhus, D.L. (1991). Measurement and control of response bias. in *Measures of Personality and Social Psychological Attitudes,* J.P. Robinson, P.R. Shaver, and L.S. Wrightsman (Eds.), San Diego: Academic Press, pp. 17–59.

Paulhus, D.L. and Reid, B. (1991). Enhancement and denial in socially desirable responding. *Journal of Personality and Social Psychology,* 60:307–317.

Peterson, C. and Seligman, M.E.P. (1984). Causal explanations as a risk factor for depression: Theory and evidence. *Psychological Review,* 91:347–374.

Peterson, C., Semmel, A., von Baeyer, C., Abramson, L.Y., Metalsky, G.I., and Seligman, M.E.P. (1982). The Attributional Style Questionnaire. *Cognitive Therapy and Research,* 6:287–300.

Quinn, R.P. and Staines, G. (1979). *Quality of Employment Survey, 1973–1977: Panel,* Ann Arbor, Mich.: Inter-University Consortium for Political and Social Research.

Rhodes, S.R. and Steers, R.M. (1990). *Managing Employee Absenteeism,* Reading, Mass.: Addison-Wesley.

Rokeach, M. (1973). *The Nature of Human Values,* New York: Free Press.

Roth, D.L. and Ingram, R.E. (1985). Factors in the self-deception questionnaire: Associations with depression. *Journal of Personality and Social Psychology,* 48:243–251.

Roth, D.L., Snyder, C.R., and Pace, L.M. (1986). Dimensions of favorable self-presentation. *Journal of Personality and Social Psychology,* 51:867–874.

Rotter, J.B. (1954). *Social Learning and Clinical Psychology,* Englewood Cliffs, N.J.: Prentice-Hall.

Rotter, J.B. (1966). Generalized expectancies for internal versus external control of reinforcement. *Psychological Monographs: General and Applied,* 80:(No. 609).

Rushmore, C.H. and Youngblood, S.A. (1979). Medically-related absenteeism: Random or motivated behavior? *Journal of Occupational Medicine,* 21:245–250.

Rynes, S.L., Weber, C.L., and Milkovich, G.T. (1989). Effects of market survey rates, job evaluation, and job gender on pay. *Journal of Applied Psychology,* 74:114–123.

Sackeim, H.A. and Gur, R.C. (1979). Self-deception, other-deception, and self-reported psychopathology. *Journal of Consulting and Clinical Psychology,* 47:213–215.

Salancik, G.R. and Pfeffer, J. (1978). A social information processing approach to job attitudes and task design. *Administrative Science Quarterly,* 23:224–251.

Seligman, M.E.P. (1975). *Helplessness: On Depression, Development, and Death,* San Francisco: Freeman.

Smulders, P.G.W. (1980). Comments on employee absence/attendance as a dependent variable in organizational research. *Journal of Applied Psychology,* 65:368–371.

Staw, B.M. and Oldham, G.R. (1978). Reconsidering our dependent variables: A critique and empirical study. *Academy of Management Journal,* 21:539–559.

Steers, R.M. and Rhodes, S. (1978). Major influences on employee attendance: A process model. *Journal of Applied Psychology,* 63:391–407.

Taylor, S.E. (1989). *Positive Illusions: Creative Self-Deception and the Healthy Mind,* New York: Basic Books.

Watson, D. and Clark, L.A. (1984). Negative affectivity: The disposition to experience aversive psychological states. *Psychological Bulletin,* 96:465–490.

Watson, D., Clark, L.A., and Tellegen, A. (1988). Development and validation of brief measures of positive and negative affect: The PANAS scales. *Journal of Personality and Social Psychology,* 54:1063–1070.

Wetzel, J.R. (1990). American families: 75 years of change. *Monthly Labor Review,* 113: 4–13.

8

COMPUTER FRIEND OR FOE? THE INFLUENCE OF OPTIMISTIC VERSUS PESSIMISTIC ATTRIBUTIONAL STYLES AND GENDER ON USER REACTIONS AND PERFORMANCE

Elizabeth J. Rozell and William L. Gardner III

ABSTRACT

This longitudinal study investigated the influence of attributional style and gender within a computer-related context. The subjects were 600 undergraduate students enrolled in an introductory MIS course. Multivariate analyses of covariance (MANCOVA) revealed that optimistic users reported more favorable computer attitudes, higher levels of computer efficacy and positive affect, and less negative affect than pessimistic users. Attributional style also accounted for differences in computer-related performance and users' causal attributions. The only gender effect identified involved user affect; female users experienced more anxiety, while males reported higher levels of positive affect. The practical implications of these findings are considered.

©St. Lucie Press CCC 1-884015-19-0 1/95/$100/$.50

INTRODUCTION

As computer applications continue to expand, individuals in all types of organizations are forced to adapt to new information technologies. For many workers, the pressures created by rapidly changing computer technologies have produced adverse cognitive, affective, and motivational consequences (Igbaria and Parasuraman, 1989; Rozell and Gardner, 1992). Indeed, cases in which employees view the computer as a "foe" rather than a "friend" are well documented (Martocchio, 1992; Meier, 1988; Muira, 1987; Williams, 1991; Zmud, 1979). Ultimately, computing problems can contribute to employee alienation and apathy. These may in turn produce adverse organizational consequences, including increases in absenteeism and turnover, and/or a commensurate decline in productivity (Williams, 1991).

Given the scope and severity of such adverse consequences, research to identify individual differences that predispose employees to react positively or negatively toward computers is warranted. Such knowledge could help practitioners to create a work environment that is conducive to the individual utilization of technology (Leitheiser, 1992; Murrell and Sprinkle, 1993; Nelson, 1990; Nelson and Chaney, 1987; Zmud, 1979). Although studies of computer systems in the workplace are plentiful, most limit their focus to one or two variables that are deemed to be crucial to computer performance. Individual differences that have been examined include computer attitudes and anxiety, computer experience, relevant abilities and skills, and computer efficacy (Dambrot et al., 1988; Dambrot et al., 1985; Igbaria and Parasuraman, 1989; Marcoulides, 1989; Morrow et al., 1986; Muira, 1987; Raub, 1981). Gender differences regarding these variables have also been identified (Collis, 1985; Stake, 1983; Wilder et al., 1985).

In an effort to provide new insights into the key determinants of individual performance on computer-related tasks, the current study explores these relationships from an attributional perspective. More specifically, a longitudinal design was employed to examine the relationships between attributional style and users' cognitive, motivational, and affective processes and subsequent computer-related performance. In addition, gender-based differences in these processes and computer performance are explored.

ATTRIBUTIONAL STYLE

Attributional style refers to a predisposition to make certain types of attributions in response to success or failure. This construct can be traced to the reformulated learned helplessness model of Abramson et al. (1978). A basic assumption of this model is that performance attributions shape future achievement-related behaviors. Abramson et al. (1978) also propose that some people develop a maladaptive attributional style that becomes manifest as a tendency to attribute negative outcomes to internal, stable, and global causes (e.g., lack of ability) and positive outcomes to external, unstable, and specific causes (e.g., a lucky break). Seligman (1990) has since described a "pessimistic" explanatory style that involves a tendency to attribute failure to internal, permanent, and pervasive causes and success to external, temporary, and specific causes. In contrast, persons with an "optimistic" explanatory style are biased toward the exact opposite pattern of attributions for success and failure.

Pessimistic persons are especially susceptible to learned helplessness. This is because their tendency to attribute failure to inadequate ability undermines their self-confidence and creates an expectation that they will perform poorly in the future. As a result, helpless individuals lose hope and stop trying; such motivational deficits in turn contribute to deficient performance on future tasks. Thus, a self-defeating pattern of causal attributions, performance expectations, effort, task performance, and subsequent causal attributions is created (Martinko and Gardner, 1982; Seligman, 1990). Several authors have advanced propositions regarding the relationships between attributional style and selected variables that are relevant within computerized work settings (Campbell, 1992; Hall and Cooper, 1991; Martinko et al., 1992). In the few cases in which such propositions have been empirically tested, the results generally suggest that computer attitudes and anxiety are related to users' attributional styles and/or causal attributions for computer-related performance (Campbell, 1992; Hall and Cooper, 1991).

Although such studies of attributional style within computer-related contexts are rare, Seligman (1990) contends that an individual's degree of pessimism or optimism serves as a determinant of success or failure regardless of the task. As such, Seligman and Schulman (1986) hypothesized and confirmed that attributional style is a significant predictor of the performance of insurance salespersons. Specifically, pessimistic explanatory styles were associated with low levels of productivity, as expected. In *Learned Optimism,* Seligman (1990) discusses several additional studies that he and his colleagues have conducted. As a group, these studies provide convincing evidence of the power of attributional style in predicting performance, affect, effort, attitudes, anxiety, and efficacy in a variety of situations.

Henry et al. (in press) provide direct empirical evidence of the potential impact of attributional style on computer-related performance. These authors administered the Attributional Style Questionnaire (ASQ) (Peterson et al., 1982) to students in a computer science programming course. Although the hypothesis that the pessimistic explanatory style would be related to the students' final course grades was not supported, the results revealed that students with an optimistic style significantly outperformed less optimistic students.

GENDER DIFFERENCES

Research on gender effects in computer-related contexts has produced conflicting findings. Most studies have found that women hold more negative attitudes toward computers than men (Arch and Cummins, 1989; Collis, 1985; Dambrot et al., 1985; Levin and Gordon, 1989; Sigurdsson, 1991; Turnipseed et al., 1990; Wilder et al., 1985). Others suggest that (1) gender is unrelated to computer anxiety or computer attitudes (Dambrot et al., 1988; Honeyman and White, 1987; Parasuraman and Igbaria, 1990; Pope-Davis and Twing, 1991; Smith, 1986) or (2) females possess more positive computer attitudes than men (Aman, 1992) and perform at higher levels on computer-related tasks (Dambrot et al., 1988).

For many years, women were excluded from a large segment of the labor market because they were perceived as lacking computer skills (Collis, 1985) and as being anxious about computers. Socialization processes may have contributed to these expectations. Muira (1987) asserts that girls are explicitly and implicitly informed that mathematical tasks, including those that require computers, are most appropriate for boys. This is because males are commonly viewed as possessing superior mathematical abilities. As a result, girls lose confidence in their mathematical skills during their pre-teen years. However, the conflicting findings reviewed above suggest that the manner in which women are socialized may be changing.

Many researchers contend that differential levels of computer experience may account for the gender effects discussed above. For instance, several studies have found that computer experience is inversely related to negative feelings toward the computer, such as negative attitudes and anxieties (Aman, 1992; Meier, 1988; Raub, 1981; Sigurdsson, 1991). Therefore, computer experience was included as an important individual attribute in the current study.

Gender differences in attributions for computer-related performance have also been identified. Stake (1983), for example, demonstrated that males were less pessimistic than females with regard to computer-related activities. Similarly, Linn (1985) found that males tended to attribute positive computer outcomes to task difficulty and chosen strategies, whereas females were most likely to attribute success to good fortune. Under failure conditions, males favored external attributions, whereas females commonly identified inadequate ability as a primary cause. Nearly identical results were obtained by Nelson and Cooper (1989), with females attributing computer-related success to good luck and males attributing failure to unstable causes. Finally, Aman (1992) showed that males expect greater success in a computer-related situation, whereas females are less confident of their abilities.

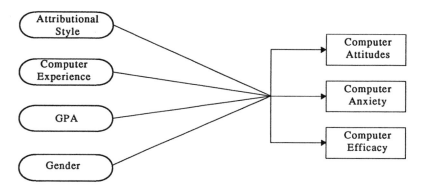

FIGURE 8.1 Individual attributes as they affect computer-related antecedent conditions.

PROPOSED MODELS AND HYPOTHESES

The models that are tested in this study are depicted in Figures 8.1 to 8.3. The initial theoretical foundation for these models is provided by Weiner's (1979) framework for studying attributions in achievement-related settings. This framework has been subsequently adapted and expanded to apply to computer-related contexts by Rozell and Gardner (1992). Each of these conceptual frameworks was used in formulating the proposed models.

Although the primary focus of the study was the impact of attributional style and gender on users' reactions to computers, GPA and computer experience were also included as important variables in the models depicted in Figures 8.1 to 8.3. GPA was used as a proxy measure of the abilities and past performance histories of the students who served as subjects. The computer experience variable reflects the users' familiarity with current technologies. This variable was included based on prior research that has documented its impact on user attitudes, anxiety, and performance (Aman, 1992; Dambrot et al., 1988; Lee, 1986; Meier, 1988; Raub, 1981; Sigurdsson, 1991).

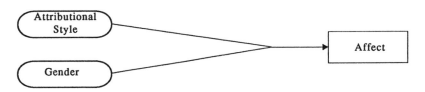

FIGURE 8.2 Individual attributes and their effect on affective states.

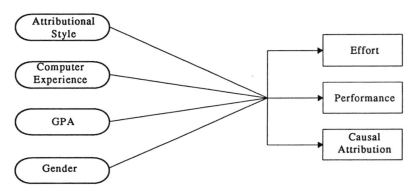

FIGURE 8.3   Individual attributes as they affect effort, performance, and causal dimensions.

The specific hypotheses to be tested are presented below. Wherever possible, directional hypotheses were advanced. For example, it was predicted that females would possess more negative computer attitudes and experience more computer anxiety and lower levels of computer efficacy than males, since most of the studies reviewed identified gender differences in this direction. However, directional hypotheses were not advanced with regard to the influence of gender on effort and performance, since the available results are contradictory.

H_1: Male users possess more optimistic and less pessimistic attributional styles than female users.

H_{2a}: Users with more optimistic attributional styles possess more favorable computer attitudes, less computer anxiety, and greater computer efficacy.

H_{2b}: Male users hold more positive attitudes toward computers, experience lower levels of computer anxiety, and possess higher levels of computer self-efficacy than female users.

H_{3a}: Users with more optimistic attributional styles experience more positive affect and less negative affect.

H_{3b}: Male users experience more positive affect and less negative affect than female users.

H_{4a}: Users with more optimistic attributional styles will exert more effort, perform at higher levels, and make different performance attributions for a computer-related task.

H_{4b}: Gender accounts for differences in users' effort, performance, and causal attributions regarding a computer-related task.

H₅ₐ: Optimistic users attribute success on computer tasks to internal, stable, and controllable causes and failure to external, unstable, and uncontrollable causes; pessimistic users exhibit exactly the opposite pattern of causal attributions.

H₅ᵦ: Male users attribute success on a computer-related task to internal, stable, and controllable causes and failure to external, unstable, and uncontrollable causes; female users will exhibit exactly the opposite pattern of causal attributions.

METHODS

Subjects

The subjects were 600 students enrolled in an undergraduate introductory management information systems (MIS) course. The sample was comprised of 57% males and 43% females; 85% of the subjects fell between the ages of 18 to 21 years. The students were fairly evenly split between juniors (32.3%), sophomores (30%), and freshmen (29.6%), with relatively few seniors (5.3%) and graduate students (2.8%).

Procedure

One week into the course, students were asked to participate in a study of people's reactions to examination performance. At this time, they completed the measures of computer attitudes, computer anxiety, computer efficacy, attributional style, and affective states described below, plus several demographic items. Immediately before the initial examination (time period 1), students were asked to indicate the amount of effort they expended in preparation for the exam. The exam was then administered. Students received their exam scores the following week, at which time they were asked to report their performance attributions and affective states. The practice of measuring self-reported effort prior to the exam, and causal attributions and affect afterward, was repeated during time periods 2 (exam two) and 3 (exam three).

Measures

Computer Attitudes.   Attitudes toward computers were measured by the 20-item scale of Popovich et al. (1987). The items assess positive and negative reactions to computers, as well as attitudes toward computers, children, and education and reactions to computerized mechanisms. The coefficient alpha of 0.80 obtained in the current study attests to the reliability of the scale.

Computer Anxiety.   A scale developed by Marcoulides (1989) was used to measure computer anxiety. The 20 items reflect possible features of computer anxiety. A coefficient alpha of 0.91 was obtained for this scale.

Computer Experience.   Computer experience was measured using a questionnaire developed by Lee (1986). The items include biographical questions about respondents' past experiences with computers. The current study obtained a coefficient alpha of 0.58 for this scale.

Attributional Style.   A scale developed by Peterson et al. (1982) was used to measure attributional style. The 48 items on the ASQ tap various dimensions of the respondents' attributions for six hypothetical positive (success) and six negative (failure) events. ASQ subscales include locus of control, stability, globality, CoPos (the composite score for positive events), CoNeg (the composite score for negative events), and CPCN (a total score, the difference between the CoPos and CoNeg scores). The latter three subscales each measure the degree to which a person possesses an optimistic or pessimistic style. As in prior studies (Seligman, 1990), the coefficient alpha of 0.73 obtained for the overall CPCN scale was higher than the corresponding alphas of every subscale, with the exception of CoNeg ($\alpha = 0.75$). Since the CPCN scale encompasses the more specific subscales, it appears to be the most comprehensive yet reliable measure.

Computer-Related Performance.   Scores on the three exams served as measures of computer-related performance. The exams measured students' knowledge of computers and computer programming skills.

Mood.   Mood was measured using the Multiple Affect Adjective Checklist (Zuckerman and Lubin, 1965). Respondents to this instrument indicate the extent to which they are experiencing various affective states. Coefficient alphas for the mood checklist averaged 0.88 across all time periods.

Reported Effort.   Nine items were developed to measure reported effort. Sample items include "How many times did you read the chapters that were on the exam?" and "How many hours did you spend in preparation for the exam?" Alpha coefficients for this measure averaged 0.76 across time periods.

Attributions.   Russell's (1982) Causal Dimension Scale was used to measure attributions. This nine-item scale assesses attributions for success or failure along three dimensions: locus of causality, stability, and controllability. The coefficient alphas for the subscales averaged 0.70 across all time periods.

Computer Self-Efficacy.   A scale created by Murphy et al. (1989) was used to measure computer self-efficacy. The 32 items on the Computer Self-Efficacy Scale assess the extent to which respondents believe they are successful in their encounters with computers. The coefficient alpha for this scale was 0.96.

Analysis

A t-test was employed to test the predicted relationship between gender and attributional style (H_1). Multivariate analysis of covariance (MANCOVA) was used to test for the effects of attributional style (H_{2a} to H_{5a}) and gender (H_{2b} to H_{5b}).

RESULTS

t-Test Results: Gender and Attributional Style

The first hypothesis predicted that male users would have more optimistic and less pessimistic attributional styles than females. A t-test was performed to test this hypothesis. Since this t-test was not significant ($t = 0.23$, d.f. = 289, $p = 0.82$), Hypothesis 1 was not supported.

Multivariate Analyses of Covariance (MANCOVA)

Tests of Assumptions

Because MANCOVA is a variation of the more basic multivariate analysis of variance (MANOVA) technique, the assumptions of MANOVA were tested. Specifically, the procedures recommended by Stevens (1986) were followed to test the assumptions that the observations are independent, the dependent variable observations follow a multivariate normal distribution in each group, and the covariance matrices of the dependent variables are equivalent in each group. The results indicated that these criteria were satisfied. Finally, since it is a requirement of MANOVA that the dependent variables be correlated, the appropriateness of this technique was assessed for each MANCOVA performed using Bartlett's test of sphericity. In every case, this test was significant ($p < 0.01$), indicating that MANCOVA is appropriate.

MANCOVA Results

For presentation purposes, the results for each pair of hypotheses (a and b) are summarized using two tables: one for the overall and gender effects and a second for the covariate(s). It should be recognized, however, that each set of hypotheses for a given time period was tested using a single MANCOVA. Moreover, although each MANCOVA tested for interaction effects, none of these tests were significant. As such, only main effects are reported.

Predictors of the Antecedent Conditions

As indicated in Table 8.1, the multivariate F-tests (Wilks Lambda) for the overall MANCOVA used to test hypotheses 2a and 2b were significant. The overall univariate F-tests that considered the joint effects of the covariates and gender were likewise significant for computer attitudes and computer efficacy, but not computer anxiety. Because the multivariate test for the effect of gender was insignificant, no support for hypothesis 2b was obtained.

The results for attributional style (CPCN) and the other covariates are summarized in Table 8.2. As this table reveals, attributional style and computer experience were significantly related to computer attitudes. Since higher scores indicate more negative attitudes toward computers, the negative beta weights suggest that optimistic and experienced users possessed more positive attitudes than pessimistic and less experienced users. Attributional style and computer experience were also significantly related to computer efficacy. Again, it was found that more optimistic and experienced users reported higher levels of computer self-efficacy. Importantly, these results are consistent with the predictions of hypothesis 2a. However, contrary to expectations, optimistic users were not less anxious about computers than pessimists.

Predictors of Affective States

The results of the MANCOVA performed to test hypotheses 3a and 3b are summarized in Tables 8.3 and 8.4. Due to the longitudinal design, the same

TABLE 8.1   MANCOVA Results for Hypothesis 2: Overall and Gender Effects

			Means	
Effect	Multivariate F-ratio	Univariate F-ratio	Males ($n = 134$)	Females ($n = 93$)
Overall	12.58***			
Computer attitude[a]		19.69***		
Computer anxiety		2.23		
Computer efficacy		35.48***		
Gender	1.85			
Computer attitude		0.75	1.91	2.00
Computer anxiety		2.41	2.26	2.41
Computer efficacy		0.64	3.16	3.10

Note: * = $p <0.05$; ** = $p <0.01$; *** = $p <0.001$.
[a] Lower scores reflect more positive attitudes.

TABLE 8.2   MANCOVA Results for Hypothesis 2a: Attributional Style

Dependent variable	Covariates	β	t
Computer attitude[a]	GPA	0.06	−1.07
	Computer experience	−0.39	6.52***
	Attributional style (CPCN)	−0.27	4.39***
Computer anxiety	GPA	0.12	−1.75
	Computer experience	−0.12	−1.76
	Attributional style (CPCN)	−0.05	−0.67
Computer efficacy	GPA	−0.02	−0.32
	Computer experience	0.55	10.01***
	Attributional style (CPCN)	0.18	3.19***

Note: $* = p <0.05$; $** = p <0.01$; $*** = p <0.001$.
[a] Lower scores reflect more positive attitudes. $n = 227$.

MANCOVA was run for each of the three time periods. Each analysis included gender as a factor and attributional style as a covariate, with the dependent variables of anxiety, depression, hostility, and positive affect.

For time period 1, the multivariate tests for the overall MANCOVA were significant (see Table 8.3). The overall univariate F-tests were also significant for anxiety, depression, hostility, and positive affect. Similar, though weaker, overall effects were obtained for time period 2. While the multivariate test was insignificant, the overall univariate F-tests were significant for anxiety, depression, and positive affect. However, neither the multivariate nor the univariate F-tests for overall effects were significant for time period 3. The lack of significant effects during the third time period may be attributable to the attrition of subjects over the course of the study, which reduced the power of the analysis. Alternatively, it could be that the relationships between attributional style and user affect weakened over time.

As indicated in Table 8.4, the covariate of attributional style was significantly related to user anxiety, depression, hostility, and positive affect in time period 1 and anxiety, depression, and positive affect in time period 2. These results are completely consistent with the prediction of hypothesis 3a that optimistic users experience more positive affect and less negative affect than pessimistic users. However, attributional style was not related to any of the affective states in the last time period.

The multivariate tests for the effects of gender alone were also significant for time periods 1 and 2 only (see Table 8.3). Whereas the univariate F-tests revealed

TABLE 8.3 MANCOVA Results for Hypothesis 3: Overall and Gender Effects

	Time period 1[a]			Time period 2[b]			Time period 3[c]		
Effect	Multivariate F-ratio	Univariate F-ratio	Means	Multivariate F-ratio	Univariate F-ratio	Means	Multivariate F-ratio	Univariate F-ratio	Means
Overall	3.93**			1.79			1.26		
Anxiety		5.62*			5.37*			1.69	
Depression		7.24**			4.69**			2.17	
Hostility		11.37**			2.21			0.00	
Positive affect		10.79**			4.14*			1.11	
Gender	7.39***			5.09**			1.90		
Anxiety		10.66**	Males 0.31 / Females 0.43		7.10**	Males 0.24 / Females 0.33		0.00	Males 0.30 / Females 0.30
Depression		0.88	Males 0.21 / Females 0.24		3.56	Males 0.20 / Females 0.26		0.50	Males 0.27 / Females 0.26
Hostility		0.52	Males 0.21 / Females 0.19		0.43	Males 0.28 / Females 0.26		0.22	Males 0.38 / Females 0.36
Positive affect		9.11**	Males 0.78 / Females 0.69		1.50	Males 0.64 / Females 0.59		2.48	Males 0.56 / Females 0.50

Note: * = p <0.05; ** = p <0.01; *** = p <0.001.
[a] n = 156 (males); n = 123 (females).
[b] n = 160 (males); n = 124 (females).
[c] n = 155 (males); n = 122 (females).

TABLE 8.4 MANCOVA Results for Hypothesis 3a: Attributional Style

Dependent variable	Time period 1[a]		Time period 2[b]		Time period 3[c]	
	β	t	β	t	β	t
Anxiety	−0.14	−2.37*	−0.14	−2.32*	−0.08	−1.30
Depression	−0.16	−2.69**	−0.13	−2.16*	−0.09	−1.47
Hostility	−0.20	−3.37**	−0.09	−1.49	−0.002	−0.04
Positive affect	0.19	3.28**	0.12	2.04*	0.06	1.06

Note: * = $p < 0.05$; ** = $p < 0.01$; *** = $p < 0.001$.
[a] $n = 279$.
[b] $n = 284$.
[c] $n = 277$.

significant gender effects for anxiety in each of the first two time periods, as well for positive affect in time period 2, the remaining univariate tests were insignificant. The means indicate that female users reported more anxiety and less positive affect than male users, as predicted. Thus, mixed support for hypothesis 3b was obtained.

Predictors of Effort and Computer-Related Performance

The results of the MANCOVA performed to test hypotheses 4a and 4b are summarized in Tables 8.5 and 8.6. As indicated in Table 8.5, the multivariate tests for the overall MANCOVAs were significant in each time period. As for the univariate F-tests, significant overall effects were found for performance in time periods 1 and 2. In addition, the univariate tests revealed significant overall effects for locus of control in time period 1 and effort in time period 2. None of the univariate F-tests for overall effects were significant in time period 3.

Each of the multivariate and univariate F-tests performed to test for gender effects was insignificant (see Table 8.5). Hence, the prediction of hypothesis 4b that gender would account for differences in users' effort, performance, and subsequent performance attributions was not supported.

The results for the covariates are summarized in Table 8.6. Attributional style was the only covariate related to self-reported effort, but only in time period 2. GPA, experience, and attributional style were associated with computer-related performance in time period 1, as was GPA in time period 2. The positive beta weights indicate that users with higher GPAs, more extensive computer experi-

**TABLE 8.5   MANCOVA Results for Hypothesis 4:
Overall and Gender Effects**

Effect	Time period 1[a]		Time period 2[b]		Time period 3[c]	
	Multivariate F-ratio	Univariate F-ratio	Multivariate F-ratio	Univariate F-ratio	Multivariate F-ratio	Univariate F-ratio
Overall	4.06***		2.90***		1.75*	
Effort		2.17		2.67*		1.62
Performance		17.50***		6.49***		1.63
Locus of control		3.35*		1.04		0.29
Stability		0.39		2.30		0.49
Controllability		1.14		1.90		1.63
Gender	0.98		0.98		0.81	
Effort		2.21		3.60		0.81
Performance		1.67		0.29		0.00
Locus of control		0.16		0.09		0.00
Stability		0.16		0.44		0.89
Controllability		0.04		0.00		3.34

Note: * = $p < 0.05$; ** = $p < 0.01$; *** = $p < 0.001$.
[a] $n = 136$ (males); $n = 99$ (females).
[b] $n = 135$ (males); $n = 98$ (females).
[c] $n = 42$ (males); $n = 42$ (females).

ence, and optimistic styles achieved higher levels of performance. However, due to the lack of consistent results, especially with respect to attributional style, only limited support was obtained for the prediction of hypothesis 4a that more optimistic users would exert more effort and perform better on computer-related tasks.

Predictors of Users' Performance Attributions

The MANCOVA results summarized in Tables 8.5 and 8.6 also provide insights into the predictors of users' performance attributions. GPA was significantly related to the stability dimension, but only for time period 2. This result suggests that, in this time period, students with high GPAs were more likely to attribute their performance to stable causes. Attributional style was related to the locus of control dimension in time period 1, and the controllability dimension in time period 3. Thus, for time periods 1 and 3 only, optimistic users were more inclined than pessimists to attribute their performance to internal and uncontrol-

TABLE 8.6 MANCOVA Results for Hypothesis 4a: Attributional Style

Dependent variables	Covariates	Time period 1[a] β	t	Time period 2[b] β	t	Time period 3[c] β	t
Effort	GPA	-0.09	-1.32	0.06	87	0.13	1.17
	Computer experience	-0.09	-1.41	-0.06	-0.96	-0.16	-1.44
	CPCN	0.08	1.29	0.17	2.56*	0.12	1.07
Performance	GPA	0.34	2.63***	0.26	4.12***	0.27	1.95
	Computer experience	0.23	3.82***	0.08	1.24	0.02	0.17
	CPCN	0.15	2.49*	0.06	0.95	0.16	1.40
Causal dimensions							
Locus of control	GPA	0.11	1.75	-0.00	-0 .02	-0.10	-0.87
	Computer experience	0.09	1.40	-0.09	1.40	0.03	0.27
	CPCN	0.15	2.40*	-0.08	-1.17	-0.01	-0.07
Stability	GPA	0.07	1.04	0.17	2.55*	0.06	0.40
	Computer experience	0.00	0.001	-0.03	-0.43	0.06	0.56
	CPCN	-0.01	-0.12	-0.02	-0.25	-0.10	-0.85
Controllability	GPA	0.10	1.44	0.08	1.22	-0.08	-0.69
	Computer experience	-0.01	-0.08	0.12	1.85	0.01	0.07
	CPCN	0.09	1.33	0.06	0.93	-0.24	-2.16*

Note: $* = p < 0.05$; $** = p < 0.01$; $*** = p < 0.001$.
[a] $n = 235$.
[b] $n = 233$.
[c] $n = 84$.

lable causes, respectively. However, since neither of these effects emerged in more than one time period, they only provide weak evidence of a relationship between attributional style and users' attributions (H_{4b}).

The preceding analysis is limited by the fact that it does not take into account the actual performance level for which the users made attributions. Because attribution research suggests that optimists and pessimists, as well as males and females, make dissimilar attributions for success and failure, performance level appears to mediate these relationships, as hypotheses 5a and 5b indicate. To test these hypotheses, the subjects were split into success (students who performed in the top 40% of the class) and failure (students whose scores fell in the bottom 40%) groups for each time period, and separate MANCOVAs were performed. However, since none of the multivariate or univariate F-tests were significant, no support for these hypotheses was obtained.

DISCUSSION

Attributional Style

As hypothesized, attributional style was significantly related to the computer attitudes, computer efficacy, affective reactions, attributions, effort, and performance of users. Optimistic users possessed more positive computer attitudes and higher levels of computer efficacy than pessimistic users. Moreover, optimistic versus pessimistic users had more positive and fewer negative affective reactions to performance feedback. Finally, the fact that attributional style was related to user performance in the first time period, even after the influence of experience and GPA were accounted for, suggests that optimists may outperform pessimists on computer-related tasks.

Importantly, these findings are highly consistent with Seligman's (1990) research. As previously noted, attributional style has been successfully used in the insurance industry to predict agents' performance (Seligman and Schulman, 1986). The present findings imply that a similar measure of optimism/pessimism may be helpful in computer-related settings. Indeed, Seligman's work suggests that people with optimistic styles may be more likely to persevere when they experience computer problems. Hence, knowledge of attributional style may be useful in identifying persons who are susceptible to learned helplessness when they encounter difficulties with computers (Martinko and Gardner, 1982).

Attributional style was also related to users' attributions, but not on a consistent basis or in the anticipated fashion. In particular, the performance attributions that optimists and pessimists made did not differ as predicted by hypotheses 5a and 5b. One explanation for these insignificant findings is that the practice of dividing the sample into high- and low-performing subgroups reduced the power of the analyses. Alternatively, it may be that this variable is not related to users' attributions as predicted by attribution theory.

Overall, the attributional style findings suggest that the negative computer attitudes, low efficacy expectations, and negative affective reactions of pessimistic users may cause them to view the computer as a "foe." Although they are forced to do "battle" with computers, they do not expect to win. In contrast, the favorable computer attitudes, high levels of computer efficacy, and positive affective states of optimistic users cause them to view computers as user-friendly tools that facilitate goal attainment. Thus, optimists appear to possess a healthier outlook toward computers.

There are several practical implications of these results. For example, the finding that pessimists held low levels of computer efficacy has important training implications. Specifically, it implies that pessimistic users may require special training to ensure that they gain confidence in their computer skills. Two approaches to training are recommended. First, awareness workshops can be

conducted to help pessimistic users learn about their tendencies to think negatively. Second, skill-building training can be provided to enable such persons to
recognize and change negative thought patterns (Seligman, 1990). The best
approach may be a combined approach, with awareness and skill-building training being included as an integral component of ongoing training programs.

The attributional style findings also have performance appraisal implications
for the manager. Given the tendency of pessimists to exhibit low levels of
computer efficacy and negative affect, managers should exercise caution when
providing performance feedback for computer-related, as well as other, tasks. In
particular, managers should supply pessimistic workers with positive feedback
whenever possible, while avoiding personal and global attributions for employee
failure. Furthermore, they should offer pessimistic and poor performing users
specific suggestions for improving their computer-related performance.

Gender Effects

Mixed findings regarding the effects of gender in a computer-related environment were obtained. Consistent with prior research and hypothesis 3b, gender
differences in users' affective reactions during time periods 1 and 2 were identified, even after the influence of attributional style was partialed out. Specifically, female users reported higher levels of anxiety, and males experienced more
positive affect. Contrary to expectations, however, gender was not related to
computer attitudes, computer anxiety, computer efficacy, effort, computer performance, or attributions for performance, once the effects of GPA, experience,
and attributional style were partialed out. In addition, female users did not exhibit
more pessimistic styles or patterns of attributions than males, as had been
suggested by prior research (Linn, 1985; Nelson and Cooper, 1989; Stake, 1983).
Thus, there was no evidence that these differential affective reactions had any
impact on users' effort, performance, or attributions.

These findings suggest that common perceptions that female users have more
negative attitudes toward computers, are more anxious and less confident about
their computer skills, and hence are less likely to exert effort and excel on
computer tasks are overly simplistic. Indeed, the results indicate that experience—not gender—was the best predictor of computer attitudes and efficacy,
while GPA and computer experience were significantly related to user performance. Hence, the gender effects found by prior researchers for computer tasks
(Arch and Cummins, 1989; Collis, 1985; Dambrot et al., 1985; Levin and
Gordon, 1989; Sigurdsson, 1991; Turnipseed et al., 1990; Wilder et al., 1985)
may have had more to do with users' experience and demonstrated abilities than
gender.

To the extent that this is true, it is clear that stereotypes characterizing women
as ill-suited for computer tasks are inaccurate and inappropriate. Furthermore,

these results imply that practitioners would be well advised to concentrate on providing female employees with opportunities to develop their computer skills and acquire computer experience, rather than assuming that they lack the required aptitude and/or desire to work with computers. Finally, when these findings are considered in conjunction with the attributional style results, it appears that managers would be better served by focusing on the computer attitudes, self-efficacy expectations, effort, and performance of pessimistic rather than female users.

FUTURE RESEARCH DIRECTIONS

The findings of this study add to the growing body of literature focusing on reactions to computer technology. The logical next step is to explore the relationships identified within a field setting using practitioners as subjects. An obvious limitation of the current research is that it was conducted within undergraduate computer classes using students as subjects and their exam scores as performance measures. As such, the extent to which the findings reflect relationships that arise in applied work settings is unclear. Still, it should also be noted that the classroom context chosen exhibited certain key attributes of a computer-based work setting, in that most subjects were motivated and held responsible for completing computer-related tasks. Thus, despite the fact that the academic setting raises concerns about the external validity of the results, the experimental context was not wholly unrealistic. However, to more fully understand the cognitive, affective, and motivational processes that shape the behavior and performance of computer users, these processes must be examined in applied work settings.

Future studies should also consider the role that the computer plays in the individual's work life as a potential moderating variable. The current study demonstrated that, in general, optimistic users exhibit more positive computer attitudes and affective reactions than pessimistic users. They also tend to display higher levels of self-efficacy and computer-related performance. It is quite possible, however, that the strength of these relationships depends upon the importance of computers to the user's job. When the computer is central to the individual's work, these relationships are likely to be especially strong. As such, a pessimistic attributional style, computer anxiety, and negative attitudes toward computers would be especially debilitating. In contrast, when the role of the computer is minor, the effects of these individual difference variables are less likely to be severe.

Research along these lines should also examine the extent to which the relationships identified generalize across computer tasks. It is suspected that the adverse effects of pessimism will be more pronounced for complex computer tasks (e.g., programming, troubleshooting), rather than simple ones (e.g., data entry), since the former require greater confidence in one's abilities. Until this assertion is empirically tested, however, its merits cannot be assessed.

The utility of attributional training represents yet another area where increased research attention is needed. Earlier, it was argued that awareness and skill-building training could serve to elevate the self-efficacy expectations, and hence the computer-related performance, of pessimistic users. This assertion is based on the success that Seligman (1990) and his colleagues have achieved using attributional training within other contexts. Nevertheless, research is required to assess the overall utility and most effective means of delivering such training for computer-related tasks. Ultimately, this stream of research could provide managers with some highly practical and effective tools for empowering and energizing the pessimistic computer user.

REFERENCES

Abramson, L., Seligman, M.E.P., and Teasdale, J. (1978). Learned helplessness in humans. *Journal of Abnormal Psychology,* 87:49–74.

Aman, J. (1992). Gender and attitude toward computers. in Proceedings of the National Educational Computing Conference, Nashville.

Arch, E.C. and Cummins, D.E. (1989). Structured and unstructured exposure to computers: Sex differences in attitude and use among college students. *Sex Roles,* 20:245–254.

Campbell, N. (1992). Enrollment in computer courses by college students: Computer proficiency, attitudes, and attributions. *Journal of Research on Computing in Education,* 25:61–73.

Collis, B. (1985). Psychosocial implications of sex differences in attitudes toward computers. *International Journal of Women's Studies,* 8:207–213.

Dambrot, F.H., Walkins-Malek, M.A., Sillings, S.M., Marshall, R.S., and Garver, J.A. (1985). Correlates of sex differences in attitudes toward and involvement with computers. *Journal of Vocational Behavior,* 27:71–86.

Dambrot, F.H., Sillings, S.M., and Zook, A. (1988). Psychology of computer used. II. Sex differences in prediction of course grades in a computer language course. *Perceptual and Motor Skills,* 66:627–636.

Hall, J. and Cooper, J. (1991). Gender, experience, and attributions to the computer. *Journal of Educational Computing Research,* 7(1):51–60.

Henry, J.W., Martinko, M.J., and Pierce, M.A. (in press). Attributional style as a predictor of success in a first computer science course. *Computers and Human Behavior.*

Honeyman, D.S. and White, W.J. (1987). Computer anxiety in educators learning to use the computer: A preliminary report. *Journal of Research on Computing in Education,* 20:129–138.

Igbaria, M. and Parasuraman, S. (1989). A path analytic study of individual characteristics, computer anxiety and attitudes toward microcomputers. *Journal of Management,* 15(3):373–388.

Lee, J.A. (1986). The effects of past computer experience on computerized aptitude test performance. *Educational and Psychological Measurement,* 46:727–733.

Leitheiser, R. (1992). MIS skills for the 1990s: A survey of MIS managers' perceptions. *Journal of Management Information Systems,* 9(1):69–91.

Levin, T. and Gordon, C. (1989). Effect of gender and computer experience on attitudes toward computers. *Journal of Educational Computing Research,* 5:69–88.

Linn, M.C. (1985). Gender equity in computer learning environments. *Computers and the Social Sciences,* 1:19–27.

Marcoulides, G.A. (1989). Measuring computer anxiety: The computer anxiety scale. *Educational and Psychological Measurement,* 49:733–739.

Martinko, M.J. and Gardner, W.L. (1982). Learned helplessness: An alternative explanation for performance deficits. *Academy of Management Review,* 7:195–204.

Martinko, M.J., Henry, J.W., and Zmud, R.W. (1992). An Attributional Explanation of Individual Reactions to Information Technologies in the Workplace, Working Paper, Florida State University, Tallahassee.

Martocchio, J. (1992). Microcomputer usage as an opportunity: The influence of context in employee training. *Personnel Psychology,* 45:529–552.

Meier, S.T. (1988). Predicting individual differences in performance on computer-administered tests and tasks: Development of the computer aversion scale. *Computers in Human Behavior,* 4:175–187.

Morrow, P.C., Prell, E.R., and McElroy, J.C. (1986). Attitudinal and behavioral correlates of computer anxiety. *Psychological Reports,* 59:1199–1204.

Muira, I.T. (1987). The relationship of computer self-efficacy expectations to computer interest and course enrollment in college. *Sex Roles,* 10:303–311.

Murphy, C.A., Coover, D., and Owens, S.V. (1989). Development and Validation of the Computer Self-Efficacy Scale. *Educational and Psychological Measurement,* 49: 893–899.

Murrell, A.J. and Sprinkle, J. (1993). The impact of negative attitudes toward computers on employees' satisfaction and commitment within a small company. *Computers in Human Behavior,* 9:57–63.

Nelson, D. (1990). Individual adjustment to information-driven technologies: A critical review. *MIS Quarterly,* 14(1):79–98.

Nelson, L.J. and Cooper, J. (1989). Sex Role Identity, Attributional Style, and Attitudes toward Computers, paper presented at the Annual Meeting of Eastern Psychological Association, Boston, March ed..

Nelson, R. and Chaney, P. (1987). Training end users: An exploratory study. *MIS Quarterly,* 11(4):547–559.

Parasuraman, S. and Igbaria, M. (1990). An examination of gender differences in the determinants of computer anxiety and attitudes toward microcomputers among managers. *International Journal of Man-Machine Studies,* 32:327–340.

Peterson, C.G., Semmel, A., von Baeyer, C., Abramson, L.Y., Metalsky, G.I., and Seligman, M.E.P. (1982). The Attributional Style Questionnaire. *Cognitive Therapy and Research,* 6:287–300.

Pope-Davis, D.B. and Twing, J.S. (1991). The effects of age, gender, and experience on measures of attitude regarding computers. *Computers in Human Behavior,* 7:333–339.

Popovich, P.M., Hyde, K.R., and Zakrajsek, T. (1987). The development of the attitudes toward computer usage scale. *Educational and Psychological Measurement,* 47:261–269.

Raub, A.C. (1981). Correlates of Computer Anxiety in College Students, unpublished doctoral dissertation, University of Pennsylvania.

Rozell, E.J. and Gardner, W.L. (1992). Computer-related performance: A model of the antecedents and consequences of user success and failure. in Proceedings of the Annual Meeting of the Southern Management Association, New Orleans.

Russell, D. (1982). The Causal Dimension Scale: A measure of how individuals perceive causes. *Journal of Personality and Social Psychology,* 42:1137–1145.

Seligman, M.E.P. (1990). *Learned Optimism,* New York: Pocket Books.

Seligman, M.E.P. and Schulman P. (1986). Explanatory style as a predictor of productivity and quitting among life insurance sales agents. *Journal of Personality and Social Psychology,* 50(4):832–838.

Sigurdsson, J. (1991). Computer experience, attitudes toward computers and personality characteristics in psychology undergraduates. *Personality and Personality Differences,* 12(6):617–624.

Smith, S.D. (1986). Relationships of computer attitudes to sex, grade-level, and teacher influence. *Education,* 106:338–344.

Stake, J.E. (1983). Ability level, evaluative feedback and sex differences in performance expectancy. *Psychology of Women Quarterly,* 8:48–58.

Stevens, J. (1986). *Applied Multivariate Statistics for the Social Sciences,* Hillsdale, N.J.: Lawrence Erlbaum Associates.

Turnipseed, D.L., Burns, O.M., and Hodges, F.J. (1990). Attitudes towards computers in an information-intense environment: A field study of the insurance industry. *Journal of Applied Business Research,* 7(4):123–130.

Weiner, B. (1979). A theory of motivation for some classroom experiences. *Journal of Educational Psychology,* 71:3–25.

Wilder, G., Mackie, D., and Cooper, J. (1985). Gender and computers: Two surveys of computer-related attitudes. Special Issue: Women, girls, and computers. *Sex Roles,* 13:215–228.

Williams, J. (1991). Negative consequences of information technology. in *Management Impacts of Information Technology: Perspectives on Organizational Change and Growth,* E. Szewczak, C. Snodgrass, and M. Khosrowpour (Eds.), Harrisburg, Pa.: Idea Group Publishing, pp. 48–74.

Zmud, R.W. (1979). Individual differences and MIS success: A review of the empirical literature. *Management Science,* 25:966–979.

Zuckerman, M. and Lubin, B. (1965). *The Multiple Affect Adjective Check List,* San Diego: Educational and Industrial Testing Service.

Section III

APPLYING ATTRIBUTION THEORY TO ORGANIZATIONAL ISSUES

Part B:
Leadership

9

ATTRIBUTIONS AND
THE EMERGENCE OF
LEADERSHIP: PATTERNS IN
EMPLOYEE RESPONSES TO
EXECUTIVE SUCCESSION*

Katherine Farquhar

ABSTRACT

Attribution processes enable leaders and followers to stabilize mutual expectations. Organization members' attributions during executive succession reduce
uncertainty and anxiety and provide early indication of how much they will see
the executive or the context as responsible for organizational changes. This
chapter reports on a study of employee attributions about the newly-arrived
president of a mid-sized corporation. Several measures were used to collect data
relating to employee attributions about the new president in four divisions of the
company. Significant differences in ratings supported the overall hypothesis that
hedonic relevance of the newcomer affected how observers (the followers)
apportioned causality.

---

*The study described in this chapter is explored more fully in the author's doctoral dissertation
(Farquhar, 1989).

INTRODUCTION

Enter the new CEO or general manager. Is she here to stay—or one more through the revolving door?…Will this one make lots of changes—or stay off our backs?…Is he really top leadership material—why'd the board pick him, anyway?…Great—the company's going to take off under a new president like her!

A new executive is the head, but is not the leader (Gibb, 1969) until the followers and other stakeholders are convinced. Leadership emerges from follower attributions over time. As "attributed influence" (Pfeffer, 1978) and a "construct by which causality for outcomes is inferred" (Lord and Maher, 1991, p. 190), leadership builds on attributions between an executive and stakeholders inside and beyond the organization. This dynamic is particularly evident during executive succession, when the uncertainty and expectations that often surround top-level transitions (Diamond, 1993; Gilmore, 1988; Kets de Vries, 1988) encourage attributions.

This study examines the role of attributional processing by organization members during the transition to a new executive. A model is presented and tested to show how the personal implications ("hedonic relevance" in Jones and Davis, 1965) of the transition affect followers' attributions of executive responsibility for organizational changes. These employees have little or no direct contact with the new executive. One's place in the organization in terms of job level, functional department, and tenure is seen as a key factor influencing leadership attributions. The model is explored by a survey of 90 employees nine months after a new president began at Renovations (pseudonym), a mid-sized manufacturing and retailing company with 2000 employees and approximately $330 million in annual sales. The challenge and utility of measuring attributions in field settings are important considerations.

BACKGROUND

The study of attributions in leadership transitions draws on two theory bases: attribution processes in leadership and executive succession.

Attribution Processes in Leadership

Attribution was once the culprit responsible for biases in followers' perceptions. Findings in leadership studies were "confounded by an attributional process" (Mitchell et al., 1977, p. 254). "Implicit leadership theory" distorted commonly used instrument scores on the survey of organizations and Leader Behavior Description Questionnaire (LBDQ) (Eden and Leviatan, 1975; Rush et al., 1977). "Ritual scapegoating" explained why coaches were fired in midseason when replacing them had little impact on team standings (Brown, 1982; Gamson and Scotch, 1964). Increased understanding of social cognition in leadership and a growing focus on leader–follower interdependence (Graen and Cashman, 1975; Herold, 1977; Hollander, 1958) strengthened appreciation for the role of attribution, as shown in Calder's (1977) "attribution theory of leadership" and Pfeffer's (1978) essay on the "ambiguity of leadership." As an extension of "naïve science," attribution theory has focused on applied elements of leadership (Calder 1977): performance appraisal dynamics (Hogan, 1987; Mitchell et al., 1981), leader–follower social networks (McElroy and Shrader, 1986), leader socialization (Jones, 1983; Pfeffer and Salancik, 1975), and leader–member relations (Martinko and Gardner, 1987).

Most attribution leadership research has emphasized the supervisor–subordinate dyad or a laboratory small group. This study applies attribution to understanding a universal leadership phenomenon in its field setting: succession dynamics in the organization. Patterns in follower attributions across organizational groupings are the focus of this chapter, and field methodology is used, building on recommendations that attribution processes be studied in the field (McElroy, 1982, p. 416).

Executive Succession Research

In recent decades, succession research elaborated the stages and dynamics of leadership transitions. Executive succession is a process (Farquhar, 1989, 1991; Gabarro, 1987) with far-reaching impact (Diamond, 1993; Gilmore, 1988; Gordon and Rosen, 1981). Current succession research examines the strategic implications of the turnover event (Cannella and Lubatkin, 1993; Hambrick and Cannella, 1993; Smith and White, 1987) and its impact on the profitability and viability of the organization.

The leadership transition includes prior conditions that have substantial impact on the situation facing the newcomer (Fredrickson et al., 1988; Gordon and Rosen, 1981; Heller, 1989). Then, the first 15 to 18 months are critical to the success of a new administration (Farquhar, 1989; Gabarro, 1987), including a time of early vulnerability when the newcomer's hold on the job is tenuous (Fredrickson et al., 1988). During this extended period of ambiguity and expectations, the executive takes charge, while followers and other stakeholders make attributions about his or her impact on the organization.

Leadership Transitions and Attributions

Wall Street and boards assume a dispositional perspective. The corporation hires a new chief to improve or sustain organizational performance (study 1 in Meindl et al., 1985) and fires ("scapegoats") the executive for poor performance (Boeker, 1992; Brown, 1982; Gamson and Scotch, 1964). This emphasis on the person is institutionalized during the search and drives pressure to perform quickly. The newcomer is seen to have qualities that should enable him or her to take charge (Lord and Maher, 1991, Chap. 10) and build on these attributions (Pfeffer, 1978). The power of such dispositional attributions is shown when boards believe in executive influence even when executives are fired in good times or kept on despite poor corporate outcomes (Meindl et al., 1985).

Attributions by organizational insiders serve a different function: anchoring the relationship between leader and followers. Researchers have examined several elements of this process. Most followers are distant observers of the leader–actor (McElroy, 1982, p. 414), and their attributions comprise a social construction of leadership (Calder, 1977; Pfeffer, 1978). Leaders make attributions that then affect followers' performance (Mitchell et al., 1981) or shape supervisory relationships (Hogan, 1987). Leaders and followers affect each other's behavior through interactive attributions in their relationships (Herold, 1977; Jones, 1983). Mapping followers' attributions during a leadership transition contributes to a wider understanding of the evolving attributional relationship between a top executive and organization members.

The changes under a new executive can substantially alter working conditions and job security. However, organization insiders may have seen executives come and go, while the place stays pretty much the same. Which will it be? This uncertainty—whether there will be a significant change or no change at all—promotes attributional processing, causing people to seek the causes of transition-related events and note cues to the company's future. In attributional terms, the leadership transition is "hedonically relevant."

Followers' Attributions in Executive Transitions

Cognitive (Pyszczynski and Greenberg, 1981) and emotional factors encourage attributions that resolve cognitive dislocation and anxiety. The ambiguity and anxiety seen among followers during many top-level leadership transitions encourage causal attributions (Fredrickson et al., 1988; Pfeffer, 1978). Followers make these attributions in a socially determined context (Martinko and Gardner, 1987). Positive and negative set information provided to laboratory subjects affects their attributions about the stimulus figure ("salience–causality link" in Yarkin et al., 1981; Taylor and Fiske, 1978, p. 256). Heightening a target's salience draws the observer's attention and increases dispositional attributions (Simonton, 1986). Affectively loaded settings activate "defensive attributional processes" of observers (Bradley, 1978).

In leadership transitions, the target figure is salient, the leader's role expectations are socially determined, and organization members have vested interests. These conditions promote "socially-mediated attributions" (Farquhar, 1989, p. 260), where expectations, symbols, and patterns of observer behavior bound the search for causality. The leader, the situation, and the organization are targets of causal attributions for transition-related changes.

Hedonic Relevance

Leadership changes signal new strategies and priorities with likely impact on followers' jobs, giving the event personal meaning. Such hedonic relevance stimulates attributional processing when an actor's behavior has "significant rewarding or punishing implications for the perceiver" (Jones and Davis, 1965, p. 237). In the present model, hedonic relevance mediates attributions by linking distant events to one's personal well-being.

The relevance of social stimuli affects how information is processed into memory (Higgins et al., 1981). Relevance has affective components: the emotions associated with an event can cause a search for causality (Isen, 1984; Kelley and Michela, 1980; Schachter, 1964). Heightened relevance is associated with a tendency toward dispositional attributions: the actor–observer bias (Jones and Davis, 1965) and fundamental attribution error (Ross, 1977) model inclinations to seek person-based explanations for events with personal impact. Executive succession includes the preconditions for "defensive attributions": dependence on the actor–leader, desires for self-enhancement and self-protection, positive presentation of the self to others, and a belief in effective control (Bradley, 1978).

This study defines hedonic relevance as the "importance" to followers of the leadership transition and seeks to understand how higher relevance relates to dispositional attributions about the new leader.

MODEL AND HYPOTHESES

The proposed model of attributions in emerging leadership measures "hedonic relevance" through three demographic factors signaling the employee's distance from the top and function in the organization: department, job classification, and tenure (Figure 9.1). Though not the sole influences on hedonic relevance, these variables stand for important social processes. Departments organize people via business function, physical setting, and work groups. This tends to homogenize followers' attributions about the new CEO based on the department's assessment of the new executive's style and priorities. Job classification is a rough indicator of two key factors: professional identification and distance from the top. The categories of manager, professional, and nonexempt (mostly clerical/secretarial) generally reflect levels from the top down. The categories of manager and professional capture the staff and line perspectives. Tenure may signify investment in the organization, with longer-term employees more vested emotionally and economically. This model presumes that patterns

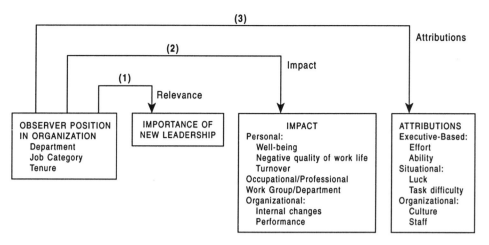

FIGURE 9.1   Relevance and attributions in leadership transitions. (1) Importance: Measures the importance or relevance to employees of the transition on a numerical scale. (2) Impact: The potential impact of the transition is seen at four levels of analysis: personal, occupational/professional, work group/department, and organization. At the personal level, that impact is seen to affect one's sense of well-being, the potential for negative outcomes, the quality of one's work life, and the likelihood that turnover will increase. At the organizational level, the impact is seen as causing internal change in areas such as policy or corporate structure and external change in terms of organizational performance. (3) Attributions: The possible targets of attributions made by employees to explain changes during the transition include the executive (executive-based), the situation (the difficulty of the task or the timing, or luck, of the transition or business conditions), and the organization (culture and work force).

in hedonic relevance emerge most clearly in such groupings where meaning is socially defined.

An employee's location in the organization affects perceptions of the importance (arrow 1 in Figure 9.1) and impact of the transition (arrow 2) and patterns in attributions about the transition (arrow 3).

Relevance

The relevance of the transition is moderated by employees' relationship to the top in terms of department, job role, and tenure. In taking charge, new executives often give priority to functional areas reflecting their own expertise (Gabarro, 1987; Kotin and Sharaf, 1967). Departments, occupations, and levels have different concerns and expectations relating to the transition, shown in their ratings of its relevance. This study examines how early perceptions of the leader reflect the interests of work units and job roles.

Hypothesis 1a: The transition will be rated as most relevant to employees in departments most directly involved with and familiar to the new executive and lowest in departments where the executive is less directly involved or familiar.

One's hierarchical position affects hedonic relevance. Managers are justifiably watchful since an early task of the new CEO is to shape the executive ranks (Gabarro, 1987). This threatens jobs or offers opportunities and certainly heightens hedonic relevance. Conversely, professionals in core functions (such as accounting or MIS) may feel that their jobs are safe regardless of prospective changes. Should the job go, their skills are marketable. Hedonic relevance for professionals may consist of "professional inoculation" from the impact of the transition.

Hypothesis 1b: The transition will be rated as most relevant to managers and least relevant to professionals.

Prospective followers who are long-timers with the organization may view the executive transition as a threat or change from the status quo. Long-term employees are expected to see the event as more hedonically relevant based on their stake in the organization. Their investment could incline them toward a favorable or an unfavorable response to new leadership, but in either event, their response should be more pronounced than that of newcomers.

Hypothesis 1c: The longer tenured employees will rate the transition as more relevant than will newcomers.

Impact

Do followers think the transition will help or harm the organization? This impact is seen most clearly by departments; those that will likely fare well under the new leader should be more hopeful that the transition will yield positive effects. However, the relevance of the transition will also heighten departmental concerns over possible negatives, since those who see high executive impact are sensitized to the risks involved. Hedonic relevance is associated with higher salience of both positive and negative effects. Departments for whom the transition is less relevant may downplay it and give less extreme ratings to the transition's impact.

Hypothesis 2:   The departments for whom the transition is the most important will give higher ratings to the positive effects and to the negative effects of the transition.

Attributions

Employees for whom the transition is very relevant seem more likely to attribute high potential to the new leader. The transition got their attention; this seems to reflect their greater interest or investment in the executive's impact. They either imagine that the newcomer will make more changes than would otherwise occur or they believe that among all the causal factors involved, the new executive has most impact.

> **Hypothesis 3a:**   Employees who rate the transition high in relevance will make significantly more dispositional attributions to the newcomer than will those who rate the transition less relevant.

The construct of hedonic relevance suggests that individuals may see the impact of executive succession in very personal terms: those who see the transition as very important will see the new executive's prospective impact in highly personal terms.

> **Hypothesis 3b:**   When the transition is relevant to respondents, they will make significantly more dispositional attributions to the executive for impact of the transition at the personal level than will those for whom the transition is less relevant.

METHOD

Sample

Data were collected at the 200-person headquarters of Renovations (pseudonym), a manufacturing/retailing firm with 2000 employees and approximately $330 million in annual sales. Four divisions totaling 110 employees were surveyed: Human Resources (HR), Floorz (a product line), Corporate Finance, and MIS/Operations (MIS). The four divisions were selected to reflect differing perspectives on the new president, Donald Suttle (pseudonym), in terms of divisional function and professional identity. Suttle came from a highly successful retailing operation and was known for his energetic, progressive, and high-profile management style. Some 36 interviews were done with executives and managers, professionals, and staff at Renovations prior to and concurrent with the survey administration. These insiders, consistent with theory, predicted that HR and Floorz would react most positively to the newcomer based on his prior history in retailing and his accessible management style. Similarly, Finance and MIS were seen as more guarded and distant. HR and Floorz were paired, and MIS and Finance were paired in the analyses to test these expectations.

Ninety surveys were returned, for an 82% return rate (HR: 91%, $n = 21$; Floorz: 83%, $n = 15$; MIS: 82%, $n = 27$; and Finance: 64%, $n = 23$). The sample fell into thirds by job category—nonexempt, professional, and managers—and was distributed evenly between men and women. Five respondents reported as members of the company's top operating group; their data were withheld from all job category analyses. The sample consisted of MIS (30%), Finance (26%), HR (23%), and Floorz (17%). There were some demographic differences among departments.

Survey

Measuring attributions is a challenge (Elig and Frieze, 1975; Porrac et al., 1983; Taylor and Fiske, 1981). Elig and Frieze (1979) tested the reliability and the face and convergent validity of three approaches: open-ended responses, ratings of statements on a one- to nine-point scale, and percentage measures to apportion causality. Scale measures emerged as the most reliable and valid approach. Percentages were vulnerable to respondent error.

A 44-item questionnaire was developed and refined through pilot testing at another site. Items were developed from data on perceptions of transition-related change from 36 interviews at Renovations and in other organizations undergoing executive succession and were guided by the research hypotheses. The survey included 29 five-point items rating the likelihood of changes in the organization (a five-point scale was used because finer gradations seemed excessive for likelihood); a check-off section where respondents indicated which of these changes they thought would be caused largely by having a new president; ten seven-point Likert-scaled attributional statements targeting the president, the company, and the transition; and a seven-item list of reasons for success of a corporate president that respondents ranked from most to least important. The measure of relevance was a one to seven rating of the importance to the respondent that Renovations has a new president. Demographic data (department, job category, tenure, and gender) were collected.

Two measures of attribution differ from traditional scales. The first is the ranking, where subjects order seven possible explanations for a president's success by their importance in running the company. This method was selected over forced allocation of percentages because a pilot study confirmed Elig and Frieze's (1979) findings of high respondent error rate. The seven items are a closed set whose ordering was measured by computing the average rating for each item. These items included three "dispositional" and four "situational" explanations (Elig and Frieze, 1975; Hogan, 1987; Weiner et al., 1971). The second measure was the ten Likert-scaled statements where respondents indicated agreement with possible attributions about the transition, the president, and the company. The Likert statements and the rank-order items (Figure 9.2) ad-

Likert Statements (survey items 30–36, 39)	Rank-Order Items (survey item 43)
DISPOSITIONAL: EFFORT It takes an exceptional amount of effort for a president to be successful at leading this company	Hard work by the president
ABILITY To run this company well, the president must have outstanding management ability	President's management ability and skills
(PERSONALITY) It's the personality of the president that really determines whether he'll be effective here	President's personality
SITUATIONAL: LUCK (TIMING) This happens to be a good point in time for a new president to be coming on board	Point in time when the president began
TASK DIFFICULTY I imagine that running Renovations right now is a more challenging management job than running most comparable companies would be	Difficulty of management job to be done now
(CONTEXT) Consumer trends, competitive factors, the economy, and other factors outside the company really cause more change than a president does	Competition/pressure from outside the company: market, consumer trends, etc.
ORGANIZATIONAL: Renovations employees can pretty much run the company with little involvement by top management	Employees' responsiveness
This company will probably stay pretty much the same no matter who is the president	

FIGURE 9.2 Likert and rank-order attribution items.

dressed the categories of effort, ability, luck (timing), and task difficulty (Heider, 1958). To better reflect the context of organizational leadership, personality was added to the dispositional items, context to the situational, and a new attributional target of organizational factors was included.

On the first survey measure, the 29 items describing changes that *might* accompany a top management transition clustered in eight scales with a mean α of 0.73 (Table 9.1). A coefficient α of 0.7 to 0.8 is accepted in measuring social attitudes (Schuessler, 1982, p. 132). That standard was relaxed in this study to 0.6 for exploratory purposes. Five scales measured positive changes and two measured negative ones. A single item, on interunit competition, comprised the ninth measure.

TABLE 9.1 Organizational Change Impact Scales

Level of analysis		Survey item scales	α coefficient
Individual			
Positive	1a.	Improvements in my personal well-being: My benefits/pay will improve New president will take interest in me I will get more recognition here	0.72
Negative	1b.	Performance pressure: Will be asked to do new duties Work conditions will be harder Greater emphasis on productivity	0.65
Positive	1c.	Enhancement in quality of work life: Employee morale will improve Employees more committed to company Increased trust in management Better employee–management communications	0.85
Negative	1d.	Decreased job stability: My position will be eliminated Layoffs will be implemented I will choose to leave Others will choose to leave	0.81
Professional	2.	Elevation of my job/profession: President will support my profession My occupation will be more energetic More promotion opportunity for my job Contributions of my job more valued	0.75
Group			
Positive	3a.	Improvement in departmental well-being: Department will get more recognition President focuses on my department My department head has more power	0.78
Negative	3b.	Lack of interunit competition: Will be more interunit competition	n/a
Organizational	4a.	Changes at the corporate level: The company will be restructured New/improved technology will come Company will adopt new goals	0.65
	4b.	Changes in our business performance: Company's fiscal outlook will improve Company's reputation will improve	0.64

Attributions were also measured by the check-off option where respondents darkened a circle next to any of the 29 changes if they believed the change would be caused largely by having a new president. Although a crude statistical measure, this gave respondents the chance to make as few or as many attributions as they wished to the executive.

RESULTS

Relevance

The transition was rated by 83% of respondents as moderately to very important.

> **Hypothesis 1a:**   The transition will be rated as most relevant to employees in departments most directly involved with and familiar to the new executive and lowest in departments where the executive is less directly involved or familiar.

This hypothesis was supported by a one-way ANOVA using planned comparisons to test differences in the mean ratings of the relevance item for HR and Floorz versus Finance and MIS. The rating of 5.6 by HR/Floorz was significantly higher than the Finance/MIS mean of 4.4 ($F[1,81] = 9.47$, $p < 0.01$).

> **Hypothesis 1b:**   The transition will be rated as most relevant to managers and least relevant to professionals.

Both parts of this hypothesis were supported. ANOVAs using planned comparisons showed that the managers' mean of 5.4 was significantly higher than that of the nonexempts and professionals ($F[1,79] = 2.38$, $p < 0.10$), and the professionals' mean of 4.7 was significantly lower than that of the managers and nonexempts ($F[1,79] = 1.68$, $p < 0.10$). (A probability standard of 0.10 was used for exploratory purposes.)

> **Hypothesis 1c:**   The longer tenured employees will rate the transition as more relevant than will newer employees.

This hypothesis was not supported by ANOVA ($F[3,84] = 0.18$, n.s.) or by tests for linear fit. Contrary to the hypothesis, the two most recent tenure categories gave nonsignificantly higher ratings to the importance (5.2 and 5.0), while the more senior categories gave lower ratings (4.9 and 4.9). The tenure item may have masked real effects by using four tenure ranges rather than a continuous tenure variable.

TABLE 9.2 ANOVA: Positive and Negative Impact Scales by Department

Impact scale	HR and Floorz	Finance and MIS
1a. Personal well-being	2.9*	2.0
1c. Quality of work life	3.4**	2.9
3a. Departmental well-being	3.8*	2.2
Negative scales		
1b. Performance pressure	3.5**	3.1
3b. Interunit competition	3.1**	2.6

Note: Mean score is on a five-point scale, where 5 is "very likely" and 1 is "not at all likely." All probabilities are one-tailed. * = $p < 0.001$, ** = $p < 0.05$. 1a: $F(1,79) = 25.13$, $p < 0.001$; 1c: $F(1,77) = 5.26$, $p < 0.05$; 3a: $F(1,76) = 75.12$, $p < 0.001$; 1b: $F(1,79) = 3.41$, $p < 0.05$; 3b: $F(1,80) = 3.33$, $p < 0.05$.

Impact

Hypothesis 2:   The departments for whom the transition is the most important will give higher ratings to the positive effects and to the negative effects of the transition.

This hypothesis was supported. HR/Floorz gave significantly higher ratings on three of the four positive impact scales (Table 9.2). The means on the business performance scale (4b) were nearly identical at 3.9 and 3.8. No hypotheses were advanced regarding the organizational changes (4a) and the professional/job status (2) scales. While ANOVA revealed no significant departmental differences on the first, the HR/Floorz combination gave an average rating of 3.8, whereas the MIS/Finance combined mean was 3.0 ($F[1,79] = 11.06$, $p \leq 0.001$). These ratings place improved professional/job status among the positive changes that respondents in the HR/Floorz pairing see as more likely to occur. The second part of the hypothesis relating to negative effects was also supported: HR/Floorz scored significantly higher on both scales.

Attributions

Hypothesis 3a: Employees who rate the transition high in relevance will make significantly more dispositional attributions to the newcomer than will those who rate the transition less relevant.

This hypothesis was supported in two tests. Chi-square analysis showed that high-relevance respondents used the check-off more often than low-relevance respondents (Table 9.3).

TABLE 9.3 Chi-Square: Relevance × Dispositional Check-Offs

	High relevance ($n = 37$)	Low relevance ($n = 23$)	Total
No attribution made	13	19	32
Attributions made	24	4	28
Total	37	23	60

Note: $X^2(1, n = 60) = 12.84$, $p < 0.05$. High relevance = (1, 2, 3) on seven-point scale. Low relevance = (6, 7) on seven-point scale.

ANOVA with planned comparisons showed that respondents in HR/Floorz made significantly more attributions per respondent than those in MIS/Finance (Table 9.4).

> **Hypothesis 3b:** When the transition is relevant to respondents, they will make significantly more dispositional attributions to the executive for impact of the transition at the personal level than will those for whom the transition is less relevant.

This hypothesis was supported (Table 9.5). ANOVA, using planned comparisons of the percentages of possible attributional selections checked in each impact category, revealed that respondents in HR/Floorz gave significantly more attributional checks for executive responsibility on three of the four individual impact scales than those in MIS/Finance. On the fourth scale, job stability (1d), there were no significant differences.

An additional analysis of patterns in attributions was performed using the mean score received by each item in the rank-order listing. These findings are reported in Table 9.6. The president's ability and skill far outrank the other dispositional items, despite the fact that interviews in this and other companies

TABLE 9.4 ANOVA: Dispositional Attributions by Unit

	Mean number of attributions	% who made attributions
HR	12.6	76% (16)
Floorz	9.6	67% (10)
Finance	7.7	65% (15)
MIS	6.6	70% (19)

Note: Planned comparison: HR and Floorz vs. Finance and MIS $F(1,56) = 10.95$; $p < 0.01$.

TABLE 9.5   ANOVA: Mean Percent of Potential Attributions Made on Individual Impact Scales by Department

	HR and Floorz	Finance and MIS
1a. Personal well-being	0.33*	0.19
1b. Performance pressure	0.44**	0.18
1c. Quality of work life	0.57**	0.38

Note: The numbers given here are in percentages. For example, in the personal well-being scale, there are three separate items with three corresponding opportunities for attributional selections. Thus, each respondent could have made between 0 and 3 attributions for that scale. The number of attributions made by each person was expressed as a percentage of the possible attributions from 0 (nothing checked on that scale) to 1.0 (for the individual who checked all three options). The respondent who checked two of the three options would have a 0.667 score. $* = p <0.05$; $** = p <0.001$. 1a: $F(1,57) = 3.52$, $p <0.05$. 1b: $F(1,57) = 13.24$, $p <0.001$. 1c: $F(1,57) = 4.91$, $p <0.05$.

during a succession elicit many comments on the newcomer's personality. Second, outside competition and employee response led the situational items. That employees saw importance in such different aspects of the situation suggests that their capacity to discriminate finely among attributional targets must be considered in designing field instruments.

ANOVAs by unit, role, and tenure yielded no significant differences on the ten Likert-scaled attributional items. Items on the president's ability and effort correlated strongly ($r = 0.53$, $p <0.001$) and were the highest ranked factors. The two organizational factors (employees run the company without the president and the company stays the same) scored lowest, although the wording of these

TABLE 9.6   Mean Ratings of Attribution Rank-Order Items

Dispositional	Rating	Situational	Rating
Ability and skill	1.7		
		Outside competition	3.2
Hard work	3.3		
		Employee response	3.5
		Task difficulty	4.3
Personality	4.7		
		Timing	5.6
Mean rating	3.2	Mean rating	4.2

Note: The closer to 1 the score is, the more important the item is rated.

TABLE 9.7 Mean Scores: Likert-Scaled Attribution Items

Dispositional	Rating	Situational	Rating
President must have outstanding management ability	6.1		
Exceptional amount of effort is needed to run company	5.4		
		Good point in time for a new president	5.3
		Outside factors cause more change	4.3
		Running Renovations is a hard job	4.3
Personality of the president determines his success	3.9		
		Employees can run company without president	3.1
		Company stays same despite president	2.8

Note: The closer to 7 the score is, the more the respondent agrees with the statement.

latter items may have introduced a desirability bias. These findings support attribution leadership theories that emphasize observers' bias to dispositions: employees assign great importance to attributes of or control by the president (Table 9.7).

DISCUSSION

This study used four measures of attribution to assess employee responses to executive succession at Renovations, a mid-sized corporation. Five of six hypotheses about employees' ratings of the importance, impact, and attributions for transition-related changes were fully or largely supported. One's department and, to some extent, one's job role affected ratings of the transition and related attributions. Tenure had no significant impact on responses to this questionnaire.

Above all, hedonic relevance translated to a more personal and dispositional orientation toward the new executive. Changing the organization's top leader was important to 83% of the sample. Employees' ratings of the importance, impact, and attributions associated with the change were more pronounced in the two divisions closest to the newcomer's apparent strengths and interests. Those who saw the transition as important and credited the president with high potential impact also personalized this impact and made more dispositional attributions to him. Implications of this study emerge in the three areas highlighted earlier: attribution theory and measurement, leadership, and executive succession.

As empirical research, this study is hampered by several important limitations. The sample was small and limited to headquarters of a single company. The survey items are not yet validated. Thus, generalizing from the findings of this study is risky. However, the study uses several approaches to measuring attributions in real settings and demonstrates important differences in employee perceptions consistent with theory. There are several additional issues raised by this study.

Attribution Theory and Measurement

If "implicit leadership theory" (Eden and Leviatan, 1975) or general schemas determined employees' responses, systematic differences in departments' ratings of the transition would not be expected; nonetheless, such differences were found. This suggests that although individuals share numerous socially determined assumptions about leaders, their judgments of a real leader are moderated by added factors. For HR/Floorz employees, Suttle's presidency opened doors and relieved anxiety and uncertainty. For MIS/Finance, there was less optimism and a reluctance to credit the president with the potential to make changes. These findings reinforce the crucial role of hedonic relevance in attributions. Employees were invested in the outcome of this change far beyond the involvement created in most lab settings. Like the subjects in Eden and Leviatan's lab study (1975), many at Renovations actually knew fairly little about Donald Suttle. Their needs and expectations relating to the president, however, yielded distinctive responses. Suttle has meaning for each employee related to his or her well-being. This meaning shapes the assumptions held about him by prospective followers during the developmental phase of the leader–follower relationship.

The social mediation of attributions needs further research, in and out of laboratory settings. Where individuals have substantial investment in the situation, and where the actor's social role has significant implications for observers' well-being, attributions may involve more emotion and complexity in cognitive processing than is usually replicated in the laboratory. Manipulating the strength of hedonic relevance and broadening the range of potential attributional targets may make laboratory research findings more useful in understanding organizational processes.

This study also raises questions about attributional targets, supporting Elig and Frieze's (1979) argument that these must be broadened. Although they are parsimonious and useful, the four classic dimensions of skill, ability, effort, and luck (Heider, 1958) can be modified to fit organizational life. Additions such as those made here should be assessed to determine whether or not they enhance our ability to understand real-time attributions. Reflecting interview data where respondents made attributions about the president, this study added personality to the dispositional options. This is an individual characteristic beyond skill and ability. For situational attributions, elements of the internal (employee response) and external (outside competition) contexts were added, important distinctions reflecting the locus of causality.

A new category of attributional target is proposed in this study: the organization. Interviews showed that employees refer to the organization in terms that straddle the constructs of situational and dispositional attributions. Although the organization *is* part of the situation, it has enduring properties (culture, history, structure) that allow people to anthropomorphize their descriptions of causality. Should the categories of "situational" and "dispositional" be expanded to incorporate the special context of organizations? The parallel in therapy settings would be the family. Both families and organizations compete with real people for observers' dispositional attributions.

Leadership Dynamics

This study reinforces and extends previous findings on attribution dynamics in leadership. Even though the new president is not accessible to most employees, she or he generates attributions from all levels and roles (although the present study was limited to those at corporate headquarters and excluded field offices). An important theme in this study is the personalizing of the new executive's impact for people who feel part of the team. At Renovations, people in the HR/Floorz units experienced Suttle's arrival very personally. They saw direct implications for their own well-being in the workplace, and the impact was measurable. Only rarely does research on executive leadership take account of the leader's impact throughout the organization (Meindl et al., 1985; Niehoff et al., 1990). Further research is needed to determine any relationship that might exist between employees' morale, commitment, and effort based on their attributions about the incoming executive. Interviews at Renovations suggested that the high impact of department on employee attributions might relate to how each division head got along with the president. Future research can help to explain how employees develop and act on their conclusions about the top leader, with particular emphasis on how and when this person is relevant to them.

In this study, the interdependence of the leader–follower relationship was set aside, and only the followers' attributions toward the top executive as leader were examined. However, research on supervisory relationships shows that supervisors' attributions affect their behavior toward subordinates (Mitchell et al., 1981). The present study must be extended by research that examines the strength and content of executives' attributions toward the organization where they are taking charge. These attributions may be based initially on information that the board and ex-executives provide about the company, its executive team, and the work force. If the fundamental attribution error is operating, organizational problems may be overly attributed to people, with the context underrated. Not only must executives' attributions for causality in their new workplace be studied, but also the interaction effects when executive and workforce attributions operate simultaneously. The simple fact of holding responsible the other party, or seeing causality elsewhere in the environment, is a powerful force driving perceptions of leadership.

Executive Succession

Executive succession is often treated as an organization-level variable measured by changes in the bottom line. The internal organizational response to the event is rarely measured.

The attributional approach used in this study provides succession researchers with a tool to measure the nature and extent of the newcomer's psychological impact on followers. This approach is developmental in that attributions of causality to the executive, the organization, and the context may shift over time, suggesting that repeated measures can model the evolving salience of the executive to followers. Indeed, the attribution approach might predict or diagnose leadership failures where organization members never credit the leader with causing positive changes. The recent publicity on President Bill Clinton's first year suggests this type of dynamic: there have been many changes, but there is a reluctance by the public to credit the President.

The attributional approach might be used to measure transformational leadership. Early in a "transformational" leader's administration, one would expect to find heavy emphasis on dispositional attributions as employees focus on the executive and his or her leadership. Over time, however, one would predict more organizational and fewer dispositional attributions, as people in the company take increased ownership for the changes.

CONCLUSION

Employee A: The reaction was," it's about time—because we had been without someone for a long time…(we felt) gee whiz, they're not having any luck getting anybody."

Employee B: I was surprised. I was thinking, "Oh, my, we got a new president? What does that mean to us?"…Are we going to go through a big organizational change, because…every time somebody comes on board, jobs are lost or policies change…What does this mean to you personally and to the company as a whole?

These are typical reactions from interviews done at Renovations concurrent with the survey. Executive succession focuses attention and raises questions throughout the corporate hierarchy (Employee B is a secretary). Implicit here are two questions: "Why did it take so long?" and "What's going to happen to us?" Both reveal the uncertainty and anxiety that employees experience, demonstrating the impetus to attributional processing.

This study adds to knowledge about the nature of and patterns in individuals' expectations and concerns at the outset of the leader–follower relationship. Since early impressions shape later conclusions, these attributions are important. In addition, the study has provided data from several approaches to measuring attributions in a field setting. The issue of accuracy and utility of attribution measurement is an important and promising avenue for social psychologists in seeking ways to make their research useful for organizations.

REFERENCES

Boeker, W. (1992). Power and managerial dismissal: Scapegoating at the top. *Administrative Science Quarterly*, 37:400–421.

Bradley G.W. (1978). Self-serving biases in the attribution process: A reexamination of the fact or fiction question. *Journal of Personality and Social Psychology*, 36:56–71.

Brown, M. (1982). Administrative succession and organizational performance: The succession effect. *Administrative Science Quarterly*, 27:1–16.

Calder, B.J. (1977). An attribution theory of leadership. in *New Directions in Organizational Behavior*, B. Staw and G. Salancik (Eds.), Chicago: St. Clair, pp. 179–204.

Cannella, B. and Lubatkin, M. (1993). Succession as a sociopolitical process: Internal impediments to outsider selection. *Academy of Management Journal*, 36:763–793.

Diamond, M. (1993). *The Unconscious Life of Organizations: Interpreting Organizational Identity*, Westport, Conn.: Quorum Books.

Eden, D. and Leviatan, U. (1975). Implicit leadership theory as a determinant of the factor structure underlying supervisory behavior scales. *Journal of Applied Psychology*, 60:736–741.

Elig, T. and Frieze, I. (1975). A Multidimensional Scheme for Coding and Interpreting Perceived Causality for Success and Failure Events: The Coding Scheme of Perceived Causality (CSPC). Manuscript No. 1069, abstracted in the *JSAS Catalog of Selected Documents in Psychology*, 5:313.

Elig, T. and Frieze, I. (1979). Measuring causal attributions for success and failure. *Journal of Personality and Social Psychology*, 37:621–634.

Farquhar, K. (1989). Employee Response to External Executive Succession: Attributions and the Emergence of Leadership, unpublished doctoral dissertation, Boston University.

Farquhar, K. (1991). Leadership in limbo: Organization dynamics during interim administrations. *Public Administration Review*, 51:202–210.

Fredrickson, J., Hambrick, D., and Baumrin, S. (1988). A model of CEO dismissal. *Academy of Management Review*, 13(2):255–270.

Gabarro, J. (1987). *The Dynamics of Taking Charge,* Boston: Harvard University Press.

Gamson, W. and Scotch, N. (1964). Scapegoating in baseball. *American Journal of Sociology,* 70:69–72.

Gibb, C. (1969). Leadership. in *The Handbook of Social Psychology,* Vol. 4, 2nd edition, G. Lindzey and E. Aronson (Eds.), Reading, Mass.: Addison-Wesley, pp. 205–282.

Gilmore, T.N. (1988). *Making a Leadership Change,* San Francisco: Jossey-Bass.

Gordon, G. and Rosen, N. (1981). Critical factors in leadership succession. *Organization Behavior and Human Performance,* 27:227–254.

Graen, G. and Cashman, J. (1975). A role-making model of leadership in formal organizations: A developmental approach. in *Leadership Frontiers,* J. Hunt and L. Larson (Eds.), Kent, Ohio: Kent State, pp. 143–165.

Hambrick, D. and Cannella, B. (1993). Relative standing: A framework for understanding departures of acquired executives. *Academy of Management Journal,* 36:733–762.

Heider, F. (1958). *The Psychology of Interpersonal Relations,* New York: Wiley.

Heller, T. (1989). Conversion processes in leadership succession: A case study. *Journal of Applied Behavioral Science,* 25(1):65–77.

Herold, D. (1977). Two-way influence processes in leader–follower dyads. *Academy of Management Journal,* 20:224–237.

Higgins, E., Kuiper, N., and Olson, J. (1981). Social cognition: A need to get personal. in *Social Cognition: The Ontario Symposium,* Vol. I, E. Higgins, C. Herman, and M. Zanna (Eds.), Hillsdale, N.J.: Lawrence Erlbaum, pp. 395–420.

Hogan, E. (1987). Effects of prior expectations on performance ratings: A longitudinal study. *Academy of Management Journal,* 30:354–368.

Hollander, E. (1958). Conformity, status and idiosyncrasy credit. *Psychological Review,* 65:117–127.

Isen, A. (1984). Toward understanding the role of affect in cognition. in *Handbook of Social Cognition,* Vol. 3, R. Wyer and T. Srull (Eds.), Hillsdale, N.J.: Lawrence Erlbaum, pp. 170–236.

Jones, E. and Davis, K. (1965). From acts to dispositions: The attribution process in person perception. in *Advances in Experimental Social Psychology,* Vol. 2, L. Berkowitz (Ed.), New York: Academic Press, pp. 219–266.

Jones, G. (1983). Psychological orientation and the process of organizational socialization: An interactionist perspective. *Academy of Management Review,* 8(3):464–474.

Kelley, H. and Michela, J. (1980). Attribution theory and research. *Annual Review of Psychology,* 31:457–501.

Kets de Vries, M. (1988). The dark side of CEO succession. *Harvard Business Review,* 66:56–60.

Kotin, J. and Sharaf, M. (1967). Management succession and administrative style. *Psychiatry,* 30:237–248.

Lord, R. and Maher, K. (1991). *Leadership and Information Processing: Linking Perceptions and Performance,* Boston: Unwin Hyman.

Martinko, M. and Gardner, W. (1987). The leader/member attribution process. *Academy of Management Review,* 12:235–249.

McElroy, J. (1982). A typology of attribution leadership research. *Academy of Management Review,* 7:413–417.

McElroy, J. and Shrader, C. (1986). Attribution theories of leadership and network analysis. *Journal of Management,* 12:351–362.

Meindl, J., Ehrlich, S., and Dukerich, J. (1985). The romance of leadership. *Administrative Science Quarterly,* 30:78–102.

Mitchell, T., Larson, J., and Green, S. (1977). Leader behavior, situational moderators, and group performance: An attributional analysis. *Organizational Behavior and Human Performance,* 18:254–268.

Mitchell, T., Green, S., and Wood, R. (1981). An attribution model of leadership and the poor performing subordinate: Development and validation. in *Research in Organization Behavior,* Vol. 3, L. Cummings and B. Staw (Eds.), Greenwich, Conn.: JAI, pp. 197–234.

Niehoff, B., Enz, C., and Grover, R. (1990). The impact of top-management actions on employee attitudes and perceptions. *Group and Organization Studies,* 15(3):337–352.

Pfeffer, J. (1978). The ambiguity of leadership. in *Leadership: Where Else Can We Go?* M. McCall and M. Lombardo (Eds.), Durham, N.C.: Duke University, pp. 13–34.

Pfeffer, J. and Salancik, G. (1975). Determinants of supervisory behavior: A role set analysis. *Human Relations,* 28:139–154.

Porrac, J., Ferris, G., and Fedor, D. (1983). Causal attributions, affect, and expectations for a day's work performance. *Academy of Management Journal,* 26:285–296.

Pyszczynski, T. and Greenberg, J. (1981). Role of disconfirmed expectancies in the instigation of attributional processing. *Journal of Personality and Social Psychology,* 40:31–38.

Ross, L. (1977). The intuitive psychologist and his shortcomings: Distortions in the attribution process. in *Advances in Experimental Social Psychology,* Vol. 10, L. Berkowitz (Ed.), New York: Academic Press, pp. 173–220.

Rush, M., Thomas, J., and Lord, R. (1977). Implicit leadership theory: A potential threat to the validity of leader behavior questionnaires. *Organizational Behavior and Human Performance,* 20:93–100.

Schachter, S. (1964). The interaction of cognitive and physiological determinants of emotional state. in *Advances in Experimental Social Psychology,* Vol. 1, L. Berkowitz (Ed.), New York: Academic Press, pp. 49–80.

Schuessler, K. (1982). *Measuring Social Life Feelings,* San Francisco: Jossey-Bass.

Simonton, D. (1986). Dispositional attributions of (presidential) leadership: An experimental simulation of historiometric results. *Journal of Experimental Social Psychology,* 22:389–418.

Smith, M. and White, M. (1987). Strategy, CEO specialization, and succession. *Administrative Science Quarterly,* 32:263–280.

Taylor, S. and Fiske, S. (1978). Salience, attention, and attribution: Top of the head phenomena. in *Advances in Experimental Social Psychology,* Vol. 11, L. Berkowitz (Ed.), New York: Academic Press, pp. 249–288.

Taylor, S. and Fiske, S. (1981). Getting inside the head: Methodologies for process analysis in attribution and social cognition. in *New Directions in Attribution Research,* Vol. 3, J. Harvey, W. Ickes, and R. Kidd (Eds.), pp. 459–524.

Weiner, B., Frieze, I., Kukla, A., Reed, L., Rest, S., and Rosenbaum, R. (1971). Perceiving the causes of success and failure. in *Attribution: Perceiving the Causes of Behavior,* E.E. Jones, D.E. Kanouse, H.H. Kelley, R.E. Nisbett, S. Valins, and B. Weiner (Eds.), Morristown, N.J.: General Learning Press, pp. 95–120.

Yarkin, K., Harvey, J., and Bloxom, B. (1981). Cognitive sets, attribution, and social interaction. *Journal of Personality and Social Psychology,* 41:243–252.

10

A MID-RANGE THEORY OF
THE LEADER/MEMBER
ATTRIBUTION PROCESS IN
PROFESSIONAL SERVICE
ORGANIZATIONS: THE ROLE
OF THE ORGANIZATIONAL
ENVIRONMENT AND
IMPRESSION MANAGEMENT

Michael E. Bitter and William L. Gardner III

ABSTRACT

This chapter presents an attributional model of the performance evaluation process within professional service organizations (PSOs). Particular attention is devoted to the impact that PSO attributes (such as absentee management, a unique supervisory structure, complex relational linkages, and highly competitive reward systems) exert on the appraisal process. The role that member impression management (IM) plays in the leader/member attribution process is also emphasized, along with biases and self-presentational concerns that may distort leader evaluations of member performance. Finally, adverse organizational consequences arising from inaccurate performance appraisals are considered, and recommendations for avoiding or minimizing these negative outcomes are advanced.

INTRODUCTION

Previous research on the attribution processes of leaders and subordinates has focused on the attributions leaders make to explain member behavior (Green and Mitchell, 1979) and the dyadic exchange of attributions in leader/member relations (Martinko and Gardner, 1987). Neither approach, however, considers the effects of the organizational environment. In particular, it seems that certain organizational attributes can impact the leader/member attribution process and affect the strategies and tactics utilized in developing vertical relationships.

The purpose of this chapter is to offer a mid-range theory that examines the leader/member attribution process within a professional service organization (PSO) environment. Since member rewards are based upon their performance, leader performance attributions represent a crucial variable in the promotion process. Further, due to the unique attributes of PSOs, it is proposed that impression management (IM) (Gardner and Martinko, 1988; Leary and Kowalski, 1990; Schlenker and Weigold, 1992) plays a key role in PSO leader/member exchanges. The propositions generated relate specifically to PSOs. Although several of the propositions could be generalized to other organizations, it is suggested that they are particularly relevant to PSOs due to the unique nature of the environment surrounding these organizations.

THE MODEL

A model of the performance evaluation process in a PSO is presented in Figure 10.1. This model extends earlier work by introducing IM as a factor that affects both leader and member perceptions, attributions, and behavior, as well as those of other leaders and members. The process begins with the member performing a task.* Task behavior is influenced by one's attributions for past behaviors and may also reflect a member's attempt to simultaneously manage the impressions of others.

---

*The term *task* is referred to in a broad sense. For example, a consultant's "task" would encompass all of the activities assigned them during a particular engagement, rather than any specific activity undertaken.

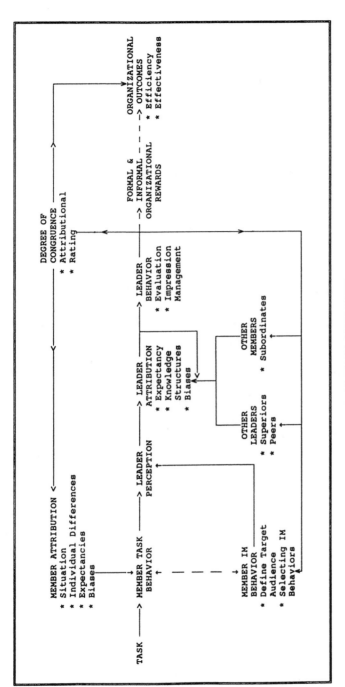

FIGURE 10.1 A model of the performance evaluation process within a PSO.

The leader perceives the member's behavior and assigns a level of relative success or failure before making an attribution for this performance. These perceptions and attributions are mediated by past experiences with the member and information received from other leaders and members. The attributions made in turn influence the leader's subsequent behavior toward the member. This response is then perceived by the member, along with other leaders and members. The leader's actions elicit behavioral responses from these individuals while updating their expectations for future behaviors. The leader's behavior also impacts the formal and informal organizational rewards a member receives. These rewards, in turn, impact the efficiency and effectiveness of the organization.

THE ORGANIZATIONAL ENVIRONMENT

PSOs operate with a primary objective of serving client needs and include public accounting, law, and consulting and investment firms. Most PSOs are structured with well-defined levels of authority. PSO employees are generally well-educated professionals who perform tasks requiring the application of expertise to unique client situations. The persons at the highest hierarchical levels are typically owner/managers (e.g., partners). Employees are hired with the intent that they progress toward ownership; those unsuitable for promotion are counseled out of the firm. As with most organizations, performance is the key variable leading to advancement and other rewards. However, the unique attributes of PSOs create barriers to purely performance-driven appraisals and hence provide greater opportunities for the use of IM by PSO employees. These unique attributes include absentee management, the supervisory structure, and informal relational linkages.

IM is the process by which "actors" direct behaviors toward "audiences" in an attempt to create and maintain desired images of themselves (Gardner and Martinko, 1988). Schneider (1981) distinguishes between two basic types of IM. The first is self-presentation, which involves the manipulation of information about the self. In the second, impressions are managed via a third party who passes the desired information on to the target (Wortman and Linsenmeier, 1977).

Gardner and Martinko (1988) assert that IM can influence individual success and promotability in organizations. Several studies have confirmed that IM can be used to make positive impressions on superiors that lead to desired rewards (Bohra and Pandey, 1984; Podsakoff, 1982; Tedeschi and Melburg, 1984). Specifically, researchers (Cardy and Dobbins, 1986; Gioia and Sims, 1986; Tsui and Barry, 1986; Wayne and Ferris, 1990; Wayne and Kacmar, 1991) have demonstrated that member IM can positively affect leader evaluations of their performance. This suggests that:

P₁: Member IM will have a pronounced effect on leader attributions for, and evaluations of, member performance in PSOs.

Absentee Management

Due to the nature of their job, PSO members often perform services at client offices, resulting in physical separation from and minimal contact with leaders. Regular observation of member behavior is usually required for leaders to make accurate attributions for member performance (Green and Mitchell, 1979). With absentee management, however, leaders have limited access to member's daily activities, resulting in little data upon which to base an appraisal (Dowell and Wexley, 1978). A danger of limited data is that the leader may incorrectly perceive member effectiveness. The more absentee management is used, the greater the ambiguity regarding member performance. IM appears to thrive on such ambiguity (Baumeister and Jones, 1978; Bradley, 1978; Fandt and Ferris, 1990; Ralston, 1985; Schlenker, 1975). Moreover, since leader ratings of members are subjective and susceptible to influence attempts (Tedeschi and Melburg, 1984; Wortman and Linsenmeier, 1977), the potential for a leader's liking of a member to bias ratings increases as ambiguity grows (Tsui and Barry, 1986; Villanova and Bernardin, 1989). Accordingly, it is proposed that:

P₂: Under conditions of absentee management, members will be highly motivated to direct IM behavior toward leaders.

Supervisory Structure

Another distinct PSO feature is its supervisory structure, where, over time, members work with many different leaders at various levels, often simultaneously. In PSOs, reward decisions are based upon the appraisals of all the leaders for whom the member has worked. Members must strive to please as many of these leaders as possible or, at least, those who exercise the most influence over the reward allocation process. Even if influential leaders are identified, members may not have the immediate and sustained access necessary to display their skills. If so, they may be motivated to employ IM through third parties. For example, a member may try to compliment a manager through a conversation with his or her administrative aide. Thus:

P₃: Members will be motivated to employ IM using third parties to overcome the constraints of the PSO environment.

Over time, members will be motivated to reduce the number of managers who directly supervise them. This might be achieved by specializing in an area of practice or through the formation of a mutually beneficial relationship with one or more leaders. By doing so, members can focus their efforts and create a strong performance history with these leaders. This reduction also allows members to concentrate their IM efforts on a few key leaders. Therefore, it is expected that:

> P_4:   Over time, members will try to reduce the number of leaders to whom they are accountable and focus their IM efforts on these leaders.

Informal Relational Linkages

Informal relational linkages among professionals are an important part of the PSO. In addition to working for several managers with differing levels of status (a formal linkage), professionals work with other members of equal or lesser rank. Forging strong informal linkages with peers and subordinates is of great importance to members seeking advancement. To succeed, they must work well with others. Hence, the performance of other members can be critical to the member's perceived success. Further, strong allies can be useful third parties for helping to manage leader impressions. This suggests that:

> P_5:   Members who cultivate favorable relations with subordinates and peers will be inclined to use them to manage leader impressions.

MEMBER BEHAVIOR

A member's behavior can be described by its focus. A member's primary behavior is aimed at completing the task at hand. However, a member's behavior might also be directed toward managing the impressions of others. Such IM behavior can be distinct or may be a part of the behaviors directed toward completion of a task. Behavior aimed at completing a task is conditioned upon a member's expectancy and ability as well as the effort exerted. This behavior may also be constrained by the situation in which the task is undertaken.

A member's past experiences lead to an awareness that perceptions of task outcomes vary. Further, leaders are not always knowledgeable about the circumstances surrounding member behavior and the corresponding outcomes that would allow them to tangibly assess performance (Green and Mitchell, 1979). As such, members realize that their actions and task outcomes could be misinterpreted by leaders, thereby producing an inaccurate performance evaluation and unjust punishment for failure or inadequate rewards for success. Schlenker

(1980) asserts that the primary motive for IM involves a desire to maximize rewards and minimize punishment. This implies that uncertainty about leader perceptions, attributions, and behaviors can cause members to hedge their positions via IM. Accordingly, it is proposed that:

P$_6$: The unique characteristics of PSOs increase the risks associated with inaccurate evaluations of member behavior. These risks, coupled with a desire to maximize rewards and minimize punishment, motivate PSO members to direct IM behavior toward their leaders.

Another concern of PSO members is that leaders may be unable to distinguish their abilities from those of others. Such a dilemma can motivate members to seek different means of influence; IM can help members portray themselves as someone with whom the leader would like to work (Ralston, 1985). Moreover, as PSO members are promoted, there is stiffer competition for fewer available formal rewards (e.g., salary increases and promotions). Since impression motivation is higher when rewards are scarce (Leary and Kowalski, 1990), motivation to use IM should increase as members advance toward ownership.

P$_7$: As members advance in the PSO, they will be increasingly motivated to utilize and intensify IM behavior toward leaders.

Once motivated, members assess the situation to determine the image they wish to convey. Next, members must choose appropriate IM behaviors to create the desired impression. The credibility and probable effectiveness of various IM options should be considered before a strategy is selected and operationalized. Depending on the audience's reactions and the salient outcomes, the chosen behaviors may be maintained or modified (Martinko, 1991).

Defining the Target Audience

To this point, the target for IM has been assumed to be the leader; however, it is also important for members seeking advancement to develop good relations with, and portray a favorable image to, peers, subordinates, and other leaders. Thus, although IM may be focused on the immediate leader, other audiences may be indirectly targeted. However, because a given IM strategy may not be effective across audiences, members concentrate on impressing competent, respected, and influential persons upon whom they depend for valued rewards and/or assistance (Leary and Kowalski, 1990). This suggests that:

P$_8$: When the size and diversity of an audience prohibits the development of an all-encompassing IM strategy, PSO members focus their IM efforts on competent, respected, and influential leaders and peers.

Selecting the IM Behavior

Members can choose from a variety of IM behaviors, including assertive and defensive tactics (Schlenker and Weigold, 1992; Tedeschi and Norman, 1985). In evaluative settings, assertive IM can convince audiences that favorable outcomes stem from the member (an attribution to internal causes). Assertive IM tactics include ingratiation and self-promotion, which are employed to secure attributions of attractiveness and competence, respectively (Jones and Pittman, 1982). Self-promotion is especially useful when members perceive that they have not been adequately recognized and rewarded in the past. Actors adopt defensive IM to protect or repair their image (Gardner, 1992). For instance, one may try to persuade others that a failure was beyond one's control (an attribution to external causes). Defensive tactics include apologies and accounts (excuses) for poor performance (Braaten et al., 1993; Kaplan and Reckers, 1993). Thus, it is advanced that:

P_9: When past success has not been adequately rewarded, members will direct assertive IM toward leaders and key peers and subordinates.

P_{10}: Members who expect sub-par task performance will direct defensive IM behaviors toward leaders and key peers and subordinates.

FACTORS MODERATING IM EFFECTIVENESS

Although there are many dispositional and situational factors that could potentially moderate the effectiveness of member IM behavior, the leader's personality and the nature of the leader/member relationship appear to be especially relevant.

Leader Personality

The personality of the leader often dictates whether an IM behavior is perceived positively or negatively. For example, ingratiatory acts may be regarded favorably by one leader, but not by another. Similarly, excuses for poor performance may be accepted sympathetically by one leader, but rejected with contempt by another. IM research suggests that, in general, persons with high approval needs and low self-monitoring abilities are more receptive to IM behavior (Gardner and Martinko, 1988; Schlenker, 1980). To the extent that members are sensitive to these and other personality traits of the leader, they are more likely to select an effective IM strategy.

Leader/Member Relationship

The nature of the relationship between the leader and member likewise impacts upon the leader's perceptions and reactions to the member's IM behavior (Wright and Ingraham, 1986). As Taylor and Koivumaki (1976) demonstrated, the closeness of a relationship can profoundly influence the kinds of attributions that one party will make for another's behavior.

LEADER PERCEPTION

Leader perception of a member's behavior includes not only the member's overt behavior, but the task outcome derived from the behavior. Task outcome is not a discrete measure; success and failure can be measured on a continuum. Although two individuals may agree that an individual has succeeded on a task, they may disagree as to the degree of success and, for that matter, as to the constitution of success. The characteristics of the environment surrounding the PSO pose potentially serious barriers to a leader's perception.

LEADER ATTRIBUTIONS

The leader's attribution of member behavior is based upon past experience. These past experiences generate both expectancy for future performance and biases that can impair the leader's ability to accurately determine causality. The leader's attribution is important because it drives leader behavior and shapes leader expectancy (Martinko and Gardner, 1987).

The Formation of Leader Attributions

Causal attributions are often categorized along the dimensions of locus of control and stability, using the taxonomy advanced by Weiner et al. (1971). By considering these dimensions in tandem, this taxonomy classifies causal attributions as internal/stable (e.g., ability), internal/unstable (e.g., effort), external/stable (e.g., task difficulty), and external/unstable (e.g., luck/chance). Importantly, research has demonstrated that the locus of control dimension is related to differential leader responses to member performance (Green and Mitchell, 1979; Martinko and Gardner, 1987). For example, leaders typically respond more punitively when they attribute member failure to low effort (an internal cause) as opposed to task difficulty (an external cause). Moreover, the stability dimension has been linked to divergent performance expectations; outcomes that are attributed to stable causes (e.g., ability, task difficulty) are expected to recur, whereas those arising from unstable causes (e.g., effort, luck) are seen as temporary (Weiner et al., 1971).

Knowledge Structures

Due to the frequency with which leaders make attributions (Green and Mitchell, 1979) and the inevitable limitations of available information, leaders often rely on knowledge structures to ascertain the cause of member behaviors. Schneider (1991) describes two basic models of category-based knowledge structures: the exemplar and prototype models. The *exemplar* model assumes that memory representations are based on concrete instances. In other words, attributes are stored at an individual level: Accountant A is shy, dedicated, ambitious, and kind; Accountant B is outgoing, dedicated, ambitious, and arrogant. In contrast, the *prototype* model assumes that an abstract representation of the prototypical attributes associated with a category (e.g., leader) is formed.

Exemplars tend to be used to evaluate individuals rather than groups. For example, a leader may compare the attributes, actions, and performance of a ratee to those of members who have excelled in the past. In contrast, prototypes are employed to summarize the attributes of an entire group (e.g., female lawyers). These prototypes may subsequently be used to form impressions of new category members. Of course, since such judgments are based on stereotypes, they may be biased. Thus leaders tend to use exemplars to appraise members they depend upon, due to the importance of accurate attributions (Neuberg and Fiske, 1987).

Although ideally based upon actual, observed performance, the evaluations completed by leaders may not accurately reflect performance because of their cognitive inability to recall member behavior, physical separation from the member, or ambiguous performance criteria (Ralston, 1985). Leaders may fill gaps in their perceptions by using exemplars or prototypes for expected performance. Hence, the appraisal completed may reflect events or actions that did not occur, but are part of the exemplar or prototype retrieved from memory (Feldman, 1981).

> P_{11}: A leader's cognitive limitations, the presence of relevant knowledge structures, absentee management, and ambiguous performance criteria reduce the accuracy of the PSO member's performance evaluations.

Attributional Biases

Since leader behavior is significantly influenced by leader attributions, attributional biases can have a potentially adverse effect on the accuracy of performance appraisals and, thus, the administration of rewards. Several

TABLE 10.1   Attributional Biases

Actor/observer bias	The tendency for observers to attribute actor behavior to dispositional causes, while actors attribute their behaviors to situational causes (Jones and Nisbett, 1972)
Self-based consensus	The tendency of people to evaluate others' behavior using their own standards, while ignoring the standards that are typical of the population (Hansen and Lowe, 1976)
False consensus effect	The tendency for people to believe that their own behavioral choices are most appropriate for the situation and are representative of the typical choice of others (Ross, 1977)
Fundamental attribution error	The tendency for individuals to overestimate the influence of dispositional factors and underestimate the impact of situational factors (Ross, 1977)
Self-serving bias	The tendency of persons to attribute their success to internal causes and failure to external causes (Bradley, 1978)
Leader expectation bias	When the member's task performance outcome coincides with the leader's expectancy, the behavior is attributed to dispositional causes; when the behavior is contrary to expectancy, the leader attributes it to situational causes (Green and Mitchell, 1979)

attributional biases that can have an impact upon the leader/member attribution process (Green and Mitchell, 1979; Martinko and Gardner, 1987) are summarized in Table 10.1. These biases also explain much of the incongruence that often arises between the attributions of leaders and members. Furthermore, such discrepancies can cause conflict resulting in dysfunctional behavior.

The Effect of Member IM Behaviors on Leader Attributions

Impression Bias

Because effective IM enhances a leader's liking of a member, it can bias his or her attributions for member performance. This is particularly likely to occur in PSOs, where conditions are ripe for the successful use of IM. When failure occurs, for instance, the leader may bypass information about task-related behavior and attribute it to external causes (Braaten et al., 1993; Kaplan and Reckers, 1993; Wood and Mitchell, 1981). Impression bias may also arise after success if IM shifts the leader's attribution toward internal causes (member ability and effort). If, however, the member's IM efforts are viewed negatively, impression bias can produce unwanted secondary impressions (Schneider, 1981; Wortman and Linsenmeier, 1977). For example, if the leader sees through an ingratiation attempt, he or she may unfairly attribute success to external factors or failure to internal factors. Therefore, it is proposed that:

P_{12}: Impression bias can significantly affect a leader's attributions for member success and/or failure, with positive bias having a favorable impact and negative bias producing adverse effects.

Gap-Filling

When there are gaps in leaders' memories of member behavior, they may attribute nonexistent behaviors to the member simply because of their situational expectations. Likewise, it seems that IM behavior can influence how leaders fill gaps in memory. Because absentee management results in barriers to observation of performance, IM behavior may provide a substitute for unobserved behavior or influence the knowledge structures invoked. This implies that:

P_{13}: Leaders' impressions of a member influence their attributions when gaps exist in their memory regarding member behavior or when no physical observation of behavior has occurred.

LEADER BEHAVIOR

The behaviors that a leader directs toward the member are driven by both the task outcome and the leader's attribution for the outcome. The primary behavior stemming from the process is the performance evaluation. The performance evaluation could be informal or formal. Informal evaluations could range from verbal feedback from a leader during or after task performance to the "mental notes" made by a leader during observation of a member's behavior.

Formal evaluations are generally written and provide a permanent record of the member's performance on a task. Unlike the typical organization, where formal performance evaluations are usually completed on an annual basis, PSOs generally evaluate performance on an interim basis because of the PSO's supervisory structure. For example, an auditor in a public accounting firm is generally given a formal evaluation after each significant engagement. The interim evaluations given by a member's various supervisors form the basis for the annual review.

The performance evaluation is the main determinant of the rewards a member receives. Further, the behaviors leaders display are, to some extent, IM tactics aimed at both the member and other organizational participants.

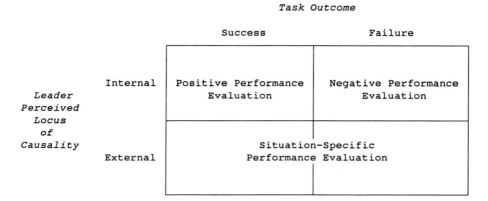

FIGURE 10.2   The impact of performance outcome and locus of causality on leader evaluations of member performance.

Performance Evaluation

A two-by-two matrix of predicted leader evaluations for member performance is presented in Figure 10.2. Its dimensions include leader attributions (using locus of causality) and task outcomes. Given perceived member success, an internal attribution to ability or effort leads to a favorable appraisal. However, if failure is perceived, an internal attribution leads to a negative rating. Alternatively, external attributions (task difficulty or luck) by the leader result in situation-specific evaluations (Green and Mitchell, 1979), whereby a member is not held accountable (or given credit) for the outcome.

Member effort is the key determinant of performance ratings (Green and Mitchell, 1979; Weiner and Kukla, 1970). While lack of ability may be correctable with training and task difficulty can be regulated by the PSO, effort is under the member's personal control. As such, low effort yielding success is acknowledged, but not highly rated, whereas failure produces negative appraisals.

Of course, this matrix is an oversimplification. Individual differences in the biases of leaders, coupled with situational factors, can greatly affect performance evaluations. For example, attributional uncertainty can contribute to inaccurate evaluations. When leaders are uncertain about the cause of a task outcome, they tend to be less extreme in their responses. Because uncertainty makes it more difficult to rule out potential causes, a discounting effect occurs that dilutes the leader's confidence in a particular attribution and hence his or her conviction to extreme responses (Kelley, 1973). Nevertheless, leaders are likely to weakly attribute member failure to internal causes, despite the presence of uncertainty, since they typically believe that member behavior is more amenable to change than the situation (Green and Mitchell, 1979).

Leader personality may also contribute to inaccurate appraisals. Leaders, like anyone else, have a desire to feel successful. The inflation of member ratings may arise from a leader's self-serving bias (Greenberg, 1984). If the member is portrayed as successful, the leader likewise feels successful. The leader's self-efficacy expectations can also affect evaluations. Villanova and Bernardin (1989) suggest that low-self-efficacy leaders tend to inflate ratings when members fail in order to avoid confrontations. Accordingly, it is proposed that:

P_{14}: Leader personality traits and self-efficacy expectations influence the extent to which they inflate or deflate member performance evaluations.

Leader Behavior as an IM Technique

Leaders who wish to promote a positive image may rely on "other-focused tactics" whereby they shape audience perceptions of their subordinates (Cialdini, 1989). High-self-monitoring leaders are especially apt to use such a strategy. Due to the formal linkages between the leader and member, positive impressions of a member cast a favorable light upon the leader. Villanova and Bernardin (1989) propose that leaders can incorporate such tactics into performance appraisals by inflating or deflating ratings. These tactics can produce benefits from both the appraised member and other leaders and members. For example, leaders may choose to inflate member ratings to increase the member's liking of them and thereby retain the member in the work group. Alternatively, a leader may deflate a rating to retain a valuable member who would otherwise be promoted. This reasoning suggests that:

P_{15}: Leaders can use performance appraisals to convey desired images toward specific leader and/or member groups.

Influences of Leader Behavior

Because a leader's reward behavior is highly visible, it can have a strong impact on the attributions and actions of others. In essence, such behavior becomes an input for other leader/member attributional processes—those of the focal member as well as those of other leaders and members (Green and Mitchell, 1979; Martinko and Gardner, 1987). Observed leader behavior can provide other leaders with useful information for updating a member's outcome history and revising their expectancies for future member performance. Information gained from the leader may also trigger rewards from other leaders. For example, positive information might cause other leaders to support a member's promotion (a formal reward) or recruit the member to work with them on a high-profile project (an informal reward).

Through observation, other leaders also learn about the focal leader. Observed behavior may give clues about the leader's management style, the fairness of the leader's evaluation techniques, and his or her ability to get along with others. Additionally, the quality of members working for the leader may reflect his or her status (Cialdini, 1989). Since leaders are usually subordinates to one or more superiors, their ratings of members may likewise be considered in assessments of their own performance (Greenberg, 1984).

A leader's behavior also influences other members' perceptions of, and behaviors toward, the member and the leader. Other members may gravitate toward or avoid the leader based on their observations. Similarly, they may associate with or avoid the member depending upon his or her apparent potential for future success (Cialdini, 1989). Finally, an understanding of member performance and leader behavior allows members to update their expectancies (Green and Mitchell, 1979; Martinko and Gardner, 1987). Knowledge of the member's standing within the PSO, coupled with updated expectancies, can permit other members to evaluate their own standing and their chances for future success (Festinger, 1954).

Finally, leader behavior can also impact a member's subsequent usage of IM behavior. Positive leader behavior may validate a member's IM behavior, whereas negative leader behavior may cause a member to reduce or alter IM behavior in the future.

LEADER/MEMBER INCONGRUENCIES

Although discrepancies may arise if leader and member perceptions of the task outcome do not match, attributional incongruencies primarily arise from biases. For example, members tend to attribute success to internal factors and failure to external factors. Leaders are biased in the opposite direction: they are inclined to view member performance as inadequate, discount member success, and attribute failure to member ability and effort (Martinko and Gardner, 1987). Further attributional incongruencies arise if members do not live up to leader expectations or when the member's behavior is contrary to what leaders would have done under the circumstances. In these situations, leaders are also likely to discount success, while attributing failure to internal factors.

Even if leader and member attributions agree, the actual evaluation may be incongruent with member expectations. Performance appraisals depend upon several factors: the situation, task difficulty, past performance by the member's peers, and individual differences. Specifically, research suggests that rating differences can occur because leaders and members have unique perspectives and focus on different facets of performance (Borman, 1974). Further, Farh and Dobbins (1989) have suggested that a member's tendency toward a "leniency bias" results in inflated self-ratings that contribute to conflict.

Results of Incongruence

Little or no conflict should arise if the leader's attributions for member behavior and/or performance ratings exceed member expectations. For example, absentee management produces ambiguity in the rating process and increases the odds of a member "getting by" with occasional poor performance. Such outcomes may validate the utility of the IM tactics used.

Jones and Nisbett (1972) suggest that the level of psychological closeness between the leader and member is directly related to agreement on attributions. Accordingly, increased psychological closeness should result in fewer instances of conflict over attributions and performance evaluations. This implies that:

P_{16}: The psychological closeness between a leader and member is inversely related to conflict over attributions and performance evaluations.

However, when the leader's attributions are less favorable or the performance appraisal is worse than expected, conflict is bound to occur. This is true whether the leader discounts the member's success or places excessive blame on the member for failure. Conflict is most likely to emerge if leader/ member differences revolve around member ability or effort. Thus, it is proposed that:

P_{17}: Incongruence between leader and member attributions and/or actual and expected performance ratings will lead to leader/member conflict, especially with regard to disputed internal attributions.

Conflict can be damaging to the leader, the member, and the organization. It impacts not only the working relationship between the two, but also may impact future behaviors. Additionally, conflict played out in front of other leaders and members may result in the loss of credibility for both parties.

IM Responses by the Member

Sometimes it is advantageous to avoid conflict and use incongruencies to manage others' impressions. This may involve accepting responsibility for negative outcomes (a public attribution), even though a member believes that it is not his or her fault (a private attribution). Alternatively, a member may attempt to preserve self-esteem by offering an account for poor performance (Kaplan and Reckers, 1993). Likewise, it may be beneficial for members to take less credit for a positive outcome, especially if they believe that the outcome has been attributed to internal causes. Modesty can help cast a member in a more positive light (Baumeister and Jones, 1978; Schlenker and Weigold, 1992).

P₁₈: P_{18}:   Members may use attributional and/or evaluation incongruencies to foster desired impressions by graciously accepting the blame for a negative outcome or exhibiting humility regarding a positive event.

Self-monitoring ability may moderate the extent to which members use incongruencies to manage impressions. Because high as opposed to low self-monitors are more attuned to their audience, they are more likely to recognize the benefits of accepting blame or offering an account for poor performance (Bradley, 1978). In addition, they possess the acting skills that are required to effectively use these strategies (Snyder, 1987).

ORGANIZATIONAL REWARDS

The reward systems of PSOs differ from those of other organizations. In most PSOs, there are few steps in the promotion ladder. Thus, formal rewards such as promotions and pay raises must be supplemented by informal rewards. Informal rewards may consist of recognition for performance, better client or industry assignments, or additional responsibilities.

Formal rewards are contingent upon the performance appraisals received by a member over time. Generally, a single evaluation does not elicit or prevent formal rewards. However, as members advance, the number of leaders for whom they work usually decreases, and the influence of these leaders increases. Thus, the linkage between a particular leader's performance evaluation and a member's rewards strengthens over time.

Even though a particular leader may not have total control over the formal rewards a member receives, he or she can attempt to influence behavior, to an extent, through the use of informal rewards. These informal rewards are based solely upon an individual leader's evaluation of a member's performance. As with the performance evaluation itself, a leader may use informal rewards as an IM tool aimed at the member or other leaders and members.

ORGANIZATIONAL OUTCOMES

The effect of biases on performance ratings also impacts the organization as a whole. As the frequency of divergence between leader and member attributions and expected and actual evaluations increases, members perceive an inadequacy in the link between performance and rewards. Such a perception could lead to lower performance and increased IM, thereby causing the PSO to perform suboptimally.

If the performance appraisal does not actually reflect member performance, the distribution of rewards and punishment will be dysfunctional. Improper reward allocations result in the suboptimal use of firm resources. Undeserved pay raises waste resources. Poor promotion decisions or client/industry assignments cost the firm revenue and reduce efficiency. Improper punishment can lead to learned helplessness. Helpless employees display motivational deficits that decrease organizational efficiency and waste resources (Martinko and Gardner, 1987).

Because of its "survival of the fittest" environment, a PSO must eventually separate from many of its employees. However, if separation occurs too soon, it can be very costly to the PSO. Whether premature separation is due to improper termination or unwarranted behavior that results in the member's resignation, biases have resulted in a suboptimal use of resources.

CORRECTIVE STRATEGIES

A unique supervisory structure and absentee management are inherent attributes of the PSO. Thus, strategies to improve the accuracy of performance evaluations and strengthen the perceived link between member behavior and rewards must be developed around these organizational characteristics.

Many times, differences in the attributions of leaders and members can be settled via verbal exchanges. Members should explain job-related problems they encounter through regular communications with leaders and during performance reviews. Leaders should listen to members who use defensive IM tactics such as justifications, accounts, excuses, or apologies (Braaten et al., 1993; Schlenker, 1980; Martinko and Gardner, 1987) to explain poor performance. Although these explanations may not always be valid or satisfactory, they can provide the leader with insights into the situation affecting performance, as well as the member.

The performance appraisal itself should be written and the outcome of the interview documented. This provides formal data that is useful in determining rewards and punishment. It also protects both the leader and member from later discrepancies. In fairness to the member, it may be useful to allow him or her to respond in writing, thus providing supplementary information for those decision makers who allocate rewards and punishment (Martinko and Gardner, 1987).

A final suggestion for improving performance evaluations and avoiding dysfunctional behavior is the use of attribution training. Such training for both leaders and members increases their awareness of biases and reduces rating errors (Martinko and Gardner, 1987). Additional training to educate leaders about IM behavior and its potential influence on performance evaluations would also help reduce impression bias (Wayne and Kacmar, 1991).

Unfortunately, much of the literature on IM has cast such behavior as an illicit, manipulative attempt to induce desired outcomes. Indeed, IM has primarily been described as an impairment to organizational success in the preceding discussion. However, IM behaviors need not be deceptive (Schlenker, 1980) or damaging. Liden and Mitchell (1988) propose that IM behaviors can be used by leaders and members to influence their exchanges. Members that employ IM behavior tend to develop more open and interactive exchanges with leaders (Wayne and Kacmar, 1991). As such, it seems plausible that IM can also help overcome some of the barriers posed by the PSO's organizational environment.

CONCLUSIONS

The model presented is not intended to fully detail the leader/member exchange or IM processes, since these have been discussed in detail by other researchers. Rather, the model highlights the linkages between these processes within a particular organizational setting. Still, many of the propositions advanced may be readily extended to research in other organizational settings.

Knowledge of the possible effects of member IM on leaders' attributions and performance appraisals could assist managers in reducing the impact of impression bias. Further, the effect of the organizational environment on performance evaluations has probably been underestimated. Again, awareness of these influences may encourage managers to develop useful approaches to working around these barriers. Ultimately, such approaches could serve to improve relations between leaders and members, while reducing the prevalence of many suboptimal and dysfunctional behaviors.

The mid-range theory outlined in this chapter describes the performance evaluation process in PSOs and points toward potential barriers to pure performance-based evaluations. As far as can be determined, this process has not been explored by researchers in the past. Before the problems of performance evaluation faced in practice are addressed, the nature of these problems must be understood. Future research should now be aimed toward empirical validation of the propositions generated and the development of methods to improve the performance evaluation process in PSOs.

REFERENCES

Baumeister, R.F. and Jones, E.E. (1978). When self-presentation is constrained by the target's knowledge: Consistency and compensation. *Journal of Personality and Social Psychology,* 36:608–618.

Bohra, K.A. and Pandey, J. (1984). Ingratiation toward strangers, friends, and bosses. *Journal of Social Psychology,* 112:217–222.

Borman, W.C. (1974). The rating of individuals in organizations: An alternate approach. *Organizational Behavior and Human Performance,* 12:105–124.

Braaten, D.O., Cody, M.J., and DeTienne, K.B. (1993). Account episodes in organizations: Remedial work and impression management. *Management Communication Quarterly,* 6:219–250.

Bradley, G.W. (1978). Self-serving biases in the attribution process: A reexamination of the fact or fiction question. *Journal of Personality and Social Psychology,* 36:56–71.

Cardy, R.L. and Dobbins, G.H. (1986). Affect and appraisal accuracy: Liking as an integral dimension in evaluating performance. *Journal of Applied Psychology,* 71:672–678.

Cialdini, R.B. (1989). Indirect tactics of image management: Beyond basking. in *Impression Management in the Organization,* R.A. Giacalone and P. Rosenfeld (Eds.), Hillsdale, N.J.: Lawrence Erlbaum, pp. 45–56.

Dowell, B.E. and Wexley, K.N. (1978). Development of a work-behavior taxonomy for first-line supervisors. *Journal of Applied Psychology,* 63:563–572.

Fandt, P.M. and Ferris, G.R. (1990). The management of information and impressions: When employees behave opportunistically. *Organizational Behavior and Human Decision Processes,* 45:140–158.

Farh, J.L. and Dobbins, G.H. (1989). Effects of self-esteem on leniency bias in self-reports of performance: A structural equation model analysis. *Personnel Psychology,* 42:835–850.

Feldman, J.M. (1981). Beyond attribution theory: Cognitive processes in performance evaluation. *Journal of Applied Psychology,* 66:127–148.

Festinger, L. (1954). A theory of social comparison processes. *Human Relations,* 7:117–140.

Gardner, W.L. (1992). Lessons in organizational dramaturgy: The art of impression management. *Organizational Dynamics,* 21(1):33–46.

Gardner, W.L. and Martinko, M.J. (1988). Impression management in organizations. *Journal of Management,* 14:321–338.

Gioia, D.A. and Sims, H.P., Jr. (1986). Cognition-behavior connections: Attributional and verbal behavior in leader–subordinate interactions. *Organizational Behavior and Human Decision Processes,* 37:197–229.

Green, S.G. and Mitchell, T.R. (1979). Attributional processes of leader–member interactions. *Organizational Behavior and Human Performance,* 23:429–458.

Greenberg, J. (1984). Inflated Performance Evaluations as a Self-Serving Bias, working paper, Columbus: Ohio State University.

Hansen, R.D. and Lowe, C.A. (1976). Distinctiveness and consensus: The influence of behavioral information on actors' and observers' attributions. *Journal of Personality and Social Psychology,* 34:425–433.

Jones, E.E. and Nisbett, R.E. (1972). The actor and the observer: Divergent perceptions of the causes of behavior. in *Attribution: Perceiving the Causes of Behavior,* E.E. Jones, D.E. Kanouse, H.H. Kelley, R.E. Nisbett, S. Valins, and B. Weiner (Eds.), Morristown, N.J.: General Learning Press.

Jones, E.E. and Pittman, T.S. (1982). Toward a general theory of strategic self-presentation. in *Psychological Perspectives on the Self,* Vol. 1, J. Suls (Ed.), Hillsdale, N.J.: Erlbaum, pp. 231–262.

Kaplan, S.E. and Reckers, P.M.J. (1993). An examination of the effects of accountability tactics on performance evaluation judgements in public accounting. *Behavioral Research in Accounting,* 5:101–123.

Kelley, H. H. (1973). The process of causal attribution. *American Psychologist,* 28:107–128.

Leary, M.R. and Kowalski, R.M. (1990). Impression management: A literature review and two-component model. *Psychological Bulletin,* 107:34–47.

Liden, R.C. and Mitchell, T.R. (1988). Ingratiatory behaviors in organizational settings. *Academy of Management Review,* 13:572–587.

Martinko, M.J. (1991). Future directions: Toward a model for applying impression management strategies in the work-place. in *Applied Impression Management: How Image-Making Affects Managerial Decisions,* R.A. Giacalone and P. Rosenfeld (Eds.), Newbury Park, Calif.: Sage Publications, pp. 259–277.

Martinko, M.J. and Gardner, W.L. (1987). The leader/member attribution process. *Academy of Management Review,* 12:235–249.

Neuberg, S.L. and Fiske, S.T. (1987). Motivational influences on impression formation: Outcome dependency, accuracy-driven attention, and individuating processes. *Journal of Personality and Social Psychology,* 53:431–444.

Podsakoff, P.M. (1982). Determinants of supervisor's use of rewards and punishments: A literature review and suggestion for further research. *Organizational Behavior and Human Performance,* 29:58–83.

Ralston, D.A. (1985). Employee ingratiation: The role of management. *Academy of Management Review,* 10:477–487.

Ross, L. (1977). The intuitive psychologist and his shortcomings: Distortions in the attribution process. in *Advances in Experimental Social Psychology,* L. Berkowitz (Ed.), New York: Academic Press, pp. 174–220.

Schlenker, B.R. (1975). Self-presentation: Managing the impression of consistency when reality interferes with self-enhancement. *Journal of Personality and Social Psychology,* 32:1030–1037.

Schlenker, B.R. (1980). *Impression Management: The Self-Concept, Social Identity, and Interpersonal Relations,* Monterey, Calif.: Brooks/Cole.

Schlenker, B.R. and Weigold, M. (1992). Interpersonal processes involving impression regulation and management. *Annual Review of Psychology,* 43:133–168.

Schneider, D.J. (1981). Tactical self-presentation: Toward a broader conception. in *Impression Management Theory and Social Psychological Research,* J.T. Tedeschi (Ed.), New York: Academic Press, pp. 23–40.

Schneider, D.J. (1991). Social cognition. *Annual Review of Psychology,* 42:527–561.

Snyder, M. (1987). *Public Appearances/Private Realities: The Psychology of Self-Monitoring,* San Francisco: W.H. Freeman.

Taylor, S. and Koivumaki, J. (1976). The perception of self and others: Acquaintanceship, affect, and actor–observer differences. *Journal of Personality and Social Psychology,* 33:403–408.

Tedeschi, J.T. and Melburg, V. (1984). Impression management and influence in the organization. in *Research in the Sociology of Organizations,* S.B. Bacharach and E.J. Lawler (Eds.), Greenwich, Conn.: JAI Press, pp. 31–58.

Tedeschi, J.T. and Norman, N. (1985). Social power, self-presentation, and the self. in *The Self and Social Life,* B.R. Schlenker (Ed.), New York: McGraw-Hill, pp. 293–322.

Tsui, A.S. and Barry, B. (1986). Interpersonal affect and rating errors. *Academy of Management Journal,* 29:586–599.

Villanova, P. and Bernardin, H.J. (1989). Impression management in the context of performance appraisal. in *Impression Management in the Organization,* R.A. Giacalone and P. Rosenfeld (Eds.), Hillsdale, N.J.: Lawrence Erlbaum, pp. 299–313.

Wayne, S.J. and Ferris, G.R. (1990). Influence tactics, affect, and exchange quality in supervisor–subordinate interactions: A laboratory experiment and field study. *Journal of Applied Psychology,* 75:487–499.

Wayne, S.J. and Kacmar, K.M. (1991). The effects of impression management on the performance appraisal process. *Organizational Behavior and Human Decision Processes,* 48:70–88.

Weiner, B. and Kukla, A. (1970). An attributional analysis of achievement motivation. *Journal of Personality and Social Psychology,* 15:1–20.

Weiner, B., Frieze, I., Kukla, A., Reed, L., Rest, S., and Rosenbaum, R.M. (1971). Perceiving the causes of success and failure. in *Attribution: Perceiving the Causes of Behavior,* E.E. Jones, D.E. Kanouse, H.H. Kelley, R.E. Nisbett, S. Valins, and B. Weiner (Eds.), Morristown, N.J.: General Learning Press.

Wood, R.E. and Mitchell, T.R. (1981). Manager behavior in a social context: The impact of impression management on attributions and disciplinary actions. *Organizational Behavior and Human Performance,* 28:356–378.

Wortman, C.B. and Linsenmeier, J.A.W. (1977). Interpersonal attraction and techniques of ingratiation in organizational settings. in *New Directions in Organizational Behavior,* B.W. Staw and G.R. Salancik (Eds.), Chicago: St. Clair, pp. 133–178.

Wright, T.L. and Ingraham, L.R. (1986). Partners and relationships influence self-perceptions of self-disclosure in naturalistic interactions. *Journal of Personality and Social Psychology,* 50:631–635.

11

THE ROLE OF COGNITIVE LOAD IN SUPERVISOR ATTRIBUTIONS OF SUBORDINATE BEHAVIOR*

Karen J. Maher

ABSTRACT

This chapter presents a theoretical argument for investigating the cognitive processes that are involved in supervisor perceptions of subordinates. It is argued that supervisor perceptions involve a complex interplay of categorization processes and attributions that contribute to the quality of leader–member exchanges. These cognitive processes contribute to the stability of leader–member exchange quality over time, in part because cognitive load prevents perceivers from engaging in thorough attributional analyses. The literature on supervisor categorization and attributions is discussed, followed by an integration of the construct of cognitive load and a discussion of contextual factors that moderate the effects of cognitive load on attributions.

*The author acknowledges the valuable comments of Dennis Dossett and three anonymous reviewers on an earlier version of this manuscript.

INTRODUCTION

The importance of supervisor attributions of subordinates in supervisor–subordinate relationships has been well-documented in the literature (e.g., Mitchell et al., 1981; Mitchell and Kalb, 1982). Supervisor attributions for subordinate performance are critical because they influence supervisor behavior toward the subordinate (Green and Liden, 1980). Green and Mitchell (1979) identified several moderators of the supervisor attribution process, including the quality of the relationship between supervisor and subordinate. However, with some exceptions (Dienesch and Liden, 1986; Wilhelm et al., 1993), there has been surprisingly little work integrating supervisor attributions with the quality of the relationship between supervisor and subordinate. One useful means of operationalizing the nature of the relationship between supervisor and subordinate is leader–member exchange (LMX) (Dansereau et al., 1975). It is argued that there is an important linkage between LMX exchange quality and attributions made by supervisors.

The purpose of this chapter is to further explicate the theoretical linkage between LMX processes and attributions in supervisor–subordinate relationships through the construct of cognitive load. To fully understand how LMX and supervisor attributions are linked, one must understand the cognitive processes that underlie both LMX perceptions and attributions; the concept of cognitive load can contribute to our understanding of these cognitive processes (Maher, 1991). Briefly, when a perceiver's cognitive resources are tapped or engaged, the perceiver is said to be under cognitive load. Cognitive load makes it more difficult for perceivers to engage in controlled processing of information.

A theoretical argument for the important role of cognitive load in supervisor attributions of subordinates is presented in this chapter. First, the literature integrating supervisor attributions and LMX is briefly reviewed. Space precludes a detailed review of the LMX literature, but the reader is referred to Liden et al. (1993) for a recent review of this literature. Next, research on cognitive load and its relevance to supervisor–subordinate relationships is discussed. Several contextual factors that may influence the amount of cognitive load perceivers experience are presented. Theoretical and research implications are then discussed.

CATEGORIZATIONS AND ATTRIBUTIONS IN LEADER–MEMBER EXCHANGES

It must be noted that the term LMX is used broadly in this chapter. LMX in this context does not refer to the construct as typically operationalized through specific measurement scales, as this construct has been criticized

(Dienesch and Liden, 1986). Instead, LMX refers to the general process of categorization that occurs in supervisor–subordinate interaction. It is useful to frame these categorization processes in terms of ingroup and outgroup labels (LMX).

The cognitive perspective presented here is based in part on categorization theory, particularly the research conducted on leadership perceptions based on subordinate categorization of superiors (Lord et al., 1984). The implications of the categorization process are relevant to the task, job, and career outcomes of leader–subordinate interaction. When an individual is categorized, much subsequent information that is encountered will be processed in terms of that category. The process of categorization, then, provides powerful cognitive structures that shape the nature of interactions among people.

Such a categorization process also operates with leader perceptions of subordinates (Feldman, 1986; Lord and Maher, 1991). Feldman suggested that at the beginning of a relationship, a leader categorizes a subordinate. This categorization leads to the formation of expectations that are consistent with the impression of the subordinate that has been initially formed. High expectations may lead to more challenging assignments, promotions, etc., and low expectations of the subordinate may lead to fewer opportunities and more distant relationships. Such a categorization process, then, can lead to different LMX relationships and the ingroup/outgroup segmentation documented by Graen and his colleagues (e.g., Graen et al., 1982).

In short, theoretical work suggests that supervisors categorize subordinates into ingroup or outgroup status. This categorization process has important implications for the quality of the LMX. Graen's work has shown that once workers are labeled as ingroup or outgroup members, these labels are likely to persist and affect subordinates' task and career opportunities. Of course, these labels are often correct; supervisors attach labels to subordinates that veridically reflect job performance. However, incorrect categorizations may become supported by expectations for behavior that become self-fulfilling prophecies, as supervisors communicate their expectations to subordinates and, in turn, subordinates respond to these expectations (Darley and Fazio, 1980).

One mechanism that enables these labels to persist over time is the attribution process. Supervisors make attributions that are consistent with their label of subordinates (Wilhelm et al., 1993). Attributions also provide a critical linkage between perceptions and behavior. Supervisor attributions serve as mediators between the behavior of the subordinate and the behavior of the supervisor (Green and Mitchell, 1979; Martinko and Gardner, 1987). Considerable research shows that supervisor attributions differ depending on the subordinate's behavior and that supervisor attributions for an employee's behavior influence the supervisor's behavior toward that employee. These attributions are an integral part of the process that leads supervisors to view subordinates in different ways.

In other words, supervisor attributions are a function of the LMX relationships supervisors have with their subordinates.

Attributions and categorizations both serve as inputs to LMX development (Dienesch and Liden, 1986). Different LMX relationships (ingroup versus outgroup) are cognitive categories that serve to guide subsequent perceptions of the subordinate. A study by Heneman et al. (1989) supports these assertions. These authors found that when subordinate performance was effective, internal attributions for ability and effort were higher for ingroup members than for outgroup members. When performance was ineffective, supervisors made more internal attributions for performance to outgroup members than ingroup members. Most recently, Wilhelm et al. (1993) found that supervisors tend to attribute high inputs by ingroup subordinates to internal factors and low inputs to external factors. In contrast, supervisors tend to attribute high inputs by outgroup subordinates to external factors and low inputs to internal factors.

Martin and Klimoski (1990) provide a further empirical link between categorization processes and attributions. In a field study, they found that attributional processes were different depending on whether the initial evaluation for a subordinate was positive or negative. If an employee was given a positive evaluation, supervisors often discounted negative behavioral episodes. On the other hand, if an employee was given a negative evaluation, negative behavioral episodes were used to help form the negative impression. These findings suggest that certain types of attributions are closely tied to a supervisor's categorization of a subordinate. Thus, categorization is a powerful mechanism that incorporates attributions for performance that are consistent with the category label.

Causal attributions, then, are related to ingroup and outgroup categories with different types of attributions connected to each type of categorization. The type of relationship that exists between managers and subordinates can influence the attributions that are made for subordinate performance. Attribution theory provides a partial basis for explaining the process of LMX development and, in particular, how perceptions consistent with the LMX are maintained over time.

Given that the quality of the LMX remains stable over time (Dansereau et al., 1975; Liden et al., 1993, Wakabayashi, et al., 1988), it is argued that attributions play a large role in this stability. As attributions are made that are consistent with an LMX category, the category label becomes even stronger as consistent information is added. One could speculate that it is not the behavior of the subordinate that is stored in memory, but the supervisor's attribution (judgment) for the behavior. Thus, attributions may be made automatically that are consistent with a category label, precluding careful causal analysis of behavior.

Despite the significant contribution of attribution theory to our understanding of the leader–subordinate interaction process, many models do not take into account the role of automaticity that is an integral part of the perceptual process.

Much of the attribution theory research is based on a rational model of information processing, derived from Kelley's (1973) causal attribution framework. Rational models have been increasingly criticized (e.g., Lord and Maher, 1990; Mitchell and Beach, 1990) in that they are often not descriptively accurate. It is argued here that leader–subordinate interactions often involve such an automatic component. Supervisors may categorize subordinates in terms of ingroups and outgroups, and these categorizations persist over time, along with attributions that are consistent with category labels, because these processes require fewer cognitive resources and proceed relatively automatically.

In summary, evidence exists which shows that LMX quality is related to differential attributions by supervisors. However, there is a need to explore further the automatic cognitive processes that contribute to supervisor attributions. It is suggested here that supervisors' perceptions of subordinates, which are the result of categorization and attribution processes, are influenced by cognitive load. Gilbert and his colleagues provide a compelling integration of attributional analysis processes and the influence of cognitive load on these processes (e.g., Gilbert et al., 1988a, 1988b). Their work explains how some types of attributions are processed more automatically than other attributions.

GILBERT'S MODEL OF THE ATTRIBUTION PROCESS

Gilbert et al. (1988b) suggest that person perception consists of three phases: categorization (identifying actions), characterization (drawing dispositional or internal inferences about the target person), and correction (adjusting dispositional inferences with information about situational constraints). These authors argue that both categorization and characterization are more automatic than the correction process. Correction is a relatively controlled process that uses a significant portion of a perceiver's processing resources (Gilbert et al., 1988b). When processing resources are available, correction is more likely to occur. When processing resources are relatively unavailable, perceivers are said to be under cognitive load, and correction is less likely to occur. Because correction is less automatic, the ability of perceivers to use situational constraint information in the judgment process is decreased under conditions of cognitive load. Therefore, perceivers rely primarily on dispositional cues when making attributions for behavior. This phenomenon is also called overattribution bias in the literature (Webster, 1993).

There is considerable empirical support for these assertions. Gilbert et al. (1988b) tested these propositions in a laboratory experiment. Subjects were asked to observe the nonverbal behavior of a videotaped target person engaged in a conversation while appearing anxious and worried. Cognitive load was manipulated by having subjects rehearse and memorize information about the topics the target was ostensibly discussing while they viewed the tape. These discussion topics served as situational constraints on the target's behavior. Half of the subjects were told the target was discussing anxiety-inducing topics, while the other half were told the target was discussing relaxation-inducing topics. Results of this study showed that subjects who were not under cognitive load used the situational constraint information (topic) to make trait judgments. In other words, subjects who were not under cognitive load rated the target as more dispositionally anxious when the topic was relaxation-inducing and rated the target less dispositionally anxious when the discussion topic was anxiety-inducing. Subjects who were under cognitive load (those who rehearsed the discussion topics while viewing the tape) did not use the situational constraint information in forming trait judgments of the target. These subjects rated the target as equally anxious whether discussing anxiety-inducing topics or relaxation-inducing topics.

Gilbert et al. (1988b) also showed that cognitive load can be increased by engaging subjects' self-regulatory processes. Subjects listened to an audio tape of a target person giving a speech and manipulated load by telling subjects they would be writing and presenting a speech themselves. This type of load manipulation was intended to cause subjects to engage in self-regulatory behavior, an activity that would tap cognitive resources. Subjects were informed that the person delivering the speech they were about to hear was told which side of the issue to defend. These instructions served as the situational constraint information; believing that the speaker on the audio tape was told which stance to take should have led subjects to conclude that the speaker was really less in agreement with the issue. Results indicated that subjects under cognitive load were more likely to rate the target's traits as being consistent with the views presented in the speech, despite the fact subjects were informed that the target was told which side of the issue to defend. These basic findings were replicated by Gilbert et al. (1988a) using self-regulation of eye movements and false ingratiation as manipulations of cognitive load in two separate studies.

Osborne and Gilbert (1992) proposed that anticipated interaction with another person would also induce cognitive load on perceivers, because their resources would be tapped by preparing for the interaction. The logic against this argument suggests that engaging in an interaction makes inferential errors more costly, and so perceivers would be more likely to seek and make use of all attribution-relevant information. However, the general finding from this series of three experiments was that subjects who engaged in the most self-regulatory efforts made the least attributional correction.

Of particular interest are the ways self-regulation was operationalized in these experiments. Subjects were led to believe they would interact with a target person after they viewed the target on a videotape. Some subjects were told they would be interviewing the target (load manipulation), while others were told they would be interviewed by the target. Subjects in the second experiment were told they would interact with a target; half were given a familiar goal (ingratiate the target) or an unfamiliar goal (disgratiate the target). The latter served as the load inducement. In the third experiment, subjects were told they would interact with either a disabled individual who uses a wheelchair (load manipulation) or a nondisabled target.

In all three experiments, subjects under cognitive load were less able to make situational attributions; they instead made more dispositional attributions for the target's behavior. These experimental manipulations of cognitive load have parallels with situations perceivers might encounter in everyday circumstances. Supervisors, in particular, might be expected to anticipate interviewing a prospective employee, giving negative feedback to a subordinate in a performance review, or interacting with disabled individuals or other "different" individuals where self-regulation might be expected to be high. Each of these situations could increase the amount of self-regulation in which supervisors engage, thereby minimizing their ability to consider relevant situational information in their judgments of targets.

In another study, Gilbert and Hixon (1991) concluded, contrary to conventional wisdom, that cognitive load may actually decrease the likelihood that a stereotype is activated. However, they also found that cognitive load can increase the likelihood that a stereotype, once activated, will be used to interpret information. The implication is that supervisors who have already classified subordinates into ingroup or outgroup status may be more inclined to use the category in subsequent perceptions and make corresponding dispositional attributions.

In summary, the finding that cognitively busy perceivers are less likely to make situational attributions for a target's behavior has been replicated across several studies conducted by Gilbert and his colleagues and appears to be a generalizable phenomenon. Their results have been replicated using a variety of tasks and under several different operationalizations of cognitive load. Taken together, these studies show that when perceivers are under high cognitive load, the correction phase in which situational attributions are made is less likely to occur. This finding suggests that careful attributional analysis by observers does not always occur because observers lack the cognitive resources to do so. If, under some circumstances, explicit causal analysis is circumvented, attributional frameworks such as Green and Mitchell's (1979) and Martinko and Gardner's (1987) models of leader–member attributions may be less helpful. Neither of these models, although acknowledging the role of relatively automatic attributional processes, fully explains why attributions over time are consistent with a cognitive category.

The implication for the quality of supervisor–subordinate relationships is that those who label individuals initially as ingroup or outgroup members (and who are cognitively busy) will fail to correct for situational constraints on performance. These perceivers will be more likely to make dispositional attributions for both success and failure, consistent with category labels. Those who are not cognitively busy when making initial categorizations may correct and allow for situational explanations for behavior.

Cognitive load may influence initial impressions and interpretations of behavior that immediately follow these first impressions, but an obvious argument to the line of thinking presented here is that over time supervisors will make attributions that more accurately reflect the subordinate's true performance level (Fedor and Rowland, 1989). In other words, perceivers are not always under cognitive load. Why can't perceivers then correct their impressions at times when their cognitive resources are not being tapped?

Consistent with this logic, Gilbert and Osborne (1989) did find that busy subjects are able to correct their causal ascriptions if given the opportunity to reflect on the stimulus material. However, these authors also suggest that in some cases subsequent corrective thought cannot reverse the effects of cognitive load on perceptions. They found that subjects, even after correcting for an inappropriate dispositional attribution, continued to make trait judgments that were consistent with the original characterization of the target. Similar findings were obtained for subjects who continued to be under cognitive load; they could not correct at a later time (Osborne and Gilbert, 1992).

Cognitive Load and Schema-Consistent Processing

Such findings are consistent with the literature on self-fulfilling prophecy and expectancy confirmation, which points to the powerful influence of initial impressions on subsequent perceptions. Darley and Gross (1983) found that subjects who agreed that information received was insufficient to make judgments of a target's academic ability nevertheless allowed the insufficient information to influence subsequent ratings of the target. Subjects allowed their initial impressions of the target to influence subsequent attributions and judgments despite an admitted lack of basis for judgment. Darley and Gross concluded that once a hypothesis is formulated, cognition is biased toward its confirmation.

These findings are consistent with the suggestion made by Lord and Smith (1983) that attributions may follow, rather than precede, information that has been automatically encoded. The automatic encoding of information using categorization processes may then bias any correction processes. In other words, a perceiver's initial categorization of a target influences encoding of subsequent information so that it interferes with correction processes. This process exemplifies what Srull and Wyer (1989) term *cognitive bolstering:* perceivers tend to review behaviors that are consistent with the label or overall concept of a person to confirm the validity of that label. Inability to correct is also consistent with literature, which shows that the processing of schema-consistent information takes fewer cognitive resources than schema-inconsistent processing (Fiske and Neuberg, 1990; Wilson et al., 1989). Thus, perceivers who lack the resources to allow situational information to influence judgments may be more likely to process information in a schema-consistent fashion. Recall that Heneman et al. (1989) found that perceivers were likely to make attributions for behavior that were consistent with the category label associated with a subordinate. That is, perceivers were more likely to make attributional judgments in a schema-consistent fashion.

From a broader perspective, these findings illustrate the pervasive consequences of on-line versus memory-based, processing (Hastie and Park, 1986). There is no simple, direct relationship between judgment and memory; perceivers can recall information that is not necessarily used to form judgments. Judgments occur spontaneously with perception, and the judgment is stored in memory, thereby affecting subsequent judgments. Even if, subsequent to initial classification, perceivers are allowed time to consider situational constraints on a target's behavior, the original dispositional attribution may persist and influence subsequent judgments about the target. It may be the case that processing capacity at the time of encoding is the most important determinant of subsequent judgments. Such a process may be particularly significant in LMXs, because initial impressions, whether accurate or inaccurate, may affect LMX quality, which can influence a subordinate's career progression and other important dyadic outcomes.

It seems, then, that the failure to correct for situational influences on behavior may have its most powerful effect at the beginning of the perceptual process, i.e., on the attributions that are made concurrently with initial categorization. Through the process of self-fulfilling prophecy and confirmation bias, these perceptions continue over time. In addition, however, there are a variety of contextual factors that contribute to the likelihood that cognitive load will have a greater long-term effect on perceptions. These factors are discussed in the following section.

CONTEXTUAL FACTORS CONTRIBUTING TO COGNITIVE LOAD

Despite the argument that initial categorization processes and attributions contribute to the quality of the LMX, it is possible for supervisors to revise their perceptions over time as they encounter repeated examples of information inconsistent with their initial impressions. By this time, however, the interaction norms between supervisor and subordinate may be so entrenched that the type of LMX relationship continues. In this section, several factors are described that may contribute to the stability of LMX through their influence on cognitive load.

These can be classified in terms of structural factors, individual differences, and motivational factors.

Structural Factors

One structural factor that may have an influence on the stability of supervisors' perceptions of their subordinates is power. Fiske (1993) presents a compelling argument that there is an interaction between power and stereotyping. The focus of Fiske's argument is on racial and gender stereotypes, but her comments apply equally well to cases of supervisor classifications of ingroups and outgroups.

Fiske (1993) suggests that those who have power in organizations do not pay attention to those without power. Supervisors, of course, have at least legitimate power over their subordinates and, most likely, other sources of power as well. Power holders do not pay attention to those without power for several reasons. First, those with power simply have more demands on their attention than those without power. Thus, managers are in positions in which their cognitive resources are being tapped to a greater extent, resulting in their perceptions remaining consistent over time. Second, Fiske argues that those in positions of power simply do not need to pay attention because their fates do not depend on those under them in the hierarchy. Power holders are thus able to engage in more superficial processing because attention is generally directed upward in the hierarchy, not downward. Finally, Fiske suggests that those who have many subordinates will pay less attention. Thus, a supervisor's span of control may also contribute to LMX stability over time. Those with a large span of control are less able to pay attention to their subordinates than those with a smaller span of control.

In short, there are several ways that power can increase the amount of cognitive load that is experienced on a daily basis by supervisors. This makes it likely that supervisors will make attributions that are consistent with initial categorizations. Moreover, subordinates may lack the social power necessary to change leaders' perceptions of them if these perceptions are inaccurate.

Individual Differences

There are several factors relating to individual difference that may also affect the amount of cognitive load experienced by perceivers. Fiske (1993), in addition to the structural factors outlined above, suggests that a supervisor's personal need for power and dominance may be a factor in perpetuating stereotypes of others. She argues that people with a high need for dominance tend to ignore stereotype-discrepant information and attend to information that is confirming.

An additional variable that influences correction processes is the individual's need for cognitive closure (Webster, 1993). Cognitive closure is defined as confident knowledge on a topic as opposed to ambiguity about that topic. This construct lies on a continuum ranging from a strong need for closure to a strong need to avoid closure. According to Webster, those with high need for closure should be less likely to adjust their perceptions for situational information and instead should "freeze" on the original dispositional attribution. Consistent information will be processed because it may help perceivers maintain their closure. Webster found that subjects high in need for closure tended to make quicker decisions and spent less time and thought on the task than those high in need to avoid closure. Those who are reluctant to commit to an opinion may have fewer overattribution effects. A possible implication is that more extreme LMX categorizations (very high or very low) could lead to greater overattribution because the supervisor has already committed to a strong view of the subordinate.

Another set of factors that have to do with individual difference is related to self-regulatory processes. Recall that Osborne and Gilbert (1992) found that the more self-regulatory processes engaged in by perceivers, the less likely they were to correct for situational explanations for behavior. One measure that is relevant here is self-consciousness—the tendency to direct attention inward or outward (Fenigstein et al., 1975). There are three dimensions of self-consciousness: private, public, and social anxiety. Private self-consciousness involves the degree to which one's thoughts are centered around one's mood and self-awareness. Public self-consciousness refers to one's concern with others' reactions to the self as a social object, including concern about physical appearance and making a good impression. Social anxiety includes concerns with speaking in front of a group and shyness (Fenigstein et al., 1975). Those high in public self-consciousness and social anxiety may be especially likely to experience cognitive load while engaging in interactions with others, because self-regulatory processes are engaged.

Thus, there are several individual differences that may affect a supervisor's ability to consider situational information in the attribution process. Supervisors higher in need for power, need for closure, and self-consciousness may be more inclined to make category-consistent attributions. Of course, although some perceivers may be high in need for closure or high in self-consciousness, these individual differences are not strictly dispositional factors. Certain factors in the environment may heighten one's self-consciousness (Carver and Scheier, 1982; Maher, 1991) or need for closure (Webster, 1993) and thus can be experimentally manipulated.

Motivational Factors

There are also several factors that influence a perceiver's motivation to exert cognitive effort to form accurate perceptions. Stangor and McMillan (1992), in their meta-analytic review of memory for expectancy-congruent and expectancy-incongruent information, found several factors that influence a perceiver's motivation to resolve incongruity. One of these factors is the strength of the perceiver's established expectation for the target. The stronger the expectation, the less motivated the perceiver might be to carefully evaluate inconsistent information. Supervisors who have categorized subordinates into ingroups or outgroups may have stronger expectancies and may not want to exert the cognitive effort necessary for revision.

Time pressure may also make perceivers less motivated to engage in careful attributional analysis. Time pressure can increase perceivers' need for closure (Webster, 1993) and increase their tendency to commit overattribution. Fatigue may also play a role in the amount of effort perceivers are willing to expend to engage in attributional analysis (Webster, 1993). Webster also acknowledges that the pleasantness of the task may influence need for closure and therefore the amount of cognitive effort expended. Those performing an unpleasant task may be more likely to engage in a "let's get this over with" mentality (Webster, 1993, p. 262) and have a high need for closure. One can imagine supervisors who are simply not interested in exerting cognitive effort toward completing what they perceive to be an onerous annual performance review of their subordinates. It may be easier to discount inconsistent information than to revise impressions.

What these factors have in common is an underlying affective component. Perceivers simply may not "like" to encounter information inconsistent with their established views. It may not only tap cognitive resources, but it may also lead perceivers to question their initial impressions, thereby increasing the tendency to maintain their impression through self-justification processes. It also may be politically advantageous for supervisors, for example, to appear consistent in their judgments of others.

In short, perceivers tend to overrate the extent to which targets' behavior corresponds to their disposition, and often perceivers fail to adjust their impression based on situational cues, because of cognitive load. Perceivers may lack the cognitive capacity to attend to the needed information for impression revision, for example, through the structural and individual difference factors discussed above. Alternatively, if information is inconsistent, perceivers may not be motivated to incorporate that information into their existing categories. The extent to which cognitive load influences perceptions, then, may be a function of both the person and the situation.

To recapitulate the main points presented in this chapter, it is argued that there is an important link between LMX and attributions that enables LMX categorizations to remain stable over time. Cognitive load is a factor that contributes to perceptual consistency even in the face of inconsistent information. There are several factors that contribute to the amount of cognitive load that may be experienced by supervisors when making judgments of their subordi-

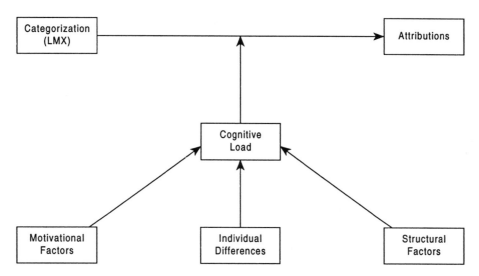

FIGURE 11.1 The role of cognitive load in LMX-related attribution.

nates. The intent of this chapter is not to argue that cognitive load is the only mechanism through which attributions contribute to LMX categorizations. However, this construct provides a starting point for studying these cognitive processes.

The relationships among the constructs discussed in this chapter are depicted in Figure 11.1. Categorizations into ingroup or outgroup status influence supervisor attributions for subordinate behavior, and this process is influenced by cognitive load. When perceivers experience cognitive load, they are less likely to make use of situational constraint information when making attributions. Individual differences, motivational factors, and structural factors all influence the amount of cognitive load experienced by perceivers.

Based on the arguments presented in this chapter, the following propositions are presented.

>**Proposition 1:** Supervisors who are under cognitive load will make more dispositional attributions for a subordinate's behavior than supervisors not under cognitive load.

>**Proposition 1a:** Dispositional attributions made by supervisors will be congruent with the initial ingroup or outgroup label.

>**Proposition 2:** Structural factors (power, span of control) will influence supervisor attributions of subordinate behavior through their influence on cognitive load.

Proposition 3: Motivational factors (strength of expectancies, time pressure, affect) will influence supervisor attributions of subordinate behavior through their influence on cognitive load.

Proposition 4: Individual differences (need for power, need for closure, self-consciousness) will influence supervisor attributions for subordinate behavior through their influence on cognitive load.

IMPLICATIONS

Research Implications

Gilbert's work on cognitive load was conducted under highly controlled laboratory conditions using primarily subjects' judgments of targets' attitudes. Researchers should transfer Gilbert's basic paradigm to supervisor–subordinate relationships in the laboratory. Although artificial, this seems to be the most appropriate first step in applying these ideas to LMX relationships. Admittedly, investigating cognitive load phenomena in field settings is problematic because it is difficult to manipulate the amount of cognitive resources available to supervisors. Perhaps the most fruitful avenue for field settings is to explore the individual difference factors described earlier in this chapter and their effects on attributions supervisors make for subordinates' behavior.

Another issue that makes the ideas presented in this chapter difficult to test empirically is the time component involved in assessing LMX relationships. To show the effects of cognitive load on LMX and associated attributions, researchers must conduct longitudinal studies. Researchers must then be prepared to measure cognitive load longitudinally as well. Further, cognitive load may play a much different role in initial impression formation than in later judgments of the target. The former may depend on relatively objective influences of load, such as performing another task at the same time as forming an impression of a target person. Motivational factors that influence the amount of cognitive resources supervisors are willing to expend, and structural factors that preclude supervisors from diverting cognitive resources to person perception, may be the more important determinants of perceptions over time.

Theoretical Implications

The view presented here is consistent with a categorization-based process of person perception and automatic processing of information. Initial impressions are powerful determinants of attribution processes and subsequent judgments. Controlled attributional analyses certainly occur, but attributions are also made automatically and may not be the mechanism that drives behavior. Rather, initial impressions, categorizations, and expectancies may be the primary determinants of behavior, with attributions serving as explanations for the categorization. In other words, attributions may serve as rationalizations for categorizations of subordinates, which can perpetuate the initial impressions of the subordinate over time. The role of automatic attributional processes in judgments of others warrants further exploration.

More research is also needed on the role of motivation factors in attributional analysis. Motivation factors may be crucial determinants of whether or not LMX categorizations persist over time despite information that is inconsistent with initial labels. Future models of supervisor attributions should consider the effect of motivation on supervisor evaluations of subordinates. Possible ways of increasing supervisor motivation to fully integrate inconsistent information should also be addressed.

Finally, although the focus of this chapter is on supervisor–subordinate relationships, the basic cognitive processes that are described are relevant in many other contexts. For example, whenever a person could be expected to engage in self-regulation, that person may be less likely to correct for situational information. Selection interviewers and recruiters may fall prey to this phenomenon if they are preoccupied with their own behavior in the interview. Power differentials between parties in selection and recruiting situations may also influence the type of attributional analysis that occurs.

REFERENCES

Carver, C. and Scheier, M. (1982). Control theory: A useful conceptual framework for personality—social, clinical, and health psychology. *Psychological Bulletin,* 92:111–135.

Dansereau, F., Graen, G., and Haga, W. (1975). A vertical dyad linkage approach to leadership within formal organizations: A longitudinal investigation of the role making process. *Organizational Behavior and Human Performance,* 13:46–78.

Darley, J. and Fazio, R. (1980). Expectancy confirmation process arising in the social interaction sequence. *American Psychologist,* 35:867–881.

Darley, J. and Gross, P. (1983). A hypothesis-confirming bias in labeling effects. *Journal of Personality and Social Psychology,* 44:20–33.

Dienesch, R. and Liden, R. (1986). Leader–member exchange model of leadership: A critique and further development. *Academy of Management Review,* 11:618–634.

Fedor, D. and Rowland, K. (1989). Investigating supervisor attributions of subordinate performance. *Journal of Management,* 15:405–416.

Feldman, J. (1986). A note on the statistical correction of halo error. *Journal of Applied Psychology,* 71:173–176.

Fenigstein, A., Scheier, M., and Buss, A. (1975). Public and private self-consciousness: Assessment and theory. *Journal of Consulting and Clinical Psychology,* 43:522–527.

Fiske, S. (1993). Controlling other people. *American Psychologist,* 48:621–628.

Fiske, S. and Neuberg, S. (1990). A continuum of impression formation, from category-based to individuating processes: Influences of information and motivation on attention and interpretation. in *Advances in Experimental Social Psychology,* Vol. 23, M. Zanna (Ed.), San Diego: Academic Press, pp. 1–74.

Gilbert, D. and Hixon, J. (1991). The trouble of thinking: Activation and application of stereotypic beliefs. *Journal of Personality and Social Psychology,* 60:509–517.

Gilbert, D. and Osborne, R. (1989). Thinking backward: Some curable and incurable consequences of cognitive busyness. *Journal of Personality and Social Psychology,* 57: 940–949.

Gilbert, D., Krull, D., and Pelham, B. (1988a). Of thoughts unspoken: Social inference and the self-regulation of behavior. *Journal of Personality and Social Psychology,* 54:685–694.

Gilbert, D., Pelham, B., and Krull, D. (1988b). On cognitive busyness: When person perceivers meet person perceived. *Journal of Personality and Social Psychology,* 54:733–740.

Graen, G., Novak, M., and Sommerkamp, P. (1982). The effects of leader–member exchange and job design on productivity and satisfaction: Testing a dual attachment model. *Organizational Behavior and Human Performance,* 30:109–131.

Green, S. and Liden, R. (1980). Contextual and attributional influences on control decisions. *Journal of Applied Psychology,* 65:453–458.

Green, S. and Mitchell, T. (1979). Attributional processes of leaders in leader–member interactions. *Organizational Behavior and Human Performance,* 23:429–458.

Hastie, R. and Park, B. (1986). The relationship between memory and judgment depends on whether the judgment task is memory-based or on-line. *Psychological Review,* 93: 258–268.

Heneman, R., Greenberger, D., and Anonyuo, C. (1989). Attributions and exchanges: The effects of interpersonal factors on the diagnosis of employee performance. *Academy of Management Journal,* 32:466–476.

Kelley, H. (1973). The processes of causal attribution. *American Psychologist,* 28:107–127.

Liden, R., Wayne, S., and Stilwell, D. (1993). A longitudinal study on the early development of leader–member exchanges. *Journal of Applied Psychology,* 78:662–674.

Lord, R. and Maher, K. (1990). Alternative information processing models and their implications for theory, research, and practice. *Academy of Management Review,* 15:9–28.

Lord, R. and Maher, K. (1991). *Leadership and Information Processing: Linking Perceptions and Performance,* New York: Routledge.

Lord, R. and Smith, J. (1983). Theoretical, information processing, and situational factors affecting attribution theory models of organizational behavior. *Academy of Management Review,* 8:50–60.

Lord, R., Foti, R., and De Vader, C. (1984). A test of leadership categorization theory: Internal structure, information processing, and leadership perceptions. *Organizational Behavior and Human Performance,* 34:343–378.

Maher, K. (1991). The Effects of Cognitive Load on Causal Attributions, Performance Ratings, Affect, and Leader–Member Exchange Quality, unpublished doctoral dissertation, Akron, Ohio: University of Akron.

Martin, S. and Klimoski, R. (1990). Use of verbal protocols to trace cognitions associated with self- and supervisor evaluations of performance. *Organizational Behavior and Human Decision Processes,* 46:135–154.

Martinko, M. and Gardner, W. (1987). The leader/member attribution process. *Academy of Management Review,* 12:235–249.

Mitchell, T. and Beach, L. (1990). "…Do I love thee? Let me count…" Toward an understanding of intuitive and automatic decision making. *Organizational Behavior and Human Decision Processes,* 47:1–20.

Mitchell, T. and Kalb, L. (1982). Effects of job experience on supervisor attributions for a subordinate's poor performance. *Journal of Applied Psychology,* 67:181–188.

Mitchell, T., Green, S., and Wood, R. (1981). An attributional model of leadership and the poor performing subordinate: Development and validation. in *Research in Organizational Behavior,* Vol. 3, B. Staw and L. Cummings (Eds.), Greenwich, N.J.: JAI Press, pp. 197–234.

Osborne, R. and Gilbert, D. (1992). The preoccupational hazards of social life. *Journal of Personality and Social Psychology,* 62:219–228.

Srull, T. and Wyer, R. (1989). Person memory and judgment. *Psychological Bulletin,* 96:58–83.

Stangor, C. and McMillan, D. (1992). Memory for expectancy-congruent and expectancy-incongruent information: A review of the social and social developmental literatures. *Psychological Bulletin,* 111:42–61.

Wakabayashi, M., Graen, G., Graen, M., and Graen, M. (1988). Japanese management progress: Mobility into middle management. *Journal of Applied Psychology,* 73:217–227.

Webster, D. (1993). Motivated augmentation and reduction of the overattribution bias. *Journal of Personality and Social Psychology,* 65:261–271.

Wilhelm, C., Herd, A., and Steiner, D. (1993). Attributional conflict between managers and subordinates: An investigation of leader–member exchange effects. *Journal of Organizational Behavior,* 14:531–544.

Wilson, T., Lisle, D., Kraft, D., and Wetzel, C. (1989). Preferences as expectation-driven inferences: Effects of affective expectations on affective experiences. *Journal of Personality and Social Psychology,* 56:519–530.

12

SUPERVISORY ATTRIBUTIONS AND EVALUATIVE JUDGMENTS OF SUBORDINATE PERFORMANCE: A FURTHER TEST OF THE GREEN AND MITCHELL MODEL*

Neal M. Ashkanasy

ABSTRACT

In this study, field supervisors' recollections of high- and low-performing subordinates were used to test the underlying propositions of the Green and Mitchell (1979) attribution model of leader–follower relations. Results supported ten out of twelve predictions relating informational cues and attributions, as well as a multivariate relationship between attributions and evaluative responses. Attributional variables were also shown to affect evaluative judgments above the direct effect of informational cues. Finally, results were interpreted as indicating that different cognitive processes are involved in evaluation of high and low levels of performance.

*The author wishes to gratefully acknowledge the assistance provided by Cindy Gallois in the design and execution of this study. The comments provided by three anonymous reviewers on an earlier draft of this manuscript are also appreciated. Finally, thanks are extended to Wendy Reid and Carolyn Alford for their assistance in coding the open-ended data.

INTRODUCTION

Calder (1977) argued that leadership is a process of social interaction and perception and should therefore be defined in terms of theories of basic social psychology such as attribution theory. One well-developed and researched model of this type is that proposed by Green and Mitchell (1979) (see Levine and Moreland, 1990). This chapter presents an application of this model to supervisors' recollections of their dealings with high- and low-performing subordinates.

The model proposed by Green and Mitchell (1979) incorporates two theoretical perspectives. The first of these is that of Weiner et al. (1971) and is based on dimensions of locus of causality and stability. These dimensions define four variables: attributions to ability (internal, stable), effort (internal, unstable), task difficulty (external, stable), and luck (external, unstable). The second theory is based on Kelley's (1971) three-dimensional informational model. This model involves a comparison of present performance with past performance (consistency), performance at other tasks (distinctiveness), and performance of others at the same task (consensus). Green and Mitchell (1979) combined the two perspectives to predict leader responses to subordinate behavior in terms of four dependent variables: (1) the leader's expectations for the subordinate's future performance, (2) the leader's aspirations for the subordinate, (3) the leader's perception of a need for closer supervision in future, and (4) the leader's behavioral response (reward or punishment). The model has been generally well supported in subsequent research (see Levine and Moreland, 1990), although it has been described as an oversimplification by Feldman (1981) and Lord and Smith (1983).

Research dealing with the Green and Mitchell (1979) model has been focused primarily on developing extensions and establishing the utility of the model across situations. Examples include Anderson (1992), Brown (1984), Brown and Mitchell (1986), Dobbins (1985), Knowlton and Mitchell (1980), Mitchell et al. (1981), Tongtharadol et al. (1991), and Wood and Mitchell (1981). The only research that has directly tested the model's underlying propositions, however, has been carried out by Ashkanasy (1989) and Ashkanasy and Gallois (1994). Ashkanasy (1989) asked subjects to respond to descriptions of hypothetical subordinate performances that varied in consistency, distinctiveness, consensus, and outcome. Results supported eleven of twelve predictions based on Kelley's (1971) principle of covariation (see Table 12.1) and a multivariate correlation between attributional and evaluative response variables. Results also indicated, however, that attributions to controllability and intentionality need to be considered (see Weiner, 1985).

In a subsequent laboratory study (Ashkanasy and Gallois, 1994), subjects

**TABLE 12.1   Predicted Effect of
Informational Cues on Causal Attributions**

Cause to which performance is attributed	Performance		
	Consistent	**Distinctive**	**Consensual**
Ability	Increase	Decrease	Decrease
Effort	Decrease	Decrease	Decrease
Task	Increase	Increase	Increase
Luck	Decrease	Increase	Decrease

Note: "Decrease" and "increase" indicate the predicted direction of effects. For example, consistent success was expected to increase attributions to ability, while consistent failure was expected to increase attributions to lack of ability.

supervised work groups composed of confederates who were cued to perform well or poorly on simple tasks. Results supported only two of the predictions listed in Table 12.1 (consistency effects on ability and luck attributions), but again provided strong support for the existence of a multivariate correlation between the attributional and evaluative variables.

The aim of the present study was to extend this program of research to field situations by an analysis of supervisors' recollections of their responses to their subordinates. The multi-method approach is important if this research program is to have practical application, and it has been adopted by other researchers in this field (e.g., Brown and Mitchell, 1986; Dobbins and Russell, 1986). By focusing on recollections, the present study addresses cognitive and memory processes and therefore provides an alternative perspective. Hurlburt and Mellencon (1987), for example, have argued that responses based on memory are implicitly different from those based on immediate perception. Nevertheless, justification for applying this perspective in the present instance has been provided by Reynolds and West (1989) and Feldman and Lynch (1988). They have shown that attributional templates, based on attitudes buried in long-term memory, play a role in organizing memory for social information. Empirical data to support this view have been obtained by Nathan and Lord (1983), who showed that cognitive categorization was responsible for halo effects in performance rating. Finally, Martin and Klimoski (1990), who examined verbal protocols in performance evaluation, found that memory retrieval could be more influential than the objective facts in shaping supervisors' judgments.

In the present study, therefore, it was expected that elements of the Green and Mitchell model would be reflected in supervisors' recollections of their judgments of subordinate behavior. Consistent with the model, variables were treated in three groups. Group 1 variables (informational cues) consist of ratings of subordinate performance in the present instance (or target performance), of the subordinate's record of performance on the same and other tasks, and of others' performance on the same task (Kelley, 1971). Group 2 (attribution) variables comprise the four attribution variables originally proposed by Weiner et al. (1971), together with the two additional dimensions (controllability, intentionality) defined by Weiner (1985). Group 3 (evaluation) variables consist of those defined in Green and Mitchell (1979): expectations for future performance, aspirations for the subordinate, need for close supervision in the future, and rewarding or punishing response. It was expected that evidence would be forthcoming to support the pattern of predictions listed in Table 12.1 (which define relationships between Group 1 and Group 2 variables). It was further expected that support would be found for a multivariate canonical relationship between Group 2 and Group 3 variables. Finally, a relationship was expected to be found between Group 2 and Group 3 variables over and above the contribution of Group 1 variables.

METHODS

Subjects

Subjects were 231 Australian workplace supervisors who worked in a variety of occupations, including education, nursing, clerical, financial and personnel administration, research, engineering, and insurance. They consisted of 131 males and 94 females (6 subjects were unspecified), with a mean age of 35.3 years (SD = 11.1). Subjects had worked, on average, 10.4 years (SD = 9.6) for their present employer, including 3.3 years (SD = 3.0) in supervisory positions, and supervised an average of 16.1 employees (SD = 21.1).

Subjects were recruited in three categories. Category 1 subjects ($n = 98$) were recruited through personal contact, direct mail, in-house distribution by firms that offered to help, and approaches by previously enlisted subjects. Category 2 subjects ($n = 79$) were mature-age, part-time psychology students, who participated in the study in order to obtain partial credit in an introductory psychology course. Category 3 subjects ($n = 54$) were employed by a large insurance company and were instructed by management to complete the questionnaire. ANOVA tests on all variables revealed no differences in responses between the three categories or across occupations.

Procedure

The study was carried out using a three-part questionnaire (described below). Questionnaires were distributed to respondents over a period of four months. Forty questionnaires were completed in group sessions. The remainder were done in the subject's time and returned by postage-paid mail. A brief outline of the study and its aims was sent to subjects who requested feedback.

Materials

The questionnaire booklet consisted of three sections: an introductory section and two sections asking for separate responses to specific incidents of subordinate performance—the first relating to poor performance and the second to high performance. The introductory section briefly explained the purpose of the study and presented a response guide for the seven-point Likert scales used in the questionnaire. Subjects were asked to provide brief demographic information and were offered mailed feedback if they supplied their name and address. (A t-test comparison of scores of the 145 subjects who were identified in this way and those who were not identified indicated no significant differences on any variable.)

Section 2 required subjects to recall a recent incident in which they had to deal with a subordinate who had performed poorly. Section 3 required subjects to recall an incident in which they had to deal with another subordinate who had performed well. In each case, subjects were asked to rate the subordinate's past performance, how the subordinate performed on other tasks, and how the subordinate's colleagues fared on the same task. This was accompanied by an open-ended section asking subjects to list the criteria they used to evaluate their subordinate's performance in this instance. Then followed a seven-point Likert-type scale that asked for a rating of the degree of high or low performance in the present instance. Following this were six Likert-type items dealing with causal explanations. These included the original four attribution variables of Weiner et al. (1971—ability, effort, task difficulty, luck—plus two additional variables suggested by Weiner (1985): controllability and intentionality. Then followed four items based on Green and Mitchell's (1979) dimensions of performance evaluation (expectation on the same task, expectation on other tasks, aspirations for the subordinate, need for close supervision). Subjects were then asked to give an indication of their actual rewarding or punishing response to the subordinate's behavior, using a behaviorally anchored seven-point scale. The scale range was from 1 (no response) to 7 (strongest possible reaction). Finally, an open-ended question asked subjects to describe their reactions using adjectives and labels.

RESULTS

Descriptive Statistics

Variables measured in the present study belong to one of three groups: Group 1: informational cues; Group 2: attribution variables; or Group 3: evaluation variables.

Group 1 variables consist of the seven-point ratings of the three informational cues of Kelley (1971)—past performance, performance on other tasks, and others' performance on the same task—followed by a rating of the subordinate's high or low performance in the present instance (or target performance). Means, standard deviations, and intercorrelations for these variables are given in Table 12.2 for both high-performing and low-performing subordinates. This table shows that subjects gave higher ratings on past performance and performance on other tasks to higher-performing subordinates. Scores for others' performances on the same task were higher for low performers than for high performers. There was also high correlation between ratings on past performance and performance on other tasks.

Group 2 variables comprise the six attribution variables (Weiner et al., 1971; Weiner, 1985). These are attributions to ability, effort, task characteristics, luck, controllability, and intentionality. Descriptive statistics for these variables are

TABLE 12.2   Means, Standard Deviations, and Intercorrelations for Informational Cues

Rating	High performance Mean	SD	Correlation[a,b] 1	2	3	4	Low performance Mean	SD
1. Target performance[c,d]	6.46	0.75	—	−0.05	−0.15	0.14	4.70	2.01
2. Past performance[d]	5.58	1.46	0.06	—	0.61	−0.09	3.67	1.87
3. Performance on other tasks[d]	6.27	0.81	0.31	0.32	—	−0.23	4.19	1.85
4. Others' performance[d]	4.51	1.78	0.01	0.19	0.05	—	5.73	1.34

Note: $n = 231$.

[a] Lower triangular matrix shows correlations for high performance; upper triangular matrix shows correlations for low performance.

[b] Critical values of r are 0.13 ($p < 0.05$) and 0.17 ($p < 0.01$).

[c] Rating is of the *degree* of high or low performance.

[d] Significant difference in mean scores across performance level.

TABLE 12.3 Means, Standard Deviations, and Intercorrelations for Attribution Variables

	High performance		Correlation[a,b]						Low performance	
	Mean	**SD**	**1**	**2**	**3**	**4**	**5**	**6**	**Mean**	**SD**
1. Ability (or lack of ability)[c,d]	6.00	1.22	—	−0.41	0.15	0.32	0.26	−0.11	3.16	2.10
2. Effort (or lack of effort)[c,d]	6.38	1.12	0.27	—	−0.18	−0.31	−0.17	0.15	5.33	2.01
3. Good (or bad) luck[d]	1.53	0.89	−0.12	−0.09	—	0.19	0.14	−0.08	1.44	0.81
4. Task easiness (or difficulty)[d]	2.12	1.37	−0.11	−0.10	0.36	—	0.39	−0.14	2.09	1.56
5. Outcome not in control	1.92	1.38	−0.09	−0.21	0.26	0.15	—	−0.11	1.71	1.25
6. Intended outcome[c]	6.26	1.06	0.15	0.07	−0.15	−0.01	−0.23	—	3.39	1.97

Note: n = 231.

[a] Lower triangular matrix shows correlations for high performance; upper triangular matrix shows correlations for low performance.

[b] Critical values of r are 0.13 (p <0.05) and 0.17 (p <0.01).

[c] Significant difference in mean scores across performance level.

[d] Text in parentheses refers to low performance.

given in Table 12.3. (Note that wording was reversed for poor performance on the first four variables.) These results demonstrate a bias toward internal attributions for high performance (see Ross, 1977), although there were no differences on external attribution (task, luck) scores across performance levels. Correlations between these variables were moderate, but generally in accord with expectations. An exception is the negative correlation between attributions for lack of ability and lack of effort for poor performance. It seems that, for poor performance, the more the outcome was attributed to lack of effort, the less it was seen to have resulted from lack of ability. For high performance, on the other hand, ability and effort were positively correlated.

Group 3 variables include five evaluative responses based on Green and Mitchell (1979): expectation on the same and other tasks, aspirations for the subordinate, need for close supervision, and rewarding/punishing response. Means, standard deviations, and intercorrelations for these variables are given in Table 12.4. As one would expect, all differences across outcome were strongly significant for these variables. Scores on all variables were correlated, although correlations between rewarding responses for high performance were relatively low.

TABLE 12.4 Means, Standard Deviations, and Intercorrelations for Evaluation Variables

	High performance		Correlation[a,b]					Low performance	
	Mean	SD	1	2	3	4	5	Mean	SD
1. Expectation on same task	6.60	0.52	—	0.77	0.59	−0.41	−0.30	4.35	2.07
2. Expectation on another task	6.37	0.71	0.53	—	0.59	−0.45	−0.28	4.81	1.75
3. Aspirations for the subordinate	6.17	1.06	0.43	0.51	—	−0.48	−0.29	3.72	1.90
4. Need for close supervision	1.91	1.13	−0.32	−0.27	−0.23	—	0.33	5.28	1.83
5. Rewarding (punishing) response[c]	4.83	1.27	0.19	0.19	0.13	−0.20	—	4.11	1.44

Note: $n = 231$. All differences in mean scores across performance level are significant.

[a] Lower triangular matrix shows correlations for high performance; upper triangular matrix shows correlations for low performance.

[b] Critical values of r are 0.13 ($p < 0.05$) and 0.17 ($p < 0.01$).

[c] Text in parentheses refers to low performance.

Open-Ended Responses

Evaluation Criteria

Frequency counts of evaluation criteria cited by subjects showed that qualitative measures of performance (good vs. bad job) were most frequently cited (25% of all criteria were in this category). Other criteria included time management (18%), face-value impressions (14%), others' evaluations (10%), adherence to procedures (8%), quantitative measures (7%), and affective response (7%). Only 10% of the criteria given included reference to Kelley-type informational cues. Overall, it appears that few subjects explicitly acknowledged the use of informational cues in forming their judgments.

Supervisor's Response to Subordinate Performance

Open-ended responses to high and low performers were coded by two assistants according to the "strength" and "concreteness" of response using seven-point scales. Inter-coder reliability was good (0.82, 0.86, respectively, for high performance, and 0.80, 0.85 for low performance), and the two variables were highly correlated ($r = 0.60$). Correlation between the mean coded measures and subjects' numerical rating of reward/punishing response, however, was only moderate (high performance: $r = 0.25$, low performance: $r = 0.18$). This result suggests that the numerical ratings on the reward/punishing response variable may reflect a subjective judgment, rather than an objective measure of outcome.

Overall, the open-ended items in the questionnaire suggest that subjects were unaware of processes of controlled categorization, believing that their evaluative judgments were formed on the basis of qualitative impressions. This finding supports Wayne and Kacmar's (1991) conclusion that impressions affect performance ratings.

Relationship Between Informational Cues and Attributions

Two-step multiple regression was used to test the hypotheses given in Table 12.1. Dependent variables for each analysis were the four attribution variables of Weiner et al. (1971). In the first step, the rating of the target performance was entered.* In the second step, the three Kelley (1971) informational cues were entered. Zero-order correlations, β-weights, and estimates of variance explained are given in Table 12.5. With the exception of effort attributions for high performance and luck attributions for low performance, a significant proportion of the variance of all the attributional variables was explained by the Kelley cues. Of the 12 predictions listed in Table 12.1, 10 were supported, either for high or low performance (or for both high and low). Overall, 13 of the 24 β-weights were significant and in the predicted direction, and there were no instances of significant effects opposite to those predicted.

Relationship Between
Attribution and Evaluation Variables

It was hypothesized that there would be a multivariate relationship between the attributional and evaluative variables. This was tested using canonical correlation for each data set.** Results are given in Table 12.6. Two canonical roots were significant for judgments of high-performing subordinates, with predictive

---

*This provided a control for halo and common method variance. Although the partialing method of controlling common method variance can be problematic when factor structures are inferred (see Podsakoff and Organ, 1986), the use of a single measure for this purpose is a statistically valid method of removing overlapping variance (see Williams and Brown, 1994). Kemery and Dunlap (1986) noted that spurious negative correlations can result, but a check of partialed and nonpartialed results found no instances of this in the present study.

**Controllability and intentionality were defined by Weiner (1985) as dimensions rather than variables. It was therefore appropriate to check and, if necessary, to control for any effect of the stability/locus variables on these dimensions (see Ashkanasy, 1989). Multiple regression on ability, effort, task difficulty/easiness, and luck resulted in $R(4,226) = 0.31$ and 0.42 for high and low performance, respectively. For intentionality, $R(4,226) = 0.21$ and 0.17. The results for controllability were significant ($p < 0.01$), while those for intentionality were marginally significant ($p < 0.05$ and $p < 0.10$, respectively). In the interest of consistency, however, it was appropriate to apply the adjustment in all cases.

TABLE 12.5   Results of Two-Step Regression of Attributions on Informational Cues

	Rating of target performance		Subordinate has a record of good past performance		Subordinate performs well on other tasks		Others perform well on this task		R^{2a}	ΔR^{2b}
	r	β	r	β	r	β	r	β		
High performance attributed to:										
Ability	0.18**	0.13*	0.16*	0.14*	0.22**	0.15*	−0.17**	−0.21**	0.11**	0.08**
Effort	0.33**	0.32**	0.04	−0.01	0.13*	0.03	0.09	0.09	0.12**	0.01
Easy task	−0.27**	−0.24**	0.04	0.08	−0.19**	−0.15*	0.13*	0.12*	0.11**	0.04*
Good luck	−0.33**	−0.28**	−0.05	0.01	−0.25**	−0.17*	0.04	0.05	0.14**	0.03*
Low performance attributed to:										
Lack of ability	−0.02	−0.04	−0.39**	−0.31**	−0.30**	−0.14*	−0.03	−0.09	0.17**	0.17**
Lack of effort	0.18**	0.16*	0.17**	0.20**	0.05	0.02	0.26**	0.26**	0.13**	0.10**
Difficult task	−0.11	−0.07	−0.09	−0.19**	0.07	0.13*	−0.23**	−0.20**	0.08**	0.07**
Bad luck	0.03	0.03	0.04	0.05	0.02	−0.01	−0.05	−0.05	0.01	0.00

Note: $* = p < 0.05$, $** = p < 0.01$.
[a] d.f. = 4226.
[b] ΔR^2 = proportion of variance explained by the Kelley (1971) informational cues.

**TABLE 12.6 Results of Canonical Analysis
of Evaluation Variables on Attribution Variables**

	High performance		Low performance	
	Root 1	Root 2	Root 1	Root 2
Canonical correlation[a]	0.99	0.39	0.98	0.45
Chi-square	1109.6	88.9	797.5	92.2
d.f.	36	25	36	25
Predictive redundancy	0.32	0.05	0.17	0.11
Canonical loadings on left-side variables (attributions)				
Ability (or lack of ability)	**0.58**	0.34	0.37	**−0.84**
Effort (or lack of effort)	**0.63**	0.17	**0.56**	**0.42**
Task easiness (or difficulty)	0.08	**0.76**	0.26	0.10
Good (or bad) luck	0.04	**0.83**	0.36	0.07
Not in control[b]	−0.03	0.01	0.01	−0.03
Intended outcome[b]	0.05	0.18	0.00	−0.31
Canonical loadings on right-side variables (evaluations)				
Expectation on same task	**0.91**	−0.29	**0.41**	**−0.83**
Expectation on another task	**0.66**	−0.28	**0.48**	**−0.69**
Aspirations for the subordinate	**0.49**	**−0.47**	0.37	**−0.82**
Need for close supervision	0.00	**0.82**	0.39	**0.78**
Rewarding (punishing) response	0.29	**−0.64**	**0.41**	**0.45**

Note: Loadings >0.40 shown in boldface type.
[a] All canonical correlations are significant ($p < 0.01$).
[b] Residual variable (see second footnote in the text).

redundancies of 0.32 and 0.05 (see Stewart and Love, 1968). The first related internal attributions to all five evaluative variables with the exception of need for supervision. The second root essentially related external attributions to perceived need for supervision.

For judgments of low performers, three roots were significant, with predictive redundancies, respectively, of 0.17, 0.11, and 0.01 (indicating that only the first two were of practical multivariate significance). The first root appears to relate effort attributions to expectations. Thus, an attribution to lack of effort resulted in a more punitive behavioral response, but was accompanied by more optimistic expectations for future performance. The second root, on the other hand, seems to have tapped the mutual exclusivity of effort and ability attributions noted earlier. In this case, attribution to a lack of effort was associated with more negative evaluative judgments, but was accompanied by a negative association with lack of ability. The implication here is that subordinates who did not perform up to their potential were the most negatively evaluated.

Contribution of Attributions Beyond Informational Cues

The final hypothesis was that attributions would significantly contribute to performance judgments beyond the contribution of the informational cues. A four-step regression model was used to test this. Variables introduced in each step were (1) the rating of the target performance, (2) the three informational cues, (3) the four attribution variables of Weiner et al. (1971), and (4) the two additional attribution dimensions suggested by Weiner (1985). Results are given in Table 12.7 for responses to high-performing subordinates and in Table 12.8 for low-performing subordinates.

Rating of target performance was included in the first step to control for halo and common method covariance (see first footnote in this chapter). It was notable that this rating accounted for up to 18% of variance for high performance, but only up to 6% for low performance, suggesting that ratings for high performance were more impressionistic than ratings for low performance. (Note that this rating was of the degree of high or low performance and followed the initial categorization of performance.) Results in respect of the second step show that evaluative responses were substantially determined by informational cues above the direct effect of performance rating (accounting for up to 46% of additional variance). Performance on other tasks was the strongest of the three cues for both high and low performance. Entry of the original four attribution variables in Step 3 resulted in significant additional explanation for expectation on the same task and rewarding response in the case of high performance, as well as a significant trend on need for supervision. The most pertinent variable was task easiness, which was positively correlated with need for supervision and negatively correlated with positive evaluative responses. In the case of low performance, on the other hand, the attribution variables resulted in significant additional explanation for ratings of expectations on the same task and aspirations for the subordinate. The variable that contributed most in this respect was lack of ability, which resulted in more negative expectations and aspirations. Finally, the two additional attribution dimensions were introduced in Step 4 as a means of controlling for the effects of the variables of Weiner et al. (1971) (see second footnote in this chapter). Results indicated that attributions of intent affected expectations for both high and low performance and aspirations for high performance, but the effects were relatively small compared to the attribution variables introduced in Step 3.

DISCUSSION

The purpose of the present research was to see if the Green and Mitchell (1979) attributional model of leadership could explain supervisors' recollections

TABLE 12.7 Results of Step-Wise Regression Analysis for High Performance

	Expectation on same task		Expectation on another task		Aspirations for subordinates		Need for close supervision		Rewarding response	
	r	β	r	β	r	β	r	β	r	β
High performance rating	0.43***	0.22***	0.38***	0.16***	0.37***	0.25***	-0.28***	-0.16***	0.18***	0.07
r^2	0.18***		0.14***		0.14***		0.08***		0.03**	
Past performance	0.18***	0.07	0.23***	0.04	0.24***	0.11	-0.14**	-0.05	0.09	0.06
Other task performance	0.44***	0.22***	0.63***	0.51***	0.46***	0.28***	-0.34***	-0.26***	0.22***	0.12
Others' performance	0.02	0.03	0.08	0.07	0.04	0.05	0.05	0.06	-0.04	-0.01
R^2	0.29***		0.44***		0.28***		0.16***		0.06***	
ΔR^2	0.11***		0.30***		0.14***		0.08***		0.03**	
High ability	0.26***	0.10	0.20***	0.03	0.26***	0.13**	-0.10	0.01	0.11	0.04
High effort	0.25***	0.08	0.17***	0.01	0.13**	-0.05	-0.06	0.03	0.05	-0.01
Easy task	-0.23***	-0.04	-0.17***	0.01	-0.17***	-0.05	0.26***	0.16***	-0.31***	-0.28***
Good luck	-0.37***	-0.17***	-0.29***	-0.09	-0.19***	0.02	0.19***	0.04	-0.13**	0.02
R^2	0.35***		0.45***		0.30***		0.185***		0.13***	
ΔR^2	0.06***		0.01		0.02		0.025*		0.07***	
Lack of control	-0.19***	-0.03	-0.12	0.00	-0.11	-0.01	-0.02	-0.09	-0.03	0.03
Intended outcome	0.28***	0.16***	0.25	0.11	0.29***	0.19***	-0.03	0.03	0.07	0.04
R^2	0.38***		0.46***		0.34***		0.195***		0.13***	
ΔR^2	0.03***		0.01		0.04***		0.01		0.00	

Note: * = $p < 0.10$, ** = $p < 0.05$, *** = $p < 0.01$.

TABLE 12.8 Results of Step-Wise Regression Analysis for Low Performance

	Expectation on same task		Expectation on another task		Aspirations for subordinates		Need for close supervision		Punishing response	
	r	β	r	β	r	β	r	β	r	β
Low performance rating	-0.16**	-0.10	-0.15*	-0.04	-0.21**	-0.11*	0.19**	0.10	0.23**	0.17**
r^2	0.03*		0.03*		0.05**		0.04**		0.06**	
Past performance	0.59**	0.31**	0.47**	0.07	0.44**	0.07	-0.30**	-0.07	-0.23**	-0.10
Other task performance	0.60**	0.34**	0.69**	0.60**	0.62**	0.50**	-0.43**	-0.31**	-0.32**	-0.23**
Others' performance	-0.08	0.04	-0.16*	0.00	-0.12*	0.07	0.22**	0.09	0.16**	0.05
R^2	0.46**		0.49**		0.41**		0.21**		0.15**	
ΔR^2	0.43**		0.46**		0.36**		0.17**		0.09**	
Lack of ability	-0.39	-0.15**	-0.29**	-0.13*	-0.35**	-0.26**	0.14*	0.10	0.02	-0.05
Lack of effort	0.18**	0.09	0.07	0.03	0.00	-0.11	0.09	0.07	0.07	0.00
Difficult task	-0.01	0.07	0.10	0.06	0.10	0.12*	-0.14*	-0.08	-0.14*	-0.07
Bad luck	0.00	0.00	0.01	-0.01	0.02	0.01	-0.07	-0.04	-0.10	-0.07
R^2	0.49**		0.50**		0.46**		0.23**		0.17**	
ΔR^2	0.03*		0.01		0.05**		0.02		0.02	
Lack of control	-0.08	-0.05	0.07	0.10	-0.02	-0.01	-0.05	-0.01	-0.06	0.00
Intended outcome	-0.14*	-0.16**	-0.15*	-0.12*	-0.04	-0.01	0.15*	0.11	0.10	0.05
R^2	0.52**		0.53**		0.46**		0.25**		0.17**	
ΔR^2	0.03*		0.03*		0.00		0.02		0.00	

Note: * = $p < 0.05$, ** = $p < 0.01$.

of their responses to subordinate performance. Results appear to suggest that this is the case. Support was forthcoming for most of the predictions given in Table 12.1 and for a canonical relationship between the attribution and evaluation variables. Results also supported an effect of attributions on evaluative judgments beyond the impressionistic contribution of informational cues. Nevertheless, comparisons across outcome and with the results of earlier studies reveal some interesting differences.

In the first instance, subjects' evaluative judgments were primarily based on an overall assessment of performance. This is clear from the analysis of open-ended responses, from the clear differences in scores across outcome, and from the high correlation between informational cues and evaluative variables. Nevertheless, the processes underlying judgments of high and low performance appear to be different. Reactions to high performance tended to be straightforward and positive, whereas low performance was viewed more cautiously.

Responses to high performance appear to have been moderated by a global assessment of performance capabilities, based on perceptions of performance on other tasks undertaken by the subordinate. This view is supported by the results of canonical correlation. These indicated that although expectation variables were affected by internal attributions, evaluative variables associated with behavioral outcomes (such as need for supervision and reward) were tempered by attribution to task easiness.

Judgments of low performance were also subject to ratings of other task performance but were more complex. This is especially evident in consideration of the canonical correlation results. The first root appears to represent a reaction to lack of effort as an unstable attribution (see Weiner et al., 1971). Thus, although the subordinate may have performed poorly (and was seen to be deserving of punishment), there was an expectation that performance in the future would improve. The second root appears to have picked up the negative correlation between attributions to lack of ability and lack of effort for poor performance. In this instance, effort attributions were associated with negative expectations and punitive responses. At the same time, lack of ability attributions were negatively associated with low expectations and punishing responses, suggesting that the most punitive judgments were reserved for subordinates who had failed to live up to their potential. Overall, it appears that responses to poor performance involved complex cognitive processes.

In summary of the contrast between high and low performance, it appears that responses to high performance were more impressionistic and based on a global assessment of performance. Assessment of poor performance, on the other hand, was more complex. This contrast is consistent with results obtained by Gioia and Sims (1986), who observed verbal interactions between managers and high- and low-performing subordinates. They found that managers actively sought causal explanations when dealing with low performers, but engaged in mutual positive conversation with high performers. Further, subordinates were given less blame for failure and more credit for success. In another study, de Jong et al. (1988) found that judges attributed high performance to internal factors, but sought excuses for low performance.

Comparing the results of the present study with the results of earlier direct tests of the Green and Mitchell (1979) model suggests a mid-way result, especially with regard to the effect of the informational cue variables. In the pencil-and-paper study (Ashkanasy, 1989), eleven of twelve predictions were supported with significant results. In the laboratory study (Ashkanasy and Gallois, 1994), on the other hand, only two of the predictions were supported. In the present study, ten of the predictions were supported (for either high or low performance). Further, the present study provided only limited support for the conclusion of the pencil-and-paper study that controllability and intentionality need to be considered. Thus, although the results obtained in the present study support the existence of an impressionistic component (Wayne and Kacmar, 1991), they also suggest that on-the-spot reactions carry over to recalled responses. As such, these results support the view of Reynolds and West (1989) and Feldman and Lynch (1988) that attributional schemata play a role in organizing memory of reactions to subordinate performances.

Finally, this study is subject to two caveats related to the use of surveys. The first is that survey data are subject to acquiescent responses set, priming, and self-selection bias; the second is that early questionnaire items can influence subsequent responses (Tourangeau et al., 1989). In the present instance, however, the clear differences apparent for reactions to high and low levels of performance provide little evidence of systematic biases in either of these respects, suggesting that responses reflect a valid attempt to recall events as they happened. Further, the results of the present research are generally consistent with those of the earlier studies, differing in only minor respects. This gives reason for confidence that the Green and Mitchell (1979) model provides at least partial explanation for supervisors' reactions to subordinate performance.

REFERENCES

Anderson, L.R. (1992). Leader interventions for distressed group members: Overcoming leaders' self-serving attributional biases. *Small Group Research,* 23:503–523.

Ashkanasy, N.M. (1989). Causal attribution and supervisors' response to subordinate performance: The Green and Mitchell model revisited. *Journal of Applied Social Psychology,* 19:309–330.

Ashkanasy, N.M. and Gallois, C. (1994). Leader attributions and evaluations: Effects of locus of control, supervisory control, and task control. *Organizational Behavior and Human Decision Processes,* 59:27–50.

Brown, K.A. (1984). Explaining group poor performance: An attributional analysis. *Academy of Management Review,* 9:54–63.

Brown, K.A. and Mitchell, T.R. (1986). Influence of task interdependence and number of poor performers on diagnoses of causes of poor performance. *Academy of Management Journal,* 29:412–424.

Calder, B.J. (1977). An attribution theory of leadership. in *New Directions in Organizational Behavior,* B.M. Staw and G.R. Salancik (Eds.), Chicago: St. Clair Press, pp. 179–204.

de Jong, P.F., Koomen, W., and Mellenbergh, G.J. (1988). Structure of causes for success and failure: A multidimensional scaling analysis of preferential judgements. *Journal of Personality and Social Psychology,* 55:718–725.

Dobbins, G.H. (1985). Effects of gender on leaders' responses to poor performers: An attribution interpretation. *Academy of Management Journal,* 28:587–598.

Dobbins, G.H. and Russell, J.M. (1986). The biasing effects of subordinate likableness on leaders' responses to poor performers: A laboratory and a field study. *Personnel Psychology,* 39:759–777.

Feldman, J.M. (1981). Beyond attribution theory: Cognitive processes in performance appraisal. *Journal of Applied Psychology,* 66:127–148.

Feldman, J.M. and Lynch, J.G., Jr. (1988). Self-generated validity and other effects of measurement of belief, attitude, intention, and behavior. *Journal of Applied Psychology,* 73:421–435.

Gioia, D.A. and Sims, H.P., Jr. (1986). Cognition-behavior connections: Attribution and verbal behavior in leader–subordinate interactions. *Organizational Behavior and Human Decision Processes,* 37:197–229.

Green, S.G. and Mitchell, T.R. (1979). Attributional processes in leader–member interactions. *Organizational Behavior and Human Performance,* 23:429–458.

Hurlburt, R.T. and Mellencon, S.M. (1987). How are questionnaire data similar to, and different from, thought sampling data? Five studies manipulating retrospectiveness, single-moment focus, and indeterminacy. *Cognitive Therapy and Research,* 11:681–704.

Kelley, H.H. (1971). Causal schemata and the attribution process. in *Attribution: Perceiving the Causes of Behavior,* E.E. Jones, D.E. Kanouse, H.H. Kelley, R.E. Nisbett, S. Valins, and B. Weiner (Eds.), Morristown, N.J.: General Learning Press, pp. 151–174.

Kemery, E.R. and Dunlap, W.P. (1986). Partialling factor scores does not control common method variance: A rejoinder to Podsakoff and Todor. *Journal of Management,* 12: 525–530.

Knowlton, W.A. and Mitchell, T.R. (1980). Effects of causal attributions on a supervisor's evaluation of subordinate performance. *Journal of Applied Psychology,* 65:459–466.

Levine, J.M. and Moreland, R.L. (1990). Progress in small group research. *Annual Review of Psychology,* 41:585–634.

Lord, R.G. and Smith, J.E. (1983). Theoretical, informational, information processing, and situational factors affecting attributional theories of organizational behavior. *Academy of Management Review,* 8:50–60.

Martin, S.L. and Klimoski, R.J. (1990). Use of verbal protocols to trace cognitions associated with self- and supervisor evaluations of performance. *Organizational Behavior and Human Decision Processes,* 46:135–154.

Mitchell, T.R., Green, S.G., and Wood, R.E. (1981). An attributional model of leadership and the poor performing subordinate: Development and validation. *Research in Organizational Behavior,* 3:197–234.

Nathan, B.R. and Lord, R.G. (1983). Cognitive categorization and dimensional schemata: A process approach to the study of halo in performance ratings. *Journal of Applied Psychology,* 68:102–114.

Podsakoff, P.M. and Organ, D.W. (1986). Self reports in organizational research: Problems and perspectives. *Journal of Management,* 12:531–544.

Reynolds, K.D. and West, S.G. (1989). Attributional constructs: Their role in the organization of social information in memory. *Basic and Applied Social Psychology,* 10:119–130.

Ross, L. (1977). The intuitive psychologist and his shortcomings: Distortions in the attribution process. *Advances in Experimental Social Psychology,* 10:173–220.

Stewart, D. and Love, W. (1968). A general canonical correlation index. *Psychological Bulletin,* 70:160–163.

Tongtharadol, V., Reneau, J.H., and West, S.G. (1991). Factors influencing supervisor's responses to subordinate's poor performance: An attributional analysis. *Journal of Management Accounting Research,* 3:194–212.

Tourangeau, R., Rasinski, K.A., Bradburn, N., and D'Andrade, R. (1989). Carryover effects in attitude surveys. *Public Opinion Quarterly,* 53:495–524.

Wayne, S.J. and Kacmar, K.M. (1991). The effects of impression management on the performance appraisal process. *Organizational Behavior and Human Decision Processes,* 48:70–88.

Weiner, B (1985). An attributional theory of achievement motivation and emotion. *Psychological Review,* 92:548–573.

Weiner, B., Frieze, I., Kukla, A., Reed, L., Rest, S. and Rosenbaum, R.S. (1971). Perceiving the causes of success and failure. in *Attribution: Perceiving the Causes of Behavior,* E.E. Jones, D.E. Kanouse, H.H. Kelley, R.E. Nisbett, S. Valins, and B. Weiner (Eds.), Morristown, N.J.: General Learning Press, pp. 95–121.

Williams, L.J. and Brown, B.K. (1994). Method variance in organizational behavior and human resources research: Effects on correlations, path coefficients, and hypothesis testing. *Organizational Behavior and Human Decision Processes,* 57:185–209.

Wood, R.E. and Mitchell, T.R. (1981). Manager behavior in a social context: The impact of impression management on attribution and disciplinary actions. *Organizational Behavior and Human Performance,* 28:356–378.

Section III

APPLYING ATTRIBUTION THEORY TO ORGANIZATIONAL ISSUES

Part C:
Group Dynamics

13

ORGANIZATIONAL POLITICS
AND CITIZENSHIP:
ATTRIBUTIONS OF
INTENTIONALITY AND
CONSTRUCT DEFINITION

Gerald R. Ferris, Dharm P.S. Bhawuk,
Donald F. Fedor, and Timothy A. Judge

ABSTRACT

Organizational politics and organizational citizenship have emerged in recent years as important, but apparently distinct, work behaviors. Indeed, one might be inclined to argue that, on the surface at least, these constructs represent polar opposites. This chapter suggests that when examining the actual behaviors themselves, in many cases politics and citizenship appear to be quite similar, if not identical. Thus, it is argued that the key distinction between organizational politics and citizenship involves a behavior labeling process that is triggered by the perceiver's attributions of intentionality. A model of the process dynamics is presented, and implications for theory, research, and practice are discussed.

©St. Lucie Press CCC 1-884015-19-0 1/95/$100/$.50

INTRODUCTION

Two important constructs have emerged in recent years in the organizational sciences to command the attention of a number of scholars. Theory and research in organizational politics and organizational citizenship have proliferated in the past decade, focusing on a number of issues including construct definition, dimensionality, and relationships with other work behaviors and attitudes. Interestingly, these two constructs and the work associated with them have progressed in parallel but unrelated fashion. That is, there has been an apparent implicit assumption that politics and citizenship are quite distinct behaviors. Indeed, one might argue that, at a surface level, these constructs represent polar opposites, with the self-interested nature of politics reflecting the antithesis of the altruistic nature of citizenship. However, closer examination of these two constructs reveals that in a number of cases, the actual behaviors specified to reflect politics and citizenship are quite similar, if not identical. Thus, if there is believed to be a fundamental incompatibility between these two constructs, it cannot be effectively reconciled at the behavioral level.

The purpose of this chapter is to provide a systematic, critical analysis of the constructs of organizational politics and organizational citizenship and to propose a conceptual model which demonstrates that the distinction between these constructs involves a behavior labeling process, triggered by the perceiver's attributions of intentionality. Thus, it is argued that the key differentiating feature between politics and citizenship is not so much the particular behaviors a person exhibits, but rather the motives or intentions attributed to the person by the perceiver in making sense of why the behaviors were displayed.

ORGANIZATIONAL POLITICS

Definition

Organizational scientists have developed different notions of what constitutes political behavior, and these notions have come from a number of different disciplines. Psychologists, sociologists, economists, and management scholars all have studied politics, albeit under such different labels as impression management, self-presentation, and ingratiation, and provided different definitions of these specific constructs.

Indeed, there are some differences across the various definitions, but they are relatively minor ones, primarily reflecting differences in disciplinary background and level of analysis. Particularly noteworthy is the convergence of the different definitions of politics on the notion of influence, although the specific manifestation of influence attempts is likely to differ somewhat across the various views. Mindful of these earlier definitional efforts and their convergence, a conceptualization of politics derived from an integration of the political and symbolic perspectives on organizational life has been developed (Ferris et al., 1991). Quite simply, organizational politics is construed in this conceptualization as the management of shared meaning by individuals, groups, or organizations. Rather than inherent properties of situations, meanings are the result of our responses to those situations and our subsequent interpretations. Whether more or less, we all have a say in the interpretations of those events, and some consensus forms, usually legitimized by organizational symbols and myths. These "shared meanings" then provide guidelines for future interpretations and organizational behavior. The idea is to manage the meaning of the actions, events, and situations to produce the outcomes desired.

Politics in Organizations

Theory and research on organizational politics have tended to focus on how the process operates in organizations (Ferris et al., 1989; Gardner and Martinko, 1988; Porter et al., 1981), the tactics used (Kipnis et al., 1980; Porter et al., 1981; Tedeschi and Melburg, 1984), and the conditions under which influence tactics are employed (Fandt and Ferris, 1990).

Political behavior has been considered in a number of organizational decision areas, including the performance evaluation process (Ferris et al., in press; Kipnis and Schmidt, 1988; Wayne and Ferris, 1990), the personnel selection process (e.g., Baron, 1989; Gilmore and Ferris, 1989), career progress and mobility (e.g., Judge and Bretz, in press), and compensation (e.g., Bartol and Martin, 1988).

Types of Behaviors

Numerous specific influence tactics have been isolated and studied in the social and organizational psychology literature (e.g., Kipnis et al., 1980; Porter et al., 1981). Tedeschi and Melburg (1984) proposed a useful taxonomy for conceptualizing the vast array of influence tactics. These behaviors are classified according to two dimensions: assertive–defensive and tactical–strategic.

The tactical–defensive category includes such behaviors as apologies, accounts (excuses and justifications), disclaimers, and self-handicapping. Tactical–assertive behaviors include ingratiation, intimidation, self-promotion, exemplification, entitlements (verbal claims of responsibility for positive events), and enhancements (Jones and Pittman, 1982). Strategic–defensive behaviors range from learned helplessness to alcoholism and drug abuse, which are typically seen as self-handicapping behaviors, whereas strategic–assertive behaviors include those aimed at developing desired reputational characteristics.

Consequences of Organizational Politics

There is general agreement that a relationship exists between the influence tactics or strategies one uses and how that person is evaluated (Schlenker, 1980). In fact, it has been shown that persons who demonstrate ingratiating types of behaviors tend to receive favorable evaluations (e.g., Jones, 1964). More specifically, other-enhancing communications (Jones, 1990), favor doing (Wortman and Linsenmeier, 1977; Wayne and Ferris, 1990), and opinion conformity (Byrne, 1969) all have been found to increase liking. Furthermore, liking has been found to be positively related to target responses, such as performance ratings (e.g., Wayne and Ferris, 1990) and reward behavior (Podsakoff, 1982). Thus, it seems that some political behaviors may affect liking, which in turn influences target responses.

The foregoing discussion of political behaviors provides an overview of the different types of tactics that have been employed in organizations, but it does not offer the specificity one might seek in attempting to understand precisely what types of behavioral actions are being discussed. Thus, it might be useful to examine sample items from two political behavior scales, which focus on the frequently studied category of ingratiation. Kipnis et al. (1980) include the following items to measure the ingratiation category:

1. Praised him or her
2. Made him or her feel important
3. Did personal favors for him or her
4. Acted in a friendly manner prior to asking what I wanted

Wayne and Ferris (1990) developed a scale called *supervisor-focused tactics,* which also reflect ingratiating types of behaviors. Several representative items are:

1. Take an interest in your immediate supervisor's personal life
2. Praise your supervisor on his or her accomplishments
3. Do personal favors for your supervisors
4. Compliment your supervisor on his or her dress or appearance

ORGANIZATIONAL CITIZENSHIP BEHAVIOR

Organ (1988) defined organizational citizenship behavior (OCB) as behaviors that are discretionary, as opposed to obligatory, and are not an enforceable requirement of the individual's job description. These behaviors are not directly or formally rewarded by the organization. Organ stressed the "nonrequired" and "noncompensated" aspects of citizenship behavior: "nonrequired contributions that are regarded by the person as relatively less likely to lead along any clear, fixed path to formal rewards" (p. 5). He argued that "Rewards for OCB are at best probabilistic in nature, uncertain of attainment, and at most an inference on the part of the individual who contemplates such returns" (p. 5).

There are two other requirements of citizenship behavior (Organ, 1988). First, citizenship behavior represents actions of individuals that, in the aggregate, improve the functioning of organizations. Second, citizenship behavior is characterized by modesty and mundaneness, so much so that any return on this is unthinkable. Is citizenship behavior limited by definition to those behaviors that are "utterly and eternally lacking in any tangible return to the individual"? Organ (1988) answered:

> Not necessarily. Over time, a steady stream of OCB of different types...could well determine the impression that an individual makes on a supervisor or on coworkers. That impression, in turn, could influence the recommendation by the boss for a salary increase or promotion. (p. 5)

Organ (1988) also has avoided the issue of intention or motive of citizenship behavior. He argued that the conditions that increase or decrease the likelihood of the occurrence of OCB, or the proximal motive for such behaviors, were not essential to the appreciation of the behavior, nor to the "recognition, definition, or understanding of it." Thus, he excluded "any necessary qualification about subjective or internally formulated motive" (Organ, 1988, p. 4).

Bateman and Organ (1983) provided the first instrument to measure OCB. The measure includes a wide array of activities on the job, and the instrument is completed by the supervisors of the employees whose behavior is studied. A representative number of the 16 items included in the instrument are presented below:

1. Assists me with my duties

2. Takes the initiative to orient new employees to the department even though it is not part of his or her job description

3. Helps others when their work load increases (assists others until they get over the hurdles)

4. Volunteers to do things not formally required by the job

5. Makes innovative suggestions to improve the overall quality of the department

6. Willingly attends functions not required by the organization, but helps in its overall image

The behaviors that were included in the instrument were presumably those that are valued by supervisors "in part because they make their own jobs easier and free their own time and energy for more substantive tasks" (Bateman and Organ, 1983, p. 588). The authors further stress that these behaviors are valued by supervisors all the more because they cannot "require" such supra-role behaviors beyond "minimally acceptable or enforceable standards" (p. 588). Thus, it is clear that OCB is conceptualized as behaviors that cannot be required but are valued by supervisors. This could make these behaviors tools in the hands of the employees for managing their supervisors' impression of them, thus creating some conceptual confusion.

To add to the welter of the conceptualization of citizenship behavior, Graham (1991) referred to the altruism factor as *neighborliness,* and Puffer (1987) called it *prosocial behavior* (and also included other behaviors that are not quite altruistic). Furthermore, Brief and Motowidlo (1986) defined prosocial behavior as behavior that is "performed with the intention of promoting the welfare of the individual, group, or organization toward which it is directed" (p. 711).

The OCB construct, then, appears to be rooted in altruism. Yet, the classical philosophical view of altruism involves the capacity of individuals to exhibit behavior that "enhances the net welfare of another at some net cost to themselves" (Krebs and Miller, 1985, p. 2). This view, of course, stands in stark contrast to reinforcement-based approaches to human behavior which contend that individuals are motivated to maximize their self-interest (i.e., gains). This raises a question concerning the extent to which OCB, as conceptualized by scholars in this area, is actually as distinct from some other organizational science constructs as one might be led to believe.

POLITICS AND CITIZENSHIP: DISTINCT OR SIMILAR?

Conventional wisdom would suggest that organizational politics and organizational citizenship are separate and distinct constructs. Indeed, the self-interested nature of politics is likely regarded as the antithesis and polar opposite of the altruistic depiction of citizenship. However, several scholars recently have critically examined the citizenship construct and have questioned its apparent altruistic underpinnings.

Graham (1991) pointed out that a major weakness in the definition of OCB is that it is defined in the context of a 2 × 2 matrix, that is, in-role versus extra-role behavior is crossed with functional versus dysfunctional behavior. She rejected the narrow "extra-role/organizationally functional" criterion of defining OCB on the grounds that the behaviors that are categorized under OCB are very difficult to classify and proposed to include forms of political behavior hitherto neglected by OCB researchers. In short, Graham proposed a drastically different approach which she terms a "political approach to OCB" by broadening the term to include all organizationally relevant individual behavior.

Schnake (1991) suggested refinement in both the definition and measurement of the OCB construct and proposed his own causal model of organizational citizenship behavior. However, he did not add to the clarification of the construct, since he used the same two dimensions of altruism and generalized compliance (also called conscientiousness), which lack consistent support in the literature. Furthermore, he introduced self-monitoring as a mediator between co-worker/leader social cues and both dimensions of OCB. Because self-monitoring is identified as an individual characteristic that affects political behavior, the distinction between OCB and political behavior is further blurred.

Fandt and Ferris (1990) called for a more careful examination of the distinctions between prosocial and political behaviors. They pointed out that on the surface, there appears to be a fundamental incompatibility between these two sets of behaviors, with politics typically being construed in a pejorative sense as inherently dysfunctional. They suggested that, on the one hand, it is quite possible that some self-interest maximizing behaviors are also advantageous to an organization and, on the other hand, the mere appearance of being altruistic can be quite self-serving. These issues of motive or intentionality and the distinction between politics and citizenship have been emphasized more recently by Ferris and his colleagues (Ferris et al., in press; Ferris et al., 1991) and by Podsakoff et al. (1993), although Ferris and Podsakoff differ somewhat in their views.

When looking at the actual behaviors that appear to reflect organizational politics and citizenship discussed in the preceding sections, the constructs appear more similar than different. For example, helping other employees could be viewed as self-presentation ("I am a helpful person") or favor exchange behavior ("I am helping now and expect help in the future"), both of which could be construed as political behaviors. Similarly, assisting the supervisor could be viewed as complimentary, other-enhancement behavior ("I want to make your job easier because I respect you"), and not complaining about minor things could be only a conformity tactic ("I am like you; therefore I do not complain"). Therefore, what appears to be the differentiating factor may well be the attributed motives or intentions.

The comparison of organizational politics to OCB might be construed in a manner similar to that in which altruism and aggression have been examined recently by Krebs and Miller (1985). They acknowledged that there has been a diversity of definitions of both constructs, and a central source of difference among the definitions is the tendency to focus on observed behaviors and not intentions or motives. This leads one to make sense of and label behaviors simply on the basis of their perceived consequences, without giving consideration to intentions, contributing to an incomplete analysis.

DIFFERENTIATING POLITICS AND CITIZENSHIP: ATTRIBUTIONS OF INTENTIONALITY

Construct differentiation is accomplished most obviously in the comparison of behaviors reflecting those constructs. However, in some cases, the differentiation is a function of the cognitive evaluation, interpretation, and assignment of meaning of observed behaviors. In this section, the concept of intentionality is presented. It is suggested that attributions regarding intentions or motives can represent a key triggering mechanism in construct definition and differentiation.

Perceived Intentionality

The motives or intentions that we perceive as the impetus for others' behavior have considerable impact on how we interpret and react to that behavior. Leary and Kowaloski (1990) proposed a model of impression management that involves two principal components: impression construction and impression motivation. Impression motivation refers to the motives for controlling others' perceptions. Fedor and his colleagues (Fedor, 1991; Fedor et al., 1989) have investigated perceived intentions in the feedback process. They reported that subordinate perceptions of the supervisor's intentions in giving feedback affected subordinate reactions to the feedback. It has also been suggested that perceptions of intentionality of behavior play a pivotal role in how individuals respond to conflict situations (Baron, 1988; Gordon and Bowlby, 1989; Thomas and Pondy, 1977). Thomas and Pondy argued that people make sense of others' behavior through their perceptions of others' intentions. Baron found that "the impact of attributing provocative actions to external causes depends, quite strongly, on the perceived sincerity of such statements" (p. 125).

Political Behavior and Intentionality

As noted in an earlier section of this chapter, the term "political behavior" is used to refer to a number of areas of the literature appearing under headings such as ingratiation, impression management, and self presentation. Collectively, this literature is quite extensive, beginning with the early works of Goffman (1959) and the significant contributions to theory and research made by Jones and his colleagues (Jones, 1964, 1990; Jones and Wortman, 1973; Jones and Pittman, 1982) and extending to the more recent efforts on political behavior in general (e.g., Gardner and Martinko, 1988; Ferris and Judge, 1991; Ferris et al., 1989; Tedeschi and Melburg, 1984; Porter et al., 1981; Kipnis et al., 1980), as well as particular types of political behavior including ingratiation (Liden and Mitchell, 1988; Ralston and Elsass, 1989; Wortman and Linsenmeier, 1977). An important issue shared in common by all of this work, implicitly or explicitly, is the important role played by the motives or intentions of the individual exhibiting these behaviors. Ralston and Elsass (1989) defined ingratiation as a covert influence factor whereby the true motive or intent behind the behavior necessarily remains hidden, and Jones and Pittman (1982) argued that "the very success of ingratiation usually depends on the actor's concealment of ulterior motivation..." (p. 179).

Intentionality and the Attribution Process

There is general agreement that intentions play a pivotal role in political behavior, and it has been suggested that observers make sense of intentionality or underlying motives through the attribution process. Wortman and Linsenmeier (1977) proposed that "...the ingratiator's task is primarily one of manipulating the attributions made by the target person he is trying to impress" (p. 135), and Porter et al. (1981) also highlighted the role of attributions of intentionality when they stated:

> The "politician" must take care to avoid having his or her behavior attributed by others to a self-serving intent. Creation of the impression that behavior is legitimate may be accomplished by acting in ways that make reliable attributions difficult. (p. 118)

Attribution theory essentially suggests that people have a fundamental tendency to search for the causes of their own and others' behavior, and it was developed by Heider (1958) with theoretical refinements and extensions provided by Jones and Davis (1965) and Kelley (1972) (for reviews see Ross and Fletcher, 1985; Weary and Arkin, 1981). People are believed to concern themselves with causal explanations in order to exercise control over important aspects of their environment (Berscheid et al., 1976; Regan, 1978). Basic to Heider's approach is the suggestion that perceivers assume an active role in making inferences about and ascribing meaning to actions, which also involves an evaluation of the underlying motives, intentions, or disposition of the actor; how the perceiver reacts to the actor is determined by this ascribed meaning, which is arrived at through inferences about the causality of the action (Regan, 1978). Therefore, motives or intentions play a central role in theories of attribution. Furthermore, attribution theory suggests that individuals explain actions either dispositionally (i.e., caused by the person) or situationally (i.e., caused by the context or situation), and the cognitive structures (e.g., inferential sets, frames, schemas) of the perceiver are important in the interpretation of such actions and the assumption of causality (Markus and Zajonc, 1985).

Theory and research in the areas of organizational politics and attribution processes have emphasized the importance of motives or intentions in perceiver reactions to actor behavior. However, while the perceived intentionality of political behavior has been suggested as important for the success of those tactics, no prior work has suggested that intentions are actually fundamental to the very nature of behavior interpretation and labeling and the differentiation of constructs.

MODEL OF INTENTIONALITY AND CONSTRUCT LABELING

It has been suggested that the primary mechanism that differentiates the construct of organizational politics and organizational citizenship is not the actual behaviors representing the two constructs because, as discussed above, in many cases the behaviors are very similar. Instead, it was argued that the differentiating mechanism is the attributions about the motives or intentions of the actor exhibiting the behavior, which serve as a triggering device to influence how the particular behavior is cognitively evaluated, interpreted, and labeled. A model depicting this behavior labeling process is presented in Figure 13.1. The model identifies a number of factors that influence the attributions that are proposed to affect behavior/construct labeling and perceiver reactions. Each of these factors is examined more closely in the following sections.

Characteristics of Actors

Effectively managing attributions of sincerity, genuineness, and positive intentionality is proposed to be influenced significantly by the personality characteristics and political skill of the actor. The particular personality characteristics considered to be critical are Machiavellianism (Mach) and self-monitoring. High Machs tend to be manipulative and adept at influencing others (Christie and Geis, 1970). Furthermore, high Machs tend to have a greater ability to control their public expression of emotional states and are better able to keep their private feelings from influencing their public behaviors. Therefore, it is suggested that high Machs will be better able to conceal their true intentions and thus manage the perceiver's attributions of intentionality.

Self-monitoring refers to the social perceptiveness and adeptness at constructing a pattern of behavior that matches or is appropriate for a given situation (Snyder, 1987). Thus, it is proposed that high self-monitors will be more effective at managing the perceiver's attributions of positive and sincere intentions.

In addition to the foregoing personality characteristics, the actor also needs to possess political skill to influence intentionality attributions. Political skill refers to the style and behavioral strategies to make one's actions appear to be sincere. The nonverbal style of persuasion, along with the verbal content, reflect

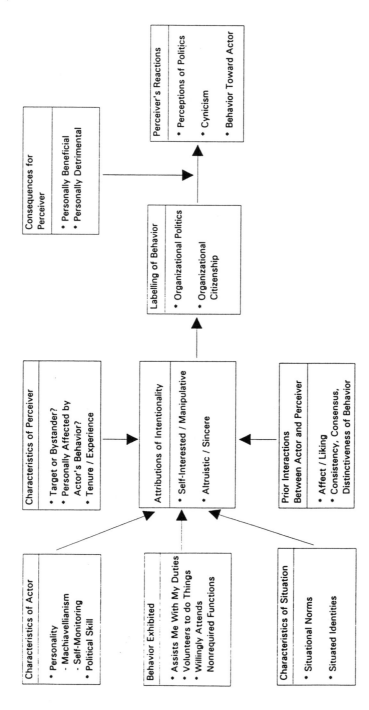

FIGURE 13.1   Model of intentionality and behavior labeling.

a critical combination determining whether or not ulterior motives are disguised (Drake and Moberg, 1986). In their study of praise, Kanouse et al. (1981) suggested that the specific language used in giving praise determines reactions, providing further testimony to the conventional belief that it is not what you say, but how you say it.

Another aspect of style and political skill has to do with the strategic expression of emotion (Hochschild, 1983; Rafaeli and Sutton, 1989; Goffman, 1959), which is designed to make actions more believable. Rafaeli and Sutton suggested that the content of displayed emotions is evident in tone of voice, language, bodily gestures, and facial expressions, and Goffman referred to such displays of emotion as "control moves," designed to influence the reactions of targets. Hochschild suggested that the ability to express certain emotions or feelings over an extended period of time may be critical to the effects of such displays and coined the term "emotional stamina" to reflect this ability. It is proposed, therefore, that political skill and style are critical to the management of intentionality attributions.

Behavior Exhibited and Characteristics of the Situation

The particular behaviors exhibited by the actor are also proposed to influence the attributions of intentionality, but since the behaviors really need to be examined in light of the situation characteristics, these two categories are examined together. The behaviors associated with politics and citizenship include the following:

- Praising one's supervisor on his or her accomplishments (politics)
- Volunteering to do things not formally required by the job (OCB)
- Assisting with others' duties (OCB)
- Acted in a friendly manner prior to asking what was wanted (politics)

These behaviors may be perceived and interpreted quite differently as a function of situational behavior norms. Porter et al. (1981) suggested that the political norms of a situation (i.e., what is and what is not acceptable) are best learned by observing the activities of others and their consequences (i.e., were those behaviors successful?). Goffman (1955) and Rafaeli and Sutton (1989) both have discussed the importance of situational norms for the successful display of emotion, and Ralston and Elsass (1989) emphasized situational norms when suggesting that the same behaviors can result in quite different inferences depending upon the style of the actor and the situation. Such factors can result in the same behaviors being perceived as deceitfully manipulative or genuinely friendly.

Thus, it seems that not all behaviors are similarly perceived or equally effective, but that situational appropriateness is a determining factor. Fiske and Taylor (1984) suggested that individuals attempt to conform to situational norms concerning their behavior in social settings. Furthermore, for every social setting, there is a social interaction pattern of behavior that conveys the optimal identity for that particular setting. This has been referred to as a "situated identity," and it is suggested that people construct patterns of situationally appropriate behavior based upon their knowledge of these situated identities (e.g., Alexander and Knight, 1971; Gergen and Taylor, 1969). Therefore, it is proposed that the particular behaviors exhibited will differentially affect attributions of intentionality as a function of the situational appropriateness of the behaviors.

In addition to exhibiting qualitatively correct behaviors for the situation, there are likely to be situational norms concerning the quantity of such behaviors demonstrated. Stereotypically, the "obvious politician" is one who frequently engages in quite transparent efforts to manipulate others and who "lays it on too thick" in terms of influence efforts, which suggests ulterior motives. Indeed, Baron (1989) found that job applicants in employment interviews could undermine their case by engaging in excessive impression management tactics, thus falling victim to the "too much of a good thing" effect. Jones (1990) cautioned ingratiators not to employ excessive tactics because strategic failure could result due to overkill. In addition to qualitatively selecting the appropriate behaviors for the particular situation, therefore, it is suggested that the quantity of the behaviors employed could affect attributions of intentionality as well.

Characteristics of the Perceiver

Several characteristics of the perceiver are proposed to influence attributions of intentionality he or she makes. First, whether the perceiver is the target of the actor's actions or simply a bystander is proposed to affect the perceiver's attributions. Targets of behaviors tend to become more engaged in the interactions, and they are more likely than bystanders to judge the behavior exhibited toward them as authentic and the actor as sincere (Jones, 1990). Bystanders tend to be less engaged and more removed from the interactions and, therefore, tend to be more scrutinizing of the actor's intentions. As noted by Jones (1964), an observer to an ingratiating interchange, for a variety of reasons, is more inclined than the target to perceive ulterior motives in the actor and discount the influence attempt. If the perceiver is the target of behavior, then it is proposed that he or she will be more likely to make altruistic or sincere attributions of intentionality. If the perceiver is a bystander, for whom the actor's overtures are not intended, he or she will be more likely to make attributions of self-interested, manipulative intentions by the actor.

A second characteristic of the perceiver believed to influence intentionality attributions is the extent to which the perceiver has a stake in, or is personally affected by, the actor's behavior. Perhaps somewhat similar to the concepts of hedonic relevance and personalism (Jones and Davis, 1965), this factor suggests that the degree to which actor behavior personally affects the perceiver will influence his or her personal involvement, which will affect the type of intentionality attributions made. In essence, the degree of personal impact and involvement can change a bystander into a target.

Third, the amount of tenure and/or experience in organizational settings is proposed to affect perceiver attributions. Presumably, less experienced perceivers might be more socially naive and more prone to be deceived by influence attempts than would more experienced, seasoned veterans. Gilmore and Ferris (1989) suggested that experienced interviewers are less susceptible to image management tactics of job applicants because they have seen such efforts many times in the past and can better assess the applicants' motives or intentions. Therefore, it is proposed that increased experience of the perceiver will increase the likelihood of making attributions of deceitful motives or intentions.

Prior Interactions Between Actor and Perceiver

The history of previous interactions between the actor and perceiver is also proposed to be an important influence on intentionality attributions. One relevant aspect of the history of interactions is the degree of affect or liking the perceiver has for the actor, and affect has been investigated with respect to its association with attributions (e.g., Porac et al., 1983). Heider (1958) suggested that attributed motives or intentionality are influenced by feelings of the perceiver toward the actor in a manner consistent with his balance principle; that is, meaning will be assigned to an actor's behavior in a manner consistent with the perceiver's degree of affect or liking toward the actor. Regan et al. (1974) found that prosocial behavior was attributed to internal causes if performed by a friend (i.e., liked) and to external causes if done by an enemy (i.e., disliked). Essentially, good people are expected to do good things, and bad people are expected to do bad things. When the observed behavior fits the perceived image of the actor, we tend to make attributions internally, to intentions and dispositions. However, when the observed behavior departs from our expectations (i.e., does not fit with our image of the actor), perceivers are more inclined to make external or situational attributions (Regan, 1978). It is proposed, then, that attributions of positive or negative intentions will follow from the consistency of behavior exhibited with perceiver affect toward the actor.

Another relevant aspect of the history of interactions between actor and perceiver borrows from Kelley's (1972) attribution model and focuses on his concepts of consistency, distinctiveness, and consensus. Consistency refers to the generality of the behavior across time and place. Distinctiveness refers to whether a behavior is expressed toward a specific target only or is used generally across all potential targets. Consensus refers to the generality of a behavior across a population of people.

For example, if an employee is punctual every day, he or she is consistent, but if the person shows up on time only on a particular day, then his or her behavior is inconsistent, and the supervisor may attribute negative intentionality. However, if an employee is generally punctual and on a particular day he or she is late, the supervisor is likely to attribute situational constraints as the cause of his or her delay. Similarly, if an employee is always helpful to his or her co-workers and when the supervisor requests him or her to help a co-worker he or she does so, then his or her behavior is not distinctive or different from normal. However, if the employee were to help a coworker only when the supervisor requested, then his or her behavior is distinctive and is likely to receive a negative attribution. Finally, if the supervisor is an aloof person, and most employees maintain a distance from him or her, and if an employee tries to be sociable and gregarious, it could be viewed negatively, simply because it is nonconsensual (not what everyone does).

Attributions of Intentionality

The foregoing factors and linkages serve as the proposed determinants of perceiver's attributions concerning the motives or intentions of the actor. These influences will collectively determine whether the perceiver will attribute the actor's behavior to positive or negative dispositional causes, that is, whether the actor is believed to behave with self-serving, manipulative intentions or with authentic, sincere ones. It is noteworthy that this model bases the behavior intentionality, interpretation, and labeling process on the implicit assumption that a dispositional and not a situational attribution will be made. Indeed, theory and research on attribution processes suggest that behavior can be attributed to either dispositional or situational causes (e.g., Ross and Fletcher, 1985). However, research has supported the well-established "fundamental attribution error," that observers reflect a tendency to make dispositional attributions for actor behavior, whereas actors tend to use situational causes as explanations (Ross, 1977). Furthermore, this model departs from conventional attribution theory and suggests that in the observation and interpretation of any behavior, even when situational factors may emerge as potential explanations, perceptions of intentionality are meaningfully factored into the cognitive evaluation process.

Labeling Behavior

Once intentionality of the behavior has been determined, these attributions to particular motives are used by the perceiver to interpret and label the actor's behavior, and it is the attributed motives that effectively distinguish between the behavior being labeled organizational politics or organizational citizenship. It is proposed that when the actor's behavior is attributed to self-interested, deceitful intentions, the perceiver will interpret and label that behavior politics. When the behavior is attributed to authentic, sincere motives, citizenship will be the label attached to the behavior.

Consequences for Perceiver and Reactions

Whereas it is argued that the focal process involved in construct labeling for organizational politics and citizenship involves the attributions of intentionality, it is suggested that both intentions and consequences of the behavior determine perceiver reactions. The research evidence on perceptions of organizational politics indicates that politics is associated with lower satisfaction and increased anxiety (e.g., Ferris and Kacmar, 1992; Gandz and Murray, 1980). However, Ferris et al. (1989) suggested that these relationships might be moderated by the extent to which politics is viewed as a threat (i.e., personally detrimental) or an opportunity (i.e., personally beneficial), and empirical support has recently been provided for this notion (Ferris et al., 1993, 1994). This conceptualization borrows from the research of James and his colleagues (James and James, 1989; James et al., 1990), who have focused on the interpretive aspect of perception and cognition in the individual experience of and assignment of meaning to work environments. Their work has suggested that the interpretation of environmental events involves a higher-order schema that is reflective of a cognitive evaluation of the judged "goodness" versus "badness" of environmental attributes. In the present conceptualization, it is proposed that both the intentions underlying the behavior and the consequences for the perceiver (i.e., personally beneficial versus personally harmful) combine to affect perceiver reactions. Therefore, it is suggested that the self-interested political behavior would lead to negative reactions by the perceiver (e.g., low satisfaction, high anxiety, etc.) when the consequences of the actor's behavior are seen as being personally detrimental for the perceiver. However, such behavior could lead to more favorable reactions when the perceiver sees personally beneficial consequences from politics. Furthermore, a similar pattern of reactions would be expected for citizenship behavior. It may be that this process could help explain the relatively high level of cynicism in the work force today, as reported by Kanter and Mirvis (1989), in addition to other employee attitudes.

It is further proposed that intentions and consequences interact to influence perceiver attitudes about and behavior toward the actor. In a recent study, Wayne et al. (1989) examined how a subordinate's use of ingratiation directed at a superior affected perceptions and attitudes of co-workers who witnessed the ingratiation attempts. Counterintuitively, the results of this study demonstrated that the bystander co-workers not only were not less satisfied, but they actually reflected significantly higher levels of both satisfaction and perceptions of fairness. Perceived intentions and consequences of the actor's behavior were not assessed in this study, but it could well be the case that bystanders made different interpretations of the observed ingratiating behavior. Perhaps sincere intentions were attributed to the actor. Alternatively, they may indeed have perceived the actor to be manipulative; however, *manipulate* has at least two quite different definitions according to Webster's dictionary (see Owen, 1986; Ferris and Judge, 1991):

1. Manage or utilize skillfully
2. Control or play upon as artful, unfair, or insidious means

The perceived intentionality and consequences of observed behavior may determine which definition one employs.

IMPLICATIONS AND CONCLUSION

In this chapter, it has been argued that to effectively differentiate the constructs of organizational politics and organizational citizenship, the actual behaviors involved must in many cases be ignored in favor of intentions. Indeed, it was suggested that the politics–citizenship distinction involves a behavior labeling process, which is triggered by the perceiver's attributions of intentionality, and a model to illustrate the process dynamics was proposed. This proposed model has some interesting and potentially important implications for theory, research, and practice.

Implications for Theory and Research

The obvious and most immediate need is to conduct empirical tests of the proposed model to assess the validity of its linkages and the proposed process. Experimental studies will be necessary initially to exercise control over, and to be able to manipulate, the desired conditions. Fedor's (Fedor et al., 1989) work is useful and instructive in this regard.

An issue that is quite interesting, and has considerable potential to be developed into an important area of research in its own right, is the political skill construct. Whereas this model suggests a number of different influences on attributions of intentionality, it is believed that the political skill of the actor is perhaps the most important influence, although this is in need of much further development. It appears to involve some combination of personality characteristics, perhaps including intelligence, shrewdness, and social awareness, along with attention to detail, language selection, and communication style. Future research should make efforts to establish the requisite dimensions of political skill and investigate how those high on this construct seem to fare in organizational life (i.e., in terms of promotions and velocity of mobility, performance appraisals, salary increases, etc.) as opposed to those low on the construct.

Implications for Practice

It seems that the notions introduced in this chapter may have implications for practice as well. Top-level managers and executives in organizations are continually called upon to inspire the masses through stimulating speeches and the articulation of a vision. Whereas the actual rhetoric of such communications is indeed important to conveying the proper message, the sincere, genuine intentions of the executive probably explain the real impact of these addresses. If it were simply to develop mastery over the English language in preparing effective speeches, an executive could attend management development seminars or simply hire a good speech writer. However, learning to be genuine, sincere, and believable defies conventional education and training and calls for alternative approaches. Perhaps this interest in managing intentions can help to explain the recent phenomenon of executives taking acting classes (Drake, 1987).

Conclusion

Organizational scientists who study employee behavior at work are indeed concerned with the consequences of actions. However, they are also quite interested in the intentions or motives underlying such actions. The problem with motives or intentions is that they defy direct observation and must be inferred, yet they are critically involved in defining behaviors and reacting to them. The constructs of organizational politics and citizenship provide good examples of how the behaviors themselves may not be the key differentiating mechanisms, but rather the intentions or motives attributed to the behaviors. The proposed model was intended to shed light on the dynamics of this process and thus to help explain the reactions of supervisors, co-workers, and subordinates to actor behavior in organizational contexts.

REFERENCES

Alexander, C.N., Jr. and Knight, G.W. (1971). Situational identities and social psychological experimentation. *Sociometry,* 34:65–82.

Baron, R.A. (1988). Attributions and organizational conflict: The mediating role of apparent sincerity. *Organizational Behavior and Human Decision Processes,* 41:111–127.

Baron, R.A. (1989). Impression management by applicants during employment interviews: The "too much of a good thing" effect. in *The Employment Interview: Theory, Research, and Practice,* R.W. Eder and G.R. Ferris (Eds.), Newbury Park, Calif.: Sage Publications, pp. 204–215.

Bartol, K.M. and Martin, D.C. (1988). Influences on managerial pay allocation: A dependency perspective. *Personnel Psychology,* 41:361–378.

Bateman, T.S. and Organ, D.W. (1983). Job-satisfaction and the good soldiers: The relationship between affect and employee "citizenship." *Academy of Management Journal,* 26:587–595.

Berscheid, E., Graziano, W., Monson, T., and Dermer, M. (1976). Outcome dependency: Attention, attribution, and attraction. *Journal of Personality and Social Psychology,* 34:978–989.

Brief, A.P. and Motowidlo, S.J. (1986). Prosocial organizational behaviors. *Academy of Management Review,* 11:710–725.

Byrne, D. (1969). Attitudes and attraction. in *Advances in Experimental Social Psychology,* Vol. 4, L. Berkowitz (Ed.), New York: Academic Press, pp. 35–90.

Christie, R. and Geis, F.L. (1970). *Studies in Machiavellianism,* New York: Academic Press.

Drake, B.H. and Moberg, D.J. (1986). Communicating influence attempts in dyads: Linguistic sedatives and palliatives. *Academy of Management Review,* 11:567–584.

Drake, G. (1987). Acting lessons for the political world. *New York Times,* February 10, p. 22.

Fandt, P.M. and Ferris, G.R. (1990). The management of information and impressions: When employees behave opportunistically. *Organizational Behavior and Human Decision Processes,* 45:140–158.

Fedor, D.B. (1991). Recipient responses to performance feedback: A proposed model and its implications. in *Research in Personnel and Human Resources Management,* Vol. 9, G.R. Ferris and K.M. Rowland (Eds.), Greenwich, Conn.: JAI Press, pp. 73–120.

Fedor, D.B., Eder, R.W., and Buckley, M.R. (1989). The contributory effects of supervisor intentions on subordinate feedback responses. *Organizational Behavior and Human Decision Processes,* 44:396–414.

Ferris, G.R. and Judge, T.A. (1991). Personnel/human resources management: A political influence perspective. *Journal of Management,* 17:447–488.

Ferris, G.R. and Kacmar, K.M. (1992). Perceptions of organizational politics. *Journal of Management,* 18:93–116.

Ferris, G.R., Russ, G.S., and Fandt, P.M. (1989). Politics in organizations. in *Impression Management in the Organization,* R.A. Giacalone and P. Rosenfeld (Eds.), Hillsdale, N.J.: Lawrence Erlbaum, pp. 143–170.

Ferris, G.R., King, T.R., Judge, T.A., and Kacmar, K.M. (1991). The management of shared meaning in organizations: Opportunism in the reflection of attitudes, beliefs, and values. in *Applied Impression Management: How Image-Making Affects Managerial Decisions,* R.A. Giacalone and P. Rosenfeld (Eds.), Newbury Park, Calif.: Sage Publications, pp. 41–64.

Ferris, G.R., Brand, J.F., Brand, S., Rowland, K.M., Gilmore, D.C., King, T.R., Kacmar, K.M., and Burton, C.A. (1993). Politics and control in organizations. in *Advances in Group Processes,* Vol. 10, E.J. Lawler, B. Markovsky, J. O'Brien, and K. Heimer (Eds.), Greenwich, Conn.: JAI Press, pp. 83–111.

Ferris, G.R., Fink, D.D., Galang, M.C., Zhou, J., Kacmar, K.M., and Howard, J.L. (1994). Political Work Environments, paper presented at the Ninth Annual Conference of the Society for Industrial and Organizational Psychology, Inc., Nashville.

Ferris, G.R., Judge, T.A., Rowland, K.M., and Fitzgibbons, D.E. (in press). Subordinate influence and the performance evaluation process: Test of a model. *Organizational Behavior and Human Decision Processes.*

Fiske, S.T. and Taylor, S.E. (1984). *Social Cognition,* Reading, Mass.: Addison-Wesley.

Gandz, J. and Murray, V. (1980). The experience of workplace politics. *Academy of Management Journal,* 23:237–251.

Gardner, W.L. and Martinko, M.J. (1988). Impression management in organizations. *Journal of Management,* 17:321–338.

Gergen, K.J. and Taylor, M.G. (1969). Social expectancy and self-presentation in a status hierarchy. *Journal of Experimental Social Psychology,* 5:79–82.

Gilmore, D.C. and Ferris, G.R. (1989). The politics of the employment interview. in *The Employment Interview: Theory, Research, and Practice,* R.W. Eder and G.R. Ferris (Eds.), Newbury Park, Calif.: Sage Publications, pp. 195–203.

Goffman, E. (1955). On face work: An analysis of ritual elements in social interactions. *Psychiatry,* 22:225–237.

Goffman, E. (1959). *The Presentation of Self in Everyday Life,* New York: Doubleday Anchor.

Gordon, M.E. and Bowlby, R.L. (1989). Reactance and intentionality attributions as determinants of the intent to file a grievance. *Personnel Psychology,* 42:309–329.

Graham, J.W. (1991). An essay on organizational citizenship behavior. *Employee Responsibilities and Rights Journal,* 4:249–270.

Heider, F. (1958). *The Psychology of Interpersonal Relations,* New York: Wiley.

Hochschild, A.R. (1983). *The Managed Heart: Commercialization of Human Feeling,* Berkeley: University of California Press.

James, L.A. and James, L.R. (1989). Integrating work environment perceptions: Explorations into the measurement of meaning. *Journal of Applied Psychology,* 14:739–751.

James, L.A., James, L.R., and Ashe, D.K. (1990). The meaning of organizations: The role of cognition and values. in *Organizational Climate and Culture,* B. Schneider (Ed.), San Francisco: Jossey-Bass, pp. 40–84.

Jones, E.E. (1964). *Ingratiation,* New York: Appleton-Century-Crofts.

Jones, E.E. (1990). *Interpersonal Perception,* New York: W.H. Freeman.

Jones, E.E. and Davis, K.E. (1965). From acts to dispositions: The attribution process in person perception. in *Advances in Experimental Social Psychology,* Vol. 2, L. Berkowitz (Ed.), New York: Academic Press, pp. 219–266.

Jones, E.E. and Pittman, T.S. (1982). Toward a general theory of strategic self-presentation. in *Psychological Perspectives on the Self,* Vol. 1, J. Suls (Ed.), Hillsdale, N.J.: Lawrence Erlbaum, pp. 231–262.

Jones, E.E. and Wortman, C. (1973). *Ingratiation: An Attributional Approach,* Morristown, N.J.: General Learning Press.

Judge, T.A. and Bretz, R.D. (in press). Political influence behavior and career success. *Journal of Management.*

Kanouse, D.E., Gumpert, P., and Canavan-Gumpert, D. (1981). The semantics of praise. in *New Directions in Attribution Research,* Vol. 3, J.H. Harvey, W. Ickes, and R.F. Kidd (Eds.), Hillsdale, N.J.: Lawrence Erlbaum, pp. 97–115.

Kanter, D.L. and Mirvis, P.H. (1989). *The Cynical Americans: Living and Working in an Age of Discontent and Disillusion,* San Francisco: Jossey-Bass.

Kelley, H.H. (1972). Attribution in social interaction. in *Attribution: Perceiving the Causes of Behavior,* E.E. Jones, D.E. Kanous, H.H. Kelley, R.E. Nisbett, S. Valins, and B. Weiner (Eds.), Morristown, N.J.: General Learning Press.

Kipnis, D. and Schmidt, S.M. (1988). Upward influence styles: Relationship with performance evaluations, salary, and stress. *Administrative Science Quarterly,* 33:528–542.

Kipnis, D., Schmidt, S.M., and Wilkinson, I. (1980). Intra-organizational influence tactics: Exploration in getting one's way. *Journal of Applied Psychology,* 65:440–452.

Krebs, D.L. and Miller, D.T. (1985). Altruism and aggression. in G. Lindzey and E. Aronson (Eds.), *Handbook of Social Psychology,* Vol. 2, 3rd edition, New York: Random House, pp. 1–72.

Leary, M.R. and Kowaloski, R.M. (1990). Impression management: A literature review and two-component model. *Psychological Bulletin,* 107:34–47.

Liden, R.C. and Mitchell, T.R. (1988). Ingratiating behaviors in organizational settings. *Academy of Management Review,* 13:572–587.

Markus, H. and Zajonc, R.B. (1985). The cognitive perspective in social psychology. in *Handbook of Social Psychology,* Vol. 1, 3rd edition, G. Lindzey and E. Aronson (Eds.), New York: Random House, pp. 137–230.

Organ, D.W. (1988). *Organizational Citizenship Behavior: The "Good-Soldier" Syndrome,* Lexington, Mass.: Lexington Books.

Owen, H. (1986). Leadership indirection. in *Transforming Leadership,* J.D. Adams (Ed.), Alexandria, Va.: Miles River Press, pp. 111–122.

Podsakoff, P. (1982). Determinants of supervisor's use of rewards and punishment: A literature review and suggestions for future research. *Organizational Behavior and Human Performance,* 29:58–83.

Podsakoff, P.M., MacKenzie, S.B., and Hui, C. (1993). Organizational citizenship behaviors and managerial evaluations of employee performance: A review and suggestions for future research. in *Research in Personnel and Human Resource Management,* Vol. 11, G.R. Ferris (Ed.), Greenwich, Conn.: JAI Press, pp. 1–40.

Porac, J.F., Ferris, G.R., and Fedor, D.B. (1983). Causal attributions, affect, and expectations for a day's work performance. *Academy of Management Journal,* 26:285–296.

Porter, L.W., Allen, R.W., and Angle, H.L. (1981). The politics of upward influence in organizations. in *Research in Organizational Behavior,* Vol. 3, L.L. Cummings and B.M. Staw (Eds.), Greenwich, Conn.: JAI Press, pp. 109–149.

Puffer, S.M. (1987). Prosocial behavior, noncomplaint behavior, and work performance among commission salespeople. *Journal of Applied Psychology,* 72:615–621.

Rafaeli, A. and Sutton, R.I. (1989). The expression of emotion in organizational life. in *Research in Organizational Behavior,* Vol. 11, L.L. Cummings and B.M. Staw (Eds.), Greenwich, Conn.: JAI Press, pp. 1–42.

Ralston, D.A. and Elsass, P.M. (1989). Ingratiation and impression management in the organization. in *Impression Management in the Organization,* R.A. Giacalone and P. Rosenfeld (Eds.), Hillsdale, N.J.: Lawrence Erlbaum, pp. 235–249.

Regan, D.T. (1978). Attributional aspects of interpersonal attraction. in *New Directions in Attribution Research,* Vol. 2, J.H. Harvey, W. Ickes, and R.F. Kidd (Eds.), Hillsdale, N.J.: Lawrence Erlbaum, pp. 207–233.

Regan, D.T., Straus, E., and Fazio, R. (1974). Liking and the attribution process. *Journal of Experimental Social Psychology,* 10:385–397.

Ross, L. (1977). The intuitive psychologist and his shortcomings: Distortions in the attribution process. in *Advances in Experimental Social Psychology,* Vol. 10, L. Berkowitz (Ed.), New York: Academic Press, pp. 174–221.

Ross, M. and Fletcher, G.J.O. (1985). Attribution and social perception. in *Handbook of Social*

Psychology, Vol. 2, 3rd edition, G. Lindzey and E. Aronson (Eds.), New York: Random House, pp. 73–122.

Schlenker, B.R. (1980). *Impression Management: The Self-Concept, Social Identity, and Interpersonal Relations,* Monterey, Calif.: Brooks/Cole.

Schnake, M. (1991). Organizational citizenship: A review, proposed model, and research agenda. *Human Relations,* 44:735–759.

Snyder, M. (1987). *Public Appearances, Private Realities: The Psychology of Self-Monitoring,* New York: W.H. Freeman.

Tedeschi, J.T. and Melburg, V. (1984). Impression management and influence in the organization. in *Research in the Sociology of Organizations,* Vol. 3, S.B. Bacharach and E.J. Lawler (Eds.), Greenwich, Conn.: JAI Press, pp. 31–58.

Thomas, K.W. and Pondy, L.R. (1977). Toward an "intent" model of conflict management among principal parties. *Human Relations,* 30:1089–1102.

Vroom, V.H. (1964). *Work and Motivation,* New York: John Wiley.

Wayne, S.J. and Ferris, G.R. (1990). Influence tactics, affect, and exchange quality in supervisor–subordinate relations: A laboratory experiment and a field study. *Journal of Applied Psychology,* 75:487–499.

Wayne, S.J., Kacmar, K.M., and Ferris, G.R. (1989). Subordinate Upward Influence Effects on Coworker Response, paper presented at the Fourth Annual Conference of the Society for Industrial and Organizational Psychology, Inc., Boston.

Weary, G. and Arkin, R.M. (1981). Attributional self-presentation. in *New Directions in Attribution Research,* Vol. 3, J.H. Harvey, W. Ickes, and R.F. Kidd (Eds.), Hillsdale, N.J.: Lawrence Erlbaum, pp. 97–115.

Wortman, C.B. and Linsenmeier, J.A.W. (1977). Interpersonal attraction and techniques of ingratiation in organizational settings. in *New Directions in Organizational Behavior,* B.M. Staw and G.R. Salancik (Eds.), Chicago: St. Clair Press, pp. 133–178.

14

REALIZING THE ADVANTAGES OF ORGANIZATIONAL INTERDEPENDENCIES: THE ROLE OF ATTRIBUTIONALLY MEDIATED EMOTIONS*

Keith G. Allred

ABSTRACT

Organizational parties exist in interdependent relationships which include both compatible and incompatible interests. Organizational theory typically focuses on either the parties' compatible or incompatible interests in explaining organizational phenomena. Thus, organizational theory fails to illuminate how parties resolve the dilemma between cooperating and competing with each other. Drawing on negotiation research and Weiner's (1985, 1986) attributional theory of emotion, it is argued in this chapter that attributionally mediated emotions play an important role in organizational parties' choices to cooperate or compete. Hypotheses for research are identified, and a model of psychological processes by which parties choose to cooperate or compete is proposed.

*I thank Christine Edwards, Connie Gersick, Harold Kelley, Barbara Lawrence, David Lewin, and Bernard Weiner for their helpful comments on earlier versions of this chapter.

INTRODUCTION

Organizations exist, it can be argued, because people can achieve more by jointly pursuing compatible interests than they can by acting independently. However, organizational parties' interests are not perfectly or uniformly compatible. Parties to the interdependent relationships which constitute organizations confront situations in which doing what is best for the other party is not clearly what is best for one's own party. Interdependence poses the threat that the other party will behave in a manner detrimental to one's own interests (Pfeffer and Salancik, 1978). The mixed-motive nature of their interdependence thus presents organizational parties with a ubiquitous dilemma. Organizational parties hesitate to cooperate fully with other parties because incompatible interests expose one's party to exploitation. Parties hesitate to pursue their interests in a selfish or competitive manner, because such action threatens to forfeit the advantages of mutual cooperation on compatible interests. How do organizational parties resolve the dilemma of whether to cooperate or compete?

Attribution research suggests possible answers. In this chapter it is argued that interdependent parties choose between the horns of the mixed-motive interdependence dilemma, in part, by looking to the other party's past behavior. In particular, it is suggested that Party A's attributions for Party B's past behavior will shape whether Party A cooperates or competes with Party B in future situations. Attributions shape future cooperative or competitive behavior via the emotions they elicit. Thus, in Kelley and Michela's (1980) terms, this conceptual analysis focuses on the implications of attributions once made rather than on the processes by which the attributions are made.

After briefly mentioning that organizational theory leaves the dilemma of mixed-motive interdependence unaddressed, the research literature on negotiation is reviewed. Because it examines interactions between parties to mixed-motive interdependent relationships, negotiation research can illuminate organizational parties' responses to mixed-motive interdependence, whereas organizational theory does not. Integrating findings from research on negotiations with Weiner's (1985, 1986) attributional theory of emotion, a model of attributional processes that play a role in interdependent parties' decisions to cooperate or compete is developed. The model suggested by Weiner's theory represents processes common to interdependent social relationships in general. The proposed model is further elaborated in terms of two mediating variables that are important in organizational contexts. By drawing on intergroup attribution research, a mediating effect for the relative organizational subunit identities of the parties is proposed. By drawing on emotion research, a mediating effect for consideration of the other party's relative power is also proposed.

ORGANIZATIONAL THEORY

A thorough review of the large and complex organizational theory literature is beyond the purposes of the present discussion. However, briefly noting some basic themes in organizational theory will identify the need for a conceptual framework that addresses the dilemmas posed by organizational interdependencies. Organizational theory began in the first half of this century by explaining organizations with a clear focus on the efficiencies of joint pursuit of corresponding interests. In espousing scientific management, Taylor (1911) argued that the true interests of management and employees were one and the same.

Classical school theorists such as Follett (1942) argued that organizational collaboration did not require compromise of one party's interests to another's. Rather, all parties simply needed to contribute to decision-making processes so that their interests could be integrated. The human relations school (e.g., Roethlisberger and Dickson, 1939) suggested means by which the formal and informal organization could be brought into harmony. Theorists of the decision-making school (e.g., Barnard, 1938; Simon, 1945) argued that organizational parties' interests were sufficiently compatible, or could be rendered so compatible, that remaining incompatible interests were rather inconsequential. The compatible interests tradition has continued in the second half of the century (e.g., Argyris, 1964; Blau and Schoenherr, 1971; Blau and Scott, 1962; Likert, 1961, 1967; Ouchi and Jaeger, 1978). A newer tradition, however, recognizes that organizational parties' interests are not perfectly compatible. Theorists such as Dalton (1959), Stone (1974), and Pfeffer (1981) explore the uses of power and politics as means by which one organizational party protects its interests and attempts to coerce the other parties to behave in the manner it desires. Conflict inevitably results from parties' attempts to coerce each other. The incompatible interests theorists' portrayal of strife-ridden organizations thus sharply contrasts with the compatible interests theorists' representation of organizations as harmonious, collaborative entities.

The tendency for organizational theory to focus on either compatible or incompatible interests creates a blind spot in the view it provides of organizational parties' behavior. Bifurcated as it is, organizational theory leaves the dilemma posed by the mix of interests unexamined (Bacharach, 1983; Bacharach and Lawler, 1980, 1981a, 1981b; Kochan and Verma, 1983; Lax and Sebenius, 1986; Strauss, 1984). A number of theorists (e.g., Bacharach and Lawler, 1980; Lawrence and Lorsch, 1967; March and Simon, 1958), including agency theorists (see Eisenhardt, 1989) and transaction cost economists (e.g., Barney and Ouchi, 1988; Williamson, 1975) do acknowledge the existence of both compatible and incompatible interests in organizational relationships. However, because they typically treat compatible and incompatible interests in isolation, the mixed-interests theorists leave the dilemma posed by mixed interests unaddressed. Alison and Mike's experience illustrates the overlooked dilemma:

> Alison and Mike were the founding partners of an interior design growth firm. Mike's genius for creating Southwest office decor combined with Alison's business acumen to build a rapidly growing, highly profitable enterprise called Southwest Spaces.
>
> However, Mike and Alison's interests were not perfectly compatible. Mike sometimes felt that Alison's bottom-line orientation compromised the artistic commitment Mike felt was critical to the success of Southwest Spaces. Alison worried that Mike's artistic commitment blinded him to the harsh business realities they had to face to be successful.
>
> As a result of their difference in perspectives, Mike and Alison disagreed over several important decisions. Their disputes had generated a degree of mutual distrust. Mike was aware that Alison thought his artistic commitment limited the quality of his decisions. As a result, he wondered if Alison actually wanted to control the firm and confine him to design. Alison realized that Mike felt that her commitment to the bottom line over design limited her ability to make appropriate decisions for Southwest Spaces. Consequently, Alison wondered if Mike wanted to control the firm and confine her to day-to-day management affairs. In fact, both had considered trying to gain more control over the direction of the firm. Each, however, had been hesitant to try anything because they recognized the needed contribution the other made. Each realized the other would be offended by a move to gain power over the other and didn't want to sacrifice the other's needed good will and commitment.*

The compatible interests school of organizational theory explains how and why Alison and Mike could join together to produce more than what they could acting independently. The incompatible interests school explains why Alison and Mike are tempted to compete with each other. However, Alison and Mike's quandary is rooted in simultaneous pulls to cooperate and to compete. Because it focuses on either compatible or incompatible interests, organizational theory cannot illuminate the processes by which Alison and Mike choose between the horns of the dilemma.

Using Alison and Mike's interaction as a touchstone, the research literature on negotiation is reviewed next. Proceeding from an assumption of mixed-

---

*This example is a somewhat stylized account from an actual organization. The names of the organization and the people have been changed to preserve anonymity.

motive interdependence, negotiation research can shed light on how organizational parties resolve the dilemma unaddressed by organizational theory.

NEGOTIATION RESEARCH

Negotiation research identifies mixed-motive interdependence as a defining characteristic of negotiation. If the relationship between the parties to the negotiation were purely cooperative and the parties' interests purely compatible, there would be nothing about which to negotiate. Similarly, if the relationship were purely competitive and the parties' interests completely incompatible, there would be little point in negotiating. Finally, if the actions of one party left the other party unaffected, there would be no need for negotiation.

Consequently, negotiation is recognized as an important process by which organizational parties strive to realize the advantages and control the disadvantages of their interdependence. Indeed, Walton and McKersie (1965, p. 3) define negotiation as "the deliberate interaction of two or more complex social units which are attempting to define or redefine the terms of their interdependence." Viewed from this interdependence perspective, negotiation is a fundamental process by which organizational parties attempt to realize the very purpose for which organizations can be said to exist. Organizational scholars (Bacharach, 1983; Bacharach and Lawler, 1980; Kochan and Verma, 1983; Lax and Sebenius, 1986; Walton and McKersie, 1965) argue that researchers can illuminate the ways in which organizations achieve effectiveness by investigating the dynamics which promote or inhibit successful negotiations.

Negotiation research has identified motivational orientation as one of the critical determinants of negotiation effectiveness. Motivational orientation is the weight a negotiator gives to the other party's interests relative to the negotiator's own interests (Carnevale and Pruitt, 1992). Whether conducted from a social psychological (see Carnevale and Pruitt, 1992; Deutsch, 1973; Lewicki and Litterer, 1985; Pruitt, 1981; Pruitt and Rubin, 1986; Rubin and Brown, 1975), game theoretic (Axelrod, 1984; Rapoport, 1960, 1970), management (Blake and Mouton, 1979; Lax and Sebenius, 1986; Rahim, 1986), industrial relations (Chamberlain and Kuhn, 1986; Walton and McKersie, 1965), or communication perspective (see Womack, 1990), negotiation studies yield a common answer to the question of how organizational parties can effectively manage their interdependence. The most viable, functional response to interdependence is for the parties to give mutual consideration and weight to the other's interests in cooperatively choosing what to do. The mutually cooperative orientation consistently results in agreements that are objectively better than the agreements resulting from any other combination of motivational orientations. Parties are more satisfied with agreements resulting from a mutually cooperative orientation. Negotiations in which at least one party has low concern for itself or the other party result more frequently in impasse or poorer agreements.

Mutually cooperative orientations achieve more and better solutions to the problems of mixed-motive interdependence in part because they prevent the ill effects of mutually selfish and/or competitive behavior. These effects are at the heart of a substantial literature on social dilemmas such as the prisoner's and commons dilemmas (see Brewer and Kramer, 1985; Messick and Brewer, 1983). In part, the superiority of the mutually cooperative orientation also stems from the fuller exchange of information and joint problem-solving that it facilitates. Through joint problem-solving based on more information, the parties are often able to discover creative arrangements which better satisfy the needs of both than would have otherwise been apparent. Walton and McKersie's (1965) notion of integrative bargaining is the most widely acknowledged explication of these effects.

It should be noted, however, that the caveat that the cooperation must be mutual to be effective is a fundamental and problematic qualification. One of the least functional responses for any given party is to unilaterally weigh the other party's interests in choosing cooperative responses while the other party chooses responses based solely on what is best for itself. For example, a cooperative response by one party to the prisoner's dilemma, or by a number of parties to the commons dilemma, makes the competitive response that much more attractive for the other parties. Similarly, if one party attempts to engage in integrative bargaining and reveals more information about its own position and preferences, the other party can use that information to its advantage and not reciprocate the exchange of information. Thus, while cooperative responses offer the best solution to the problem of mixed-motive interdependence, they increase the threat and impact of exploitation.

Negotiation research thus demonstrates the critical role motivational orientation plays in realizing the advantages and managing the disadvantages of interdependence. The evidence of the superiority of the mutually cooperative response also raises the question of how parties choose and maintain the preferable cooperative orientation in the face of heightened potential exploitation. Current research investigating the determinants of motivational orientation itself is sparse in contrast to the abundance of research on the implications of motivational orientation. In their theorizing, negotiation researchers generally posit the existence of different motivational orientations without seriously examining the source of motivational orientation. In their empirical studies, negotiation researchers have often simply manipulated motivational orientation in laboratory settings.

Those researchers who have explored the determinants of motivational orientation have typically explained it in one of two ways. First, motivational orientation is conceived as an innate individual difference. People cooperate or compete because they are cooperative or competitive people. Second, motivational orientation is explained as a strategic choice based on a rational assessment of the negotiation situation. People consider issues such as the degree of compatibility of interests, the length of relationship, and the power of the other party when deciding whether to cooperate or compete.

Both explanations seem reasonable and have received some empirical support (see Carnevale and Pruitt, 1992; Rubin and Brown, 1975; Thompson, 1990 for reviews). Certainly, people do vary in how cooperative, competitive, or individualistic they are. It seems just as reasonable to argue that people will tend to be more cooperative when a rational assessment of the situation indicates that it is in one's own best interest to cooperate.

However, both individual difference and strategic choice explanations have their limitations. Invoking cooperative and competitive dispositions to explain all cooperative and competitive behavior is rather tautological. Furthermore, the individual difference explanation fails to account for substantial changes in motivational orientation within one person across different situations (Carnevale and Pruitt, 1992; Thompson, 1990). Explaining motivational orientation exclusively in terms of a rational assessment of what will promote one's own interests seems inadequate to explain the many observable conflict behaviors that are manifestly self-destructive. The conclusion of Alison and Mike's interaction can illustrate the shortcomings of existing explanations of parties' behavior in situations of mixed-motive interdependence:

> Steve, the accountant at Southwest Spaces, had arrived to discuss the firm's business plan and tax strategy for the coming year with Alison and Mike. However, Mike, facing several design deadlines, occasionally left the meeting to give feedback to some of the firm's designers. When he returned after one such departure, Steve mentioned that they had been discussing the need for Southwest Spaces to incorporate for tax and liability reasons. Steve explained that the process was simple and involved naming a board of directors. Mike suspected that Alison initiated the idea to wrest control from him. He said he wasn't interested in incorporating and immediately left the conference room again.
>
> Concerned that Mike was making a hasty decision without understanding its implications, Alison attempted to explain the rationale for incorporating further when Mike returned. Mike interpreted Alison's behavior as proof that she was trying to take control away from him. He insisted he would not agree to incorporate and left the room again. As Mike considered what Alison had done, he became convinced that her behavior reflected her lack of respect for his perspective. Angered, his opposition to incorporation mounted. Mike vowed to keep Southwest Spaces as it had been. As Alison considered Mike's behavior, she became convinced that his actions reflected an arrogance

and lack of respect for the expertise she brought to the endeavor. She was angered that he would consider his own judgment so superior to hers as to dismiss her recommendation without listening to her rationale. Alison determined not to back down, but to demand that they incorporate.

As each acted according to his/her interpretation of each other's motives, each became more convinced that his/her interpretation of the other was correct. The relationship deteriorated and, following an extended legal battle, Mike bought out Alison's interests. The company's capital was strained, sales decreased, costs increased, and design quality was neglected as Mike endeavored to continue independent of Alison.

If Alison and Mike's motivational orientations are to be explained in terms of predispositions toward cooperation or competition, what accounts for each person's shift from a mutually cooperative to a mutually competitive orientation? Although there seems to be some calculation of self-interest involved, it is difficult to explain Alison and Mike's behavior as the result of purely rational and strategic choices in pursuit of their interests. The strategic choice explanation portrays a process far more dispassionate than what appears to have occurred between Alison and Mike.

Indeed, one important determinant of motivational orientation which seems to be operating in Alison and Mike's interaction but which is lacking in both individual difference and strategic choice explanations is the role of emotions. Over two centuries ago, de Callieres (1716) observed that passions ruled princes' behavior in negotiations. Emotionally charged interactions analogous to Alison and Mike's are commonly observable among interdependent parties in organizations today. However, an analysis of the role emotions might play in determining the motivational orientations of interdependent parties toward each other is essentially nonexistent in modern research on negotiations (Shapiro, 1992a, 1992b). The question of how organizational parties achieve the advantages and control the disadvantages of interdependence is addressed next by broadening the analysis of motivational orientation antecedents. Specifically, the role that attributionally mediated emotions play in determining motivational orientation is examined.

ATTRIBUTION AND EMOTION

Initiated by Heider (1958), research over the past few decades has established the importance of attribution as a social process. In order to adapt effectively in social contexts, attributionists argue, it is necessary not only to understand how another party is behaving, but why they are so behaving. Kelley (1984) has observed that recent theories of emotion (e.g., Abelson, 1983; Averill, 1982; de Rivera, 1977, 1984; Roseman, 1984; Weiner, 1985, 1986; see also Frijda, 1988 for a review) explain emotional responses in attributional terms. According to cognitive appraisal emotion theorists, attributions elicit adaptive behaviors via the discrete emotions to which attributions give rise. Kelley further argues that attributionally mediated emotions have developed as adaptations specifically to the challenges posed by interdependent relationships. Parties choose how to act toward another party, he suggests, by looking to their partner's past behaviors. The interpretation or attribution one makes for a partner's past behavior elicits an emotional response that motivates and directs future behavior toward that partner appropriate to the interpretation of the past behavior. The previous discussion of organizational theory and negotiation research suggests that a challenge people commonly face in organizations is the dilemma between cooperating and competing with others with whom they are interdependent. Weiner's attributional analysis of emotion in particular can be understood as a description of how humans adapt to the dilemma between cooperating and competing.

Weiner (1985, 1986) argues that people search for causes of an event, particularly if an event's outcome is important, unexpected, or negative. As do other cognitive appraisal theorists, Weiner posits that the discrete emotions that causal attributions elicit direct people's behavior. The particular emotional response, Weiner argues, is a function of the position of an attribution along several abstract dimensions that underlie all causal attributions. One of those abstract dimensions, the degree to which a cause is under the volitional control of a party, has implications for social or other-directed emotions. Consequently, the control lability dimension is particularly relevant to the present analysis. When one perceives that another person's behavior negatively affects one, one will be more angry with that person to the extent that one construes the cause of that person's behavior to have been controllable by him or her. The more uncontrollable the cause one attributes for the same behavior, the less angry with that person one will be. In the preceding scenario, Mike believed Alison insisted on incorporating out of selfishness and greed. Mike likely perceived Alison's selfishness and greed to be controllable by her. Consequently, he was angry with her. Of course, if Mike had believed that Alison wanted to incorporate because she foresaw genuine tax and liability threats, he, recognizing her inability to control such threats, would likely have been less angry.

Parties similarly experience more gratitude for another party's positive behavior to the extent they attribute their behavior to controllable causes. For example, Mike might have believed that Alison continued to discuss tax strategy with Steve out of consideration for Mike. Mike might have positively interpreted her recommendation to incorporate, construing it to be Alison's way of saving him from detailed and tedious tax discussions, which he dislikes anyway, so that he could attend to his design deadlines. Recognizing Alison's consideration as controllable by her, Mike would likely have felt gratitude toward Alison. However, if Mike believed that Alison saved him from detailed tax discussions simply because Steve's time was limited and a conclusion had to be reached, Mike might have judged the cause of Alison's behavior to be less controllable by her (i.e., there was no freedom of choice) and would therefore have felt less gratitude.

Weiner's attributional analysis of anger and gratitude can be understood as an adaptation to the dilemma posed by mixed-motive interdependence. Working in tandem, gratitude and anger aim to realize the advantages and control the disadvantages of interdependence. When another party appears to be choosing the cooperative orientation, one can similarly respond with a cooperative orientation in order to achieve the advantages of interdependence that accrue from the mutually cooperative response. Gratitude can serve just this function. The cognitive antecedent of gratitude is a perception that another party, due to a cause controllable by that party, behaved positively toward another person. In other words, the other party chose to behave in a manner that benefited that person. The behavioral consequence of gratitude is to reciprocate the cooperative motivational orientation toward that party. Formally stated:

Hypothesis 1:   Gratitude toward another party will lead to greater regard for that party's interests.

When a party with whom one is interdependent acts, in contrast, without regard for one's interests, the motivational orientation research suggests one's interests are threatened. In such circumstances, one is particularly exposed to exploitation if one chooses a cooperative response, but will be less exposed if one also acts simply out of regard for one's own interests. Furthermore, a competitive response may serve to signal the other party that the competitive response will be less than ideal, possibly inducing the party to change its orientation. Anger can serve just this function. The cognitive antecedent of anger is an interpretation that a party with whom one is interdependent has behaved in a manner detrimental to one's own interests for a reason controllable by that party. In other words, the other party chose to behave in a harmful manner.* The behavioral consequence of anger is to elicit an individualistic or competitive response. Formally stated:

---

*Other emotional responses to the perceptions that another party chose to harm one are, of course, also possible. For example, a perception that a very powerful other chose to seriously harm one may lead to fear. Identification of all emotional responses to perceived harmful behavior by another is beyond the scope of the present analysis (see de Rivera 1977, 1984; Roseman, 1984 for further treatment of the issue). For purposes of the present discussion, it is simply argued that anger is one important emotional response to behavior that is perceived to be detrimental. When anger is elicited, the behavioral response will be as hypothesized.

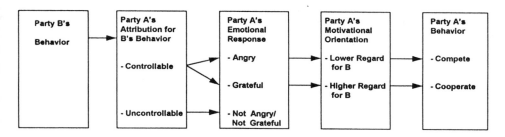

FIGURE 14.1 Attributional/emotional responses to mixed-motive interdependence.

Hypothesis 2: Anger toward another party will lead to less regard for that party's interests.

The relationship posited between attributionally mediated emotions and motivational orientation can be combined with relationships established in existing research into the model of psychological processes by which parties choose to cooperate and compete represented in Figure 14.1. Substantial empirical research testing Weiner's theory supports the linkages from behavior to attribution and from attribution to emotion (see Weiner, 1985, 1986). The vast research literature on the consequences of motivational orientation previously reviewed supports the linkages from motivational orientation to behavior. The proposed model thus moves beyond previous explanations of parties' cooperative and competitive choices. In contrast to individual difference explanations, the attributionally mediated emotions explanation accounts for variations in motivational orientation across situations. The proposed model also supplements the dispassionate and calculative processes specified by strategic choice explanations by elaborating the role emotions play. The model represented in Figure 14.1 applies to any social situation in which parties are interdependent and have imperfectly compatible interests. However, the basic linkages may be subject to modification in various social circumstances. In particular, it is argued here that two common and important characteristics of organizational relationships—organizational subunit group identities and power relationships—will modify the role of attributionally mediated emotions.

GROUP IDENTITY EFFECTS

Organizations are composed of numerous subunits. Although they can and do identify with the organization as a whole, individuals typically also identify themselves with the subunits to which they belong. Indeed, individuals' identification with an organizational subunit (e.g., division) often comprises their primary group identity within organizational contexts (Kramer, 1991). Organizational subunits exist in various mixed-motive interdependent relationships with other organizational subunits. Accordingly, the model represented in Figure 14.1 should account for organizational subunits' decisions to cooperate or compete with each other.

The adaptiveness of the behavioral responses that emotions elicit depends in part on the accuracy of the attributions that give rise to the emotions. Although people are known to be rational in large measure in the rules they use to interpret information to arrive at attributions (Harkness et al., 1985; Heider, 1958; Kelley, 1967; McArthur, 1972), their rationality is limited. Consistent with Simon and March's (March and Simon, 1958; Simon, 1945) general observations about the limits on rationality in decision-making, people are also bounded in the rationality with which they attribute the causes of other people's behavior. In part, these attributional errors appear to be the result of cognitive heuristics employed to cope with a complex world, as Simon and March observed. In part, these errors also may have self-enhancing motivational roots (Bradley, 1978; Zuckerman, 1979). Whatever the cause, research suggests that interdependent parties will tend to overattribute their partner's behavior to their partner's personal dispositions and underattribute the behavior to situational causes (Jones and Nisbett, 1972; Miller, 1976; Schneider and Miller, 1975; Ross, 1977; Sillars, 1981; Snyder and Jones, 1974; Watson, 1982). Thomas and Pondy (1977) have specifically documented pronounced attributional biases in corporate disputes. The evidence suggests this tendency may be particularly true when the other party's behavior negatively affects the attributor.

The emotional explanation of motivational orientation presented in Figure 14.1 can thus explain the kind of self-destructive competitive behaviors implied by Alison and Mike's experience. Mike seems to have overattributed Alison's behavior to her selfishness and greed. Conversely, he seems to have underattributed her behavior to the genuine tax and liability threats Steve was identifying. Mike's resulting anger thus elicited a response that may have been overly competitive. Alison similarly seems to have overattributed Mike's behavior to his selfishness and arrogance and underattributed his behavior to the threat incorporation implied to him. Alison's resulting anger also may have elicited an overly competitive response. The interaction thus degenerated into the self-perpetuating and self-destructive kind of conflict that strategic choice and dispositional theories of motivational orientation would have difficulty explaining.

The common attributional biases that Mike and Alison seem to have encountered can be exacerbated when attributing the cause of a party's behavior who is not a member of the groups with which one identifies (see Brewer, 1979; Brewer and Kramer, 1985; Hewstone, 1988, 1990; Messick and Mackie, 1989; Tajfel, 1982 for reviews). Referred to as the "ultimate attribution error" by Pettigrew

(1979) and the "intergroup attributional bias" by Hewstone (1990), people tend to attribute negative behaviors to dispositional causes more frequently when the person is an outgroup member than when the person is an ingroup member. Particularly under circumstances of highly incompatible interests and/or hostility between the groups, people will also tend to attribute positive behavior to situational causes more frequently when the actor is an outgroup member than when the actor is an ingroup member. Although the intergroup bias research has not focused on the controllability dimension of attributions per se, it is suggested here that people typically perceive dispositional causes for interpersonal behavior (e.g., selfishness or kindness) to be more controllable than situational causes. Accordingly, the following hypotheses are proposed:

Hypothesis 3a: Parties will attribute an outgroup member's negative behavior to more controllable causes than they will an ingroup member's negative behavior.

Hypothesis 3b: As a result of attributions to more controllable causes, parties will feel more anger toward an outgroup member than they will toward an ingroup member for a negative behavior.

Hypothesis 3c: As a result of higher levels of anger following a negative behavior, parties will exhibit less regard for an outgroup member's interests than they will for an ingroup member's interests.

Hypothesis 4a: Parties will attribute an outgroup member's positive behavior to less controllable causes than an ingroup member's positive behavior.

Hypothesis 4b: As a result of attributions to less controllable causes, parties will feel less gratitude toward an outgroup member than they will toward an ingroup member for a positive behavior.

Hypothesis 4c: As a result of lower levels of gratitude following a positive behavior, parties will exhibit less regard for an outgroup member's interests than they will for an ingroup member's interests.

POWER RELATIONSHIP EFFECTS

In addition to being characterized by subdivision into smaller groups, most organizations are also characterized by their hierarchical nature. Consequently, the relative power of the parties is another important feature of organizational relationships. It is suggested that power relationships, like group identity, will modify the causal pattern determining motivational orientation specified in Figure 14.1. However, it is proposed here that consideration of the other party's power will affect motivational orientation at a different phase of the process than consideration of the other organizational party's group identity does. While the effect of group identity on motivational orientation begins with attributional processes, considerations of another party's power relative to one's own will intervene at the point of the motivational orientation/behavior linkage. In other words, attributions for the other party's behavior, and the attendant emotions and motivational orientation, will not vary systematically according to differences in power relations. However, according to Frijda's (1988) "law of care for consequence," the effect of motivational orientation on behavior will vary systematically according to power considerations. Frijda argues that although emotions do tend to be absolute in the behavior they elicit, the behavioral implications do admit of other considerations of the environment. Accordingly, Frijda describes the

> ...law of care for consequence: Every emotional impulse elicits a secondary *impulse that tends to modify it in view of its possible consequences.* The major effect is response moderation. (emphasis in original, Frijda, 1988, p. 355)

Within an organizational environment of mixed-motive interdependent relationships, power may modify the behavioral implications of emotions identified in the proposed model. In particular, the behavioral responses to which anger gives rise via motivational orientation are likely to be modified by considerations of the other party's power. In this chapter, anger has been characterized as a response to protect oneself from exploitation in its less pronounced, more defensive manifestations. In its more pronounced and offensive manifestations, anger is an attempt by a party to induce a change in the negative behavior of the other party by withdrawing needed cooperation or by behavior that is antagonistic or punitive. However, if the other party is more powerful, anger is likely to be perceived as less instrumental in either protecting oneself from exploitation or inducing change in the other party's behavior. Moreover, drawing a more powerful other into a pattern of using one's power to induce desired behavior may obviously lead to negative repercussions. Consequently, whereas a subordinate will likely feel anger toward a superior, and a corresponding low regard for that superior's interests, he or she is not likely to behave as competitively toward a superior as a result of that anger as he or she will toward a peer. On the other hand, recognition that the other party is more powerful is not likely to moderate the behavioral implications of gratitude. Accordingly, the following hypothesis is proposed:

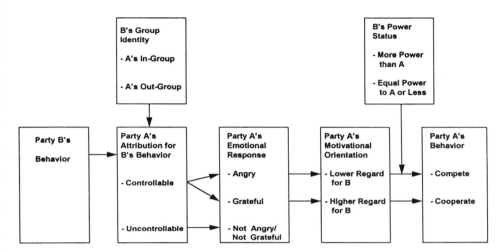

FIGURE 14.2 Attributional/emotional responses to organizational mixed-motive interdependence.

Hypothesis 5:   Anger toward a more powerful party will lead to smaller shifts toward less regard for the other party's interests than anger toward a party of equal power.*

CONCLUSION

The group identity and power hypotheses modify the model of basic human responses to situations of mixed-motive interdependence represented in Figure 14.1. The roles of these common organizational variables are incorporated in Figure 14.2. The model in Figure 14.2 also addresses the dilemma unaddressed by organizational theory. Organizational parties look to another party's past behavior to choose whether to cooperate or compete with that party. The model also supplements the explanations of motivational orientation offered in the

---

*As noted previously, it is also possible that one might have a different emotional response, such as fear, to being harmed by a powerful other. Thus, the change in motivational orientation due to consideration of the other's power would be mediated by another emotion. However, it is suggested here that a rather ominous behavior by a much more powerful party is necessary to elicit a truly fearful response as opposed to an angry response. Consistent with the hypothesis here proposed, Gibson (1994) found that organizational members often felt anger toward a superior who harmed them in some way, but suppressed the expression of anger.

literature on negotiations. By incorporating the roles of attributions and emotions, the proposed model can explain the variations in motivational orientation of one party across situations that eluded individual difference explanations. The attributionally mediated emotions explanation also addresses the difficulties strategic choice models have in explaining the emotionally charged, self-perpetuating, and self-destructive patterns into which organizational parties sometimes fall while navigating the difficulties of mixed-motive interdependence.

The further understanding of the determinants of motivational orientation implied by the proposed model suggests means by which parties might maintain the preferable mutually cooperative orientation. For example, the proposed model suggests one might prevent self-defeating intraorganizational conflict through organizational policies and structures that enhance members' identification with the organization as a whole relative to identification with particular subunits. Following the prescriptions the model might produce, organizational parties may be able to more effectively navigate the pitfalls of interdependence in order to more fully realize its advantages

REFERENCES

Abelson, R.P. (1983). Whatever became of consistency theory? *Personality and Social Psychology Bulletin,* 9:37–54.

Argyris, C. (1964). *Integrating the Individual and the Organization,* New York: Wiley.

Averill, J.R. (1982). *Anger and Aggression: An Essay of Emotion,* New York: Springer-Verlag.

Axelrod, R. (1984). *The Evolution of Cooperation,* New York: Basic Books.

Bacharach, S.B. (1983). Bargaining within organizations. in *Negotiating in Organizations,* M.H. Bazerman and R.L. Lewicki (Eds.), Beverly Hills, Calif.: Sage Publications, pp. 360–374.

Bacharach, S.B. and Lawler, E.J. (1980). *Power and Politics in Organizations,* San Francisco: Jossey-Bass.

Bacharach, S.B. and Lawler, E.J. (1981a). *Bargaining: Power, Tactics, and Outcomes,* San Francisco: Jossey-Bass.

Bacharach, S.B. and Lawler, E.J. (1981b). Power and tactics in bargaining. *Industrial and Labor Relations Review,* 34:219–233.

Barnard, C.I. (1938, reissued 1968). *The Function of the Executive,* Cambridge, Mass.: Harvard University Press.

Barney, J.B. and Ouchi, W.G. (Eds.). (1988). *Organizational Economics,* San Francisco: Jossey-Bass.

Blake, R.R. and Mouton, J.S. (1979). Intergroup problem solving in organizations: From theory to practice. in *The Social Psychology of Intergroup Relations,* W.G. Austin and S. Worchel, (Eds.), Monterey, Calif.: Brooks/Cole.

Blau, P.M. and Schoenherr, R.A. (1971). *The Structure of Organizations,* New York: Basic Books.

Blau, P.M. and Scott, W. (1962). *Formal Organizations,* San Francisco: Chandler.

Bradley, G.W. (1978). Self-serving biases in the attribution process: A reexamination of the fact or fiction question. *Journal of Personality and Social Psychology,* 8:56–71.

Brewer, M.B. (1979). In-group bias in the minimal intergroup situation: A cognitive–motivational analysis. *Psychological Bulletin,* 86(2):307–324.

Brewer, M.B. and Kramer, R.M. (1985). The psychology of intergroup attitudes and behavior. *Annual Review of Psychology,* 36:219–243.

Carnevale, P.J. and Pruitt, D.J. (1992.) Negotiation and mediation. *Annual Review of Psychology,* 43:531–582.

Chamberlain, N.W. and Kuhn, J.W. (1986). *Collective Bargaining,* 3rd edition, New York: McGraw-Hill.

Dalton, M. (1959). *Men Who Manage,* New York: John Wiley and Sons.

de Callieres, F. (1716, reissued in 1976). *On the Manner of Negotiating with Princes,* A.F Wyte (trans.), Notre Dame, Ind.: Notre Dame University Press.

de Rivera, J. (1977). A structural theory of the emotions. *Psychological Issues,* 10(4), Monograph 40.

de Rivera, J. (1984). The structure of emotional relationships. in *Review of Personality and Social Psychology,* Vol. 5, P. Shaver (Ed.), Beverly Hills, Calif.: Sage Publications, pp. 116–145.

Deutsch, M. (1973). *The Resolution of Conflict: Constructive and Destructive Processes,* New Haven, Conn.: Yale University Press.

Eisenhardt, K.M. (1989). Agency theory: An assessment and review. *Academy of Management Review,* 14(1):57–74.

Follett, M.P. (1942). *Dynamic Administration: The Collected Papers of Mary Parker Follett,* H.C. Metcalf and L. Urwick (Eds.), New York: Harper and Row.

Frijda, N.H. (1988). The laws of emotion. *American Psychologist,* 43(5):349–358.

Gibson, D. (1994). Emotional scripts and organization change. in *Advances in Organization Development,* Vol. 3, F. Massarik (Ed.), Norwood, N.J.: Ablex.

Harkness, A.R., DeBono, K.G., and Borgida, E. (1985). Personal involvement and strategies for making contingency judgments. *Journal of Personality and Social Psychology,* 49:22–32.

Heider, F. (1958). *The Psychology of Interpersonal Relations,* New York: Wiley.

Hewstone, M. (1988). Attributional bases of intergroup conflict. in *The Social Psychology of Intergroup Conflict,* W. Stroebe et al. (Eds.), New York: Springer-Verlag.

Hewstone, M. (1990). The "ultimate attribution error"? A review of the literature on intergroup causal attribution. *European Journal of Social Psychology,* 20:311–335.

Jones, E.E. and Nisbett, R.E. (1972). The actor and the observer: Divergent perceptions of the causes of behavior. in *Attribution: Perceiving the Causes of Behavior,* E.E. Jones et al. (Eds.), Morristown, N.J.: General Learning Press.

Kelley, H.H. (1967). Attribution theory in social psychology. in *Nebraska Symposium on Motivation,* D. Levine (Ed.), Lincoln: University of Nebraska Press.

Kelley, H.H. (1984). Affect in interpersonal relations. in *Review of Personality and Social Psychology,* Vol. 5, P. Shaver (Ed.), Beverly Hills, Calif.: Sage Publications, pp. 89–115.

Kelley, H.H. and Michela, J. (1980). Attribution theory and research. *Annual Review of Psychology,* 31:457–501.

Kochan, T.A. and Verma, A. (1983). Negotiations in organizations: Blending industrial relations and organizational behavior approaches. in *Negotiating in Organizations,* M.H. Bazerman and R.J. Lewicki (Eds.), Beverly Hills, Calif.: Sage Publications, pp. 13–32.

Kramer, R.M. (1991). Intergroup relations and organizational dilemmas: The role of categorization processes. *Research on Organizational Behavior,* 13:191–228.

Lawrence, P. and Lorsch, J. (1967). *Organization and Environment,* Cambridge, Mass.: Harvard University Press.

Lax, D.A. and Sebenius, J.K. (1986.) *The Manager as Negotiator,* New York: The Free Press.

Lewicki, R.J. and Litterer, J.A. (1985). *Negotiation,* Homewood, Ill.: Richard D. Irwin.

Likert, R. (1961). *New Patterns of Management,* New York: McGraw-Hill.

Likert, R. (1967). *The Human Organization,* New York: McGraw-Hill.

March, J.G. and Simon, H.A. (1958). *Organizations,* New York: John Wiley and Sons.

McArthur, L.A. (1972). The how and what of why: Some determinants and consequences of causal attribution. *Journal of Personality and Social Psychology,* 22:171–193.

Messick, D.M. and Brewer, M.B. (1983). Solving social dilemmas: A review. in *Review of Personality and Social Psychology,* Vol. 4, L. Wheeler and P. Shaver (Eds.), Beverly Hills, Calif.: Sage Publications, pp. 11–44.

Messick, D.M. and Mackie, D.M. (1989). Intergroup relations. *Annual Review of Psychology,* 40:45–81.

Miller, A.G. (1976). Constraint and target effects in the attribution of attitudes. *Journal of Experimental Social Psychology,* 12:325–339.

Ouchi, W.G. and Jaeger, A.M. (1978). Type z organization: Stability in the midst of mobility. *Academy of Management Review,* 3:305–314.

Pettigrew, T.F. (1979). The ultimate attribution error. *Journal of Personality and Social Psychology,* 5:461–476.

Pfeffer, J. (1981). *Power in Organizations,* Marshfield, Mass.: Pitman.

Pfeffer, J. and Salancik, G.J. (1978). *The External Control of Organizations: A Resource Dependence Perspective,* New York: Harper and Row.

Pruitt, D.G. (1981). *Negotiation Behavior,* New York: Academic Press.

Pruitt, D.G. and Rubin, J.Z. (1986). *Social Conflict: Escalation, Stalemate, and Settlement,* New York: Random House.

Rahim, M.A. (Ed.). (1986). *Managing Conflict in Organizations,* New York: Praeger.

Rapoport, A. (1960). *Fights, Games and Debates,* Ann Arbor: University of Michigan Press.

Rapoport, A. (1970). Conflict resolution in the light of game theory and beyond. in *The Structure of Conflict,* P.G. Swingle (Ed.), New York: Academic Press.

Roethlisberger, F.J. and Dickson, W.J. (1939, reissued 1966). *Management and the Worker: An Account of a Research Program Conducted by the Western Electric Company, Hawthorne Works, Chicago,* Cambridge, Mass.: Harvard University Press.

Roseman, I.J. (1984). Cognitive aspects of emotions and emotional behavior. in *Review of Personality and Social Psychology,* Vol. 5, P. Shaver (Ed.), Beverly Hills, Calif.: Sage Publications, p. 11–36.

Ross, L. (1977). The intuitive psychologist and his shortcomings: Distortions in the attribution process. in *Advances in Experimental Social Psychology,* Vol. 10, L. Berkowitz (Ed.), New York: Academic Press.

Rubin, J. and Brown, B.R. (1975). *The Social Psychology of Bargaining and Negotiation,* New York: Academic Press.

Schneider, D.J. and Miller, R.S. (1975). The effects of enthusiasm and quality of arguments on attitude attribution. *Journal of Personality,* 43:693–708.

Shapiro, D.L. (1992a). The Importance of "Considering" Grievants' Expressed Views: What Does This Mean? paper presented at the annual meeting of the Academy of Management, Las Vegas.

Shapiro, D.L. (1992b). New Developments in Workplace Fairness Issues, preconference symposium, Conflict Management Division, annual meeting of the Academy of Management, Las Vegas.

Sillars, A.L. (1981). Attributions and interpersonal conflict resolution. in *New Directions in Attribution Research,* Vol. 3, J.H. Harvey, W. Ickes, and R.F. Kidd (Eds.), Hillsdale, N.J.: Erlbaum, pp. 279–305.

Simon, H.A. (1945, reissued 1976). *Administrative Behavior,* New York: The Free Press.

Snyder, M.L. and Jones, E.E. (1974). Attitude attribution when behavior is constrained. *Journal of Experimental Social Psychology,* 33:435–441.

Stone, K. (1974). The origins of job structures in the steel industry. *Review of Radical Political Economics,* 6(2):61–95.

Strauss, A. (1984). *Negotiations,* San Francisco: Jossey-Bass.

Tajfel, H. (1982). Social psychology of intergroup relations. *Annual Review of Psychology,* 33:1–39.

Taylor, F.W. (1911, reissued 1967). *The Principles of Scientific Management,* New York: W.W. Norton.

Thomas, K.W. and Pondy, L.R. (1977). Toward an "intent" model of conflict management among principal parties. *Human Relations,* 30:1089–1102.

Thompson, L. (1990). Negotiation behavior and outcomes: Empirical evidence and theoretical issues. *Psychological Bulletin,* 108(3):515–532.

Walton, R.E. and McKersie, R.E. (1965). *A Behavioral Theory of Labor Negotiations,* New York: McGraw-Hill.

Watson, D. (1982). The actor and observer: How are their perceptions of causality different? *Psychological Bulletin,* 92:682–700.

Weiner, B. (1985). An attributional theory of achievement motivation and emotion. *Psychological Review,* 92:548–573.

Weiner, B. (1986). *An Attributional Theory of Motivation and Emotion,* New York: Springer-Verlag.

Williamson, O.E. (1975). *Markets and Hierarchies: Analysis and Antitrust Implications,* New York: Free Press.

Womack, D.F. (1990). Applied communications research in negotiation: Implications for practitioners. in *Theory and Research in Conflict Management,* M.A. Rahim (Ed.), New York: Praeger, pp. 32–53.

Zuckerman, M. (1979). Attribution of success and failure revisited, or: The motivational bias is alive and well in attribution theory. *Journal of Personality,* 47:245–287.

15

FIXING BLAME IN
n-PERSON ATTRIBUTIONS:
A SOCIAL IDENTITY MODEL
FOR ATTRIBUTIONAL
PROCESSES IN
NEWLY FORMED
CROSS-FUNCTIONAL GROUPS

Don Michael McDonald

ABSTRACT

Cooperation is not always achieved within cross-functional groups. When discrepancies over interactions occur, pre-existing social structures, such as departmental affiliation, may bias the selection of attributional targets (selection of who is to blame) and thereby affect cooperation in newly formed groups. This research advances attributional theory into groups where more than one actor may be the target of attribution (*n*-person attributions) and demonstrates empirically that pre-existing group relationships may cause differential ascriptions of blame within groups involved in cooperative processes.

©St. Lucie Press CCC 1-884015-19-0 1/95/$100/$.50

INTRODUCTION

Cross-functional groups are important to organizations because they link valuable resources within organizations. Cross-functional groups, which may take the form of task forces, committees, project teams, quality circles, and task groups of all types, are comprised of representatives from various pre-existing groups within larger organizations. They can easily be critical elements in Total Quality Management and reengineering efforts. Cross-functional groups require cooperation among members, i.e., willingness to help others in the process of achieving one's own objective(s).

Cooperation within cross-functional groups is important to organization success because it contributes toward unified direction (Bonnet, 1986; Eckhardt, 1987; Kanter, 1983), synergy (Sparrow and Pettigrew, 1988), and sustained competitive advantage. Cooperation is threatened by suboptimization (Deming, 1986) or subgroup optimization (Schwartz-Shea, 1991). Suboptimizing occurs when actors (individuals or groups) pursue objectives to their parochial interests and fail to achieve the best interest of the larger group or organization. This is a failure in cooperation. Competitive advantage for one organization over others exists if the organization can gain a resource or resources that other organizations do not have and cannot copy (Porter, 1987). If competitive advantage is to be sustained (i.e., be an advantage that competitors are unable to neutralize through duplicating it or drawing it away), then the resources that comprise it are best constituted across individuals in the group or organization, not within single individuals or the materials and technologies they use (Barney, 1986). Working relationships and social structures, which depend on cooperation, constitute such resources (Ulrich, 1991).

Cooperation does not always occur in groups formed across departmental lines (Brown et al., 1986; Dougherty, 1992). In her exploratory study of 18 new product efforts in five firms in the computer communications and chemical materials industries, Dougherty documented significant failure in cooperation between technology and marketing groups as they attempted to join together to solve corporate problems. Dougherty claims that even though cooperation across departments is important to commercial success of new products, new product development efforts seldom achieve it. Dougherty not only argues that cooperation failure occurs in organizations, but also implies that it is negatively related to productivity.

Cooperation may be affected by group member response to discrepancy. Discrepancy is defined here as the perception by an observer that the actions of another are contrary to expectations of cooperation. Discrepancy does not necessarily require malice, but it is a condition in which cooperation and understanding of intent can no longer be assumed by the observer, and the assumption of malice may be an option. Discrepancy does not require conflict in objectives, but simply differences in objectives. Interpretation of the discrepancy depends on the observer. When cross-functional groups assemble, their members can be expected to come with different views on desired outcome. Even if objectives are independent (i.e., they can be achieved at the same time without compromise or interdependence), discrepancies are inevitable, and group members must resolve discrepancies effectively in order to continue to work together in a cooperative manner (Bettenhausen and Murnighan, 1985).

The present research explores one possible reason for failure of cooperation in cross-functional groups: misdirected attributions of blame in response to discrepancies during group interactions. For the sake of parsimony, the scope of the present research is limited. The context of interest is newly formed, cross-functional groups. The phenomena under study are attributional responses of group members to discrepancies related to the pursuit of independent objectives. This analysis sought to investigate within-group phenomena common to all group members; therefore some elements of the social structure were held constant. No hierarchical, role, or status differences were included, because these may result in different attributional experiences from one group to another (Berger et al., 1992; Martinko and Gardner, 1987). Sequences and channels of interaction among members are defined the same for all group members in order to prevent differential access to resources from being a factor. The findings of the present research may be generalizable beyond these limitations, but that is left to future research.

ATTRIBUTION AS AN EXPLANATION FOR COOPERATION FAILURE

Attribution (and attributional) theory is an appropriate base for developing a model of discrepancy response in the context of newly formed cross-functional groups. Attribution refers to an observer's inference of the cause of behavior (either in themselves or others), and the attributional process suggests that the attributor's future (behavior) is in some way affected by the attribution (Ross and Fletcher, 1985). Attribution theory posits that attributions may be precipitated by the observation of discrepancy (Hastie, 1984). The following selective review of literature makes clear that attribution theory readily links observations of discrepancy to willingness to cooperate and that attributions can be biased.

Discrepancy leads to attributions of cause. Heider (1944, 1958), commonly acknowledged as the father of attribution theory, refers to his theory as common-sense or naive psychology, because he attempts to explain how the typical, untrained layperson might attribute cause to another person's outcomes. "In common-sense psychology (as in scientific psychology) the result of an action is felt to depend on two sets of conditions, namely, factors within the person and factors within the environment." (Heider, 1994, p. 82). The internal–external dimension continues to be central to most attribution models. Jones and Davis (1965) and Jones and McGillis (1976) state that attribution takes place when the actor who is to make an attribution (the observer) decides if behavior is caused by its actor (target) or its particular setting (environment). Jones and McGillis (1976) conclude that information about intent comes only from unique effects of actions, i.e., actions that are inconsistent with expectations of the observer. "When intentional behavior departs from expectations, the observer gains insight about the actor's personality and motives" (Crittenden, 1983).

Attributions of cause affect willingness to cooperate. As Kelley (1971, p. 22) explains, "The attributor is not simply an attributor, a seeker after knowledge; his latent goal in gaining knowledge is that of effective management of him[/her]self and [the] environment." Weiner (1974) exemplifies this point when he states that attribution of responsibility (whether or not the actor had control over environmental conditions) affects the observer's willingness to help the actor. By so doing, Weiner links the attribution of responsibility to willingness to cooperate with the needs of others. Weiner's (1974, 1986) attributional process model is respected as one of the most comprehensive attributional models developed.

Weiner (1974) notes that response in the attributional process may be biased by the observer's self-interest. Elliott (1989) builds on Weiner's research to hypothesize about differences between an observer's attributions about him/herself and attributions about another. Using the four characteristics of attribution of Weiner et al. (1972), Elliott found empirical evidence that subjects more heavily credit their own outcomes with effort, ability, and difficulty of a situation and less with luck than they do the outcomes of other actors under the same circumstances. This suggests a connection between self-interest as a motive and biased interpretations of the actions of others. This is consistent with Forsyth (1980), who argued that both the causes and consequences of attributions vary according to the function that attribution serves for the observer.

Self-interest may also bias recall of causal events. Nisbett and Wilson (1977) contend that observers are sometimes unaware of a stimulus, unaware of the response, and/or unaware that the stimulus has affected the response. They contend that when people attempt to report on their cognitive processes, they do so not on the basis of any true introspection, but based on a priori, implicit causal theories of plausible causes. Report is accurate only if real cause seems plausible and salient to the observer.

SOCIAL IDENTITY AS A FACTOR IN ATTRIBUTION BIAS

Social identity theory advances attribution theory into social contexts, providing a basis for bias and its consequences beyond the dyad. "Social identity is an individual's knowledge that he/she belongs to certain social groups together with some emotional and value significance to him/her of the membership" (Tajfel, 1972, p. 292). Social identity suggests that actors categorize people and assign themselves to a category in order to ascribe meaning to themselves within a social context (Doise et al., 1988). This occurs automatically when any person is placed in a new social context, and it has long been the basis for theories of social attribution (Deschamps, 1973–74). Social identity ties self-interest to the characteristics and actions of others. Once categories are established in the perceptions of individuals, individuals attribute qualities to others based on the implications these qualities have upon themselves. Empirical evidence indicates that attribution of characteristics to other groups (outgroups) is made in a fashion that will preserve the social identity of one's own group (ingroup) and enhance its value (Deschamps, 1973–74; Brewer, 1985). When ingroups and outgroups are defined within larger groups, the effect can be detrimental to cooperation in the larger context (Brewer and Schneider, 1990).

n-PERSON ATTRIBUTIONS

Most advancement of attribution theory beyond the dyad leaps directly to the intergroup level, ignoring intragroup phenomena. Social identity theory has been used to explain observer bias about outgroup member characteristics in general (e.g., Augoustinos, 1990) and outgroup members specifically (e.g., Hewstone et al., 1982), but not for selectivity bias within the observer's own group (intragroup). *n*-Person groups (i.e., groups larger than a dyad) have been studied in the context of social dilemmas (Dawes, 1980). Few, however, have considered attributions in *n*-person groups, and those who have (Van Lange et al., 1989, 1990) explore social dilemmas without the aid of social identity theory. Social identities that create partitions within a group may cause cooperation failure in intragroup processes, even when objectives are not in conflict. The author could find no test of *n*-person group cooperation when objectives were not in conflict.

Social identity theory can make salient the selection of targets of attribution in *n*-person groups. The target of attribution may be in question if an observer is exposed to more than one actor at a time. The observer may not be accurate in noting who perpetrated any given act. Social identity theory suggests that observers may be biased in recalling who perpetrated actions that the observer deems discrepant, if who the perpetrator is has salience for the observer's self-interest (Howard and Rothbart, 1980). If this occurred within a group, it would constitute an *n*-person attribution bias. Social identity links self-interest to actions attributed to others (Brewer, 1985). Discrepancy by definition occurs when another's actions are perceived as contrary to an observer's expectations, and the observer of an ingroup member is more likely to expect the actions to be more like his or her own, given the same opportunity. Observance of discrepancy in an ingroup member is inconsistent with a tendency to perceive ingroup members as like oneself, but observance of discrepancy in an outgroup member is not. Recall of events is linked to congruence (Nisbett and Wilson, 1977); therefore, recall of who perpetrated an action deemed discrepant is linked to social identity. Target selection can thus be based on selective recall of who the actor was.

MODEL

Weiner's (1974, 1986) attributional process model lends itself to inclusion of target selection in *n*-person groups. Weiner states that the process begins with an event that is not consistent with desired goals of the observer, followed by a causal search. According to Weiner, the search is affected by "a large number of variables...including past history information, causal rules, and communications from others" (p. 79). At this juncture, search for the target in *n*-person groups can be included, followed by what Weiner defines as the next step—the attribution of cause. Weiner refers to causal antecedents of attribution as the weighing of specific information and hedonic bias, and it involves achievement and affiliation. Evidence shows that if an observer perceives him/herself as in a category common to the actor, attribution is biased (Stephan, 1977). It may also be that differential affiliations among group members bias identification of the target of attribution. Adapting Weiner's (1974, 1986) model to include social identity factors in *n*-person groups (Figure 15.1), the sequence becomes (1) assembly of a new group, (2) categorization of group members and assignment of self to a category, (3) occurrence of discrepancy, (4) selection of target, and (5) attribution of cause.

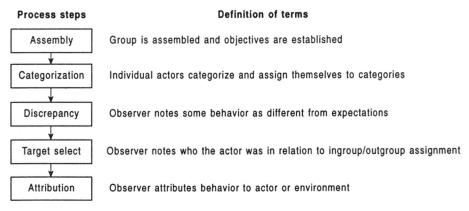

Process steps　　　　　　　　　　　　**Definition of terms**

Assembly	Group is assembled and objectives are established
Categorization	Individual actors categorize and assign themselves to categories
Discrepancy	Observer notes some behavior as different from expectations
Target select	Observer notes who the actor was in relation to ingroup/outgroup assignment
Attribution	Observer attributes behavior to actor or environment

FIGURE 15.1　A social identity model of attributional processes in *n*-person groups.

Social identity theory suggests at least two hypotheses about attributions within n-person groups. One pertains to the selection of target and the other to attribution of cause. First, selection of targets may be biased by whether observers perceive potential targets as ingroup or outgroup members. Since discrepancy occurs over actions contrary to what the observer would have done, and observers tend to perceive ingroup members as more similar to themselves (Tajfel, 1972), even seeking out similarities once categories are established (Tajfel, 1974), social identity theory predicts that observers will tend to recall discrepancies as perpetrated by outgroup members more often than they will by ingroup members.

In newly formed cross-functional groups, previous group experience may be a sufficient basis for social identity bias. The basis for categorization in social identity theory may be any factor(s) about the individual that can be used to differentiate him/herself from some others, but not from all others. Tajfel (1974) notes that the individual is simultaneously a member of "numerous social groups, and that membership contributes, positively or negatively, to the image that [one] has of [one]self" (p. 69). This suggests that awareness of membership extends beyond the context in which an individual may find him/herself at any given time.

Previously established social identities may be brought to bear in current groups. As noted earlier, it would not be unusual for cross-functional groups to have two or more members from each of several functional groups within the larger organization. It is also logical that individuals would seek to meet identity needs by drawing categorization lines around previously established relationships represented in the present assembly, rather than ignoring them in favor of establishing categories that cut across previously established relationships.

> **Hypothesis 1:** When observers of discrepancy in newly formed n-person groups have a previously established basis for identifying with some group members and not with others, observers will tend to report outgroup members as perpetrators of discrepant actions disproportionately more often than they will ingroup members.

Once the perpetrator of the discrepant action has been selected by the observer, fundamental attribution error (Ross and Fletcher, 1985) may occur based on social identity. When negative outcomes are involved, observers tend to attribute the environment as the cause for attributions about themselves, whereas they see actors more as the cause for attributions about others (Elliott, 1989). Social identity theory, however, suggests that observers will tend to perceive ingroup members as more similar to themselves, i.e., they will reflect upon themselves in evaluating an ingroup member's behavior (Brown, 1984; Tajfel, 1972). Attribution of responsibility to ingroup members reflects on the observer.

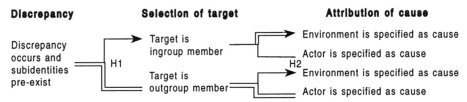

FIGURE 15.2 Response to discrepancy in *n*-person attributions. Double line represents tendency predicted by hypotheses.

Social identity theory therefore suggests that observers may be biased toward attributing discrepancies more toward the environment if the selected targets are ingroup members and more toward actors if selected targets are outgroup members.

> **Hypothesis 2:**   When members in newly formed *n*-person groups observe discrepancies with actors with whom they have a previously established basis for identity, observers will tend to attribute cause more toward environments than actors, whereas if they do not have a basis, they will tend to attribute the cause disproportionately more toward actors than environment.

The hypothesis sequence described above is graphically represented in Figure 15.2. Once discrepancy occurs, observers tend to select outgroup members as perpetrators of the discrepant action. If selected actors are ingroup members, observers tend to attribute discrepant actions to environments. If selected actors are outgroup members, observers tend to attribute discrepant actions to actors.

METHOD

A laboratory experiment was used to test the above hypotheses. Subjects were 84 university juniors and seniors who had worked on graded group projects in management classes (about ten weeks at the time of testing). Advance arrangements were made with course instructors for students to be randomly assigned to groups for the course projects. This assignment created the previously existing social identities required for manipulation. *n*-Person (experimental) groups were constructed of four subjects—two pairs of subjects, each pair from a different class project group. Two pairs created a condition of ingroup and outgroup within the same *n*-person experimental group.

Gender was blocked. All pairs and all *n*-person groups were either all male or all female. Gender is suspect as a status variable affecting disagreement

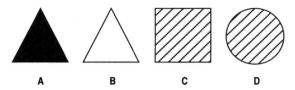

A   B   C   D

FIGURE 15.3   One possible arrangement of four cards. If cards in positions B and C were interchanged, both objectives would be completely met for these four cards.

resolution (Berger et al., 1980), attributions (Crittenden and Wiley, 1980), and social identity (Amancio, 1989) and as such may affect cooperation in task groups (Berger et al., 1992; Garza and Borchert, 1990). No older (e.g., second career) students were placed into groups to prevent age from being a status issue.

An independent objective interaction was adapted* to generate discrepancies among subjects within n-person groups. The task was to assemble a single row of cards from piles of cards dealt to the subjects individually (a kind of four-handed solitaire). Subjects were handed instructions to read silently before they took turns placing cards into a single row. Two of the instructions specified that no two cards of the same color (among a choice of three) were to be arranged consecutively. The other two instructions specified that no two cards of the same shape (among a choice of three) were to be arranged consecutively. After all cards were on the table, subjects were allowed to change card positions, one per sequential turn, until all subjects were satisfied with the arrangement. No talking was allowed during interaction. Both objectives could be achieved simulta-neously, but both could also be achieved with moves that contradicted the other objective. Figure 15.3 demonstrates how the shapes objective could be contra-dicted while meeting the colors objective (cards A and B), how the colors objective could be contradicted while meeting the shapes objective (cards C and D), and how both could be achieved simultaneously (cards B and C).

Discrepancy was defined as one subject recognizing that another placed a card in the row in a way that contradicted the first subject's understanding of the objective. Eighteen cards (two sets of three colors and three shapes each) were dealt to the subjects in an identical distribution for each n-person group. Figure 15.4 illustrates how instructions and seating were arranged so that each subject had instructions different from the subject with whom he or she had previously worked as well as different from one subject with whom he or she had not. Objectives were alternated around the table to increase the likelihood of discrepancy occurring during play. Discrepancies occurred randomly, and all

---

*The author would like to thank Inter-Dynamics for permission to adapt its copyrighted materials for use in academic research.

SUBJECT B
Identity 1, with
Color Objective

SUBJECT C
Identity 2, with
Shape Objective

SUBJECT A
Identity 1, with
Shape Objective

SUBJECT D
Identity 2, with
Color Objective

FIGURE 15.4 Arrangement of subjects in *n*-person groups to achieve different objectives across previous social identities.

subjects became observers within a group as the cards were played and later rearranged.

After interaction was completed, all subjects were asked to complete a questionnaire. One question asked, "Did some player make a move different from your initial understanding of the game? If so, what is the place letter of the player whom you first observed making such a move?" (Each seat position was labeled A, B, C, or D.) Hypothesis 1 suggests that observers will tend to notice or report more first occurrences of contradiction in outgroup subjects than in ingroup subjects. The questionnaire also asked for attributions of cause, but did not initially impose predetermined options on the subjects. Instead, they were asked the open-ended question, "What was your first thought as to the reason for this discrepancy?" This was intended to reduce hegemony. (By suggesting that the instructions were a possible alternative cause before the subjects had an opportunity to reply might affect response.) Afterward, subjects were asked to choose from among a list of statements the one that best represented their open-ended response. Options included the actor (other player) or the environment (rules of the game). Hypothesis 2 suggests that the rules of the game would be indicated more often for ingroup targets than for outgroup targets and that the actors would be marked more often for outgroup targets than for ingroup targets.

Hypothesis 1 was analyzed by chi-square goodness of fit, i.e., chi-square as a test against a mathematically known ratio of occurrence. The known ratio was the ratio of cross-identity (outgroup) to within-identity (ingroup) occurrences of contradictory moves. When a contradictory move occurred, one subject would not detect it—the one with the same objective as the actor. Contradiction would occur for the other two observers simultaneously—one who identified with the actor and one who did not. The ratio of first contradictory moves occurring for an ingroup member and an outgroup member was therefore exactly one to one. This was true in every case, but discrepancies, by definition, only occurred when contradictions were noted by observers. The chi-square was therefore computed from the ratio of discrepancies reported against outgroup members versus those reported against ingroup members, with an expected value of 50% each.

Hypothesis 2 was analyzed by chi-square as a test of independence, i.e., as a test for difference between ratios of measured frequencies. The independent variable was the manipulation that the observer either did or did not have a previously existing basis for identity with the target. The dependent variable was ratios of notations by observers that they either attributed the cause toward the target–actor or toward the environment. The design of the experiment is such that the environment is in fact the cause of contradiction, but the measure considered for Hypothesis 2 is not based on general tendency to choose one cause over the other. It is based on the difference in that tendency toward ingroup and outgroup members.

RESULTS

Data were analyzed on 78 subjects who interacted in 19 groups. Data from some subjects were disqualified because corresponding subjects did not report noting discrepancies, they failed to report with whom discrepancies were first observed, or they noted on the questionnaire that they had friendships with group members other than intended by the manipulation. As a further manipulation check, subjects were asked to report on the questionnaire which other subject they would prefer to work with again later. Of those subjects who came to the experiment with a member from their course group, only 10.7% indicated someone other than that group member (defined as ingroup member in this research). This is even after experiencing discrepancy in objectives. Table 15.1 presents the data by hypothesis along with p-values of the chi-square calculations. Hypothesis 1 pertains to identity as a factor in selection of target, and Hypothesis 2 pertains to identity as a factor in attribution of cause.

TABLE 15.1 Chi-Square Analysis of Ingroup–Outgroup Bias in *n*-Person Groups

	Group affiliation		
	Outgroup	Ingroup	Chi-square results
Identity as a factor in selection of target			
Reported	48	30	$p < 0.0415$
Identity as a factor in attribution of cause			
Actor	17	16	
Environment	29	10	$p < 0.0444$

Data show that subjects reported outgroup members as targets of discrepancy significantly more frequently than ingroup members. This supports the prediction in Hypothesis 1 that selection of targets of attribution in cases of discrepancy may be biased toward outgroup members, with discrepancies made by ingroup members being overlooked more often.

Hypothesis 2 was not supported by these data. In fact, results were significant for the exact opposite effect. Once actors were selected by observers, observers tended to report attributing ingroup actors as the cause over the environment, but tended to report attributing environment as the cause over outgroup actors.

DISCUSSION AND IMPLICATIONS

Research Design

This research utilized an independent objective interaction to generate conflict among members of newly formed small groups. This may be a useful alternative to the generation of conflict through social dilemmas (Dawes, 1980), because it more readily allows study of conflict over shared, but not universally shared, objectives. This is a condition common in organizations (Bacharach and Lawler, 1980).

Implications for Understanding Within-Group Processes in Organizations

It cannot be concluded from the present research that cooperation will fail within groups that are composed from multiple members of pre-existing groups (e.g., typical cross-functional groups in organizations). Groups from which experimental pairs were drawn did not specialize their prior group activities based on particular functions, as would be the case in cross-functional groups formed in organizations. Their identities were assumed to be based on work on a common goal. The model and test do suggest, however, that selection of members to blame for undesirable outcomes during group interactions may be biased by previously established identities. This may in turn affect willingness to cooperate within cross-functional groups. The isolation of this phenomenon suggests the need for further research in the area of within-group attributional processes and their relation to within-group cooperation.

The present research also has important implications for the growing interest in management of diversity (e.g., Jackson and associates, 1992; Jackson et al., 1993). Gender was blocked in the present research, but the findings suggest that further study of *n*-person groups may be fruitful with the manipulation of gender, race, and other factors.

Implications for Advancement Theory

Several contributions are made by the present research toward a better understanding of within-group attributional theory. First a definition is offered for n-person attributions, making obvious the need to advance attribution theory into this area. Second, a model is offered for the attributional process in n-person groups. This model extends Weiner's (1974, 1986) attributional process model by locating the social identity phenomenon as one causal antecedent of attribution and incorporates the selection of target as an additional step prior to actual attribution of that cause.

This research also advances the integration of attribution theory and social identity theory, pointing out some usefulness as well as limitations in current theory development. The laboratory test on actual small group interactions presents evidence that social identity is a factor to be reckoned with in attributional processes within groups and that previous group experiences may affect categorization in newly formed groups.

Of particular interest is the contradiction of findings for Hypothesis 2. Even though the results are contrary, social identity is obviously a factor, or the results of testing based on pre-existing identities would not be significant. Social identity theory may need further advancement to explain this phenomenon. One possibility is that salience of the ingroup actor is increased by social identity because the ingroup member's actions reflect on the observer. The observer becomes more critical of untenable actions in the ingroup actor. This is consistent with Shaver (1970), who presents evidence that observers hold actors more responsible when the importance of outcomes increases. Another possibility is that social identity causes the observer to assume homogeneity with other ingroup members, not only in ability but also in interpretation of the problem. This would prevent the observer from considering that the ingroup actor may have a different objective. A third explanation is that observers simply dropped their previously established identities when discrepancies occurred. Although subjects had worked together in their course groups extensively, the experiments took place at the end of the term, when subjects were no longer dependent on each other for course grades. Tajfel (1974) states that observers may abandon their social identity if maintaining it is contrary to self-interest. This third explanation seems plausible as to why observers would not favor ingroup members over outgroup members, but it does not explain why observers would disfavor ingroup members over outgroup members.

The preceding discussion suggests that n-person groups must be further explored by attribution theory and that integration with social identity theory may be a fruitful approach. At the same time, it suggests that further theory development and/or testing is required if social identity theory is to adequately predict behavior in n-person groups.

REFERENCES

Amancio, L. (1989). Social differentiation between "dominant" and "dominated" groups: Toward an integration of social stereotypes and social identity. *European Journal of Social Psychology,* 19(1):1–10.

Augoustinos, M. (1990). The mediating role of representations on causal attributions in the social world. *Social Behaviour,* 5(1):49–62.

Bacharach, S.B. and Lawler, E.J. (1980). *Power and Politics in Organizations,* San Francisco: Jossey-Bass.

Barney, J. (1986). Organization culture: Can it be a source of sustained competitive advantage? *Academy of Management Review,* 11:656–665.

Berger, J., Rosenholtz, S.J., and Zelditch, M., Jr. (1980). Status organizing processes. *Annual Review of Sociology,* 6:479–508.

Berger, J., Norman, R.Z., Balkwell, J.W., and Smith, R.F. (1992). Status inconsistency in task situations: A test of four status processing principles. *American Sociological Review,* 57(6):843–855.

Bettenhausen, K. and Murnighan, J.K. (1985). The emergence of norms in competitive decision-making groups. *Administrative Science Quarterly,* 30:350–372.

Bonnet, D. (1986). The nature of the R&D/marketing co-operation in the design of technologically advanced new industrial products. *R&D Management,* 16:117–126.

Brewer, M.B. (1985). The role of ethnocentrism in intergroup conflict. in *Psychology of Intergroup Relations,* 2nd edition, S. Worchel and W.G. Austin (Eds.), Chicago: Nelson-Hall, pp. 88–102.

Brewer, M.B. and Schneider, S.K. (1990). Social identity and social dilemmas: A double-edged sword. in *Social Identity Theory: Constructive and Critical Advances,* D. Abrams and M.A. Hogg (Eds.), New York: Springer-Verlag, pp. 169–184.

Brown, R.J. (1984). The effects of intergroup similarity and cooperative vs. competitive orientation on intergroup discrimination. *British Journal of Social Psychology,* 23(1): 21–33.

Brown, R., Condor, S., Matthews, A., and Wade, G. (1986). Explaining intergroup differentiation in an industrial organization. *Journal of Occupational Psychology,* 59(4):273–286.

Crittenden, K.S. (1983). Sociological aspects of attribution. in *Annual Review of Sociology,* Palo Alto: Annual Review, pp. 425–446.

Crittenden, K.S. and Wiley, M.G. (1980). Causal attribution and behavioral response to failure. *Social Psychology Quarterly,* 43:353–358.

Dawes, R.M. (1980). Social dilemmas. *Annual Review of Psychology,* 31:169–193.

Deming, W.E. (1986). *Out of the Crisis,* Cambridge, Mass.: MIT, Center for Advanced Engineering Study.

Deschamps, J. (1973–74). Attribution, social categorization and intergroup representations. *Bulletin de Psychologie,* 27(13–14):710–721.

Doise, W., Turner, J.C., Rabbie, J.M., and Horwitz, M. (1988). Individual and social identities in intergroup relations. *European Journal of Social Psychology,* 18(2):99–111.

Dougherty, D. (1992). Interpretive barriers to successful product innovation in large firms. *Organization Science,* 3(2):179–202.

Eckhardt, G.W. (1987). Organizational health through change. *Organization Development Journal,* 5(2):33–36.

Elliott, G.C. (1989). Self-serving biases in the face of reality: The effect of task outcome and potential causes on self–other attributions. *Human Relations,* 42(11):1015–1032.

Forsyth, D.R. (1980). The functions of attributions. *Social Psychology Quarterly,* 43(2): 184–189.

Garza, R.T. and Borchert, J.E. (1990). Maintaining social identity in a mixed-gender setting: Minority/majority status and cooperative/competitive feedback. *Sex Roles,* 22(11–12): 679–691.

Hastie, R. (1984). Causes and effects of causal attribution. *Journal of Personality and Social Psychology,* 46:44–56.

Heider, F. (1944). Social perception and phenomenal causality. *Psychological Review,* 51: 358–374.

Heider, F. (1958). *The Psychology of Interpersonal Relations,* New York: Wiley.

Hewstone, M., Jaspars, J., and Lalljee, M. (1982). Social representations, social attribution and social identity: The intergroup images of "public" and "comprehensive" schoolboys. *European Journal of Social Psychology,* 12(3):241–269.

Howard, J.W. and Rothbart, M. (1980). Social categorization and memory for in-group and out-group behavior. *Journal of Personality and Social Psychology,* 38(2):301–310.

Jackson, S.E. and associates. (1992). *Diversity in the Workplace: Human Resources Initiatives,* New York: Guilford Press.

Jackson, S.E., Stone, V.K., and Alvarez, E.B. (1993). Socialization amidst diversity: The impact of demographics on work team oldtimers and newcomers. in *Research in Organizational Behavior,* Vol. 15, L.L. Cummings and B.M. Staw (Eds.), Greenwich, Conn.: JAI Press, pp. 45–109.

Jones, E.E. and Davis, K.E. (1965). From acts to dispositions: The attribution process in person perception. in *Advances in Experimental Social Psychology,* Vol. 2, L. Berkowitz (Ed.), New York: Academic Press.

Jones, E.E. and McGillis, D. (1976). Correspondent inferences and the attribution cube: A comparative reappraisal. in *New Directions in Attribution Research,* Vol. 1, J.H. Harvey, W. Ickes, and R.F. Kidd (Eds.), Hillsdale, N.J.: Erlbaum, pp. 389–420.

Kanter, R.M. (1983). *Change Agents: Innovation in Organizations,* New York: Simon and Schuster.

Kelley, H.H. (1971). *Attribution in Social Interaction,* Morristown, N.J.: General Learning Press.

Martinko, M.J. and Gardner, W.L. (1987). The leader/member attribution process. *Academy of Management Review,* 12:235–249.

Nisbett, R.E. and Wilson, T.D. (1977). Telling more than we can know: Verbal reports on mental processes. *Psychological Review,* 84(3):231–259.

Porter, M.E. (1987). From competitive advantage to corporate strategy. *Harvard Business Review,* 65(3):43–59.

Ross, M. and Fletcher, G.J.O. (1985). Attribution and social perception. in *Handbook of Social Psychology,* Vol. 2, G. Lindzey and E. Aronson (Eds.), New York: Random House, pp. 73–122.

Schwartz-Shea, P. (1991). Understanding subgroup optimization: Experimental evidence on individual choice and group processes. *Journal of Public Administration Research and Theory,* 1(1):49–73.

Shaver, K.G. (1970). Defensive attribution: Effects of severity and relevance on the responsibility assigned for an accident. *Journal of Personality and Social Psychology,* 14(2): 101–113.

Sparrow, P.R. and Pettigrew, A.M. (1988). Strategic human resource management in the UK computer supplier industry. *Journal of Occupational Psychology,* 61(1):25–42.

Stephan, W.G. (1977). Stereotyping: The role of ingroup–outgroup differences in causal attribution for behavior. *Journal of Social Psychology,* 101:255–266.

Tajfel, H. (1972). La catégorisation sociale. in *Introduction à la Psychologie Sociale,* Vol. 1, S. Mosovici (Ed.), Paris: Larousse.

Tajfel, H. (1974). Social identity and intergroup behavior. *Social Science Information,* 13: 65–93.

Ulrich, D. (1991). Using human resources for competitive advantage. in *Making Organizations Competitive: Enhancing Networks and Relationships across Traditional Boundaries,* R.H. Kilmann et al. (Eds.), San Francisco: Jossey-Bass, pp. 129–155.

Van Lange, P.A., Liebrand, W.B., Kiers, H.A., and Zwaal, W. (1989). Redenen voor en attributies van keuzegedrag in een *n*-personen prisoner's dilemma (Reasons for and attributes of choice behavior in an *n*-person prisoner's dilemma). *Nederlands Tijdschrift voor de Psychologie en haar Grensgebieden,* 44(5):225–234.

Van Lange, P.A., Liebrand, W.B., and Kuhlman, D.M. (1990). Causal attribution of choice behavior in three *n*-person prisoner's dilemmas. *Journal of Experimental Social Psychology,* 26(1):34–48.

Weiner, B. (1974). Achievement motivation as conceptualized by an attribution theorist. in *Achievement Motivation and Attribution Theory,* B. Weiner (Ed.), Morristown, N.J.: General Learning Press, pp. 3–48.

Weiner, B. (1986). *An Attributional Theory of Motivation and Emotion,* New York: Springer-Verlag.

Weiner, B., Frieze, I.H., Kukla, A., Reed, I., Rest, S., and Rosenbaum, R.M. (1972). Perceiving the causes of success and failure. in *Attribution: Perceiving the Causes of Behavior,* E.E. Jones, D.E. Kanouse, H.H. Kelley, R.E. Nisbett, S. Valins, and B. Weiner (Eds.), Morristown, N.J.: General Learning Press.

16

THE EFFECT OF DEMOGRAPHIC DIVERSITY ON CAUSAL ATTRIBUTIONS OF WORK GROUP SUCCESS AND FAILURE: A FRAMEWORK FOR RESEARCH*

Leonard Karakowsky and J.P. Siegel

ABSTRACT

Characteristics of the work group can influence how co-workers assign responsibility for the causes of their group's success or failure in the performance of organizational goals. This chapter develops a theoretical framework for understanding the impact of demographic diversity on group members' causal attributions of responsibility for their work group's successes or failures. It is proposed that demographic diversity represents a critical influence on group member causal attributions through its impact on social integration and work group efficacy. This attribution process is moderated by a number of work group variables, including the reward system and work group history.

*The authors wish to thank Glen Whyte, Martin Evans, Jia Lin Xie, and the anonymous reviewers for the Florida State Symposium on Attribution Theory for their comments on this chapter.

INTRODUCTION

Barley (1990) observed that change in technological environments has encouraged organizations to place increasing emphasis on work groups. In manufacturing as well as other technologies, reliance has shifted from individual workers to teams (Ancona, 1990). This increasing emphasis on groups or teams underscores the increasing importance of adequately addressing the factors that influence group effectiveness (Goodman et al., 1982). Hackman and Morris (1975) identified three components of group effectiveness: group performance, satisfaction of group member needs, and the ability of the group to exist over time. Hackman and Morris' (1975) model asserts that intragroup actions play a critical role in achieving group effectiveness. This suggests that the relations among group members will play a major role in group processes and the ultimate achievement of group effectiveness.

One facet of group behavior that will clearly impact intragroup relations is the manner in which group members share credit or blame for group successes and failures. How work group members assign relative responsibility for the causes of their group's successes or failures has important implications for the effective functioning of the group. Consistent with Schlenker and Miller's (1977b) observation, studies of attribution biases in the group context have revealed processes in groups that can produce bitter rivalries among the group members regarding their retrospective perceptions of the relative contributions to group effort. If members possess radically different perceptions of the relative contributions to group effort, they will have different opinions concerning the proper division of rewards among the group members and will perceive inequities based on their perceptions of member contributions (Adams, 1965; Walster et al., 1973). Clearly, then, attribution processes do have important implications for intragroup relations and consequently can impact work group effectiveness and productivity.

A major trend that will clearly impact the dynamics of work group relations is the increasing emphasis on demographic diversity in the workplace. Both the popular press and the academic literature have repeatedly acknowledged the increasingly diverse nature of the work force, including the demographic characteristics of race, ethnicity, gender, and age (e.g., Johnston and Packer, 1987). It is estimated that by the next decade, a major portion of all net additions to the U.S. work force will be ethnic minorities, including many immigrants from Asian and Latin American countries (Fullerton, 1987). Numerous management scholars (e.g., Alderfer, 1991; Cox and Blake, 1991) have urged researchers to address more fully the impact of diversity on organizational behavior. The sparse research that has addressed the impact of diversity on work group dynamics has provided mixed views of the consequences. For example, while a number of studies have supported the notion that heterogeneous groups perform better than homogeneous groups on creative and judgmental tasks (Jackson, 1992), the research has also suggested that diversity can generate interpersonal processes that impede group productivity (Steiner, 1972). Clearly, much more knowledge is needed concerning the impact of diversity on the functioning of work groups in order to ensure that organizations and their members can effectively adapt to a diverse environment.

One specific area that needs to be addressed concerns the impact of demographic diversity on how co-workers share group successes and failures in the performance of organizational goals. Certainly adapting to a culturally diverse workplace requires an understanding of those elements that impact how work groups share success and failure in the performance of organizational goals. In order to address this issue, two questions must be answered. First, how does the work group context influence the manner in which individuals assign relative responsibility for group success or failure? Second, how does the composition of the group, or, more specifically, how does demographic diversity in the group, influence how these attributions are made?

The intent of this chapter is to provide an examination of the effect of the work group context, specifically demographic diversity in the work group, on individual causal attributions of group success or failure in achievement situations. First, the research that has examined individual causal attributions in achievement situations is briefly reviewed. Second, the literature that has extended these concepts to the group context is examined. Third, a theoretical framework is presented that explains the role of demographic diversity in influencing causal attributions among work group members. The presentation of an integrated framework, along with testable research propositions, is intended to encourage a systematic course of research aimed at the development of a comprehensive model for understanding the attributional processes involved in the work group context.

CAUSAL ATTRIBUTIONS IN ACHIEVEMENT SITUATIONS

In order to understand the process of attribution among members of a work group, it is first useful to examine the literature regarding individual causal attributions. Attribution theory examines the role of cognitive and perceptual factors in individual reactions to events (Heider, 1958; Jones and Davis, 1965; Kelley, 1967, 1973; Weiner, 1972, 1974, 1985, 1986). Specifically, attribution theory explains the processes through which individuals attempt to assign causes for particular behavior or outcomes.

Evans (1986) indicated the importance of considering the role of attributions within the broader class of variables that deal with motivation to perform in the workplace. While individuals usually increase their goals after a success (Locke and Latham, 1990; Locke et al., 1984) and lower their goals after a failure, these typical shifts occur only when particular kinds of attributions are made (Weiner, 1986). In his integrated model of motivation, Evans (1986) indicated that when an achievement task is completed, final feedback is provided, and the individual compares performance against the initial goal. It is at this stage that the major attributional processes occur (Weiner, 1986). When the individual compares performance against a goal or standard, there are two possible outcomes: success or failure (Evans, 1986). According to attribution theory, it is at this point that the individual will engage in a search for causes of the success or failure. The source that the individual chooses for the cause of success or failure will have broad implications for his or her affective reaction to the outcome, sense of efficacy for future task performance and subsequent goal level (Evans, 1986).

According to attribution theory, individuals rely on social and situational information cues to assign causes for performance outcome/behavior (Heider, 1958; Jones and Davis, 1965; Kelley, 1967; Weiner, 1986). Heider (1958) asserted that individuals must integrate the cues linked to outcomes/responses as a means to infer the factors that generated them. Weiner et al. (1972) posited that achievement behavior is cognitively mediated by attributions of causality to one or more of four factors: level of ability, amount of effort expended, level of difficulty of the task, and amount of luck. Weiner (1986) classified these factors along three separate dimensions including *locus*, *stability*, and *controllability*, as follows: internal (ability and effort) and external (task difficulty and luck), stable (ability and task difficulty) and unstable (effort and luck), controllable (effort) and uncontrollable (ability, task difficulty, luck).

The research in attribution theory has found evidence that people do engage in a process that involves the analysis of achievement outcomes and the assignment of causes to these outcomes (e.g., Feather and Simon, 1971; Frieze and Weiner, 1971; Luginbuhl et al., 1975; Rosenbaum, 1972; Weiner et al., 1972; Weiner and Kukla, 1970). Why a particular pattern of attributions is generated (e.g., external versus internal) depends largely on the antecedents of the causal attributions. This chapter is fundamentally concerned with exploring those antecedents that play a critical role in influencing causal attributions in the work group context and, more specifically, the effect of demographic diversity on group members' causal attributions. In addition, it is the impact on self-attributions that is of central interest in this chapter. The question, as implied earlier, essentially asks how a member of a demographically diverse work group assigns causality for the work group's success or failure.

The Antecedents of Causal Attributions

The theoretical framework proposed below is based on the assertion that demographic diversity in the work group impacts causal attributions through its effect on the salience of three broad sources of attributions. These sources, classified by Kelley and Michela (1980) in their review of the literature, include *motivation-based, expectations-based,* and *information-based* antecedents of attributions.

First, according to attribution theory, individuals are motivated to evaluate a situation in order to understand why an outcome/event occurred (Heider, 1958; Jones and Davis, 1965; Kelley, 1967; Weiner, 1985). Individuals are motivated to engage in this process because of the need to maintain a sense of "cognitive mastery" over the environment (Kelley, 1967). Further, the research has identified a common pattern among individual causal assignments for success and failure in achievement situations regarding the locus (internal/external) dimension. The tendency for individuals to attribute success to internal factors and failure to external factors has been explained through the concept of "ego defense," i.e., self-serving biases (e.g., Adler, 1956; Allport, 1937; Heider, 1958; Kelley, 1967; Chacko and McElroy, 1983; Weiner, 1986). Egocentric attributions provide a means to increase or maintain self-esteem of the actor by permitting a person to take credit for success and avoiding blame for failure (Heider, 1958; Schlenker, 1973). The ego-based origin of internal attributions of success and external attributions of failure has been supported in a number of research efforts that identified the protection of self-esteem as the source of such attributions (Frieze and Weiner, 1971; Feather, 1969). Empirical support has been received for this notion of ego-based attribution elsewhere in the literature (e.g., Clapham and Schwenk, 1991; Luginbuhl et al., 1975; Miller, 1976; Mitchell et al., 1981; Weiner and Kukla, 1970).

Second, Bem (1972) and Miller and Rose (1975) argued that alternate explanations to egocentric attribution may also explain the differential attributions of success and failure. One major alternative discussed in the literature is based on the notion of expectations, that is, expectations regarding task performance as the primary source for causal attributions. The research has found support for the view that behavior/performance that is expected (i.e., consistent with beliefs about the individual) will be attributed to stable internal factors (i.e., ability), and unexpected behavior/performance is attributed to unstable or external factors (i.e., effort or luck) (e.g., Deaux, 1976; Feather, 1969; Frieze and Weiner, 1971; McMahan, 1973; Regan et al., 1974). With respect to self-attributions, the research has suggested that expectancy of success (the belief in one's ability in relation to task difficulty, intended effort, anticipated luck) will generate a pattern of causal attributions similar to that mentioned above (Weiner, 1985). For example, the results of Feather and Simon's (1971) study suggested that expectations of success on a task that stemmed from an individual's self-confidence in his or her ability to perform would generate internal attributions for (expected) success and external attributions for (unexpected) failure. On the other hand, expectations of failure (due to a lack of confidence in ability) would generate attributions of (unexpected) success to external factors and (expected) failure to internal factors (lack of ability). In both cases, unexpected outcomes resulted in attributions to external factors and expected outcomes were assigned to internal factors.

Third, attributions of causality can be generated from information-based antecedents. For example, Kelley (1967) asserted that the performance outcome is attributed to the factor with which it is seen as covarying. Specifically, the outcome will be perceived as covarying with the stimulus, the person, the time, or a combination of these factors. Kelley (1967) posited that, in addition to the actual outcome, three sources of information are used to make these attributions: consistency (relative consistency of the individual's performance over time), consensus (comparable performance of individual's performance with others' performance), and distinctiveness (degree to which performance on the task differs from other tasks).

While the attribution research can be separately classified based on the elements of motivation, beliefs, and information, it is important to keep in mind that these factors may interact to generate a given set of attributions. Each factor can be considered as a cue that the individual will process to varying degrees as a source for generating causal explanations of performance. Further, as the research has indicated, it is the salience of these cues that will govern the ultimate source of attributions in an achievement situation. As Kelley and Michela (1980) explained, the effect is attributed to the cause that is most salient in the perceptual field at the time the effect is observed. Consistent with Evans' (1986) observation, the research has supported this notion of cue salience (e.g., MacArthur, 1972; Taylor and Fisk, 1975). For example, an important task for which an individual takes complete responsibility will be high in ego involvement. Therefore, the salience of this cue will be a critical factor in determining the subsequent pattern of attributions.

How do these attribution tendencies change in the group setting? Moreover, how will a critical element of the work group context—demographic diversity—influence the pattern of attributions group members generate following group success or failure in a task? These questions are specifically addressed in the following sections.

Extending Attribution Theory Concepts to the Work Group Context

As discussed above, the research in attribution theory has found evidence that people do engage in a process that involves the analysis of achievement outcomes and the assignment of causes to these outcomes. The application of attribution theory to the group setting suggests that individuals as members of a group also generate a naive theory of the relationship between group characteristics and group outcomes. Knowledge of performance acts as the primary cue in the formation and reporting of group members' perceptions of group processes and individual behavior (e.g., Downey et al., 1979). That is, knowledge of a group's performance will influence the type of characteristics that its members attribute to the group and its processes. In other words, information-based attribution, as described earlier in the individual context, applies equally to the group context. However, the key question is how the ego-based and belief-based sources of attribution transfer to the group context.

The research has supported the notion that the egocentric bias continues to operate in the group context. The tendency for group members to attribute success to internal causes and to defer personal responsibility for group failure has received empirical support (e.g., Schlenker, 1975; Schlenker et al., 1976). This, in effect, reproduces in the group setting the individual attribution based on the egocentric bias discussed earlier. For example, Schlenker (1975) examined the patterns of egocentric attributions in a cooperative group setting and found that subjects perceived greater causative responsibility for their group's performance following a group success rather than a group failure. Caine (1975), Medow and Zander (1965), Schlenker et al. (1976), and Wolosin et al. (1973) found similar support for the ego-based attribution tendency extended to the group setting. However, other studies have suggested that the process may be somewhat less egocentric than this research implies. For example, Schlenker et al. (1976) and Forsyth and Schlenker (1977) found that while members of successful groups feel more responsible for the group's performance than members of failing groups, the members did not see themselves as more or less responsible than the average group member of their own group. Moreover, it was found that group members raised their evaluations of the responsibility of all group members following a successful group performance and lowered their evaluations of the responsibility of all group members following a failing group performance.

Schlenker and Miller (1977b) suggested that to an individual group member, other group members can be perceived as either (1) an external variable (e.g., group-other) whose influence on the group can be perceptually minimized or maximized to increase or decrease personal responsibility for the outcome or (2) an extension of the self (e.g., group-internal), which should be protected in the same way that egocentric attribution protects individual self-esteem. This conceptualization of causal attributions in the group context, based on the modification of the Weiner et al. (1972) classification by Zaccaro et al. (1987), distinguishes four causal loci for attribution: member-internal (self only), group-internal (group and self), group-other (group excluding the self), and environment (external to the group, i.e., task difficulty or luck). According to the egocentric view of attributions, group members will tend to claim personal responsibility for group success (member-internal) and tend to attribute group failure to other members (group-other) (e.g., Schlenker et al., 1976). Similar support for the existence of an egocentric attribution tendency in the group context can be been found elsewhere in the literature (e.g., Caine, 1975; Medow and Zander, 1965; Forsyth and Schlenker, 1977; Schlenker et al., 1976; Wolosin et al., 1973; Schlenker, 1975). Although the research has offered some indication of the impact of group context on causal attributions, it has not provided a systematic examination of important work group characteristics, such as demographic diversity, on members' causal attributions.

Far less research attention has focused on the notion of belief-based (or expectations-based) attribution in the group context. The research needs to more fully explore two fundamental questions: First, what elements of the group context (i.e., demographic diversity) influence expectations of group success or failure? Second, how do these expectations or beliefs impact the resultant causal attributions that group members generate following group success or failure?

The research that has examined belief-based attribution in the lone-performer context, as discussed above, suggested that individuals develop expectations of success or failure prior to performance of a task, based on expectations concerning their ability or expectations concerning the task difficulty. Whether success/ failure was expected/unexpected will determine the subsequent pattern of attributions. The question can then be more specifically addressed: in what way does membership in a group change expectations concerning performance? More specifically, what characteristics of the work group affect an individual's belief in the ability to successfully perform a task? To answer these questions, it is useful to first consider the concepts of self-efficacy and group efficacy.

Self-efficacy represents one's belief in one's ability to perform a task (Bandura, 1977, 1982). This theory states that people who possess low self-efficacy will have difficulty in dealing with environmental demands, as opposed to those maintaining high self-efficacy, who can sufficiently cope with environmental demands. Bandura suggested that self-efficacy theory can be extended to groups. For example, Gist (1987) suggested that *groupthink* (Janis, 1972) can be considered as an effect of unrealistically high group efficacy perceptions as reflected in the excessive optimism and illusions of invulnerability characteristic of this phenomenon.

What types of attributions will be made by members of a group subject to high efficacy perceptions? According to the logic of the expectations-based view of attributions, high perceived group efficacy will likely generate group-internal attributions for (expected) success and environment attributions for (unexpected) failure. That is, a belief in the work group's ability to perform successfully (high perceived work group efficacy) should encourage the group member to acknowledge the group as a cause of (expected) success (group-internal) and defer (unexpected) failure to causes outside the work group (environment). Low perceived group efficacy would generate group-internal attributions for (expected) failure and environment attributions for (unexpected) success. The nature of these causal attributions is further discussed below. In addition, this chapter examines an issue that has not been adequately addressed in the literature: the relationship of demographic diversity to group efficacy and the implications for group member causal attributions.

The preceding discussion of ego-based and belief-based sources of causal attributions provides a useful framework for exploring the impact of demographic diversity on work group members' causal attributions for group success or failure. Specifically, the influence of work group diversity on these direct antecedents of causal attributions is examined in the following sections.

THE EFFECT OF DEMOGRAPHIC DIVERSITY ON ATTRIBUTIONS OF SUCCESS AND FAILURE IN THE WORK GROUP

The proposed framework for understanding the impact of demographic diversity in the work group on group members' causal attributions is outlined in Figure 16.1. According to this framework, two general classes of attribution antecedents, ego-based and belief-based (expectation-based) sources, are significantly

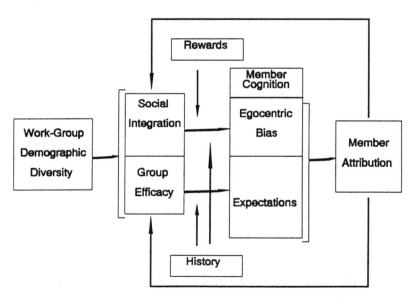

FIGURE 16.1   The impact of demographic diversity on causal attributions in the work group.

influenced by demographic diversity in the work group. The effect of demographic diversity on individual causal attributions is posited to occur through its impact on the salience of several important work group characteristics or situational cues. This is consistent with the notion that the salience of situational or personal cues affects the nature of causal attributions (Kelley and Michela, 1980).

The framework suggests that demographic diversity will influence the egocentric tendency to claim responsibility for group success (member-internal) and to defer responsibility for failure to co-workers (member-other). The effect of diversity on causal attributions will occur through its impact on the salience of several characteristics of the work group, including group cohesiveness, social identity, and social integration. Similarly, demographic diversity will influence the salience of the belief-based cues or antecedents of causal attribution through its impact on beliefs or expectations regarding the group's ability to perform successfully (group efficacy).

This framework also suggests that the impact of diversity on causal attributions will be modified by the nature of the work group reward system and the work group's history. The following sections include a discussion of the effects of each characteristic or factor on the pattern of attributions individuals will generate following work group success or failure. In addition, the effects of each factor are summarized in the form of a research proposition.

Social Integration

The framework (Figure 16.1) suggests that demographic diversity affects group member causal attributions of work group success or failure through its impact on social integration. The concept of social integration has been viewed as a combination of the elements of group cohesiveness and social identity (O'Reilly et al., 1989). Consequently, it will be useful to begin this examination with a discussion of the implications of cohesiveness and social identity for attributions in the work group. Following these discussions, the influence of social integration and the role of demographic diversity in the attribution process are delineated.

Although no generally accepted definition of group cohesiveness exists, it has been defined as the total field of forces that act to keep members within a group (Festinger, 1950). Other commonly used definitions include mutual positive forces (Lott and Lott, 1965) and attraction-to-the-group (Pepitone and Kleiner, 1957). Cohesive groups have been characterized by integrated cooperation among group members, egalitarian behavior (e.g., Mikalachki, 1969), loyalty among group members, and concern for feelings of other group members (Cartwright and Zander, 1968; Shaw, 1971). The level of group cohesiveness has important implications for member attributions following group success or failure in performance.

As discussed earlier, the research has emphasized the general tendency of individual group members to claim greater personal responsibility for their group's performance after a group success rather than failure. Schlenker and Miller (1977a) argued that one of the factors determining whether the group members will be denied credit for success or blamed for failure is the degree to which the other group members are viewed as an extension of the self. When this occurs, the other members will be equally protected by the egocentric bias (Wortman, 1970). Based upon these elements, Schlenker and Miller (1977a) suggested that cohesion should decrease a member's tendency to blame a group defeat on other group members or minimize credit given for group success. On the other hand, members of noncohesive groups will have little incentive to consider factors other than the maximization of self-esteem when attributing causes of success and failure. This assertion is in line with the results of Schlenker and Miller's (1977a) study, which indicated that members of noncohesive groups displayed a greater tendency than members of cohesive groups to maximize their relative contributions to group success and minimize their relative contributions to group failure.

Proposition 1:   The level of work group cohesiveness will be negatively related to the level of egocentric bias in individual group member causal attributions of group success or failure.

One key characteristic that can be used to distinguish groups is the concept of social identity (Tajfel and Turner, 1979). According to social identity theory, people tend to classify themselves and others into various social categories such as organizational or group membership (Tajfel and Turner, 1985). One consequence of social identity is the tendency of the individual to support the values and actions of the group and internalize the perception of the group image as more desirable compared to other groups (Turner, 1982). Group members can enhance self-esteem by increasing the desirability associated with their social categories (Tajfel and Turner, 1979). Based on this reasoning, group members can influence social identity through the attributions they make for the behavior of ingroup and outgroup behaviors (Hewstone et al., 1982). That is, attributions will be made to favor the ingroup image (Hewstone et al., 1982). Zaccarro et al. (1987) suggested that member-internal and group-internal attributions for success can maintain and/or raise self-esteem by enhancing both personal and social identity. Similarly, negative self-evaluations can be avoided by attributing failure to other group members (group-other) or to factors outside the group (environment).

Based on the assertions of social identity theory, a group member who strongly identifies with the work group is less likely to claim sole responsibility for group success (member-internal) and blame others for group failure (group-other)—the typical pattern of egocentric attributions. Rather, success will be shared with co-workers (group-internal), and failure will be deferred to causes outside the group (environment). This pattern of attributions will enhance or protect the value of the social categorizations and social identity to a group member and thereby facilitate increases in self-esteem (Hewstone et al., 1982).

> **Proposition 2:**   The level of work group identity will be negatively related to the level of egocentric bias in individual group member causal attributions of group success or failure.

Social Integration and Demographic Diversity

The notion of social identity, along with the concept of group cohesiveness, can be viewed, parsimoniously, as elements within the construct of social integration. Social integration is a multifaceted phenomenon that can be viewed as the degree to which an individual is psychologically linked to others in a group (O'Reilly et al., 1989). It can, more specifically, be considered as a reflection of attraction to the group, satisfaction with other members of the group, and social interaction among the group members (Katz and Kahn, 1978). Consequently, the implications of cohesiveness and social identity for the egocentric bias should be identical for social integration: an individual who is satisfied with his or her group, who feels an attraction to the group, and who interacts with the group should consider the group as an extension of the self. Based on the above reasoning, attributions should be made that preserve the group and the self in high regard; group failure should be deferred to sources outside of the group, and group success should be shared among co-workers.

In summary, based on Propositions 1 and 2, a third proposition can be generated regarding the relationship of social integration and the egocentric bias.

> **Proposition 3:**   The level of social integration in work groups will be negatively related to the level of egocentric bias in group member causal attributions of group success and failure.

The previous discussions presented a number of propositions regarding the impact of work group characteristics on members' causal attributions. The critical question is how work group diversity influences the level and direction of the effects of these cues on group members. How does diversity or homogeneity among variables such as culture, gender, age, and race within groups influence the assignment of credit and blame among co-workers? According to the model proposed in this chapter, it is the impact of group diversity on the level of social integration that influences the ultimate pattern of attributions that co-workers generate. Essentially then, it is necessary to consider how the level of social integration differs depending on the heterogeneity or homogeneity of these key work group characteristics.

The research has supported the notion that relative similarity of group members can affect measures of social integration (Festinger, 1954; Newcomb, 1961). The research has also supported the existence of an association between similarity in a number of demographic variables (including race, education, and age) and social integration (e.g., Hoffman, 1985; Ward et al., 1985; Tsui and O'Reilly, 1989). O'Reilly et al. (1989) studied the relationships among group demography, social integration, and turnover using 20 actual work units and 79 respondents. They found that heterogeneity in group tenure was associated with lower levels of group social integration. In other words, as demographic diversity (heterogeneity) increases in the work group, social integration decreases. Based on the preceding arguments, as social integration decreases, the level of egocentric bias in attributions will increase. In summary, then, as diversity in the work group increases, the level of egocentric bias among group members' causal attributions of responsibility for group success or failure will increase.

> **Proposition 3a:** Demographic diversity in the work group will be positively related to the level of egocentric bias in individual group member causal attributions of group success or failure.

Work Group Efficacy and Demographic Diversity

How does demographic diversity in a work group influence group efficacy perceptions? This is an area in critical need of research. Before addressing this question however, it is necessary to understand the implications of the work group context for the belief-based (expectations-based) antecedents of causal attributions.

As the preceding discussion indicated, the concepts of self-efficacy and group efficacy (Bandura, 1982) are relevant to the examination of individual and group expectations regarding the ability to successfully perform a task. Lindsley et al. (1994) defined collective efficacy in terms of the group's belief that it can successfully perform a specific task. According to the expectations-based view, discussed previously, high perceived group efficacy would generate group-internal attributions for (expected) success and group-external attributions for (unexpected) failure. This pattern is in clear opposition to the results of purely ego-based attribution (indicated earlier). On the other hand, low perceived group efficacy would generate group-internal attributions for (expected) failure and environment attributions for (unexpected) success.

> **Proposition 4:** High perceived group efficacy will reduce the effects of the egocentric bias in group member causal attributions of work group success and failure.

Gist (1987) and Earley (1993) suggested that a measure of group efficacy could reflect individuals' perceptions of their group's capability. Based on this view, the question to be addressed is how group diversity affects an individual's perception of his or her group's ability to successfully perform a task. Little research has attempted to explore the implications of demographic diversity on this group-based conceptualization of efficacy. An examination of this relationship is necessary in order to understand the impact of diversity on causal attributions via the effect on belief-based (expectations-based) sources of causal attributions.

The influence of demographic diversity on expectations of group success (group efficacy) can be viewed through two fundamental sources. First, heterogeneous work groups may simply be comprised of individuals whose race, culture, or sex generate different sets of causal attributions. Second, demographic diversity in a work group can encourage particular patterns of belief-based attributions due to individual member beliefs regarding the ability of their group to perform given the demographic make-up of the group. In this case, stereotypes and biases regarding race, culture, or sex will influence the beliefs regarding the group's ability to perform. Each of these two broad sources of influence is discussed below.

Earley (1993) suggested that cultural beliefs can influence efficacy perceptions through shaping early childhood efficacy experiences. For example, individuals raised in collectivist cultures are more likely to feel most efficacious working in groups (with ingroup members) as opposed to working alone, since this reflects their cultural preferences or values. On the other hand, individuals raised in individualist cultures experience reduced perceptions of efficacy in the group context (Earley, 1993). This research implies that culture can influence the beliefs regarding ability to perform as a group. Demographically diverse work groups that include individuals with a variety of cultural preferences (e.g., for collectivism or individualism) will consequently generate differing expectations regarding the ability to operate successfully as a group. This influence on efficacy will then generate the pattern of expectations-based attributions discussed above.

The work of Betancourt and his associates (e.g., Betancourt et al., 1992; Betancourt and Weiner, 1982) indicates the critical influence of culture on causal attributions. Consistent with the observation of Betancourt and Lopez (1993), there is significant research evidence to suggest that cultural or value orientation influences attributional processes. Specifically, the dimensional properties of attributions (locus, stability, and controllability) and their psychological consequences do vary among different cultures (e.g., Betancourt and Weiner, 1982). For example, in a comparison of causal attributions of Chilean and U.S. respondents, Betancourt and Weiner (1982) found that Chileans perceived the external causes as more external, the stable causes as less stable, and the controllable causes as less controllable. This in itself has important implications for understanding the process of causal attributions in demographically diverse work groups. Based on this view, a mix of different cultures in the work group can bring to the group a mix of different patterns for assigning causality for group success and failure. In addition to this, cultural differences in perceptions of causality also reflect different expectations regarding the group's ability to succeed, as discussed below.

While the existence of cultural differences in attributional styles is, of course, significant in itself, the implications for group efficacy are of particular interest here. For example, cultural differences in perceived controllability (e.g., Betancourt, 1990; Betancourt et al. 1992; Betancourt and Weiner, 1982; Kluckhohn and Strodtbeck, 1961) imply differences in beliefs regarding group expectations of future success. Obviously, a group that perceives its outcomes (i.e., success or failure) as largely uncontrollable will likely exhibit lower group efficacy than a group that views the causes of its performance as more controllable.

Proposition 4a: Cultural diversity in the work group will influence causal attributions directly through culturally specific attributional styles and indirectly through the impact on group efficacy.

The second broad source of influence on belief-based attribution arising with demographic diversity derives from group member stereotypes or biases. Numerous scholars have argued that stereotypes influence causal attributions by providing a source of expectancies about behavior (e.g., Deaux, 1976; Jones and McGillis, 1976). The research that has examined the effects of stereotypes on causal attributions has often found that a performance outcome (success or failure) that is consistent with stereotype-based expectancies is attributed to internal (and stable) causes (e.g., ability), whereas stereotype-inconsistent performance is attributed to external (or unstable) causes (e.g., task characteristics, luck, or effort) (e.g., Heilman, 1983; Nieva and Gutek, 1980). Consistent with this view, a number of research studies have found that external or unstable sources (e.g., luck) are often assigned as causal explanations for the success of women or blacks (e.g., Deaux and Emswiller, 1974; Greenhaus and Parasuraman, 1993; Ilgen and Youtz, 1986; O'Leary and Hansen, 1984).

The relationship of stereotypes and causal attributions is clearly represented in Pettigrew's (1979) notion of the ultimate attribution error, which is an extension of the fundamental attribution error (Heider, 1958; Ross, 1977) in the group context. The tendency to underestimate situational factors and overestimate personal factors as causes of group behavior or outcomes certainly captures the nature of the stereotype-based attributions discussed above. Further, the notions of ingroup and outgroup categories (from social identity theory), discussed earlier, have important implications for the process of stereotype-based attributions in groups. For example, Taylor and Jaggi (1974) suggested the existence of ethnocentric attribution in groups whereby group members make internal attributions for the positive behavior of other ingroup members and external attributions for their negative behavior, while the opposite pattern of attributions is made for outgroup members. This hypothesis has received some support elsewhere in the literature (e.g., Hewstone and Ward, 1985; Jackson et al., 1993).

What are the implications of racial or sex-based stereotypes for individual member expectations of group success or failure? Clearly, these stereotypes can affect group members' expectations of other group members' ability to perform successfully within the group. Consequently, for example, a male group member who feels that the female members of the group are less competent (less ability) will generate relatively lower expectations regarding the group's overall ability to succeed. Similarly, a highly heterogeneous group whose members harbor many stereotypes regarding other members' ability to perform will generate specific expectations regarding overall group performance potential. Negative stereotypes or biases will generate low efficacy perceptions (expected failure, unexpected success), with the corresponding pattern of attributions described above.

> **Proposition 4b:** The existence of stereotypes/biases in demographically diverse work groups will influence perceived group efficacy and consequently influence the pattern of group member causal attributions of group success and failure.

MODERATORS OF THE RELATIONSHIP BETWEEN DEMOGRAPHIC DIVERSITY AND ATTRIBUTIONS OF SUCCESS AND FAILURE IN THE WORK GROUP

There are a number of factors that can moderate the relationship between demographic diversity and attributions of group success or failure. The following sections identify two key moderators of this relationship, including the work group's reward systems and history (level of familiarity with co-workers' abilities).

Reward Systems

Caine and Schlenker (1979) and Zaccarro et al. (1987) suggested that when status and role differentiations within a group are based primarily on perceived individual contributions, then self-serving biases (i.e., egocentric attributions) will dominate in the group context and resemble the lone-performer attribution pattern. When reward or resource allocations are based on member contributions to the group, member-internal attributions will increase following successful group performance. An individual who perceives remuneration to be linked to performance will be motivated to attribute a greater proportion of success to himself or herself (member-internal) rather than to other group members. Similarly, failure will be assigned to causes external to the self (i.e., group-other or environment). In summary, the presence of status, reward, and role differentiation will increase the strength of the egocentric bias in causal attributions.

How might a reward system enhance or impede the presence of the egocentric bias in a demographically diverse work group? Competition, as outlined above, will be exacerbated by racial and gender biases when rewards are given for individual contributions. That is, rewards that distinguish individual member performance will increase the presence of egocentric attributions and consequently magnify the impact of diversity in the work group. Basing rewards on entire group effort is one method of reducing the egocentric pattern of attributions.

> **Proposition 5:**   The level of perceived association between rewards and individual contributions is positively related to the level of egocentric bias in causal attributions of group success and failure.

> **Propositions 5a:**   The effect of demographic diversity on group member causal attributions will be modified by the presence and nature of the group reward systems.

Work Group History

Different work groups obviously will have different life spans. The research has largely focused on temporary work groups constructed for the purposes of laboratory study. Therefore, typically the members of the group were unfamiliar with each other. The empirical research has not adequately addressed the effect of work group experience and familiarity on attributions of work group success and failure. What is the impact of work group history on member attributions of success or failure? Genuine knowledge of other group members' ability and effort, along with an understanding of group processes, should influence the attribution pattern individuals generate.

Downey et al. (1979) suggested that performance cues may be less salient as group members have more time to observe, analyze, and internalize the actual behavior of their group members. The results of their study indicated that although the attribution effect exists in newly formed groups, it disappears in mature groups. That is, attributions of success and failure can be based on information other than performance of the group. Information on the ability of group members, for example, will influence perceived relative contributions to group success or failure.

It can be predicted then that the greater the familiarity of the co-members' efforts/abilities, the lower will be the tendency of members to rely on egocentric attributions to assign credit and blame. Based on these assumptions, one can argue that differences in demographically homogeneous and heterogeneous groups will diminish as the members establish a greater familiarity with one another (e.g., Watson et al., 1993). However, a number of questions regarding the temporal factors need to be addressed. For example, what impact does continual success or failure have on attributions of group success or failure? With regard to this question, Siegel and Bowen (1973) found that attributions of group success may be affected by previous feedback of success and failure. This re-emphasizes the importance of considering the history of the group and its past successes and failures as a means to understand the pattern of attributions its group members generate.

> **Proposition 6:**   The history or level of familiarity with co-worker performance is negatively related to the egocentric bias in causal attributions of success and failure.

> **Proposition 6a:**   The effect of demographic diversity on group member causal attributions of group success and failure will be modified by the history (level of familiarity) of the group.

CONCLUSIONS

This chapter makes at least two important contributions to the management literature. A consideration of work group context on causal attributions has not received sufficient research attention. This chapter has attempted to apply attribution theory in order to understand how work groups share success and failure. Second, this chapter has addressed an area of increasing concern to managers: demographic diversity in work groups. A theoretical framework was presented that integrated elements of attribution theory and group-level concepts in order to contribute to an understanding of the impact of demographic diversity on individual attributions of success and failure following work group performance. The analysis presented in this chapter suggests that characteristics of the work group can influence how its members assign responsibility for group success and failure. While there is a tendency among individuals to generate egocentric attributions (the motivation-based antecedent), the work group context and, specifically, the existence of demographic diversity in the group can provide additional cues which will enhance or impede this attribution bias. This chapter also addresses the expectations-based antecedent of attributions by examining the impact of demographic diversity on group efficacy perceptions. In summary, the impact of diversity on causal attributions is hypothesized to occur through its impact on several group-level factors, including social integration and work group efficacy. According to the proposed framework, reward systems and work group history can moderate the impact of diversity on causal attributions.

Clearly, the pattern of causal attributions that group members generate will have important consequences for the future functioning of the group. As illustrated in Figure 16.1, the nature of the attributions will feed back into the group process via the variables of social integration and group efficacy. There is much research evidence, as indicated above, to support the view that causal attributions regarding achievement outcomes do affect expectations regarding future performance, and consequently group efficacy will be influenced by the causal attributions generated. As suggested above, causal attributions that imply little group control over outcomes (e.g., Betancourt and Weiner, 1982) will tend to undermine group efficacy and lead to downward efficacy–performance spirals (Hackman, 1990; Lindsley et al., 1994). Similarly, the pattern of causal attributions will also influence the extent to which group members come to identify with each other as members of one ingroup. As the initial discussion indicated, intragroup relations are affected by the perceptions individuals generate concerning the members' relative responsibility for the work group's success or failure. Attributions based on ingroup and outgroup identities may unfortunately serve to further polarize or alienate different race-, sex-, or culture-based classes of individuals in the work group and consequently place further emphasis on ingroup and outgroup distinctions. This will reduce the level of social integration within the work group.

The increasing presence of demographic diversity in the workplace underscores the practical importance of considering the impact of diversity on causal attributions. In order to ensure that heterogeneous work teams function effectively, the cognitive elements at play in the assignment of credit and blame for work group successes and failures must be better understood. This chapter is intended to encourage a systematic course of research that will examine this important issue in fuller detail.

REFERENCES

Adams, J.S. (1965). Inequity in social exchange. in *Advances in Experimental Social Psychology,* Vol. 2, L. Berkowitz (Ed.), New York: Academic Press.

Adler, A. (1956). *The Individual Psychology of Alfred Adler,* H. Ansbacher and R. Ansbacher (Eds.), New York: Basic Books.

Ajzen, I. (1971). Attributions of disposition to an actor: Effects of perceived decision freedom and behaviourial utilities. *Journal of Personality and Social Psychology,* 18:144–156.

Ajzen, I. and Holmes, W. (1976). Uniqueness of effects in causal attribution. *Journal of Personality,* 44:98–108.

Alderfer, C.P. (1991). Changing race relations in organizations: A critique of the contact hypothesis. *Canadian Journal of the Administrative Sciences,* 8(2):80–89.

Allport, G.W. (1937). *Personality: A Psychological Interpretation,* New York: Holt.

Ancona, D.G. (1990). Outward bound: Strategies for team survival in an organization. *Academy of Management Journal,* 33:334–365.

Bandura, A. (1977). Self-efficacy: Towards a unifying theory of behavioural change. *Psychological Review,* 84:191–215.

Bandura, A. (1982). Self-efficacy mechanism in human agency. *American Psychologist,* 37:122–147.

Barley, S. (1990). The alignment of technology and structure through roles and networks. *Administrative Science Quarterly,* 35:61–103.

Bem, D. (1967). Self-perception: The dependent variable of human performance. *Organizational Behaviour and Human Performance,* 2:105–121.

Bem, D. (1972). Self-perception theory. *Advances in Experimental Social Psychology,* 6:1–62.

Betancourt, H. (1990). An attribution–empathy model of helping behavior: Behavioral intentions and judgements of help-giving. *Personality and Social Psychology Bulletin,* 16:573–591.

Betancourt, H. and Lopez, S. (1993). The study of culture, ethnicity, and race in American psychology. *American Psychologist,* 48:629–637.

Betancourt, H. and Weiner, B. (1982). Attributions for achievement-related events, expectancy, and sentiments: A study of success and failure in Chile and the United States. *Journal of Cross-Cultural Psychology,* 13:362–374.

Betancourt, H., Hardin, C., and Manzi, J. (1992). Beliefs, value orientation, and culture in attribution processes and helping behavior. *Journal of Cross-Cultural Psychology,* 23:179–195.

Caine, B. (1975) Attributions of Responsibility in Cooperative Groups with Leadership, paper presented at the Southeastern Psychological Association Convention, Atlanta.

Caine, B. and Schlenker, B. (1979). Role position and group performance as determinants of egotistical perceptions in cooperative groups. *Journal of Psychology,* 10:149–156.

Cartwright, D. and Zander, A. (1968). *Group Dynamics: Research and Theory,* 3rd edition, New York: Harper and Row.

Chacko, T. and McElroy, J. (1983). The cognitive component in Locke's theory of goal setting: Evidence for a causal attribution interpretation. *Academy of Management Journal,* 26:104–118.

Clapham, S. and Schwenk, C. (1991). Self-serving attributions, managerial cognition, and company performance. *Strategic Management Journal,* 12:219–229.

Cooper, H. and Lowe, C. (1977). Task information and attributions for academic performance by professional teachers and role players. *Journal of Personality,* 45:469–483.

Cox, T. and Blake, S. (1991). Managing cultural diversity: Implications for organizational competitiveness. *Academy of Management Executive,* 5:45–56.

Deaux, K. (1976). Sex: A perspective on the attribution process. in *New Directions in Attribution Research,* Vol. 1, J.H. Harvey, W.J. Ickes, and R.F. Kidd (Eds.), Hillsdale, N.J: Erlbaum, pp. 335–352.

Deaux, K. and Emswiller, T. (1974). Explanations for successful performance on sex-linked tasks: What is skill for the male is luck for the female. *Journal of Personality and Social Psychology,* 29:80–85.

Downey, H., Chacko, T., and McElroy, A. (1979). Attribution of causes of performance: A constructive, quasi-longitudinal replication of Staw (1975) study. *Organizational Behaviour and Human Performance,* 24:287–299.

Earley, P. (1993). East meets west meets mideast: Further explorations of collectivist and individualistic work groups. *Academy of Management Journal,* 36:319–348.

Evans, M. (1986). Organizational behaviour: The central role of motivation. *Yearly Review of Management of the Journal of Management,* 12:203–222.

Feather, N. (1969) Attribution of responsibility and valence of success and failure in relation to initial confidence and task performance. *Journal of Personality and Social Psychology,* 13:129–144.

Feather, N. and Simon, J. (1971). Causal attributions for success and failure in relation to expectations of success based upon selective or manipulative control. *Journal of Personality,* 39:527–541.

Feldman, J. (1981). Beyond attribution theory: Cognitive performance processes in performance appraisal. *Journal of Applied Psychology,* 66:127–148.

Festinger, L. (1954). A theory of social comparison processes. *Human Relations,* 1:117–140.

Forsyth, D. and Schlenker, B. (1977) Attributing the causes of performance: Effects of performance quality, task importance, and future testing. *Journal of Personality,* 45:220–236.

Frieze, J. and Weiner, B. (1971). Cue utilization and attributional judgement of success and failure. *Journal of Personality,* 39:591–601.

Fullerton, H. (1987). Labour Force Projections: 1986–2000. *Monthly Labor Review,* September, 19–29.

Gist, M. (1987). Self-efficacy: Implications for organizational behaviour and human resource management. *Academy of Management Review,* 23(3):472–485.

Goodman, P., Atkin, R., and Ravlin, E. (1982). Some Observations on Specifying Models of Group Performance, paper delivered at a symposium on Productive Work Teams and Groups, American Psychological Association Convention, Washington, D.C.

Greenhaus, J. and Parasuraman, S. (1993). Job performance attributions and career advancement prospects: An examination of gender and race effects. *Organizational Behaviour and Human Decision Processes,* 55:273–297.

Hackman, J. (1990). *Groups that Work (and Those that Don't),* San Francisco: Jossey-Bass.

Hackman, J. and Morris, C. (1975). Group tasks, group interaction process, and group performance effectiveness: A review and proposed integration. in *Advances in Experimental Social Psychology,* L. Berkowitz (Ed.), New York: Academic Press.

Heider, F. (1958). *The Psychology of Interpersonal Relations,* New York: Wiley

Heilman, M. (1983). Sex bias in work settings: The lack of fit model. in *Research in Organizational Behavior,* Vol. 5, L.L. Cummings and B.M. Staw (Eds.), Greenwich, Conn.: JAI Press., pp. 269–298.

Hewstone, M. and Ward, C. (1985). Ethnocentrism and causal attribution in Southeast Asia. *Journal of Personality and Social Psychology,* 48:614–623.

Hewstone, M., Jaspars, J., and Lalljee, M. (1982). Social representations, social attribution and social identity: The intergroup images of "public" and "comprehensive" schoolboys. *European Journal of Social Psychology,* 12:241–269.

Himmelfarb, S. and Anderson, N. (1975). Integration-theory applied to opinion attribution. *Journal of Personality and Social Psychology,* 31:1064–1071.

Hoffman, E. (1985) The effect of race–ration composition on the frequency of organizational communication. *Social Psychology Quarterly,* 48:17–26.

Ilgen, D. and Youtz, M. (1986). Factors affecting the evaluation and development of minorities in organizations. in *Research in Personnel and Human Resource Management: A Research Manual,* K. Rowland and G. Ferris (Eds.), Greenwich, Conn.: JAI Press, pp. 307–337.

Ilgen, D., Mitchell, T., and Fredrickson, J. (1981). Poor performers: Supervisors' subordinates responses. *Organizational Behaviour and Human Performance,* 27:386–410.

Jackson, S. (1992). Team composition in organizational settings: Issues in managing an increasingly diverse work force. in *Group Process and Productivity,* S. Worchel, W. Wood, and J. Simpson (Eds.), Newbury Park, Calif.: Sage, pp. 138–173.

Jackson, L., Sullivan, L., and Hodge, C. (1993). Stereotype effects on attributions, predictions, and evaluations: No two social judgements are quite alike. *Journal of Personality and Social Psychology,* 65:69–84.

Janis, I. (1972). *Victims of Groupthink,* Boston: Houghton Mifflin.

Johnston, W.W. and Packer, A.H. (1987). *Workforce 2000: Work and Workers for the Twenty-First Century,* Indianapolis: Hudson Institute.

Jones, E. and Davis, K. (1965). From acts to disposition. in *Advances in Experimental Social Psychology,* L. Berkowitz (Ed.), New York: Academic Press.

Jones, E. and McGillis, D. (1976). Correspondent inferences and the attribution cube: A comparative reappraisal. in *New Directions in Attribution Research,* Vol. 1, J.H. Harvey, W.J. Ickes, and R.F. Kidd (Eds.), Hillsdale, N.J.: Erlbaum, pp. 389–420.

Katz, D. and Kahn, R.L. (1978). *The Social Psychology of Organizations,* New York: Wiley.

Kelley, H. (1967). Attribution theory in social psychology. in *Nebraska Symposium on Motivation,* D. Levine (Ed.), Lincoln: University of Nebraska.

Kelley, H. (1972). Causal schemata and the attribution process. in *Attribution: Perceiving the Causes of Behaviour,* E. Jones, D. Kanouse, H. Kelley, R. Nisbett, S. Valins, and B. Weiner (Eds.), Morristown, N.J.: General Learning Press.

Kelley, H. (1973). The process of causal attribution. *American Psychologist,* 28:107–128.

Kelley, H. and Michela, J. (1980). Attribution theory and research. *Annual Review of Psychology,* 31:457–501.

Kluckhohn, F. and Strodtbeck, F. (1961). *Variations in Value Orientations,* Evanston, Ill.: Row, Peterson.

Lindsley, D., Brass, D., and Thomas, J. (1994). Efficacy–Performance Spirals, unpublished manuscript.

Locke, E. and Latham, G. (1990). *A Theory of Goal Setting and Task Performance,* Englewood Cliffs, N.J.: Prentice-Hall.

Locke, E., Frederick, E., Lee, C., and Bobko, P. (1984). The effect of self-efficacy, goals, and task strategies on task performance. *Journal of Applied Psychology,* 69:241–251.

Lott, A. and Lott, B. (1965). Group cohesiveness as interpersonal attraction: A review of relationships with antecedent and consequent variables. *Psychological Bulletin,* 64: 259–309.

Luginbuhl, J., Crowe, D., and Kahan, J. (1975). Causal attributions of success and failure. *Journal of Personality and Social Psychology,* 31:86–93.

McArthur, L. (1972). The how and what of why: Some determinants and consequences of causal attributions. *Journal of Personality and Social Psychology,* 22:171–193.

McArthur, L. and Post, D. (1977). Figural emphasis and person perception. *Journal of Experimental and Social Psychology,* 13:520–535.

McMahan, I. (1973). Relationships between causal attributions and expectancy of success. *Journal of Personality and Social Psychology,* 28:108–114.

Medow, H. and Zander, A. (1965). Aspirations of group chosen by central and peripheral members. *Journal of Personality and Social Psychology,* 1:224–238.

Mikalachki, A. (1969). *Group Cohesion Reconsidered: A Study of Blue Collar Work Groups,* London, Ontario: University of Western Ontario.

Miller, D. (1976). Ego involvement and attributions for success and failure. *Journal of Personality and Social Psychology,* 34:901–906.

Miller, D. and Rose M. (1975). Self-serving biases in the attribution of causality: Fact or fiction. *Psychological Bulletin,* 82:213–275.

Mitchell, T.R., Green, S.G., and Wood, R.E. (1981). An attributional model of leadership and the poor performing subordinate: Development and validation. in *Research in Organizational Behavior,* Vol. 3, L.L. Cummings and B.M. Staw (Eds.), Greenwich, Conn.: JAI Press, pp. 197–234.

Newcomb, T. (1961). *The Acquaintance Process,* New York: Holt, Reinhart & Winston.

Newston, D. (1974). Dispositional inference from effects of actions: Effects chosen and effects forgone. *Journal of Experimental and Social Psychology,* 10:489–496.

Nieva, V. and Gutek, B. (1980). Sex effects on evaluation. *Academy of Management Journal,* 5:267–276.

O'Leary, V. and Hansen, R. (1984). Sex as an attributional fact. in *Nebraska Symposium on Motivation,* D. Levine (Ed.), Lincoln: University of Nebraska, pp. 133–177.

O'Reilly, C.A., III, Caldwell, D.F., and Barnett, W.P. (1989). Work group demography, social integration and turnover. *Administrative Science Quarterly,* 34:21–37.

Pepitone, A. and Kleiner, R. (1957). The effects of threat and frustration on group cohesiveness. *Journal of Abnormal and Social Psychology,* 54:192–199.

Pettigrew, T. (1979). The ultimate attribution error: Extending Allport's cognitive analysis of prejudice. *Personality and Social Psychology Bulletin,* 5:461–476.

Regan, D., Straus, E., and Fazio, R. (1974). Liking and the attribution process. *Journal of Experimental Social Psychology,* 10:385–397.

Rosenbaum, R. (1972). *A Dimensional Analysis of the Perceived Causes of Success and Failure,* unpublished doctoral dissertation, University of California, Los Angeles.

Ross, L. (1977). The intuitive psychologist and his shortcomings: Distortions in the attribution process. in *Advances in Experimental Social Psychology,* Vol. 10, L. Berkowitz (Ed.), San Diego: Academic Press, pp. 174–221.

Schlenker B. (1973). Self-image maintenance and enhancement: Attitude change following counterattitudinal advocacy. in Proceedings of the 81st Annual Convention of the American Psychological Association, Montreal.

Schlenker B. (1975). Group members' attributions of responsibility for prior group performance. *Representative Research in Social Psychology,* 6:96–108.

Schlenker, B. and Miller, R. (1977a). Group cohesiveness as a determinant of egocentric perceptions in cooperative groups. *Human Relations,* 11:1039–1055.

Schlenker, B. and Miller, R. (1977b). Egotism in groups: Self-serving biases or logical information processing? *Journal of Personality and Social Psychology,* 35:755–764.

Schlenker, B., Soraci, S., Jr., and McCarthy, B. (1976). Self-esteem and group performance as determinants of egocentric perceptions in cooperative groups. *Human Relations,* 29:1163–1176.

Shaw, M. (1971). *Group Dynamics: The Psychology of Small Group Behavior,* New York: McGraw-Hill.

Siegel, J. and Bowen, D. (1973). Process and performance: A longitudinal study of the reactions of small task groups to periodic performance feedback. *Human Relations,* 26(4)433–448.

Steiner, I. (1972). *Group Process and Productivity,* New York: Academic Press.

Tajfel, H. and Turner, J. (1979). An integrative theory of intergroup conflict. in *The Social Psychology of Intergroup Relations,* W.G. Austin and S. Worchel (Eds.), Monterey, Calif.: Brooks/Cole.

Tajfel, H. and Turner, J. (1985). The social identity theory of intergroup behavior. in *Psychology of Intergroup Relations,* 2nd edition, S. Worchel and W.G. Austin (Eds.), Chicago: Nelson Hall, pp. 7–24.

Taylor, S. and Fiske, S. (1975). Point of view and perceptions of causality. *Journal of Personality and Social Psychology,* 32:439–445.

Taylor, D. and Jaggi, V. (1974). Ethnocentrism and causal attribution in a South Indian context. *Journal of Cross-Cultural Psychology,* 5:162–171.

Trope, Y. (1974). Inferential processes in the forced compliance situation: A bayesian analysis. *Journal of Experimental and Social Psychology,* 10:1–16.

Tsui, A.S. and O'Reilly, C.A., III. (1989) Beyond simple demographic effects: The importance of relational demography in superior–subordinate dyads. *Academy of Management Journal,* 32:402–423.

Turner, J.C. (1982). Towards a cognitive redefinition of the social group. in *Social Identity and Intergroup Relations,* H. Tajfel (Ed.), Cambridge: Cambridge University Press.

Walster, E., Berscheid, E., and Walster, G.W. (1973). New directions in equity research. *Journal of Personality and Social Psychology,* 25:151–176.

Ward, R.A., La Gory, M., and Sherman, S.R. (1985). Neighborhood and network age concentration: Does age homogeneity matter? *Social Psychological Quarterly,* 48:139–149.

Watson, W.E., Kumar, K., and Michaelsen, L.K. (1993). Cultural diversity's impact on interaction process and performance: Comparing homogeneous and diverse task groups. *Academy of Management Journal,* 31:590–602.

Weiner, B. (1972). *Theories of Motivation: From Mechanism to Cognition,* Chicago: Markham.

Weiner, B. (1974). *Achievement Motivation and Attribution Theory,* Morristown, N.J.: General Learning Press.

Weiner, B. (1979). A theory of motivation for some classroom experiences. *Journal of Educational Psychology,* 71:3–25.

Weiner, B. (1985). An attributional theory of achievement motivation and emotion. *Psychological Review,* 92:548–573.

Weiner, B. (1986). *An Attributional Theory of Motivation and Emotion,* New York: Springer-Verlag.

Weiner, B. and Kukla, A. (1970). An attributional analysis of achievement motivation. *Journal of Personality and Social Psychology,* 15:1–20.

Weiner, B., Frieze, I., Kukla, A., Reed, L., Rest, S., and Rosenbaum, R.M. (1972). Perceiving the causes of success and failure. in *Attribution: Perceiving the Causes of Behaviour,* E.E. Jones, D.E Kanouse, H.H. Kelley, R.E. Nisbett, S. Valins, and B. Weiner (Eds.), Morristown, N.J.: General Learning Press.

Weiner, B., Hechhausen, H., and Meyer, E. (1972a). Causal ascriptions and achievement behavior. *Journal of Personality and Social Psychology,* 2:239–248.

Weiner, B., Hechhausen, H., Meyer, W., and Cook, R. (1972b). Causal ascription and achievement motivation: A conceptual analysis of effort and re-analysis of locus of control. *Journal of Personality and Social Psychology,* 21:239–248.

Wolosin, R.J., Sherman, S.J., and Till, A. (1973). Effects of cooperation and competition on responsibility attribution after success and failure. *Journal of Experimental Social Psychology,* 9:220–235.

Wortman, C.B. (1970). A Theory of Defensive Attribution, major area paper submitted to the Psychology Department, Duke University.

Zaccaro, S.J., Peterson, C., and Walker, S. (1987). Self-serving attributions for individual and group performance. *Social Psychology Quarterly,* 50(3):257–263.

17

DISTRIBUTIVE JUSTICE NORMS AND ATTRIBUTIONS FOR PERFORMANCE OUTCOMES AS A FUNCTION OF POWER*

Walter J. Ferrier, Ken G. Smith, Kenneth J. Rediker, and Terence R. Mitchell

ABSTRACT

This research is an investigation of how power differentials (i.e., the amount of difference in power between group leaders and subordinates) influence the attributions for group success and failure and the distributive justice norms that prevail within the group. The research also investigates whether the group's performance level or changes in the leader's power moderates attributional and distributive justice patterns.

Consistent with the hypotheses, group performance was found to have a direct effect on group members' internal and external attributions. Members from high-performing groups make greater internal attributions than do individuals from low-performing groups. Moreover, individuals from low-performing groups make greater external attributions than do individuals from high-performing groups. No significant main effects for power or power change on attributions were found, but interactions of power with group performance were consistent with theoretical expectations.

---

*Each author contributed equally to this manuscript.

©St. Lucie Press CCC 1-884015-19-0 1/95/$100/$.50

The results for distributive justice norms are also consistent with theoretical expectations, especially for individuals who gained power. Overall, the results indicate that attributions and distributive justice norms are contingent on both power levels and group performance. These results are discussed in terms of their contribution to our understanding of how power and power change influence group norms and behavioral processes.

INTRODUCTION

Power plays a central role in the understanding of organizational behavior (Pfeffer, 1981, 1991; Astley and Sachdeva, 1989; Frost, 1987). The literature concerned with organizational functioning emphasizes power and issues surrounding its acquisition and distribution as a key feature for understanding the way in which things get done (Emerson, 1962; Bacharach and Lawler, 1980; Pfeffer, 1981, 1992).

The present research is a preliminary investigation of how the amount of difference in power influences the attributions and perceptions of equality and cooperation between individuals working on a common task. The research also investigates whether the performance level or changes in power moderate these relationships. That is, does a change in performance or leader power change group interactions and performance attributions? The theoretical background for the research is grounded in the recent work of Kipnis (1976, 1987, 1991) and Kabanoff (1991) and is concerned with how power and its use affect the power user and the relationship between power users and their targets.

The practical reasons for studying this issue are fairly obvious. With acquisitions and takeovers, people's power positions are changing as is the configuration of power in existing groups (Hambrick and Cannella, 1993). Power and responsibility shift when downsizing occurs. Moreover, the recent implementation of self-managed teams has reduced the power differentials within groups. A review of the relevant literature is helpful, therefore, in highlighting several key aspects of power within organizational settings and relevant hypotheses.

BACKGROUND

Distribution rules or norms within groups have an important impact on group process. Rules that emphasize equity are based on providing outcomes commensurate with inputs. Equality norms suggest that outcomes are more or less equally divided among group participants. More specifically, where the leader has strong power relative to that of group members, an equity norm (personal outcomes should be commensurate with inputs) should prevail. In contrast, where the group leader has little power relative to the power of group members, an equality norm should emerge (everyone gets the same outcomes regardless of inputs).

A number of writers have discussed the fact that different distribution rules operate in the organizational context (Deutsch, 1985; Sampson, 1986), but the equality and equity rules seem to be the most prevalent and significant for understanding influence processes and group dynamics (Meindl, 1989). Based on the work of Meindl (1989) and his own theoretical framework, Kabanoff (1991) argues that the development and the impact of these norms are a result of the distribution of power within the group. Kabanoff's (1991) explanation for these conjectures is that low power differences between individuals will be characterized by free discussion, participation by everyone, active involvement of the leader, open debate, and social cohesiveness. Such interactions are likely to represent equality norms. Alternatively, where power differences are great, there will be increased competition, social distance, and one-way communication. These interactions are likely to be characterized by equity norms. Kabanoff (1991) does not argue that one rule is better than the other. On the contrary, he suggests that different distribution rules result in different behaviors, and these behaviors will be more or less successful depending on the context (i.e., the prevalence of other leader behaviors, the task environment, etc.).

Kipnis (1987, 1991), on the other hand, takes a much more normative stand while focusing on slightly different issues. First, based on his earlier research, Kipnis (1972, 1976) argues that power is corrupting. He has demonstrated that leaders who have high power tend to create social distance from subordinates, attribute group success to their own leadership skills, and blame subordinates or the nature of the task itself for failure. Blaming other individuals or the environment for group failure is consistent with the so-called self-serving bias—the tendency to externalize negative outcomes (Ross, 1977; Fiske and Taylor, 1991). However, reviews of this literature (Bradley, 1978; Zuckerman, 1979; Miller and Ross, 1975) suggest that the findings for internalizing success are stronger than those for externalizing failure. Fiske and Taylor (1991) summarize the research by saying that "there is more evidence that people take credit for success—the self-enhancing bias—than that they deny responsibility for failure—the self-protective bias" (p. 79).

Kipnis' (1987, 1991) recent work has focused on what he calls the metamorphic effects of power. He argues that as people gain power over others they are slowly transformed. More specifically, he proposes that the acquisition and use of power "can change the influencing agent's values, beliefs, and behavior in unanticipated and unwanted ways" (Kipnis, 1987, p. 34). As people acquire and use their power successfully, they will come to believe more positive things about themselves and negative things about their subordinates. If they use strong influencing tactics, they will tend to see themselves as the influencing agent for the successful actions of others. They will see themselves as brighter, stronger, and more effective than less powerful colleagues. These leaders' behaviors will change as well. They will increase their monitoring of subordinates, decrease subordinates' participation in decision making, and become more socially distant. In other words, both the absolute differences in power and changes in power should influence behavior in the direction for self-serving bias.

Both authors appear to agree that power differences may produce different sorts of behavior. However, Kipnis (1987) tends to focus on the leaders' causal attributions for successful and unsuccessful events and how these attributions change over time. To date, no research has actually examined experimentally what happens when people *acquire* power or have their power *reduced*; so far, the metamorphic effects of power have been based on cross-sectional data. One purpose of the following study was to observe the effects of power and changes in power on the leaders' attributions and behaviors. The following hypotheses are consistent with past attribution research:

Hypothesis 1a: Individuals (members and leaders) in high-performing groups will make more internal attributions for performance than will individuals in low-performing groups.

Hypothesis 1b: Individuals (members and leaders) in low-performing groups will make more external attributions for performance than will individuals in high-performing groups.

The following hypotheses are based on Kipnis' ideas:

Hypothesis 2a: High-power leaders will make more internal attributions for *success* than will low-power leaders.

Hypothesis 2b: High-power leaders will make more external attributions for *failure* than will low-power leaders.

Hypothesis 3a: Leaders who experience a gain in power will increase their level of internal attributions for *success*; leaders who experience a loss in power will decrease their level of internal attributions for *success*.

Hypothesis 3b: Leaders who experience a gain in power will increase their level of external attributions for *failure*; leaders who experience a loss in power will decrease their level of external attributions for *failure*.

As mentioned, Kabanoff (1991) has focused on a contingency or fit model of power distribution rules. His emphasis has been on the different types of behaviors and processes that emerge when power differences are high or low. However, as with Kipnis, no empirical research has verified or rejected Kabanoff's propositions. Therefore, the second purpose of the research was to test whether the interpersonal interactions in a group with a low-power leader were more cooperative and participative than interpersonal interactions in a group with a high-power leader.

> **Hypothesis 4a:**   Individuals (members and leaders) will experience greater equality and cooperation in groups where the leader has low power than in groups where the leader has high power.

> **Hypothesis 4b:**   Individuals (members and leaders) of groups where the leader becomes more powerful will experience a decrease in the level of equality and cooperation; individuals (members and leaders) of groups where the leader becomes less powerful will experience an increase in the level of equality and cooperation.

In the following research, subjects were part of a three-person managerial team working on a simulated business game. Some of the individuals on these teams acquired power while others had it taken away. Attributions for performance outcomes and various aspects of equality and cooperation were measured to assess the impact of power differences and changes in power.

METHOD

Organizational Simulation

A research setting was sought that would allow the researchers to manipulate the level of power and power changes over time. Many authors have argued for the use of simulations to study the dynamic aspects of organizational behavior. The current study utilized Thompson and Stappenbeck's *The Business Strategy Game* (1990), a computer-based simulation requiring teams of students to compete against one another in a simulated athletic footwear industry over the course of an entire semester. At two points throughout the simulation—the experiment's midpoint and the final day—the researchers administered a questionnaire to all participants. The level of power was manipulated at the beginning of the game and was changed just after the midpoint.

Sample

The experiment was conducted with several sections of senior-level undergraduate students (who were members of a business strategy course) at two large universities. Each course section was comprised of eight teams. A total of 33 teams, averaging four individuals per team, participated in the experiment. The game was played over a 10- to 12-week period. Teams were required to render decisions weekly in the functional areas of marketing, production, logistics, human resource management, and finance. The total number of students participating in the experiment was 111. However, due to absences on the days the questionnaires were administered, 207 questionnaires were completed out of a possible 222 from two administrations of the questionnaire.

To induce the requisite level of seriousness and professionalism, the final outcome of the simulation was included in the final course grading scheme. This condition created a simulated "market" system of rewards and punishment and also seemed to evoke students' vigilance toward free riders within the team.

The elegance and sophistication of the simulation created the opportunity for each team to receive detailed feedback of its performance relative to other teams competing in the game. Such information was provided weekly and was used in the teams' subsequent decisions regarding the re-evaluation of its strategies.

Manipulation of Power

Three aspects of power were assessed: position power (leader versus member), power level (high versus low power for leader), and power change (increase versus decrease for leader). Team members selected a team chief executive officer (CEO). Each remaining team member was given the title of executive vice president (EVP). In doing so, power was ascribed by team members to the CEO through the election process. This power difference served as the manipulation of *position power.*

One half of the selected CEOs in each course section were randomly assigned a high level of power. The remaining teams had a CEO in title only or a low level of power. Each team was then briefed by the instructor as to the role of the CEO versus that of each EVP. High-power CEOs were charged with several key responsibilities above and beyond those of each EVP and the low-power CEOs:

1. To formally evaluate each EVP weekly on the basis of participation, preparation, and contribution to team activities
2. To prepare an organizational chart indicating responsibilities delegated to each EVP
3. To serve as the sole contact point for all instructor–team communications
4. To review and formally sign off on all weekly decision sheets

As noted, low-power CEOs and EVPs were told that their ranks were simply titular formalities. This difference in power served as the manipulation of *power level.*

TIME 1   TIME 2

	TIME 1	TIME 2
HIGH	a	b
LOW	c	d

POWER

FIGURE 17.1   CEO power status by time and power.

The execution of the game was divided into two time periods. At the simulation midpoint, which delineates time period 1 (TIME1) from time period 2 (TIME2), the course instructors informed each team as to a change in CEO responsibility. TIME1 high-power CEOs (Figure 17.1, cell a) were relieved of their additional duties for the remainder of the simulation and were left with low power at TIME2 (cell d). This process changed the power level and identifies the *loss-of-power* condition, but not loss of position power.

Conversely, TIME1 low-power CEOs (cell c) were charged with the same additional responsibilities as TIME1 high-power CEOs, thus making them TIME2 high-power CEOs (cell b). This identifies the *gain-of-power* condition.

Questionnaire

At the end of both TIME1 and TIME2, a questionnaire was administered to all participants to assess attributions and perceptions of equality and cooperation. The questionnaire cover sheet contained summary performance information for each team. All of the questions employed five-point Likert scales with a score of 5 indicating definite agreement with the statement and a score of 1 indicating total disagreement.

Causal Attributions

Weiner (1980, 1985, 1986) has developed and successfully tested a theory of attribution in achievement-related contexts. According to Weiner (1980), the four most frequently used attributions are ability, effort, task difficulty, and luck. In addition, ability and effort are seen as internal attributions, whereas task difficulty and luck are seen as external attributions. Weiner (1985, 1986) also suggests that a stable (ability, difficulty) versus unstable (effort, luck) distinction is important.

Eight questions were developed to assess four types of causal attributions. The questions were slightly modified to reflect whether the respondent was a CEO or EVP and whether the respondent was from a high-performing or a low-performing team.

The external unstable dimension was addressed by two questions: "Our company's performance was due to events beyond our control" and "Our company's performance was due to [good/bad] luck" (depending on the performance condition) ($\alpha = 0.91/0.72$; TIME1/TIME2). The external stable dimension was assessed by: "Our company's performance was due to the demands of other schoolwork" and "Our company's performance was due to the difficulty of the game" ($\alpha = 0.87/0.89$; TIME1/TIME2). The internal stable dimension for the CEOs was assessed by: "Our company's performance was due to my knowledge" (EVPs responded to the CEO's knowledge) and "Our company's performance was due to my ability" (EVPs responded to the CEO's ability) ($\alpha = 0.96/0.95$; TIME1/TIME2). The internal unstable dimension for the CEOs was assessed by: "Our company's performance was due to my level of effort" (EVPs responded to the CEO's level of effort) and "Our company's performance was due to actions taken by me" (EVPs responded to the actions taken by the CEO) ($\alpha = 0.97/0.81$; TIME1/TIME2). These questionnaire items are summarized in Table 17.1.

Distributive Justice

The questionnaire also contained six items to assess the level of equality and cooperation within each group, which ranged from: "Each member of our team was treated as an equal" to "Each member of our team had his or her input equally considered" to "Members of our team were treated according to the level of their contribution" (reverse coded). This equality measure had reliabilities of $\alpha = 0.78$ and $\alpha = 0.76$ for TIME1 and TIME2, respectively. Higher scores for this composite measure would indicate an equality norm. Low scores would indicate the absence of an equality norm or the presence of an equity norm. Again, these items are summarized in Table 17.1.

Other Variables

Position power (CEO versus EVP) and the level of power (high versus low) were coded as dichotomous variables, which differentiate individuals with high power from those with lower power. Time was also coded as a dichotomous variable which captures the temporality of change in power across the two time periods.

Performance was coded as high or low and was based on each teams' relative

**TABLE 17.1   Summary of Results of
Questionnaire on Causal Attributions**

Variable	Sample questionnaire items	Alphas (Time 1/ Time2)	No. of factor items
Attribution scales	**"Our company's performance was...**		
External unstable	...due to events beyond our control" ...due to bad/good luck"	0.91/0.72	2
External stable	...due to the demands of other schoolwork" ...due to the difficulty of the simulation"	0.87/0.89	2
CEO internal stable	...due to my knowledge" ...due to my ability"	0.96/0.95	2
CEO internal unstable	...due to my level of effort " ...due to the actions taken by me "	0.97/0.81	2
Distributive justice scales	**"During team decision meetings...**		
Distributive justice	...team members were treated as equals" ...team members had their input equally considered" ...team members were treated according to their level of contribution" ...each team member had an equal influence on decisions" ...team members tried to help one another" ...team members really cooperated with one another"	0.78/0.76	6

rank within each course section. The median was used as a cutoff point to distinguish high-performing teams from low-performing teams.

RESULTS

Manipulation Checks

The questionnaire contained six items designed to check the strength of the power manipulation. These items ranged from "The CEO was given the power to carry out the responsibilities of the Business Strategy Game" to "The CEO has the responsibility to formally review and sign each week's decision sheet." These six items were combined into a single scale ($\alpha = 0.90$). Individuals associated with the high power manipulation had significantly higher scores on this scale than did individuals associated with the low power manipulation ($F = 49.566$, $p < 0.001$). In addition, individuals who moved from low power to high power reported significantly higher scores in TIME2 than in TIME1 ($F = 31.830$, $p < 0.001$). Individuals who moved from a high-power to a low-power condition also reported significantly lower scores in TIME2 than in TIME1 ($F = 15.934$, $p < 0.000$). There were no significant differences between EVPs and CEO on these ratings ($F = 0.042$, $p < 0.837$). Thus, it appears that the manipulation of power levels and change in power were successful.

Attribution Hypotheses

All of the hypotheses were tested with one-way MANOVA. In these first analyses, the four attribution variables served as dependent variables whereas position power, level of power, change in power, and the level of performance served as independent variables.

Hypotheses 1a and 1b, which predicted that causal attributions would vary with performance levels, were supported ($F = 17.094$, $p < 0.001$; see Figure 17.2). Indeed, at the univariate level, each of these attribution variables was significantly different at the 0.01 level across the high/low performance conditions. Consistent with Hypotheses 1a and 1b, high-performing individuals make greater internal attributions than do individuals from low-performing groups. Moreover, low-performing individuals make greater external attributions than do individuals from high-performing groups.

There were no significant main effects of position power, power level, or change of power on attributions. Consistent with Hypotheses 2 and 3, the analysis proceeded to a more complex level by examining the moderating effects

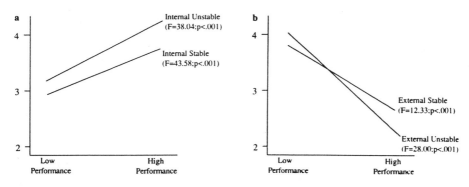

FIGURE 17.2 Effects of performance on internal and external attributions. MANOVA $F = 17.094$, $p < 0.001$. (a) Internal attributions; (b) external attributions.

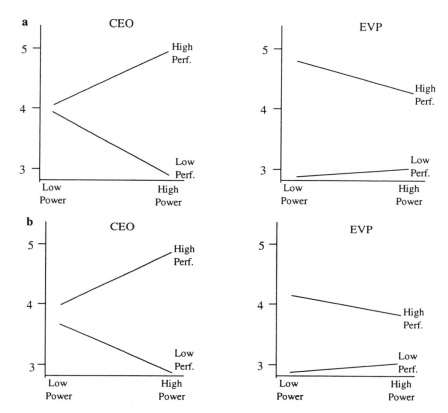

FIGURE 17.3   Internal attributions by level of power, performance, and position power. (a) Unstable: $F = 2.901$, $p < 0.10$. (b) Stable: $F = 2.679$, $p < 0.10$.

of performance. First, a four-way MANOVA was run to test the overall hypothesis that attributions would vary as a function of performance, power level, and change in power (time). The four-way MANOVA was not significant ($F = 0.890$, $p < 0.49$). However, a three-way MANOVA with position power, performance, and power level was significant ($F = 2.626$, $p < 0.05$), indicating some contingent support for Hypotheses 2a and 2b.

In analyzing variations in attributions as an interactive function of team performance, position power, and power level, three of the four attribution variables were significant or marginally significant at the univariate level (see Figures 17.3a, 17.3b, and 17.4a), internal unstable ($F = 2.901$, $p < 0.10$), internal stable ($F = 2.679$; $p < 0.10$), and external unstable ($F = 3.683$, $p < 0.05$). The external unstable attribution was not significant (Figure 17.4b). Thus, when controlling for each subject's position power within the team, only conditional support for the arguments of Kipnis and Kabanoff was found.

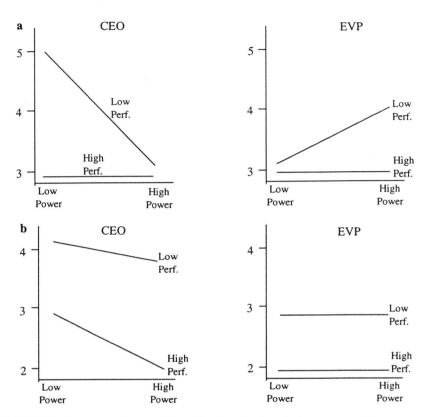

FIGURE 17.4 External unstable attributions by level of power, performance, and position of power. (a) $F = 3.683$, $p < 0.05$; (b) $F = 1.590$, $p < 0.50$.

For internal attributions in the high-power condition, high-performing CEOs tend to attribute more of the group's high performance to their own effort and actions (unstable; Figure 17.3a) and knowledge and ability (stable; Figure 17.3b) than do low-performing CEOs. This finding is consistent with Hypothesis 2a. However, in the low-power condition, internal (stable and unstable) attributions between high- and low-performing CEOs seem not to differ significantly. For the EVPs, no significant differences or interactions between power and performance are apparent. Thus, the internal attributions for the EVPs reflect the level of team performance rather than power differences.

For external stable attributions, CEOs from high-performing teams in both high- and low-power conditions seemed not to attribute their success to external factors, as expected (see Figure 17.4a). However, low team performance seemed to differentiate high- and low-power leaders in their external stable attributions. In the high-power condition, high- and low-performing CEOs do not differ significantly. However, in the low-power condition, low-performing CEOs were more likely to blame external stable factors for their team's performance than high-performing CEOs. This finding is consistent with Hypothesis 2b. External unstable attributions were found not to be significantly different in the team performance, power, and position power interaction. In fact, Figure 17.4b illustrates that external stable attributions differ by team performance alone. These data seem to support the statements by Fiske and Taylor (1991) that internalizing attributions for success are stronger than the externalizing effects for failure.

In conclusion, there is some support for Hypothesis 2 concerning the level of power and causal attributions. However, the relationship seems to be moderated by the teams' level of performance and position power and is more complex than originally hypothesized.

There is no support for Hypothesis 3 concerning the metamorphic effects of power. In fact, attributions do not seem to vary with time or the change in power. Observations from the game and the data seem to suggest that those CEOs losing power continued to act as if they retained their original level of power, whereas those who gained power made modest changes in leadership behavior. This seems to indicate that the actual use of power and influencing behaviors by high-power individuals in the first time period and/or the maintenance of their position as leader (CEO) from TIME1 to TIME2 allows a high-power condition to persist despite the experimental manipulation of a change in power.

Distributive Justice Hypotheses

Hypotheses 4a and 4b concerned the effects of position power, power level, and change in power on distributive justice behaviors (see Table 17.1). This hypothesis was tested with two-way ANOVA. The distributive justice variable (high scores = equality; low scores = equity) served as the dependent variable, and position power, the level of power, and change of power were each used individually as independent variables. Overall, there was no support for the main effects (power level, position power, and time) or the simple interaction (power × time) hypotheses (H4a and H4b).

A four-way ANOVA was run to test for more complex interactions; namely, that distributive justice behaviors vary as a function of position power, power levels, change in power (time), and performance. Performance was included as a control. There was no support for a four-way interaction ($F = 0.153$, $p < 0.75$). However, there was a significant three-way interaction among position power, change in power (time), and performance ($F = 6.132$, $p < 0.01$). Figures 17.5a and 17.5b depict gain-of-power groups having low power in TIME1 moving to high power in TIME2 and loss-of-power groups having high power in TIME1 moving to low power in TIME2. Both groups are further differentiated as to their performance levels.

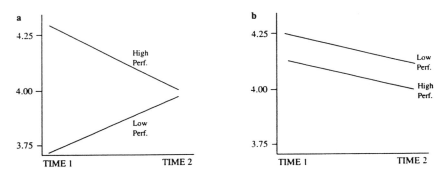

FIGURE 17.5   Distributive justice by power level, change of power, and performance ($F = 6.132$, $p < 0.01$). (a) Gain-of-power condition; (b) loss-of-power condition.

The most pronounced results concern individuals from gain-of-power teams (Figure 17.5a) in both performance conditions. As members of high-performing groups experience a leader who gains power, the distribution justice scores decrease, thus indicating a significant shift away from an equality norm. This result is consistent with Hypothesis 4b. However, members of low-performing groups with a leader who gains power experience a gain in equality. This result is inconsistent with Hypothesis 4b, which could be explained by the fact that out of 33 teams used in the experiment, only 2 teams experienced a change in performance from TIME1 to TIME2. Thus, when poor performance levels persisted, members of low-performing groups with a leader who gained power might have been worried about the team's final performance outcome (and thus their course grades) and took on equal responsibility to improve the team's performance in TIME2.

The persistence of performance could also help explain the results for loss-of-power teams illustrated in Figure 17.5b. Specifically, individuals from high-performing teams where the leader loses power experience a decline in the level of equality. This is inconsistent with Hypothesis 4b. Perhaps these individuals prefer the performance and power status quo of TIME1. As a result, individuals from these teams may be apt to let a highly productive, high-power leader influence the team's direction even more so in TIME2, since the team was doing so well without equal participation from all team members (equity norm).

Individuals from low-performing teams with a leader who lost power also experience a decline in the level of equality. This result is also inconsistent with Hypothesis 4b and may be due to the unwillingness of these individuals to share equally in the team's misfortunes and/or the possibility of holding each other more accountable for their individual contributions (equity norm) in TIME2.

In conclusion, the form of the relationship between power and distributive justice norms depends on the level of performance. Although the results in the loss-of-power condition are mostly inconsistent with Kabanoff's level-of-power hypothesis, the results for the gain-of-power condition are consistent with Kabanoff and highlight the moderating effect of performance and perhaps the mediating effects of attributions. When performance is good, individuals attribute outcomes to themselves and are perhaps less likely to cooperate and treat each other as equals as they gain power (since they see themselves as agents of success). Recalling that performance levels persisted between TIME1 and TIME2, and low-power CEOs in TIME1 were given "additional duties and responsibilities" in TIME2, then low-performing, gain-of-power CEOs might avoid becoming scapegoats by encouraging equality-building behaviors within the team.

CONCLUSION

This study initially sought to examine how power differentials and changes in power altered attributions, perceptions, and group distributive justice processes. While fundamental attribution biases were supported, the results indicate that the relationship among power, performance, and group functioning is quite complex in that performance is a key contingency variable. Indeed, the relationship among power level, position power, changes in power within the team, and group performance appears to be highly interactive.

These data suggest that the proposed theories of power, power change, performance, and attributions need to be more precise. The data presented suggest that behavioral and attributional patterns probably stabilize over time and that it is difficult to create change in these patterns as a result of changes in power alone. This is particularly true of leaders who were forced to give up their power and influence over subordinates. This suggests that loss-of-power leaders change their behaviors (as perceived by subordinates) and their attributions very little.

In addition, these results suggest that it would appear to be quite relevant for most organizational and group settings to consider group performance as an integral part of this system. The data clearly show not only that the relationship between a leader and subordinates differs as a function of group success, but also that their behavior and attribution patterns are highly sensitive to performance. Normatively, power and power use are to be directed toward group and/or organizational achievement. It is the achievement or nonachievement of goals (reflected in performance levels) that seems to both influence attributions of responsibility and alter subsequent leader/subordinate interactions.

In summary, these results paint a very complex picture of power and its use. Absolute power and power differentials appear important in terms of attributions and group processes. However, whether performance is good or bad and whether power is gained or lost seems to moderate these relationships. More precise theories and empirical tests of these relationships are clearly needed to fully understand the dynamics of power.

REFERENCES

Astley, W.G. and Sachdeva, P.S. (1989). Structural sources of interorganizational power: A theoretical synthesis. *Academy of Management Review,* 9:104–113.

Bacharach, S.B. and Lawler, E.J. (1980). *Power and Politics in Organizations,* San Francisco: Jossey-Bass.

Bradley, G.W. (1978). Self serving biases in the attribution process: A re-examination of the fact or fiction question, *Journal of Personality and Social Psychology,* 36:56–71.

Deutsch, M. (1985). *Distributive Justice: A Social Psychological Perspective,* New Haven, Conn.: Yale University Press.

Emerson, R.M. (1962). Power dependence relations. *American Sociological Review,* 27: 31–40.

Fiske, S.T. and Taylor, S.E. (1991). *Social Cognition,* New York: McGraw-Hill.

Frost, P.J. (1987). Power, politics, and influence. in *Handbook of Organizational Communication: An Interdisciplinary Perspective,* F.M. Jablin, L.L. Putman, K.H. Roberts, and L.W. Porter (Eds.), Newbury Park, Calif.: Sage.

Hambrick, D.C. and Cannella, A.A. (1993). Relative standing: A framework for understanding departures of acquired executives. *Academy of Management Journal,* 36:733–762.

Kabanoff, B. (1991). Equity, equality, power and conflict. *Academy of Management Review,* 16:416–441.

Kipnis, D. (1972). Does power corrupt? *Journal of Personality and Social Psychology,* 24:33–41.

Kipnis, D. (1976). *The Powerholders,* Chicago: University of Chicago Press.

Kipnis, D. (1987). Psychology and behavior technology. *American Psychologist,* 42:30–36.

Kipnis, D. (1991). The technological perspective. *Psychological Science,* 2:62–69.

Meindl, J.R. (1989). Managing to be fair: An exploration of values, motives, and leadership. *Administrative Science Quarterly,* 34:252–276.

Miller, D.T. and Ross, M. (1975). Self serving biases in the attribution of causality: Fact or fiction, *Psychological Bulletin,* 82:213–225.

Pfeffer, J. (1981). *Power in Organizations,* Marshfield, Mass.: Pitman.

Pfeffer, J. (1992). *Managing with Power: Politics and Influence in Organizations,* Boston: Harvard Business School Press.

Ross, L. (1977). The intuitive psychologist and his shortcomings: Distortions in the attribution process. in *Advances in Experimental Social Psychology,* Vol. 10, L. Berkowitz (Ed.), New York: Academic Press, pp. 173–220.

Sampson, E.E. (1986). Justice ideology and social legitimation. in *Justice in Social Relations,* H.W. Bierhoff, R.L. Cohen, and J. Greenberg (Eds.), New York: Plenum Press, pp. 87–102.

Thompson, A.A. and Stappenbeck, G.V. (1990). *The Business Strategy Game,* Homewood, Ill.: Irwin Press.

Weiner, B. (1980). *Human Motivation,* New York: Holt, Rinehart and Winston.

Weiner, B. (1985). An attributional theory of achievement motivation and emotions. *Psychological Review,* 92:548–573.

Weiner, B. (1986). *An Attributional Theory of Motivation and Emotion,* New York: Springer-Verlag.

Zuckerman, M. (1979). Attribution for success and failure revisited, or: The motivational bias is alive and well in attribution theory, *Journal of Personality,* 47:245–287.

Section IV

AN AGENDA FOR RESEARCH AND APPLICATION

18

AN ALTERNATIVE PERSPECTIVE ON ATTRIBUTIONAL PROCESSES*

Robert G. Lord

INTRODUCTION

Attribution theories have historically attempted to explain how ordinary people make causal attributions in the areas of social and self-perceptions by analogy to the process of scientific reasoning. In essence, typical theories present attributions as arising from largely rational, explicit processes that constitute a "naive psychology" or "a naive version of the method used in science" (Kelley, 1973, p. 109). For example, Kelley suggested that perceivers use covariation information in a manner analogous to analysis of variance in order to assign causality to those factors that systematically covary with outcomes. Although researchers recognized that perceivers may not be very precise scientists, the idealized model of perceivers as thoughtful, analytic information processors provided a standard to which many results were compared. Through contrast to this scientific analogy, the examination of many types of attributional errors gained meaning. Many of the chapters in this book continue this view, applying it to the explanation of attributions in organizational contexts.

*The author would like to thank Rosalie Hall and Elaine Engle for commenting on an earlier version of this manuscript.

ALTERNATIVE ANALOGIES FOR ATTRIBUTIONS

Perceiver-as-Scientist Analogy

In considering future directions for attribution theory, the perceiver-as-scientist analogy should be reconsidered. On the positive side, it has produced a number of systematic ways of organizing the content from attributional questions (Weiner et al., 1971), reasonable measures of causal dimensions (Henry and Campbell, 1995; Kent and Martinko, 1995; Russell, 1982), many complex theories concerning attributional processes themselves (Hilton and Slugoski, 1986; Jones and Davis, 1965; Kelley, 1973; Lipe, 1991), and a variety of interesting applications (Martinko and Gardner, 1987; McElroy, 1982; Mitchell and Wood, 1980), including those presented in this book.

However, there are many other considerations that indicate the inadequacy of this perceiver-as-scientist analogy. First, Gilbert's (1989) work on attributional reasoning, which was reviewed in this book by Maher (1995), suggests that social perceptions proceed first through very fast comprehension and categorization steps which require few attentional resources to produce trait ascriptions. Given sufficient attentional resources, perceivers can correct these dispositional inferences for situational explanations of behavior in a manner that is generally consistent with functioning as "naive scientists." Gilbert's research indicates, however, that social perceptions are generally well formed before such situational corrections, implying that explicit attributional reasoning involves an after-the-fact adjustment to social perceptions, not a necessary antecedent, as suggested by early theorists (e.g., Jones and Davis, 1965). Consistent with this viewpoint, earlier chronometric work by Smith and Miller (1983) also indicates that many trait ascriptions are made without the benefit of explicit causal analysis.

Second, the general importance of perceptual factors in shaping causal reasoning is inconsistent with the perceiver-as-scientist analogy because it shows that causal understanding occurs early on in the stream of processing stimulus information. Thus, in most social perceptions, causal understanding may occur before explicit, conscious reasoning processes become involved. Further, causal understanding may be based on processes that are unknown to perceivers and, therefore, are not subject to scientific scrutiny by the perceiver. For example, Storms' (1973) work on actor–observer biases showed that these biases could be reversed by using videotapes of interactions to reverse the visual perspective of actors and observers. Taylor and Fiske (1978) provided many examples of perceptual salience affecting causal attributions. Phillips and Lord (1981) showed that leadership perceptions and causal attributions were strongly influenced by the camera angle from which stimuli were videotaped. They made videotapes from two concurrent cameras that made the target individual more or less central in a visual field, but clearly showed exactly the same target behavior. This manipulation had substantial effects on leadership ratings and causal attributions.

Third, although not typically considered by attribution theory researchers, the extensive research on text comprehension suggests that readers understand text by building a causal understanding of a story (Fletcher and Bloom, 1988). That is, readers attempt to build a causal path linking an opening to its outcome. Links in this path are built by connecting antecedent conditions to their consequences. When antecedents cannot be easily linked to consequences, they are held in working memory longer, producing greater accessibility and more retrieval cues for unlinked as compared to linked antecedents. The important point in this research is that causal understanding occurs at a very micro level—linking clauses or successive sentences (Fletcher et al., 1990). Such reasoning is too fast for causal analysis using scientific or quasi-scientific processes, and explicit causal reasoning would interfere with text understanding by creating an additional working memory load. Further, such causal understanding occurs very early in the comprehension processes, before conscious reasoning processes become involved.

These three very different areas of research—cognitive load explanations of fundamental attribution errors, perceptual factors in causal attributions, and text comprehension research—indicate that scientific reasoning may be too slow and may consume too many attentional resources to provide a general model of attributional processes in dynamic situations. Further, in most natural situations, causal understanding is an early part of the comprehension process that occurs without awareness and in a relatively automatic manner (see Lord and Smith, 1983). In this chapter, an alternative analogy that is not subject to these limitations is suggested. It provides a complement to the perceiver-as-scientist viewpoint emphasized by most extant attribution theory research.

Perceiver-as-Primitive-Processor Analogy

In this chapter, researchers concerned with attribution theory are urged to consider an alternative model of social perceivers and actors: prehistoric man. This view depicts perceivers as primitive processors of information, reacting to situations and other individuals using prelinguistic, affectively laden, implicit processes.

Early humanoids relied on their causal understanding to effectively manage a number of human and nonhuman threats to survival, develop effective social relations, and manage difficult living situations. However, it seems unlikely that they could reason in a scientific manner. With much less developed language, it is likely that spatial and temporal factors and visual images played a very important role in their causal understanding. It is also likely that the causal understanding of our prehistoric ancestors had a very different quality, being more intuitive, more implicit, and more directly linked to actions. Prehistoric perceivers could not describe and may even have been unaware of their attributional processes.

Though radically different from the perceiver-as-scientist viewpoint, the perceiver-as-primitive-processor analogy is just as appropriate to the topics investigated by attribution theorists or researchers concerned with organizational behavior. Attributions in organizations are generally not the central focus of perceivers and for this reason may depend on evolutionarily older, nonconscious processes which can still operate when higher level processing capacities are used for other tasks.

The perceiver-as-primitive processor analogy could lead directly to alternative theories of attributional processes, different measures of attributions, and a variety of new applied concerns that will extend the scope of attribution theory. This analogy is also quite relevant to many of the chapters on attribution theory presented in this book.

A key aspect of the primitive processor analogy is that critical attributional processes may operate implicitly, outside of the awareness of information processors. Nisbett and Wilson (1977) raised this possibility years ago. Interestingly, recent work in cognitive science has emphasized subsymbolic cognitive architectures (see Lord and Maher, 1991) which involve information processes that are not directly accessible to individuals. Research has also linked implicit processing capabilities with an evolutionarily older part of the brain (Reber, 1992; Reber et al., 1991; Seger, 1994), which is another reason for the analogy to primitive perceivers.

Implicit processing has a number of qualities not shared by more explicit, scientific processing that make it a very reasonable candidate for carrying out a number of attributional tasks. Thus, attributional research should seriously consider the possibility that implicit as well as explicit processes are required to adequately understand how both contemporary and prehistoric perceivers form causal judgments. In addition, this chapter is intended to demonstrate that implicit attributional processes are important to organizational scientists.

In the remainder of this chapter, what we know about implicit learning and implicit memory is summarized. How these implicit processes may produce attributional understanding, how implicit and explicit attributional processes may be related, how such implicit attributional processes can be measured, and how this perspective relates to other theories regarding information processing in organizations are explored later in the chapter.

IMPLICIT PROCESSING AND CAUSAL UNDERSTANDING

Defining Characteristics

Seger (1994) defines *implicit learning* in terms of four characteristics, which are shown in Table 18.1. First, knowledge is not fully accessible to consciousness. That is, subjects cannot provide a full (or in many cases any) verbal account of what they have learned. Second, the information learned is more complex than simple associations or frequency counts. Simple information may also be implicitly learned, but it is much more likely to be explicitly noticed and therefore learned through explicit processes. Third, implicit learning is an incidental or unintended consequence of processing stimuli. In other words, implicit learning occurs in conjunction with other activities involving relevant stimuli. As such, implicit learning is a plausible candidate for explaining how social perceptions or causal understanding naturally emerge in conjunction with other activities. A fourth and final defining characteristic of implicit learning is that it is preserved in amnesia and, therefore, uses neural structures other than the hippocampal memory system. Implicit learning relies on the basal ganglia, association areas of the cortex, and the frontal lobes. These brain structures evolved earlier than the hippocampal memory system. Being more basic, the implicit memory system is more robust in that it shows less loss of information over time and is affected less by physical insult than the hippocampal memory system. Thus, it may be a superior system for retaining information as critical to survival as causal understanding.

Implicit learning differs from *implicit memory* in some important ways, although the two systems overlap a great deal (Seger, 1994). Research on implicit memory uses single stimuli which are generally words, whereas research on implicit learning involves complex patterns of nonverbal stimuli. In addition, implicit learning is affected by attentional factors, whereas implicit memory is not influenced by attentional manipulations. Given these distinctions, the position taken here is that the literature on implicit learning is more relevant to understanding person perceptions and attributional reasoning in dynamic organizational situations than the literature on implicit memory.

TABLE 18.1   Defining Characteristics of Implicit Learning

1. Minimal accessibility to consciousness

2. Involves complex rather than simple patterns

3. Incidental or unintended consequence of processing stimuli

4. Uses *primitive* brain systems involving the basal ganglia, association areas of cortex, and frontal lobes, rather than more recent hippocampal memory system

Implicit Capabilities

What can be learned implicitly? The answer to this critical question that is emerging from recent research is that a wide variety of tasks can be learned implicitly. What can be learned depends on both the structure of the stimulus and the response modality investigated (see Seger, 1994, p. 167). Only capabilities that seem directly relevant to attributional issues are included here.

Research clearly indicates that covariation information can be learned implicitly and that the use of covariation information is central to a number of attribution theories (Hilton and Slugoski, 1986; Jones and Davis, 1965; Kelley, 1973; Lipe, 1991). Additionally, research shows that people can also learn associations among features of visual stimuli using implicit processes (Seger, 1994). Implicit learning is capable of building prototypes that abstract patterns of covariation from visual exemplars. Thus, there appears to be a clear capability to implicitly learn the type of pictoliteral categories that Brewer (1988) believes underlie automatic aspects of social classifications.

Covariation between features of visual stimuli and verbal labels can also be learned implicitly, implying that the connection of trait labels to appearance information may be learned implicitly. Such implicit learning may be critical to the development of social stereotypes. For example, Lewicki (1986) presented pictures of women along with verbal descriptions of their personalities. Based on such information, subjects implicitly learned covariations between the hair length of the stimuli and certain personality traits. Being implicit, such information would be outside of awareness, but could provide the basis for subsequent intuitive judgments of personality based on such stimulus features. Similarly, Carlston and Skowronski (1994) recently reported five studies using a savings-at-relearning paradigm showing that trait inferences spontaneously made from behavioral descriptions were implicitly associated with pictures of the person allegedly producing these behaviors.

Many functional relationships can also be learned implicitly since implicit processes can link variables appearing at different points in time (Seger, 1994). Such learning seems directly relevant to learning cause–effect relationships that link temporal antecedents with consequences. Implicit systems also can manage visual or temporal relations that are too complex for explicit learning. Thus, attributions in complex social situations such as those involving groups or leader–subordinate interactions may be based on implicit learning. Relationships that are partially masked because of random factors can also be learned implicitly, whereas random factors are very disruptive to explicit learning (Seger, 1994).

Conceptual fluency—the ability to generalize from implicit learning to evaluating novel stimuli—is also implicit. For example, judgments of grammaticality or being "well formed" can be made based on implicit learning (Seger, 1994).

Though they have not yet been investigated, it seems likely that "social grammars" involving such constructs as norms, scripts, or cultural specifications can also be learned implicitly. Such factors are important in understanding attributions because causality is more likely to be ascribed to "abnormal" than normal actions (Hilton and Slugoski, 1986), and normality may be defined implicitly.

"Rare" behaviors may also be interpreted using different processes than common behaviors (Johnson et al., 1994). For example, Johnson et al. note that although causal analysis for rare events is based on covariation, common events tend to be explained in terms of more common dispositions. That is, attributors look for the disposition most capable of generating the outcome rather than the disposition that most highly covaries with an outcome. Thus, attributing causality to factors such as leadership may be based on a generative force principle rather than a covariation principle. Generative force learning may be implicit, reflecting dynamic learning capabilities, which are discussed subsequently.

Conceptual fluency can also provide a basis for recognition judgments. For example, novel stimuli that are consistent with past implicit learning are recognized as being familiar. Thus, conceptual fluency can generate schema-consistent rating errors, which plague many applied areas such as performance appraisal. Implicit matches to stereotypes may also lead one to implicitly recognize stereotypic stimulus characteristics. More directly related to attributional concerns, such false recognitions might provide an indirect basis for measuring trait ascriptions (see Lord, 1985; von Hippel et al., 1993).

Prediction and control can also be learned implicitly. Dynamic relations, which involve learning the consequences of manipulating certain parameters, can be learned implicitly (Berry and Broadbent, 1988; Seger, 1994). Broadbent's work is particularly relevant to organizational science because it uses a simulation of complex management decisions to investigate implicit learning. Such work shows that intuitive understanding may have an implicit basis that directly links actions to consequences. If dynamic relations are organized into sequences of actions and consequences, then dynamic learning might also provide the basis for implicit learning of scripts. Such cognitive structures can guide actions and social perceptions (Lord and Kernan, 1987) as well as provide a basis for causal understanding.

In summary, many of the processes that have been investigated in the context of attribution theory can occur implicitly. Further, since implicit learning occurs while stimuli are being consciously processed for other purposes, such leaning is germane to social processes in organizations. Social processes may involve unnoticed background to more central organizational tasks or events. Some of the processes just discussed are summarized in Table 18.2 and their relation to many of the attributional principles addressed in this book is illustrated.

TABLE 18.2   Implicit Learning Capacities and Attributional Processes

Implicit capacity	Related attributional process
Covariation learning	Causal analysis for rare events
Generative force learning	Causal analysis for common events
Feature relations in stimuli	Prototype learning
Association between visual stimuli and verbal labels	Stereotypes and pictoliteral categories
Temporal relations	Cause–effect linkages
Conceptual fluency	
Grammaticality	Social correctness
Familiarity	Schema-consistent recognition Affective reactions
Dynamic learning	Behavior–consequence learning

Relation Between Implicit and Explicit Processes

The position argued in this chapter is that primitive implicit information processes and more contemporary explicit processes operate concurrently in all situations. As Seger (1994) notes, explicit and implicit processes are specialized. They reflect separate and very different processing capacities, are produced by different brain structures, and align with different explanations of how attributional analyses occur. Implicit learning plays a larger role in perceptual and motor learning, unstructured learning, learning of complex relationships, and learning based on nonsalient information. Explicit learning, in contrast, emphasizes verbal information and more structured learning situations (e.g., formal schooling). In spite of these differences, the prehistoric and scientific capabilities may frequently combine to produce social perceptions and attributional understanding.

How these very different processes are combined presents an interesting issue for future attribution theory research. There is very little research on the interaction of implicit and explicit processes; comments in this section, therefore, are only suggestions.

One possibility is that people do *not* integrate the outcomes of implicit and explicit processes, but instead rely on one while ignoring the other. Attributional processes in many organizational situations may overtly be designed to use explicit information and processes (e.g., performance appraisal); however, the extent to which such processes can be separated from more intuitive implicit processes needs careful investigation. In many instances, it may be difficult to explicitly suppress spontaneously occurring thoughts (Wegner, 1992) or affect (Wegner, 1994), particularly if under sufficient cognitive load.

Another important consideration in relating implicit and explicit processes is that in most learning situations, implicit knowledge develops before explicit knowledge. Implicit knowledge related to social perceptions and causal understanding may provide a leading system that structures later explicit processes. For example, behaviors such as frequency of verbal behavior, which may be encoded automatically (Hasher and Zacks, 1979), serve as an initial basis for social differentiation in terms of leader–member relations (Stein and Heller, 1979). Once an individual is labeled a leader, he or she may be seen as a more important cause of subsequent outcomes. Thus, in newly formed groups or superior–subordinate dyads, implicit processes might be expected to be critical in initially differentiating among individuals and forming structures that are later confirmed and reinforced by explicit processes. In short, explicit causal processes may reflect the consequences of earlier implicit processes.

Another important area where conceptual fluency may link implicit and explicit learning is in affective relations (Seger, 1994). It seems probable that implicit learning provides a basis for explicit affective reactions such as liking or trust. Thus, on-line processing of social information (Hastie and Park, 1986) may involve implicit learning for which only the end results are explicitly accessible. Interestingly, Wayne has shown that liking may be more critical than subordinate performance in determining the nature of leader–member exchanges, and affective reactions are formed very early in dyadic relations (Liden et al., 1993; Wayne and Ferris, 1989).

Seger (1994) indicates that learning proceeds best when implicit and explicit factors reinforce each other, as when implicitly learned information is explicitly explained. Thus, prior implicit learning can be demonstrated in terms of increased efficiency or "savings" in explicit learning (Carlston and Skowronski, 1994). However, there are also instances when implicit and explicit processes work in opposition. Research indicates that strongly held explicit beliefs can override implicit processes. Consistent with this perspective, it is generally found that in hiring decisions, information on job qualifications overrides age- or gender-related stereotypes which may involve more implicit learning.

However, the subtleness of such processes is illustrated by Gilbert's (1989) work on corrections for situational causes of behavior. If Gilbert's work is interpreted as showing that very fast *implicit* comprehension and categorization processes can be corrected by *explicit* situational information, then this work can be viewed as illustrating that implicit and explicit attributional information can be synthesized. The most important conclusion seems to be that a synthesis of implicit and explicit information requires attentional resources and will not occur under high load conditions.

When causality is ascribed to situational factors ("corrected" in Gilbert's terms), it may be necessary to ignore or suppress implicitly produced trait ascriptions. As shown by Wegner's (1992, 1994) work on affect and thought suppression, thoughts or affect cannot be effectively suppressed under high load. Thus, Gilbert's findings of greater internal attributions under high load may reflect general self-regulatory constraints. Indeed, this logic suggests that fundamental attribution errors may reflect implicit processes associated with person perceptions that have not been effectively integrated with explicit information about situations. To the extent that suppression capacity varies across individuals, this logic also implies that there would be individual differences in the propensity to make fundamental attribution errors.

IMPLICATIONS FOR THEORY AND METHODOLOGY

Implicit attributional processes pose obvious problems with respect to measurement. The predominant approach to measuring causal attributions has been to ask subjects about the content of attributional judgments. (See chapters in this book by Henry and Campbell [1995] or Kent and Martinko [1995] for examples.) That is, subjects are asked to assess the importance of various dispositional or situational causes for events. However, since subjects are unaware of implicit processes or their effects, subjects cannot simply be asked to describe their implicit attributional reasoning. Neither can it be determined whether explicit causal ratings reflect the effects of implicit processes, explicit processes, or the joint effects of both types of processes. Thus, from a methodological perspective, implicit processes are a potentially troublesome source of error in investigating explicit processes, and implicit processes seem to be without a basis for direct measurement.

More careful consideration, however, indicates that implicit attributional processes are still open to scientific investigation. With few exceptions, attribution theory has not only adopted "naive psychology" as its subject matter, but has also used many common sense ideas as a basis for theory and methodology (Calder, 1977). One common sense idea, which is usually incorrect, is that scientific processes should be empirically investigated by linking key constructs to indicators that scientists can directly sense. For example, whereas a lay person may expect astronomers to test theories by directly observing the movement of stars or planets through telescopes, it is more likely that astronomers are examining traces created by the phenomena of interest. Stars may emit radio signals that are studied by astronomers, and their motion is indicated by shifts in the spectrum of emitted light.

In a similar manner, it is likely that implicit as well as explicit attributional processes can be investigated by the traces these phenomena create. In general, we want to separate the effects of perceptual and visual processes, which tend to be more implicit, from conceptual (symbolic) or verbal processes, which tend to be more explicit (see von Hippel et al., 1993). Explicit processing related to attributions should have direct effects on conceptually related measures such as recognition memory or recall. For example, Hamilton et al. (1990) found that more difficult attributional processing led to greater recall of sentences. Similarly, more extensive perceptual processing should impact on measures that are implicit or visually oriented. For example, von Hippel et al. (1993) found that implicit perceptual memory items (word-stem completion or word-fragment completion) showed greater accuracy under conditions that facilitated implicit perceptual processing. von Hippel et al. also found that schematic processing, which is conceptual, inhibited perceptual encoding of information.

Traces of Attributional Processes

A number of "traces" that may be created by both implicit processes and explicit processes related to social perceptions and attributional analyses are briefly described in this section. Such traces could be used to build indirect measures of either implicit or explicit measures of attributions. If the aim is to determine whether trait ascriptions are formed implicitly or explicitly, this topic may be assessed by comparing the relative accuracy of implicit measures and explicit measures (see von Hippel et al., experiment 3, for an example). Potential implicit measures include perceptual identification of briefly presented (30 ms or less) stimuli, word-fragment completion, and word-stem completion; explicit measures include more traditional verbal memory measures such as recognition accuracy.

Explicit memory processes may also provide important traces of schema use. It has been suggested elsewhere that recognition ratings of nonpresent behaviors can provide important indicators of underlying schemas (Lord, 1985). Such approaches have been used to demonstrate the use of leadership schemas as compared to goal-based scripts (Foti and Lord, 1987). As already noted, the use of conceptual schemas can inhibit reliance on perceptual processes (von Hippel et al., 1993).

Chronometric measures can also reflect the traces of attributional processing. As mentioned earlier, Fletcher et al. (1990) used a trace methodology to investigate the effects of attributional processing on text comprehension. They reasoned that when antecedents could not be easily linked to consequences, they would be retained in working memory longer, thereby slowing reading time. In addition, probe items related to unlinked antecedents (which are retained in working memory) should be responded to faster than probe items related to sentences where causal antecedents have already been linked to consequences. That is precisely what they found.

Chronometric measures are based on the notion of an associative long-term memory network that is searched in parallel based on cues available in working memory and their association with stored information. Therefore, both processes that strengthen association with salient cues and processes that retain such cues in working memory should affect accessibility. It would be expected that implicit attributional processes such as learning covariation information or generative relations would impact primarily on strength of association. Thus, the ability of one category feature to activate another, or the ability of a disposition to explain a behavior, may depend primarily on associations that are learned implicitly and are outside of conscious awareness.

Such implicit processes may have a wide range of effects that affect both implicit and subsequent explicit processing. For example, implicit covariation or generative information may make certain types of causal explanations salient while inhibiting alternative explanations. Such effects may occur in social perceptions, as when leaders are seen as being causally responsible for organizational performance (Lord and Maher, 1993) because perceivers believe leadership is capable of producing good (or bad) performance outcomes. Alternatively, these implicit effects can occur in self-perceptions such as when depressives see themselves as being responsible for poor outcomes but not for successes (Abramson et al., 1978). Qualities associated with negative self-images (e.g., being stupid) are believed to be capable of generating bad outcomes but not good outcomes. More explicit processes, such as behavioral ratings, can also be affected by implicitly learned information. For example, the factor structure of leadership behavior ratings can be reproduced almost exactly in ratings of fictitious individuals for whom no behavioral information is available (Rush et al., 1977). Such effects show that ratings can be reproduced based on classification information (leader/nonleader) and the implicit association (prototypicality) of behaviors within this category.

In summary, there are a number of important traces that can provide evidence of attributional processes, such as trait ascriptions, use of schemas, or implicit causal reasoning. These traces include structural measures of data, false recognition data, implicit memory measures, presence of information in working memory, or accessibility of information in long-term memory.

To measure implicit processes, researchers may also make use of conceptual fluency relations to show the effect of implicit processes on explicit measures. It has already been noted that implicit learning can have explicit effects on liking and recognition measures. Generative linkages between traits and common behaviors may also be based on implicit learning. Implicit effects may also be reflected in behavioral prediction because a key aspect of dynamic learning is understanding the impact of manipulated factors on future outcomes. Measures of perceived control might also be used as indicators of implicit understanding of a situation. Similarly, confidence measures might reflect reactions to implicit learning in specific task domains. Such effects have promise, but because such techniques use explicit responses, techniques will have to be developed to separate prior implicit learning and explicit effects that occur when responses are made.

CONCLUSIONS

A fundamental distinction between explicit and implicit processing systems has been stressed in this chapter. These systems have been linked to different brain structures that developed in different evolutionary periods and which reflect distinct processing capacities. It has been argued elsewhere (Lord and Maher, 1990) that what is needed is an expanded view of information processing that goes beyond rational models of information processing to recognize the potential for individuals to operate more like limited capacity, expert, or cybernetic processors. An obvious question is whether there is any relation between these four "modes" of information processing and the implicit–explicit processing distinction. The relations posited in Table 18.3 are offered as arguments that there is. Each of these types of processing and its relation to attributions is discussed briefly in the following sections.

Rational Processing

Rational processing is closely aligned to explicit learning and explicit processing. It involves deliberate, conscious processing that makes exhaustive use of information and requires extensive attentional resources. It is the type of processing that is most consistent with the attribution theory analogy to "naive scientists." However, capability to engage in rational processing is limited by two major factors. First, it requires extensive attentional resources and considerable time, which may not be consistent with the demands of real tasks. Second, frequently all relevant information cannot be accessed from the small portion of available knowledge that is momentarily activated in working memory. For this reason, other models of information processing may be more descriptively accurate for many tasks, including causal attribution (Lord and Maher, 1990).

Limited Capacity Processing

Limited capacity processing involves substituting heuristics or schema-based judgments for more exhaustive reasoning. It would be predominantly implicit if subjects relied on intuitive, affective, or perceptual factors. Such factors are common bases for social judgments and causal analysis. In contrast, heuristic

TABLE 18.3 Proposed Relation of Implicit and Explicit Processing to Rational, Limited Capacity, Expert, and Cybernetic Processing Modes

Processing mode	Explicit	Implicit	Explicit and implicit
Rational	Yes		
Limited capacity			
Formal heuristics	Yes		
Intuition		Yes	
Affect		Yes	
Perceptions		Yes	
Expert			
Knowledge	Yes	Yes	
Recognition		Yes	
Information access		Yes	
Deep structures			Yes
Meta-monitoring			Yes
Compiled skill	Yes		
Cybernetic			
Temporal relations		Yes	
Dynamic learning		Yes	
Functional learning			Yes
Covariation information			Yes

processes that relied on formal rules or a more conceptual basis would emphasize explicit processes.

Limited capacity processes are of interest to attributional theorists because they have been generally thought to be the reason for errors in attributional reasoning, such as fundamental attributional errors. Limited capacity processes fit with the view of perceivers as "cognitive misers" who are unwilling to devote adequate time or attentional resources to attributional issues. The view of perceivers as prehistoric processors creates another way to understand limited capacity processes and attributional "errors"—that is, these processes rely on evolutionarily older, more implicit processing capabilities. Rather than being abbreviated rational or scientific processes, limited capacity processing may result from alternative processing capabilities that are better suited to some attributional and perceptual tasks.

Expert Processing

Much of the enhanced performance of experts comes from their ability to substitute knowledge for processing (Logan, 1988; Newell, 1990). It is likely that extensive implicit learning occurs in the 10,000 hours of task experience that characterize the typical expert, which allows experts to process information in a qualitatively different manner (Chi et al., 1988; Lord and Maher, 1990). Experts are much better at recognizing key aspects of problems and retrieving appropriate information from memory, which are largely implicit processes. On the other hand, experts' use of deep rather than surface structures to understand problems could involve either explicit or implicit processes. Experts' greater meta-monitoring skills are probably dependent on implicit (see Lord and Levy, 1994) as well as explicit processes. However, the "compiled" skills of experts should not be considered to be the products of implicit learning because they originate in explicit processes (Seger, 1994).

Attributional reasoning would be expected to rely heavily on expert processing in domains in which attributors are very experienced. Thus, expert processing should characterize self-perceptions, perceptions of very familiar others, and assessment of causality for personal events or events involving very close individuals. Expert processing should also characterize domains in which one has well-developed schemas. Thus, there are many attributional areas in which implicit and explicit processing capacities combine to produce expert-level causal understanding.

Cybernetic Processing

Cybernetic processing characterizes repetitive tasks for which feedback is readily available. It involves multiple time perspectives associated with interpreting past outcomes and forming future expectations (Lord and Maher, 1990). Since most task and social interactions are repetitive, cybernetic processing is critical to understanding attributional processing. Because implicit processes are geared toward understanding temporal relations, it is expected that they are critical in understanding cybernetic processing. Dynamic learning, covariation information, and functional learning can all be implicit; thus it would be expected that cybernetic processing would be heavily dependent on implicit learning.

Several substantive domains of concern to attribution theorists seem particularly dependent on cybernetic processing. On-line social judgments (Hastie and Park, 1986) are cybernetic by definition. It was suggested earlier that these judgments may depend primarily on implicit processes, particularly when they are affectively based. Self-related judgments of task competency (self-efficacy, expectancies) and causal responsibility may also depend on cybernetic processes that are largely implicit, particularly when tasks involve perceptual or motor capacities. Finally, strategy development on repetitive tasks may be a largely implicit cybernetic process, although repeated failure can trigger more explicit considerations of strategy (Wofford and Goodwin, 1990).

In summary, the generally explicit processes of the rational information processing mode fit the perceiver-as-scientist analogy for assessing causality. Alternative models—limited capacity, expert, and cybernetic processing—rely more on implicit processes. To the extent that these alternative models describe causal analysis and social perceptions in organizations, the perceiver-as-primitive-processor analogy may be more appropriate.

REFERENCES

Abramson, L.Y., Seligman, M.E., and Teasdale, J.D. (1978). Learned helplessness in humans: Critique and reformulation. *Journal of Abnormal Psychology,* 87:49–74.

Berry, D.C. and Broadbent, D.E. (1988). Interactive tasks and the implicit–explicit distinction. *British Journal of Psychology,* 79:251–272.

Brewer, M.B. (1988). A dual process model of impression formation. in *Advances in Social Cognition,* Vol. 1, T.K. Srull and R.S. Wyer, Jr. (Eds.), Hillsdale, N.J.: Erlbaum, pp. 1–36.

Calder, B.J. (1977). An attribution theory of leadership. in *New Directions in Organizational Behavior,* B.M. Staw and G.R. Salancik (Eds.), Chicago: St. Clair Press.

Carlston, D.E. and Skowronski, J.J. (1994). Savings in the relearning of trait information as evidence for spontaneous inference generation. *Journal of Personality and Social Psychology,* 66:840–856.

Chi, M.T.H., Glaser, R., and Farr, M.J. (Eds.). (1988). *The Nature of Expertise,* Hillsdale, NJ: Erlbaum.

Fletcher, C.R. and Bloom, C.P. (1988). Causal reasoning in the comprehension of simple narrative texts. *Journal of Memory and Language,* 27:235–244.

Fletcher, C.R., Hummel, J.E., and Marsolek, C.J. (1990). *Journal of Experimental Psychology: Learning, Memory, and Cognition,* 16:233–240.

Foti, R.J. and Lord, R.G. (1987). Prototypes and scripts: The effects of alternative methods of processing information. *Organizational Behavior and Human Decision Processes,* 39:318–341.

Gilbert, D.T. (1989). Thinking lightly about others: Automatic components of the social inference process. in *Unintended Thought,* J.S. Uleman and J.A. Bargh (Eds.), New York: Guilford Press.

Jones, E.E. and Davis, K.E. (1965). From acts to dispositions: The attributional process in person perception. in *Advances in Experimental Social Psychology,* Vol. 2, L. Berkowitz (Ed.), New York: Academic Press.

Hamilton, D.L., Grubb, P.D., Acorn, D.A., Trolier, T.K., and Carpenter, S. (1990). Attributional difficulty and memory for attribution-relevant information. *Journal of Personality and Social Psychology,* 59:891–898.

Hasher, L. and Zacks, R.T. (1979). Automatic and effortful processes in memory. *Journal of Experimental Psychology: General,* 108:356–388.

Hastie, R. and Park, B. (1986). The relationship between memory and judgment depends on whether the judgment task is memory-based or on-line. *Psychological Review,* 93:258–268.

Henry, J.W. and Campbell, C. (1995). A comparison of the validity, predictiveness, and consistency of a trait versus situational measure of attributions. in *Attribution Theory: An Organizational Perspective*, M.J. Martinko (Ed.), Delray Beach, Fla.: St. Lucie Press.

Hilton, D.J. and Slugoski, B.R. (1986). Knowledge-based causal attributions: The abnormal conditions focus model. *Psychological Review*, 93:75–88.

Johnson, J.T., Boyd, K.R., and Magnani, P.S. (1994). Causal reasoning in the attribution of rare and common events. *Journal of Personality and Social Psychology*, 66:229–242.

Jones, E.E. and Davis, K.E. (1965). From acts to dispositions. in *Advances in Experimental Social Psychology*, Vol. 2, L. Berkowitz (Ed.), New York: Academic Press.

Kelley, H.H. (1973). The process of causal attribution. *American Psychologist*, 28:107–128.

Kent, R.L. and Martinko, M.J. (1995). The development and evaluation of a scale to measure organizational attributional style. in *Attribution Theory: An Organizational Perspective*, M.J. Martinko (Ed.), Delray Beach, Fla.: St. Lucie Press.

Lewicki, P. (1986). Processing information about covariations that cannot be articulated. *Journal of Experimental Psychology General: Learning, Memory, and Cognition*, 12:135–146.

Liden, R.C., Wayne, S.J., and Stilwell, D. (1993). A longitudinal study on the early development of leader–member exchanges. *Journal of Applied Psychology*, 78:662–674.

Lipe, M.G. (1991). Counterfactual reasoning as a framework for attribution theories. *Psychological Bulletin*, 109:456–471.

Logan, G.D. (1988). Toward an instance theory of automatization. *Psychological Review*, 95:492–527.

Lord, R.G. (1985). Accuracy in behavioral measurement: An alternative definition based on raters' cognitive schema and signal detection theory. *Journal of Applied Psychology*, 70:66–71.

Lord, R.G. and Kernan, M.C. (1987). Scripts as determinants of purposeful behavior in organizations. *Academy of Management Review*, 12:265–277.

Lord, R.G. and Levy, P.E. (1994). Moving from cognition to action: A control theory perspective. *Applied Psychology: An International Review*, 43:335–367.

Lord, R.G. and Maher, K.J. (1990). Alternative information processing models and their implications for theory, research, and practice. *Academy of Management Review*, 15:9–28.

Lord, R.G. and Maher, K.J. (1991). Cognitive theory in industrial and organizational psychology. in *Handbook of Industrial and Organizational Psychology*, 2nd edition, Vol. 2, M.D. Dunnette and L. Hough (Eds.), Palo Alto, Calif.: Consulting Psychologists Press.

Lord, R.G. and Maher, K.J. (1993). *Leadership and Information Processing*, New York: Routledge.

Lord, R.G. and Smith, J.E. (1983). Theoretical, information processing, and situational factors affecting attribution theory models of organizational behavior. *Academy of Management Review*, 8:50–60.

Maher, K.J. (1995). The role of cognitive load in supervisor attributions of subordinate behavior. in *Attribution Theory: An Organizational Perspective*, M.J. Martinko (Ed.), Delray Beach, Fla.: St. Lucie Press.

Martinko, M. and Gardner, W. (1987). The leader–member attribution process. *Academy of Management Review*, 12:235–249.

McElroy, J. (1982). A typology of attribution leadership research. *Academy of Management Review*, 7:413–417.

Mitchell, T. and Wood, R. (1980). Supervisor's responses to poor performance: A test of an attribution model. *Organizational Behavior and Human Performance*, 25:123–138.

Newell, A. (1990). *Unified Theories of Cognition,* Cambridge, Mass: Harvard University Press.

Nisbett, R.E. and Wilson, T.D. (1977). Telling more than we can know: Verbal reports on mental processes. *Psychological Review,* 84:231–259.

Phillips, J.S. and Lord, R.G. (1981). Causal attributions and perceptions of leadership. *Organizational Behavior and Human Performance,* 28:143–163.

Reber, A.S. (1992). The cognitive unconscious: An evolutionary perspective. *Cognition and Consciousness,* 1:93–133.

Reber, A.S., Walkenfeld, F.F., and Hernstadt, R. (1991). Implicit and explicit learning: Individual differences and IQ. *Journal of Experimental Psychology: Learning, Memory, and Cognition,* 17:888–896.

Rush, M.C., Thomas, J.C., and Lord, R.G. (1977). Implicit leadership theory: A potential threat to the internal validity of leader behavior questionnaires. *Organizational Behavior and Human Performance,* 20:93–110.

Russell, D. (1982). The Causal Dimension Scale: A measure of how individuals perceive causes. *Journal of Personality and Social Psychology,* 42:1137–1145.

Seger, C.A. (1994). Implicit learning. *Psychological Bulletin,* 115:163–196.

Smith, E.R. and Miller, F.D. (1983). Mediation among attributional inferences and comprehension processes: Initial findings and a general method. *Journal of Personality and Social Psychology,* 44:492–505.

Stein, R.T. and Heller, T. (1979). An empirical analysis of the correlations between leadership status and participation rates reported in the literature. *Journal of Personality and Social Psychology,* 11:1993–2002.

Storms, M.D. (1973). Videotape and the attribution process: Reversing actors and observers' points of view. *Journal of Personality and Social Psychology,* 27:165–175.

Taylor, S.E. and Fiske, S.T. (1978). Salience, attention, and attribution: Top of the head phenomena. in *Advances in Experimental Social Psychology,* Vol. 11, L. Berkowitz (Ed.), New York: Academic Press.

von Hippel, W., Jonides, J., Hilton, J.W., and Narayan, S. (1993). Inhibitory effects of schematic processing on perceptual encoding. *Journal of Personality and Social Psychology,* 64:921–935.

Wayne, S.J. and Ferris, G.R. (1989). Influence tactics, affect, and exchange quality in supervisor–subordinate dyads. *Journal of Applied Psychology,* 75:487–499.

Wegner, D. (1992). You can't always think what you want: Problems in the suppression of unwanted thoughts. in *Advances in Experimental Social Psychology,* Vol. 25, M.P. Zanna (Ed.), New York: Academic Press, pp. 193–224.

Wegner, D.M. (1994). Ironic processes of mental control. *Psychological Review,* 101:34–52.

Weiner, B., Frieze, I., Kukla, A., Reed, L., Rest, S., and Rosenbaum, R.M. (1971). Perceiving the causes of success and failure. in *Attribution: Perceiving the Causes of Behavior,* E.E. Jones, D.E. Kanouse, H.H. Kelley, R.E. Nisbett, S. Valins, and B. Weiner (Eds.), Morristown, N.J.: General Learning Press.

Wofford, J.C. and Goodwin, V.L. (1990). Effects of feedback on cognitive processing and choice of decision style. *Journal of Applied Psychology,* 75:603–612.

19

FINAL COMMENTS

Mark J. Martinko

The diversity of the contributions to this book makes it difficult to integrate the findings into a cohesive set of conclusions. Moreover, at this creative stage in the development of the field, a wide variety of research issues, topics, and theoretical options are probably most appropriate. Nonetheless, when considering the body of work as a whole, several issues emerge and deserve comment.

The first issue is the level of analysis. As indicated in Chapter 2, attribution theory is not a single theory but a set of theories that address issues of causal ascription. Thus, within the current text, theories of intrapersonal, dyadic, and group attributional processes have been suggested. When considering any one of these chapters, it sometimes appears that the variables, dimensions, and propositions are incongruent with prior theory. For the most part, these differences in perspective are a function of the different levels of analysis: intrapersonal, dyadic, and group. Moreover, at times, the incongruencies partially derive from attempts to force theory from one level of analysis onto another. As a result, one clear recommendation emanating from this research is that researchers and theoreticians need to be explicit regarding the level of analysis and theoretical grounding for their work.

A second issue raised concerns the nature of attribution processes. Lord's analogy of primitive versus rational man is a powerful one. Given the emphasis on parsimony, one is tempted to explain attributional processes primarily in terms of either Weiner's model of explicit processing or in terms of implicit learning. However, as the strong inference approach suggests, much more is likely to be gained by empirical contrasts of these two perspectives. As is often the case, it is likely that both perspectives are useful within particular behavioral domains. In addition, recognizing the extensive validation of Weiner's theory, it also seems reasonable to postulate that these implicit and explicit processes may operate in parallel and, in some cases, may be integrated. Thus, the contrasts between these rational versus implicit models are likely to be particularly beneficial in identifying both theoretical boundaries and parameters and in providing a realistic account of the processes by which individuals, groups, and organizations approach causal analysis.

A third set of issues permeating all of the chapters is concerned with measurement. Included within these issues are the questions of whether to measure attributional explanations or dimensions, which dimensions to measure, and whether or not traditional measurers accurately represent causal reasoning. The resolution of these issues is very much dependent upon our understanding of the basic nature and functions of attributional processes. Clearly, different causal explanations, dimensions, and measures are relevant for different behavioral domains. Although standardizing measures may be desirable in order to compare and contrast findings, it must also be recognized that measures must be varied and adapted across behavioral domains.

The notion of attributional styles also received considerable attention. Although work on attributional styles within organizational contexts has been limited, this area of research appears promising. Although there is evidence for a generalized cross-situational attributional style, it appears that the construct of attributional style is most valid in situations that have a moderate level of specificity. Although the measure of organizational attributional style proposed by Kent and Martinko appears promising, it may also be that measures that are still more specific are needed. Thus, there may be identifiable attributional styles which apply to specific domains such as interacting with peers, interacting with superiors, and intrapersonal problem-solving. Only additional research will answer these questions.

Another issue, which was embedded within the issue of level of analysis, is the target of attribution theory and its general perception by organizational researchers. As pointed out in Chapter 2, current textbooks on organizational behavior treat attribution theory primarily as a theory of interpersonal perception. The research and applications in the current text should help to demonstrate that there are multiple attributional models and applications for these models. In particular, the work on Weiner's model of achievement motivation demonstrates the crucial role that attributional processes play in intrapersonal motivation, particularly with respect to their influence on expectancies. Thus, it appears that more attention to attributional processes in intrapersonal models of motivation within the organizational sciences is warranted. In addition, however, the research presented in this book both suggests and points to a relatively new level of analysis for attribution theory: the group and organizational level. As Weiner indicated in Chapter 1, the nature of organizations and the unique problems they present stretch the parameters of current theory. The current text is intended to provide a balanced account of prior work and current issues so that theory development is informed by prior theoretical work and does not stumble forward haphazardly.

In conclusion, it is hoped that this book has at least partially fulfilled its role and function of providing a reference work that demonstrates the validity and potential of attributional perspectives within an organizational context. The works in this book make it clear that applying attribution theory to organizational contexts is not simply a matter of translating theory from one context to another. The nature and dynamics of organizations present new theoretical challenges and problems. The aim of the current text is to illuminate these issues and shed enough light so that the process of theory development and application can move forward without too many unnecessary detours.

INDEX

DATE DUE

DE 18 '04			

DEMCO 38-296

Please remember that this is a library book, and that it belongs only temporarily to each person who uses it. Be considerate. Do not write in this, or any, library book.